METROIMPERIAL INTIMACIES

PERVERSE MODERNITIES

A Series Edited by Jack Halberstam and Lisa Lowe

METROIMPERIAL INTIMACIES

FANTASY, RACIAL-SEXUAL
GOVERNANCE, AND THE
PHILIPPINES IN U.S.
IMPERIALISM, 1899–1913

Victor Román Mendoza

DUKE UNIVERSITY PRESS   DURHAM AND LONDON   2015

Printed in the United States of America on acid-free paper ∞
Typeset in Minion Pro by Westchester Book group

Library of Congress Cataloging-in-Publication Data
Mendoza, Victor Román, [date] author.
Metroimperial intimacies : fantasy, racial-sexual governance, and the
Philippines in U.S. imperialism, 1899–1913 / Victor Román Mendoza.
pages cm—(Perverse modernities)
Includes bibliographical references and index.
ISBN 978-0-8223-6019-3 (hardcover : alk. paper)
ISBN 978-0-8223-6034-6 (pbk. : alk. paper)
ISBN 978-0-8223-7486-2 (e-book)
1. Imperialism—Social aspects—Philippines—History—
20th century. 2. United States—Territories and possessions—
History—20th century. 3. Colonial administrators—Philippines—
Attitudes—History—20th century. 4. United States—Foreign
relations—Philippines. 5. Philippines—Foreign relations—United
States. I. Title. II. Series: Perverse modernities.
E183.8.P6M46 2015
327.7305990904—dc23
2015022771

Cover art: Philippines, May 3, 1898; Everett Collection Inc. / Alamy.

Duke University Press gratefully acknowledges the University of
Michigan College of Literature, Science, and Arts and the University
of Michigan Office of Research, which provided funds toward the
publication of this book.

CONTENTS

As an almost pathological introvert—an off-the-charts Enneagram type 5 with a strong 4 wing—I've always found it difficult to let go of my writing, presuming to work things out by myself. But reading other scholars' acknowledgments, another symptom of my introversion and expression of my 5-ness, has reminded me that it takes communities to write a book, and I'm exceedingly grateful to all those who've let me into theirs.

As a predental (?!) undergraduate student, though, writing a book wasn't originally in my plans. But my closest undergraduate professors, Alec Marsh, David Rosenwasser, and Jill Stephen, who first exposed me to postcolonial studies in their Irish literature reading group, showed me how intellectually and creatively satisfying critical analysis could be. I thank them, and Tom Cartelli, for putting up with that fledgling feminist-theoryhead English major. Barbara Gorka, from my other major, helped consolidate my Spanish after my time in the other colonial Philippine metropole.

When I started graduate school at the University of Illinois, Urbana-Champaign (to which I would return years later), Michael Bérubé, Tim Dean, Stephanie Foote, Janet Lyon, and Joe Valente (most of whom have since left) offered me the space to synthesize critical theory. Among my fellow graduate students at Illinois, I fondly recall Sarah Blackwood, Gabriel Cervantes, Mudita Chawla, Joshua Eckhardt, Melissa Girard, Praseeda Gopinath, Scott Herring, Ed McKenna, Deepti Misri, Dahlia Porter, Rochelle Reeves, and Rychetta Watkins. Matthew Gambino, who was pursuing a doctorate in history and a medical degree, was a solid interlocutor and friend and even after earning his paradox (sorry, Matt, for the awful pun) has continued to be generous to me in both of his fields of expertise.

At the University of California, Berkeley, Wendy Brown, Anne Cheng,

Ian Duncan, Richard Halpern, Colleen Lye, Sharon Marcus, Franco Moretti, Chris Nealon, Michael Rubenstein, and Trinh T. Minh-ha were exemplary, brilliant models of teaching, scholarship, and mentorship. I credit Sharon Marcus, who assigned some five book reviews during her graduate seminar, for teaching me how to write. And Trinh Minh-ha affirmed how important it was for me to pursue a doctorate in English as a person of color—she also encouraged me to go out on a limb creatively and theoretically. Caren Kaplan, meanwhile, took a gamble in hiring me as her research assistant; she was exceedingly magnanimous in training me, caught me up to speed on transnational feminisms, and continues to school me from afar. Karen Tongson reached out to me upon my arrival at Cal and took me out to lunch, even as she was on her way out the door. My friends in graduate school made that place and time less diffuse and traumatizing: Carlo Arreglo, Kelvin Black, Sylvia Chong, Kristin Fujie, Christine Hong, Jhoanna Infante-Abbatantuono, Marissa Lopez, Ryan McDermott, Franklin Melendez, Slavica Naumovska, Hoang Nguyen, and Monica Soare. Josephine Park, finishing up her degree, was an aspirational mentor. Funding from the Eugene Cota-Robles Fellowship and the Dean's Normative Time Fellowship made graduate school viable.

It was at Berkeley that I shifted my interests from Victorian British literature to U.S. ethnic and transnational studies—specifically, Asian American history, culture, and theory. Teaching Asian American literature with Anna Leong in the Ethnic Studies Department consolidated my knowledge. Colleen Lye's seminar on the field was terrifying, exacting, and invaluable, and it was in that context that I wrote what would be my first publication. (That essay became the germ of this book's implicit project to decolonize the term "queer.") Colleen, in turn, became a terrifying, exacting, and invaluable reader of my dissertation. During my doctoral qualifying exam, Michael Omi asked me a hard question about activism, Philippine-U.S. colonial history, and *bakla* counter-protestors around *Miss Saigon*; despite my probably elliptical answer, he agreed to serve on my committee and was incredibly careful in reading. José David Saldívar, my dissertation chair, has always had my back, intellectually and professionally. To borrow from one of his favorite writers, his mentorship is where the real work got done. José's continual readership and fierce support, despite our not seeing each other in far too long, have been brilliant and exemplary.

A lectureship and, later, a postdoc in Asian American studies brought me back to Urbana-Champaign, where a lot had changed. Kent Ono, who was integral to the growth of Asian American studies at Illinois into the vibrant, intellectual force it is now, was charitable in hiring and mentoring me. New friends Lisa Cacho, Shelley Cohen, David Coyoca, Rachel Dubrofsky, Augusto Espiritu,

Sara Clarke Kaplan, Kirstie Dorr, Mary Ellerbe, Viveka Kudaligama, Soo Ah Kwon, Shelley Lee, Marie Leger, Brian Locke, Shoshana Magnet, William Maxwell, Ryan McKean, Alex Mobley, Lisa Nakamura, Fiona Ngo, Mimi Nguyen, Pia Sengsavanh, Junaid Rana, Ricky Rodríguez, Siobhan Somerville, Julia Walker, and Yutian Wong were my political and intellectual kin in the cornfields. Joan and Ellen McWhorter were formative in my becoming. Caroline Yang was a fierce comrade to commiserate and plot with. Jennifer Chung and Kevin Lam took horrifying road trips with and for me. Susan Koshy was an incisive reader and is a tremendous model of scholarship. To Martin Manalansan, who was my unofficial mentor during the postdoc, I owe a boundless *utang ng loob* for his ongoing and unrelenting guidance, critique, friendship, and advocacy. He has made so much possible.

Metroimperial Intimacies wouldn't be the book that it is without the University of Michigan, Ann Arbor. Grants from the Rackham Graduate School helped me hire research assistants; a grant from the Office of the Vice President of Research and the College of Literature, Science, and the Arts (LSA) backstopped research expenses; a publication subvention from the LSA and the Office of Research aided with production costs; and the Institute for the Research of Women and Gender both awarded seed grants and provided course relief through the Junior Faculty Scholars Program. The administrative staff members Donna Ainsworth, Vanessa Debus, Karen Diedo, Jatell Driver, Aimee Germain, Jane Johnson, and Shelley Shock have helped me figure out how things work. Michael Schoenfeldt, chair of the English Department, has protected my time; Elizabeth Cole and Valerie Traub, who have chaired Women's Studies, have been overwhelmingly supportive, sage, and kind. Many thanks to my fabulous friends and colleagues who have offered me a feeling of belonging, most especially because they took time to engage with my work seriously and generatively and on the level of ideas: Evelyn Alsultany, Naomi Andre, Michael Awkward, Sara Blair, Andre Brock, Anne Curzan, Maria Cotera, Deirdre de la Cruz, Manan Desai, Leela Fernandes, Sarah Fenstermaker, Roxana Galusca, Susan Go, Dena Goodman, Sandra Gunning, Hui Hui Hu, Deborah Keller-Cohen, Aliyah Khan, Anna Kirkland, Larry La Fountain-Stokes, Madhumita Lahiri, Emily Lawsin, Peggy McCracken, Josh Miller, Candace Moore, Susan Najita, Lisa Nakamura, Esther Newton, David Porter, Megan Sweeney, Ruby Tapia, Valerie Traub, Ruth Tsoffar, Robert Wyrod, and Melanie Yergeau. My formal mentors—Leela, Valerie, and Maria—were absolutely essential to my reconceptualizations of this book: thank you all for your gracious critique and scrupulous labor. Your commitment to my work is unparalleled, and your labor isn't lost on me. Since we arrived, Candace has been my writing buddy, my productivity police, and my

A2BFF. I have also been lucky to have outstanding research assistants: Amanda Healy, James Hixon, Alex Ngo, and Sara Spiller. Amanda, especially, worked with me continually and was a great reader and a super-sleuth. Polly Rosenwaike trimmed my prose. Several graduate students ("my favorites") have made Ann Arbor feel less like perpetual winter: Cass Adair, Jennifer Alzate, Maryam Aziz, Karin Bashir, Sony Bolton, Jesse Carr, Faithe Day, Joseph Gamble, David Green, Amanda Healy, Ai Binh Ho, Dawn Kaczmar, Meryem Kamil, Mika Kennedy, Jenny Kwak, Joo Lee, Peggy Lee, Lillian Li, Cecilia Morales, Janee Moses, Michael Pascual, Kenny Pass, Veronica Rabelo, Gabby Sarpy, Mejdulene Shomali, Adeeba Talukder, Malcolm Tariq, Vivian Trương, and Sunhay You. I owe you each a flower. A manuscript workshop at Michigan, conducted expertly by Valerie Traub, furnished generative feedback from brilliant colleagues Maria Cotera and Ruby Tapia and from three of my heroes from elsewhere: Roderick Ferguson, Joe Ponce, and Siobhan Somerville. Their careful readings and critique have been inestimable, pressing me both to underscore what knowledges the archives I consider have to bear, and, borrowing from Lisa Lowe, to remain "unfaithful to the original" vis-à-vis LGBTQ studies.

Despite the evidence so far, I really *am* an introvert, as those of my friends here in Ann Arbor not already mentioned, those who have left, and those elsewhere can attest. To the first—Maya Barzilai, Deborah Berman, Stephen Berrey, Russell Bucher, Amy Sara Carroll, Rosie Ceballo, Clare Croft, Manan Desai, Margot Finn, Senait Fisseha, Jodi Greig, Colin Gunckel, Brandi Hughes, Holly Hughes, Shazia Iftkhar, Michael Jordan, Khaled Mattawa, Sara McClelland, Shani McLoyd, Ellen Muehlberger, Daniel Ramirez, Cody Walker, and Gillian White—I hope that by the time you read this I will have reemerged as a person again. To the second—Andrew Bell, Christine DeLisle, Vince Diaz, Maria-Paz Esguerra, Sarah Gambito, Sugi Ganeshananthan, Jason Gavilan, Francine Harris, Van Jordan, Scott Kurashige, Nadine Naber, Sri Nair, Atef Said, Thida Sam, and Sarita See—you are missed. To Julie Keenan, Shirleen Robinson, and the late Linda Underhill, who helped me keep my bearings and sanity during a shared detour through Gettysburg, I am grateful. Vanita Reddy has been my fellow brown, anti-normative, feminist anti-imperialist-in-arms, ideal intended audience, and intellectual compass. Meanwhile, many scholar friends not already listed have been exceedingly generous with their support and critical feedback at various moments in the process of writing: Anjali Arondekar, Nerissa Balce, Lucy Mae San Pablo Burns, Denise Cruz, Robert Diaz, Kale Fajardo, Gayatri Gopinath, Jin Haritaworn, Jennifer Ho, Hsuan Hsu, Paul Kramer, Eng-Beng Lim, Anita Mannur, Karen Miller, Dylan Rodriguez, Cathy Schlund-Vials, Harrod Suarez, Anantha Sudhakar, and Chris Vials.

Research for this book came from disparate archival sources. Thanks to staffs at the Bancroft Library (Berkeley); the Bentley Historical Library (Ann Arbor); the Special Collections Library (Ann Arbor); the Newberry Library (Chicago); the Chicago Historical Museum, especially Jill Austin and Jessica Herczeg-Konecny; the National Archives (Washington, DC); the Canton Lyric Opera Company, especially Joseph Rubin; and genealogists Miranda Gerholt and Michelle Centers. An East-of-California Asian American Studies workshop at Penn State helped me hone a chapter; many thanks to Tina Chen, Miliann Kang, Sue Kim, and Judy Wu for their gracious feedback and mentorship.

Despite my first having submitted to him what was essentially my dissertation, Ken Wissoker spent an hour out of his conference schedule many years ago to walk me to one of his off-site cafés so we could talk about my work. His simple, off-hand assurance then that my project, however inchoate at the time, was "a Duke book" was enough for me to keep revising it. He has since been an intellectually engaged interlocutor and attentive editor. I appreciate his thoughtfulness in picking such erudite (anonymous) readers; their suggestions have made the book genuinely better. Many thanks also to Jade Brooks, Susan Deeks, Sara Leone, Bonnie Perkel, and Christine (Choi) Riggio at Duke University Press for their helpfulness, responsiveness, and pleasantness, as well as Eileen Quam for the index. And it is an honor to be included in Duke's Perverse Modernities series; I am indebted to J. Jack Halberstam and Lisa Lowe for their confidence.

Finally, I am lucky to have a huge kinship system in many places across the metroempire: the Mendozas, the Reyeses, the Galans, the Fariñases, and the Bolinas. To Christian Reyes, Jennifer Wildermuth-Reyes, and Virgie and Manuel Galan, thanks for letting this nomad continually crash your Bay Area homes. Cousins Christian, Christina, Victor, Michelle, and Joanne, especially: I hope to visit your world again soon. Ann Hwang, Seong-Ho Shin, and Jennifer Wade have been loyal friends and are amazing humans. I gladly owe Sandie and Surinder Bolina at least half a year's Chicago mortgage and condo dues; Jas, I'm placing a reservation at your place now. John, Jessica, and Kai Mendoza are constant reminders of where I come from and what I want to get back to. John's musicianship humbles me; still, he doesn't find it too demeaning to mash up a *Les Miz*, Bon Jovi, and *Phantom* medley on the piano every time we see each other. I am privileged to have such patient, supportive, and caring parents (even though I didn't become a dentist). I thank my dad, Conrad, for not letting me be embarrassed when I was a kid by how I danced in secret—and for unwittingly making me a feminist. My mom, Lumen, proofread my first ever sentence and added a semicolon to it. For her love, care, and guidance, I do not have adequate expressions of gratitude; so, I hope to take her travelling abroad as a down payment. Finally, my favorite Vulcan/Cylon/Enneagram type 1, Pardip Kaur Bolina, has been a solid, sure, and patient partner. P: your commitment to social justice, your brilliance, your perspective, your resilience and your ability to make me laugh in the face of everything leave me awestruck. You have helped me in so many ways to finish this book, and for that I dedicate it to you. It's the best—and the least—I can offer.

The ascendancy of U.S. empire in the Philippine archipelago at the turn of the twentieth century enabled a proliferation of unexpected and unprecedented social and sexual intimacies—some real, most imagined—between the figure of the Philippine autochthonous subject and other peoples, intimacies that threatened to exceed U.S. empire's biopolitical consolidation of the normal. These intimacies emerged in various forms of largely neglected state and cultural productions, a strange archive of which *Metroimperial Intimacies* assembles: in laws and institutions emerging in the metropole and the archipelago that managed perversion; in a court-martial scandal concerning Filipino soldiers abused by their white superior officer; in local and major newspapers; in political cartoons about the new colonial subjects of the United States; in a hit Broadway musical comedy about the Philippines by a white man who had companionships with men; and in serial journals by *pensionadas* and *pensionados*, Philippine students receiving government scholarships to pursue education in U.S. universities.

These disparate archival remains allow us alternative entries into the vicissitudes of the racial-sexual management over a range of bodies within both the colonial archipelago and the metropole. Presenting us with intimacies imperceptible until now, this archive furnishes different routes of access to the social and the historical. *Metroimperial Intimacies* argues that the kinds of intimate and even perverse relations between the figure of the Philippine subject and other people that emerge are not peripheral or contrary to the heteromasculinizing, genocidal project of U.S. imperialism but constitutive of it.

The various forms of state documents and cultural production about the Philippines and the Philippine colonial subject I examine in this book were adumbrated by numerous social fantasies about other figures. Drawing on contemporaneous public discourses not only about African Americans, Native Americans, and Asian migrants, but also about the vagrant, the sodomite, the invert, the pervert, the degenerate, the fairy, the bachelor, the New Woman, the dandy, and the polygamist, the imperial and metropolitan fantasies swirling about this cultural production were unruly, varying sometimes to the point of incommensurability or contradiction with each other. As I lay out in the pages that follow, the Philippine subject was effeminized (even "fairyfied") yet hypermasculine, militarily ferocious yet unmanly, physically enviable yet unfit, Oriental yet Negro, a stylish fop yet perpetually naked, stupid yet scheming, evolutionarily rearguard yet overly civilized, a passive bottom yet an encroaching sexual menace, unfit for testimony yet culpable for what they confessed to. The particular effects on identity formation that fin-de-siècle metropolitan fantasies had, moreover, may have since become so diffuse within (or so absorbed by) normative metropolitan life as to seem, by now, indiscernible—which is why this book is not concerned with questions about contemporary "identity" much at all. Still, I suggest that these fantasies about the Philippine colonial subject saturated turn-of-the-century U.S. metroimperial discourses that were anxiously attempting to organize human difference. In supporting the management of intimacy both within the metropole and its colony, they were a crucial linchpin in the biopolitics of empire.

If, as John D'Emilio has argued, the rise of capitalism in the United States during the nineteenth century led to the formation of "lesbian and gay identity," and if, as Vladimir Lenin posited, imperialism is the "highest stage of capitalism," then how does U.S. imperial-colonial war in the Philippines fit into the story of emergent sexual identifications?[1] Although *Metroimperial Intimacies* does not deploy so conventionally materialist a critique as these citations suggest, this question remains at the heart of my inquiry about racial-sexual governance. As many scholars working at the intersections of critical race studies, gender studies, and sexuality studies have argued, racial, gendered, and sexual categories are not fixed and transhistorical. Rather, they prove unstable and conditional, contingent on changing historical, cultural, spatial, legal, and temporal contexts. Their modes of emergence, moreover, transform those contexts in turn. A few historians and literary scholars (Kristin Hoganson, Gail Bederman, Amy Kaplan) have cogently discussed the shifting intersections of race and gender around the Philippine-American War (1899 to its official end in 1902). Yet the imperial-colonial presence of the United States in the Philippines at the turn of the twentieth century—which would persist for almost ninety years in the form of military and settler occupation during that century, and endure in the forms of transnational surplus labor, tourism, strategic geopolitical positioning and counterterrorist securitization (as embodied by the Philippines-U.S. Visiting Forces Agreement of 1999), during this one—has been largely overlooked by scholars as an event that would have affected the vicissitudes of the mutual formations of race, gender, and sexuality in the United States.[2]

To put it more strongly, no scholarly works tracing the histories of sexuality in the United States, including those few that take into account the messiness of racial formations at the fin de siècle, examine how the early years of U.S. imperial colonialism in the Philippines affects such histories. Nor has any book-length study in Philippine American, Asian American, ethnic, or critical race studies—including the many that consider these fields as they intersect with gender and sexuality—considered how the emerging control over sexuality in the U.S. metropole also appeared in the early period of Philippine colonial governance, when colonial administrators "were prolific producers of social categories," and within the knowledge-making discourses in the metropole around the native Philippine subject.[3] The first gap might be explained by the historical disavowal in the United States of empire in the Philippines more generally, one that endures in LGBTQ and sexuality studies; as M. Jacqui Alexander has thrown down, contemporary queer theory in particular "eviscerates histories of colonialism and racial formation."[4] The second speaks not only to a scarcity of documents in the U.S. colonial archive that concern questions of sexuality in any capacity but also to the fact that social categories of sexuality did not look at the turn of the twentieth century as they do now. I don't intend merely to fill these areas of oversight but to claim that any history of sexuality in the United States remains incomplete without a consideration of imperial colonialism abroad and that studies of U.S. empire miss a lot when they do not take seriously the role that sexual regulation had in the formation of colonial governance. *Metroimperial Intimacies* fleshes out the ways in which, as Kandice Chuh has provocatively argued, "the history of the formation of 'Filipino' and 'Filipino American' identity formations, from a U.S. perspective, is also a history of sexuality."[5]

In her influential book *Queering the Color Line: Race and the Invention of Homosexuality* (2000), Siobhan Somerville claims that "it was not merely a historical coincidence that the classification of bodies as either 'homosexual' or 'heterosexual' emerged at the same time that the United States was aggressively constructing and policing the boundary between 'black' and 'white' bodies."[6] Following Somerville's critical lead, *Metroimperial Intimacies* seeks to further "queer" the color line that marks off racial oppression by examining how U.S. imperial expansion into the colonial archipelago affected the nascent classification of bodies—not just "black" and "white" or, for that matter, "heterosexual" and "homosexual"—within the colonial metropole. When W. E. B. Du Bois famously inveighed against the "color line" as the "problem of the Twentieth Century," he identified not only African Americans suffering the injustices of segregation and state-sanctioned white supremacy but also the people of the newly acquired Philippines, Puerto Rico, Cuba, Guam, and Hawai'i—the "twenty millions of brown and black people under the protection of the American flag."[7] In the face of what he called "the new imperial policy," Du Bois located the opportunity for cross-racial solidarities, the opportunity for varied "dark men and women" to vex the very drawing of the "line." Addressing fellow African Americans, he asked, "What is to be our attitude toward these new lands and . . . the masses of dark men and women who inhabit them? Manifestly it must be an attitude of deepest sympathy and strongest alliance. We must stand ready to guard and guide them with our vote and our earnings. Negro and Filipino, Indian and Porto Rican, Cuban and Hawaiian, all must stand united under the stars and stripes for an America that knows no color line in the freedom of its opportunities."[8] Despite Du Bois's cautioning to an emergent black middle class against U.S. imperialism and his pleas of "sympathy" for the United States' new colonial subjects, the color line continued well into the twentieth century to do a lot of work in consolidating not only white supremacist hegemony but also the specious binary (between black and white) of U.S. racial difference that cannot account for bodies that remain outside of it. More, Du Bois's rallying cry demonstrates that the United States' "new imperial policy" left one having to imagine (to conceive of an "attitude toward") racial others somewhere out there, off the U.S. metropolitan grid. For most of the U.S. public, the island inhabitants of the Philippines were out of sight, and despite U.S. colonialism's increasingly effective policing strategies in the colonial archipelago, the Philippine "dark men and women" remained in the imperial imagination just as amorphous as Du Bois's word "masses" implies. As I show in the pages that follow, such ambiguity was embedded in a variety of discourses, including the visual and the legal.

To get at these far-off and dark masses, *Metroimperial Intimacies* takes the varied modes of state and cultural production concerned specifically with the Philippine-American War as the site of imperialism's varied fantasies. Imperialism's cultural fantasies, as paradoxical as it might seem, offered the U.S. public a kind of reality about those far-off, vague colonial masses. While it might sound ephemeral, fantasy, like the Marxian concept of ideology—or, for that matter, like the categories of "race," "gender," and "sexuality"—"has a material existence."[9] Throughout this book, my understanding of fantasy draws from a psychoanalytic conceptualization, although psychoanalysis does not always motor the book's primary interpretive method or explicitly shape its idiom. Still, as psychoanalytical thinkers' understanding of fantasy varies widely; as the writing of Jacques Lacan (on whose understanding of fantasy I draw most and whose jargon I will, whenever possible, limit here to endnotes) is notoriously vexing to read; and as fantasy itself is conceptually and ontologically unruly, it is perhaps useful for me to gloss how I understand the term throughout the book. My understanding might not fully jibe with how the concept of fantasy is typically rendered in popular culture—that is, as a misty, dreamlike narrative that momentarily takes one away from everyday reality and in which one meets up with one's ideal life or, sometimes, one's worst fear. I don't depart far from this rendering, but I lock in on two particular functions. First, fantasy protects; second, fantasy enables one to locate one's desire.

Fantasy protects. Fantasy shields one from encountering some terrible, terrifying, or potentially traumatic scene, thought, or condition.[10] Throughout this book, such a terrifying scene or condition often emerges in the context of the knowledge formation in and of social worlds—around the Philippines, the "Filipina/o," the pervert, the invert, the degenerate, for example.[11] The fantasy scenario functions as a placeholder, filling out with its positive contents some constitutive void in one's knowledge production, the negation—the empty, inassimilable space—inhering in both one's ordering systems and one's social relations. By "ordering systems" here I mean the varied and intersecting governing, knowledge-making schemas of state bureaucracy, biopolitics, capitalism, militarism, heteronormativity, the sex/gender system, the law, language, discourse, history, nationalism, racial hegemony, colonialism, imperialism, and racial-sexual governance.[12] Fantasy conceals the fact that the ordering system by which one perceives, understands, or makes intelligible one's everyday sense of reality is built around a gap, a fundamental impossibility, an un-domesticatable something that not only resists linguistic representation but also eludes all attempts at historicization.[13] This is how fantasy is protective: it obscures the fact that, as much as one might want to, one can't know everything.[14] It also shields one from the fundamental, a priori alienation from another person or population—more specifically from that person's or population's radical alterity and inassimilable difference[15]—and provides the grounds (however shaky) of intersubjectivity.

This protective function of fantasy relates to another: in enabling one to elude terrifying truths, fantasy stages one's desire. This point nuances how one might usually understand the relationship between fantasy and desire— that is, the more typical rendering in popular culture that one desires what one lacks and that one must therefore fantasize when what one desires is out of reach. Slavoj Žižek renders it this way:

> Fantasy is usually conceived as a scenario that realizes the subject's desire. This elementary definition is quite adequate, on condition that we take it *literally*: what the fantasy stages is not a scene in which our desire is fulfilled, fully satisfied, but on the contrary a scene that realizes, stages, the desire as such. . . . Desire is not something given in advance, but something that has to be constructed—and it is precisely the role of fantasy to give the coordinates of the subject's desire, to specify its object, to locate the position the subject assumes in it. It is only through fantasy that the subject is constituted as desiring: *through fantasy, we learn how to desire.*[16]

Challenging the critique that psychoanalysis remains incompatible with historicism, Žižek posits that in psychoanalytic thought desire is not transhistorical but must be produced—"constructed"—out of history and the social. The fantasy scene does not satisfy some pre-given desire; the fantasy scene produces desire, showing subjects their objects, even if the former aren't fully conscious of how to apprehend or assimilate the latter. Whatever content one finds in the fantasmatic scene keeps desire going. To put these two functions of fantasy together, fantasy protects one from the traumatizing truth of the impossibility of totalizing knowledge, of completely satisfying one's desire, by constructing and reconstructing desire with different configurations of historical knowledge and, once in a while, with new knowledge altogether.

Fantasy works like the police officer whose other duty Louis Althusser *doesn't* talk about: the cop in this case doesn't say, "Hey, you there!" as in Althusser's scenario but, rather, to shield "you" from some gruesome scene insists, "There's nothing to see here," while waving you to keep moving.[17] Lauren Berlant puts this production or mapping out of desire vis-à-vis repeated fantasy in terms of monogamous, "romantic love": "love is a formal promise and an aspiration of projection, mirroring, and repetition. It is a fidelity to a form that only exists in its recurrence. . . . This is how intimates who repulse each other can remain coupled when it is no longer fun. They ride the wave of love's phantasmatic contract with imminent mutual transparency, simultaneity, and completion all too well."[18] The comforting pleasures inhering in the everyday commitment rehearsed between the intimates Berlant describes find their support in the culturally manufactured fantasy of romantic love that conceals their real malaise. The intimates' desire is realized, continually constructed, in their repetition of love's demands to form, in their adherence to love's convention. Love is a cop—and a cop-out. Or to call up a bad joke about stale relationships from a 1998 *Saturday Night Live* sketch: when an incongruous white, heterosexual couple—the exuberant "joyologist" (Molly Shannon) and the mellow, seashell arts-and-crafter (Matthew Broderick)—are asked by a talk-show host (Ana Gasteyer) how they have managed to stay together for two whole weeks, they answer the obvious: "role-playing, role-playing, role-playing." In imagining the other as someone else, these two have not failed; their repeated performances reanimate the desires they otherwise might not recognize as such. Thanks to fantasy, failure is not an option.

Still, even as fantasy protects from the fundamental incoherence of one's relation to the world, it is in that very function already articulated to that traumatic incoherence. To make more exact an earlier iteration, even as fantasy protects one from a terrifying condition, it also ambiguously mediates one's ineluctable relation to that condition.[19] Indeed, as Lacan himself would put it, fantasy seeks to "colonize" that traumatic, unruly space.[20] It is precisely as this ambiguous connection between the ordering system and all that remains inassimilable to it, however, that fantasy, a mediation in which all social beings in various ways participate, allows us to locate the individual's relation to the social. As Gilles Deleuze and Félix Guattari maintain, "Fantasy is never individual; it is *group fantasy*."[21] Tim Dean cogently expands the relationship between the individual and the social to the individual and the national: "fantasy offers itself as an indispensable concept for discussing subjectivity and sociality together, without reducing one to the other. . . . This concept justifies our speaking of social fantasy or national fantasy, since fantasy, no matter how private it may seem, is not a strictly individual phenomenon. . . . The idea of 'social fantasy' is not merely a metaphor or a result of viewing the collective analogically, as it were an individual. Rather, the concept of fantasy inscribes how a dimension of sociality . . . inhabits the innermost, ostensibly private zone of the subject."[22]

As Dean's distinction between subjectivity and sociality makes clear, referring to a "social" or "national"—or, for that matter, *imperial*—fantasy does not imply that all individuals fantasize about the same things, that fantasy, despite its unruly nature, is so easily domesticated. Rather, it means that the desire realized in one's fantasy is determined externally, by what Fredric Jameson calls the "political unconscious," on one hand, and by sociality, on the other.[23] Indeed, not only does one figure out through fantasy one's social role in the nation or empire by approximating what that formation—and what its others— might want from one; nations and empires themselves apprehend through fantasy their social status vis-à-vis the geopolitical arena. Fantasy mediates the social, the "national," the colonial—indeed, fantasy plays a "central, constitutive role" in the formation of the modern state, as Jacqueline Rose has argued in a different settler colonial context.[24] What's more, as Rey Chow offers in her critique of Althusser's narrative of ideological interpellation, fantasy also enables one—more specifically, for Chow, the ethnic minority—to negotiate the risks involved in resisting not only the interpellative hailing of the law but also its horrifying opposite, the "*terror of complete freedom.*"[25] I attempt to capture such navigating, specifically between resistance to both imperial fantasy and the terrifying "complete freedom" from, it in chapter 5, where I track Philippine students' responses to racial-sexual governance within the U.S. imperial metropole. For now, though, I want to emphasize that precisely because individuals within a particular social field risk encountering both the limits of that field or system and the things that exceed them, social fantasy in its protective and desire-realizing functions takes shape. Moreover, U.S. empire finds its support not only in the fantasies of totalizing knowledge about other populations, but also in its purporting to protect its shifting borders from the terrifying elements external to them through an aggregation of some fantasmatic notion of legitimate violence—in the "fantasy of omnipotence," as Chandan Reddy puts it, "that is definitional to the military of a Western nation-state and that codes its own terror as civilization."[26]

The archive I assemble in this book reveals what I refer to as U.S. metroimperial fantasies, by which I mean the accreted and often disparate social fantasies circulating across the Pacific—between the imperial-colonial arena in the Philippines and the imperial metropole of the contiguous United States. "Metroimperial" serves as shorthand to account for the formations of knowledge production that subtended the transformation of the United States from an imperial, settler-colonial republic expanding its borders westward during the eighteenth century and nineteenth century ("Manifest Destiny") to the overseas settler-colonial and administrative empire it became at the turn of the twentieth century. Indeed, because of the United States' ascendancy into imperial form in the Philippines and other sites in the Pacific at this time, I find it no longer compelling to talk about the United States as a "nation," since this term, as Benedict Anderson has suggested, implies a stability of border constitutions, however "imagined" they might be.[27] As Amy Kaplan has elegantly argued, the very idea of U.S. national borders became increasingly vexed within legal and public discourse as the republic swelled, anarchically, to an overseas empire at the fin de siècle.[28] "Metroimperial" exposes the fantasy-production of a U.S. "nation," a signifier of sovereignty, modernity, and care that has enabled subjects to look away from, or worse rationalize, a U.S. empire's barbaric violence. It captures more precisely the often imprecise, transpacific transits of white supremacist annihilation and racial-sexual management of both autochthonous Philippine subjects and a range of other perverse and/or racialized bodies. I will thus most often refer to the "U.S. metropole" when referring to the center of U.S. empire, located within the spatially contiguous United States. Likewise, I use the term "imperialism" to account for the direct control and administrative discourses that the United States exerted and deployed over the Philippine territory and its peoples. "Colonialism" in this book describes the settlement of, the legal and capitalist establishment of direct political sovereignty over, and the exploitation of local resources of the Philippine territory and its peoples.[29] The phrase "metroimperial fantasies" thus expresses the synchronic legal, material, ideological, cultural, and social exchanges across transpacific space. These exchanges were not always consistent, homogenous, or fluid, but uneven and messy. By staging the desires of the new transpacific empire, metroimperial fantasies protected empire's will to knowledge. Indeed, as I demonstrate in chapters 1 and 2 especially, colonial administrators' sharing in these fantasies had a direct impact on colonial state governance.

Individuals participated in these social fantasies differently. While "benevolent assimilation," the euphemistic phrase that President William McKinley used to describe imperial expansion, was riddled with and sought to project related imperial fantasies—of the Progressivist uplift of barbaric peoples, of the non-necessity of state military violence, of the mission to domesticate the wild—Du Bois, as we have seen, had his own fantasies of "masses" living and dying on the U.S. imperial color line that belted the world and sought for most of his life to imagine alternative global intimacies in the age of empire.[30] However unruly—and perhaps because of their unruliness—these fantasies simultaneously concealed and attested to the limits of colonial surveillance and knowledge production, U.S. imperial self-identification, and racial-sexual management in both the colonial Philippines and the U.S. metropole. As Rose reminds us, "Fantasy's supreme characteristic is that of running ahead of itself. . . . Fantasy has been where statehood takes hold and binds its subjects, and then, unequal to its own injunctions, lets slip just a little."[31]

While considering such a seemingly immaterial thing as imperial fantasy and thus psychoanalytic in impulse, *Metroimperial Intimacies* remains methodologically a queer-of-color historicist study of discourses constituting the Philippine subject.[32] There was, to repurpose Michel Foucault's famous thesis in *The History of Sexuality* (1976), a proliferation of discourse around the autochthonous Philippine subject, an "institutional incitement to speak about it, and to do so more and more; a determination on the part of the agencies of power to hear it spoken about, and to cause *it* to speak through explicit articulation and endlessly accumulated detail."[33] Foucault's "it" here is not, of course, the Philippine subject but "sex," but his description of the incitement to discourse—and his account of agencies of power determined to hear "it" speak—aptly conveys the will to knowledge, of colonial administrators and the U.S. public writ large, about the Philippine colonial subject and sex. For the bureaucrats of the U.S. civil government in the Philippines, as well as the U.S. public, the autochthonous Philippine people were marked by various racializing "knowledges" that accrued out of the complex dialectic of racial discourses and visual images coming, on one hand, from the imperial metropole around Native Americans, African Americans, and Asian immigrants and, on the other, from on-the-ground colonial administrations' modes of information gathering and inherited governing practices from imperial Spain. Still, that Foucault here isn't talking about the Philippine native—and, after all, why would he be?—might also be read within the context of his general inattention to imperialism and colonialism in his genealogies of sexuality (an inattention, as I have already suggested, that many studies of sexuality in the U.S. context seem to have inherited).[34] Thus, my historicist reading of discourses of sexuality in the U.S.-Philippine metroimperial context deploys analytical methods developed and histories traced by scholars engaging in the convergence of sexuality studies with histories of metropolitan intracolonialism and U.S. colonialism abroad, a convergence that Roderick Ferguson has dubbed "queer of color critique."[35] I turn to some of the work of these scholars in the next section, where I offer a snapshot of the history of racial-sexual governance in the U.S. metropole as a backdrop to my examination of metroimperial intimacies that emerged during the Philippine-American War. Before making that turn, though, I should explain the other term of the book's title.

Throughout this book, I refer to *intimacy* as a zone of close social or sexual connections between individuals, expressed by a range of practices or behavior, happening in what gets marked off as private space, even as these connections and practices are managed, conducted, or prohibited by the state, capital, and public convention. Arriving out of multiple intellectual genealogies—namely, postcolonial theory, ethnic studies, queer theory, and feminist studies—this working definition posits intimacy as an event of friendship, love, erotic contact, or sexual desire, conditioned out of real and imagined constraints.[36] Even as one might presume it primarily an expression of interiority—its Latin etymology ("innermost") guides this association—intimacy remains always implicated in various bodies' negotiations of spatial proximity, social contact, and the construction (and transgression) of the private sphere.[37] Like fantasy, intimacy is determined from without. Within the U.S. metroimperial context I examine, intimacies are conducted by the social and state regulation of marriage, by military law, by newly installed municipal legislation in the archipelago, by the colonial bureaucratic state, by transpacific geographies, by the social effectivity of capital, by gossip. Under the surveillance of the metroimperial gaze, the most improper intimacies appear in—or run off to—sometimes surprising geographic places: on the battlefield, in the colonial military barracks, under a mango tree in the tropics, in water closets, in the bedroom, at bars, at immigration inspection stations, in brothels, in seasonal laborers' sleeping quarters, in a classroom, on the beach at Manila Bay, at college, at boardinghouses, off stage, in a makeshift grave. That some of these intimacies are legible as such in the colonial archive attests to the extent that the metroimperial state and the social world shape the forms that intimacy takes and where it might be relegated to—that is, the extent to which, as Jasbir Puar puts it, the "distribution of intimacy is crucial to sexual-racial biopolitical management of life."[38] It also attests to the extent to which the state and public cultures imagine, apprehend, and record intimacy—and fail to. Thus, even if, as I demonstrate in the pages that follow, gender-sexual deviance was not the primary target of metroimperial biopolitical statecraft, it was nonetheless constitutive of such management. *Metroimperial Intimacies,* to evoke Rose's language, zeroes in on the intimacies that try to give the state the slip.

In focusing on the intimacies that emerged in the face of the imperial violence of the Philippine-American War, I do not attempt to obscure the "material historical arrangements" of "genocidal state violence" that, as Dylan Rodriguez powerfully contends, has underwritten Philippine American politics and subjectivity since colonization.[39] Rather, I attempt to capture the "diffusion" of imperial state "terror," to borrow from Saidiya Hartman.[40] *Metroimperial Intimacies* thus contributes to the scholarship in Philippine, Philippine American, comparative ethnic, gender, and sexuality studies by revealing how the state of imperial violence might shape the everyday social life of various agents—who is primed to become intimate with whom and why—at the moment of overseas imperial ascendancy, during the time of war. Metroimperial intimacy is not separate from colonial state rule; it emerges as a result of and in spite of it. As Ann Stoler puts it, "To study the intimate is not to turn away from structures of dominance but to relocate their conditions of possibility and relations and forces of production."[41] This book demonstrates how intimacies between Philippine subjects and others might emerge unexpectedly in the thick of colonial violence. But it also shows how colonial violence and the necessarily uneven networks of power it establishes inhere as fundamental components of such intimacies—however much the enabling fantasies of friendship, love, or desire compel intimates to see things otherwise. Without an examination of such intimacies, we would miss the full range and diffusion of white supremacist imperialist violence on forms of sexuality and interiority. What's more, we would miss the ways in which certain modes of interpersonal connection might recuperate, even as they might be seemingly incidental to or an excess of, the violence of imperial governmentality. After all, the obverse of McKinley's famous "benevolent assimilation" coin might not be militarized violence but, rather, *intimacy*.

Racial-Sexual Governance and the U.S. Imperial Metropolitan State

The fin-de-siècle Philippine-American War and United States' subsequent colonial occupation of the Philippines transpired when the U.S. state increasingly legislated and managed the formations of racial-sexual categories within the metropole. When discussing the U.S. metropolitan state throughout this book, I largely follow Max Weber's understanding of the state as the community holding a monopoly over the "legitimate" use of violence, as well as administrative, military, and financial power.[42] When it comes to the colonial Philippines, however, the definition of "state" that I work from follows Wendy Brown, who, drawing from Foucault's understanding of power as "both intentional and nonsubjective," describes the state as "not a thing, system, or subject but a significantly unbounded terrain of powers and techniques, an ensemble of discourses, rules, and practices, cohabiting in limited, tension-ridden, often contradictory relation with one another."[43] Brown's description of the state as "significantly unbounded terrain of powers and techniques" in fact perfectly captures the U.S. imperial colonial state in the Philippines. The U.S. colonial state in the Philippines emerged as "a political institution" that was, as Julian Go puts it, "geographically distant and juridically distinct from, but subordinate to, the metropolitan government."[44] The U.S. metropolitan state, in other words, had to be stretched, "significantly unbounded," to rule, via its monopoly of violence and administrative power, its colonial territory from afar.[45] To that end, the U.S. colonial state in the Philippines amassed its own, impressive assemblage of governing powers and techniques, including police and constabulary forces, taxation agencies, courts, and legal and economic policies, none of which was necessarily subject to the U.S. federal system or legal statutes.[46]

I discuss the formation of the U.S. colonial state in the Philippines, focusing specifically on its inchoate modes of racial-sexual regulation, in chapter 1. Here, I sketch the metropolitan backdrop for such regulation. The U.S. metropolitan state played a powerful role in determining nascent racial-sexual formations within U.S. borders. U.S. metropolitan statecraft by the beginning of the twentieth century was cohering into an organized biopolitical ensemble that aspired to identify, manage, and regulate a plurality of bodies that were emerging onto the metropolitan scene in order to entrench white heterosexual hegemony. As scholars such as Claudia Tate, Eithne Luibhéid, Chandan Reddy, Margot Canaday, Roderick Ferguson, Nayan Shah, Peggy Pascoe, and Siobhan Somerville have cogently demonstrated, as the fin-de-siècle state attempted to regulate racialized bodies—immigrants, native peoples, an emergent black middle class—under the cover of preserving metropolitan well-being, it simultaneously consolidated white supremacy and invented normative gender and sexual comportment according to the ideal of the reproductive family.

The U.S. metropolitan state was not by this time, however, a consolidated, coherent surveillance system. Rather, the state was fortifying itself precisely against the plurality of bodies in seeming need of management, populations whose increased appearance in public spheres, particularly in sprawling urban and port spaces, was enabled by the late nineteenth-century economic boom and the liberal developmentalist ethos it exceeded.[47] We might even regard the metropolitan state itself at the turn of the century as a shifting set of practices, as an *event* of governmentality emerging most clearly at the moment it acted on and was recognized by the social worlds it sought to govern.[48] Faced at once with various social transformations—transitions from agrarian to industrial to corporate capitalism and subsequent labor unrest; a growing population of U.S.-born people, "nonnative" aliens, and aspiring immigrants; the recently instituted rule of segregation in the wake of the failed state project of Reconstruction; the increased presence of mostly white women in the workforce and public life; and the economic expansion capped by overseas military conquest, for example—the U.S. metropolitan state was in the process of assembling adequate forms of regulation of the bodies and behavior of the people within its imagined borders. Touting the growing spirit of Progressivism and its middle-class values around social reform and economic uplift, such a project necessitated reforming the governance over economic policies, industrialization, and urbanization, on one hand, and bodies and populations, on the other.

The state's effort to regulate race and sexuality simultaneously within the metropole in the late nineteenth century and early twentieth century was at times explicit. State-supported biopolitical management of newly emancipated African Americans during the late nineteenth century, for example, took the form of liberal governance over marriage. In antebellum slave states, blacks had no access to legal marriage; it was only after emancipation that African Americans were also freed from their inability to make legal contracts for labor and marriage.[49] Former slaves' newly granted rights to contract work and to contract marriage were thus mutually supportive, and both marked the trajectory toward inclusion in metropolitan citizenship. The Freedmen's Bureau had in fact compelled African American men in particular into both finding wage work and legally marrying black women. (Not incidentally, the Freedman's Bureau was created by the U.S. War Department, the same administrative unit that governed military life in the colonial Philippines.) Thus, by the late nineteenth century, African Americans "were well aware of the social value invested in marriage as a sign of meritorious citizenship." The heterosexual, marital contract for blacks, as long as it kept intimacies within the race, proved "the sanctioned sign of civilization."[50] Moreover, the mode of compulsory heterosexuality deployed to "uplift" black American respectability was intimately articulated to another mode of civic participation: enlistment in the overseas imperial military.[51]

Yet some laws governing African Americans did not explicitly circumscribe acceptable sexual behavior. Scholars engaged in queer-of-color critique have shown how the state's management of racial formation relied on assumptions of and, in turn, privileged hetero-erotic reproductivity. In the wake of the landmark *Plessy v. Ferguson* (1896), for example, U.S. laws actively sought to demarcate and consolidate the racial categories of "black" and "white" to fortify the state-sanctioned institutionalization of racist segregation that until then had only been practiced de facto. As Siobhan Somerville cogently argues, however, *Plessy* was not just about stabilizing racial difference. The material legacies of slavery—signaled by African Americans' historical lack of property rights—inscribes the plaintiff Homer Plessy's black body as nonnormative specifically within the white, heteronormative economy of the post-Reconstruction liberalist United States. As Somerville puts it, "Those whose bodies were culturally marked as nonnormative lost their claim to the same rights as those whose racial or sexual reputation invested them with cultural legitimacy, or the property of a 'good name.'"[52] The alleged need, moreover, for the state-sanctioned practice of racial segregation that *Plessy* instantiated found its basis in the widespread social panic about black men's alleged sexual intractableness.[53] The hysterical need to protect the chastity of (presumed heterosexual) white women from (presumed hyper- and heterosexual) black men called for the state-sanctioned separation of races in public and private spheres. Hence, *Plessy* demonstrates that the state's "simultaneous efforts to shore up and bifurcate categories of race and sexuality in the late nineteenth and early twentieth century were deeply intertwined."[54] The proliferation of state and federal antimiscegenation laws shortly after would be the most explicit culmination of such intertwining.

Federal legislation restricting immigration and property rights, especially of various individuals and populations from Asia during the late nineteenth century and early twentieth century, also attested to this intertwining of racial formation and the emergence of sexual identities. Producing as objects of racial-sexual governance the figures of the Asiatic, the Oriental, the Hindoo, the alien, the Chinaman, the Jap, and the Filipino (among other categories of social and state-endorsed nomenclature), numerous exclusion acts and prohibitions on property emerged out of white nativist animus around labor and class antagonism.[55] Immigrant exclusion acts, for example, worked implicitly to affirm through legislation the natural citizenship of both white and black bodies against the fundamentally inassimilable "Asiatic" body. The Page Law of 1875, enacted just ten years after emancipation and thus addressing capitalism's alternative source of cheap labor, prohibited the immigration of female Chinese laborers. This law would simultaneously govern sexuality: legislators presumed that Chinese women were entering the country for "lewd and immoral purposes"; that they were prostitutes spreading venereal disease, threatening the nation's "monogamous morality."[56] Thus, under the rubric of care, this early immigration law not only barred populations arriving from Asia but also managed proper heterosexual conduct within the metropole. It fortified the implicit whiteness and heteronormativity of the state by identifying and excluding those "perverse" masses whose exclusion would guarantee racial-sexual hegemony.

Immigrant exclusion, moreover, initiated the state's production of perverse "strangers" within the metropole.[57] One long-term result of this restriction of the immigration of working-class Chinese women, besides setting a precedent for subsequent immigration acts, was the formation in the late nineteenth century and early twentieth century of Chinese bachelors' societies. As Nayan Shah has demonstrated, these oft-policed communities were widely constructed as degenerate hordes of feminized men engaging in perverse acts within conspicuously homosocial spaces.[58] Indeed, the state management of immigrant space, especially when measured by legal rights to property, would also come to govern modes of intimacy, sociality, and sexuality for Asian migrants and settler communities throughout the early twentieth century.[59]

Conversely, even as the legislated barring of allegedly perverse Chinese women sought to ensure in advance the impossibility of Chinese marriage in the United States (and thus the long-term domestic settlement of Chinese laborers), hetero-monogamy at the turn of the twentieth century would in very rare instances legitimate the access of other Asian immigrants. As Eithne Luibhéid has shown, immigration laws sometimes privileged the conjugal relationship and the sexual forms it implies.[60] As it did for African Americans around the turn of the twentieth century, heterosexual marriage—as long as it was intraracial—promised migrants from Japan a modicum of recognition by the state. Luibhéid points out that the Gentlemen's Agreement of 1908, which allowed Japanese men already settled in the United States to send for picture brides from their country of origin, affirmed the hetero-monogamous values of the state while also closing off possibilities for interracial marriage. Other state policies enforced during this time made relations between Asians and whites illegal or otherwise produced them as immoral or perverse.[61] In sum, these instances of governance over marriage demonstrate that state-sanctioned racializing policies at the turn of the twentieth century were motivated by, invested in, and advanced the production of socially acceptable sex and sexuality, the classification of the normal and the deviant, and white supremacy.

It was also at this time that the state was just beginning to identify—in order to punish—those figures who were then deemed variously "degenerates," "sodomites," "inverts," "queers," or "fairies" (among other categories of social and state-endorsed nomenclature) and who by the mid-twentieth century would be captured more popularly under the umbrella term "homosexuals." The consolidation of state governance in fact necessitated an increased understanding of what counted as "perversion" in the first place. Many scholars tracing the social, cultural, and legal histories of perverse (and normal) sexual categories and identities in the U.S. metropole have drawn on Foucault's famous argument in the first volume of *The History of Sexuality* regarding the production of the "homosexual" in the "West." While same-sex erotic and social practices have always occurred, it was only during the late nineteenth century, through the discursive invention of the homosexual in sexology and criminology, that, Foucault claims, one's sexual acts constituted the entirety of one's social being, and thus a sexual identity.[62] While scholars examining the history of sexuality in the United States typically agree with Foucault's argument that the "homosexual" was discursively "invented," several have refined when, where, and how this invention occurred.[63] Margot Canaday in particular has recovered how nonnormative sexual identities emerged before U.S. state bureaucratic power. By the end of the nineteenth century in the United States, sexological and popular discourses were still developing the terms that would characterize the recently invented homosexual and heterosexual; the state, lagging behind, was far from recognizing or deploying these characterizations. Still, as Canaday argues, while "this was a state that was a long way from being fully mobilized against homosexuality," it was "beginning to have a vague sense of what it was looking for."[64] At the same time that physicians and sexologists in the United States were categorizing and pathologizing inverts—figures who were alleged to have "inverted" their gender identification—and, eventually, homosexuals, juridical measures increasingly sought to punish those who were deemed perverts, branded particularly according to their behavior or somatic characteristics. As the visibility (and range of characteristics) of so-called abnormals rose, state bureaucratic tactics of surveillance and containment proliferated. Not incidentally, several of these measures were implemented to prevent men who practiced "sodomy" from enlisting in the military, which was just starting to make its way to colonial sites abroad.[65]

While physicians and sexologists studied mostly white, bourgeois subjects to determine what constituted the supposed nature of the invert and the homosexual, the turn-of-the-century state often enforced its nascent policing of deviant gender and sexuality over mostly nonwhite immigrants, many of whom it deemed perverse aliens.[66] The recently inaugurated Bureau of Immigration's exclusion of would-be immigrants from the United States during the late nineteenth century and early twentieth century did not use the language around the sodomite, pederast, or homosexual. Instead, an immigrant's capacity for "moral turpitude," her or his purported "racial degeneracy" as indicated by allegedly malformed or inadequate genitalia, or, most significant, her or his perceived proclivity to become a state-sponsored "public charge" and so drain government resources all indicated the immigrant's inherent sexual pathology.[67] As Canaday puts it, "Aliens were occasionally excluded or deported for sexual perversion during the early twentieth century, and it is possible to see in such cases the development of a rudimentary apparatus to detect and manage homosexuality among immigrants."[68] The fin-de-siècle state thus developed measures of what constituted sexual "perversion" and "degeneracy" through the governance of a wide range of bodies, even those not necessarily engaged in homoerotic acts or somehow demonstrative of same-sex desire.[69] Such governance found as its target the figure of "degeneration." As Canaday summarizes, "Sexual deviance was linked to racial difference—among Europeans as well as Asians—through the pseudoscience of degeneracy. Early twentieth-century sexology posited a number of contradictory explanations for sexual perversion, but an etiology based on the idea of racial degeneracy seemed to have most captured the attention of immigration officials."[70] The state's broader understanding of perversion and the alternative forms of sociality that emerged as a response to increased regulation would come not only to affect the status of the Philippines in relation to the metroimperial state, as I track in the next section, but also shape the very racial-sexual form of the Philippine subject.

Four aspects of turn-of-the-century state regulation of race and sexuality will be particularly important to the chapters that follow. First, the metropolitan state's regulation of racial difference consistently presumed, consolidated, and enforced appropriate—that is, intraracial, hetero-erotic, marital, reproductive, and noncommercial—sexuality and intimacy. Second, especially in the absence of the clearly defined "homosexual," the categorization and identity of "perverts" remained, to the gaze of the nascent U.S. bureaucratic state and its regulatory agents, still emergent and amorphous. Despite this inexactness about its target, however, the state did not stop looking, and it continually relied on racializing discourses to sharpen its gaze. Third, the U.S. metropolitan state form itself was in the process of consolidating, refining, and dispersing its biopolitical techniques of power in bureaucratic form; it was still building its apparatuses of gathering various forms of U.S. "life and its mechanisms into the realm of explicit calculations."[71] Nonetheless, and fourth, the "immaturity" of U.S. metropolitan state-form did not deter aspirations to imperial power abroad. Even as the bureaucratic form of the metropolitan state was unstable, going through unprecedented, unpredictable growth, U.S. imperialism nevertheless ventured to exert state governmentality over its new colonial territories and ambiguously racialized-sexualized subjects abroad.

The Philippine-American War in Metroimperial Consciousness

The Philippine-American War unsettled already precarious racial relations in the post-Reconstruction United States. It also disturbed the increasing variance of sexual practices and identities. An allegedly unexpected, accidental consequence of the late nineteenth-century Spanish-American War and Cuban-American War, the Philippine-American War has generally been forgotten. This war between Philippine anticolonial *insurrectos* (insurgents) and an ascendant U.S. colonial military, capped the United States' status as a new empire; in relation to other imperial nations participating in late nineteenth-century land grabbing, it also marked the United States as a new *kind* of empire. U.S. imperialism's purported benevolent assimilation of the archipelago and its natives, supported by the rhetoric of democratic exceptionalism and motivated by turn-of-the-century ambitions of Open Door liberalism, strategic geopolitical positioning, new markets for a surplus of domestic-made goods, and the shoring up of American masculinity, effected a radical upheaval of the status quo in the United States, generating social relations among people who otherwise might not have had contact.[72] Most of these unprecedented relations were often violent and abusive, but some, as this book demonstrates, were also imagined as intimate.

It is useful here to sketch briefly and in linear fashion the Philippine-American War from a popular metropolitan perspective. While the U.S. public could not have known all the details of the war—an impossibility in totalizing knowledges, to be sure—the popular press labored to keep the public up to speed. Journalists' and soldiers' narratives of the war, and some of their main characters, regularly appeared not only in national news outlets but also in smaller, regional newspapers. Indeed, the Philippine-American War was the first U.S. war to be conducted, via telegram communications, in real time.[73] Moreover, as the war progressed, the press increasingly (as I demonstrate in the chapters that follow) presumed a fair bit of the public's familiarity with far-off colonial life.

The casting of the Philippine revolution from imperial tyranny as an "insurrection" gained traction among the U.S. public, especially when the revolution was compared to the earlier "splendid little war" that led up to it: the Spanish-American War of 1898. Prior to the outbreak of the earlier war with Spain, U.S. national news coverage had been amping up the public's sympathies with the Cuban revolutionaries against the Spanish empire. Illustrations and photographs, such as those used by the yellow press journalism of Joseph Pulitzer and William Randolph Hearst, sensationalized especially the dehumanizing effects of Spanish General Valeriano Weyler's *reconcentración* campaign of anticolonial Cuban *insurrectos* of 1896, during which some two hundred thousand Cubans were decimated.[74] The new invention of moving pictures also roused patriotic feelings for U.S. military intervention and a budding desire for overseas imperial expansion.[75] In short, U.S. metropolitan media produced a "spectatorial lust" for war: popular support of both retaliation against Spanish imperial atrocities against Cuban peoples and the recently established home-rule government of Cuba Libre soon swelled into jingoistic military fervor.[76] Yet it was not until the explosion in February 1898 of the U.S. battleship *Maine* moored at Havana—which the United States public quickly attributed to Spanish military aggression—that a hitherto neutral President McKinley decided to declare war on the Spanish imperial military in late April of that year.

Presented now with the opportunity to prove economic, technological, military, and hetero-masculine power beyond the frontier-pushing, American "Indian–hating," westward movement of Manifest Destiny, the U.S. military acted swiftly.[77] The Spanish-American War in fact lasted only sixteen weeks. The spoils-dividing Treaty of Paris of 1898, between the United States and Spain, consolidated the former's status as an imperial-colonial power, forcing Spain to waive sovereignty over Puerto Rico and cede directly to the United States the island territories of Cuba, Guam, and the Philippines. Over the last of these (which the United States bought from Spain for $20 million), unlike the islands in Latin America (with the exception of Puerto Rico), the United States declared its complete sovereignty, in the name of care, devotion, and duty. Thus ended the United States' venture in fin-de-siècle competitive imperialism, a land-grabbing foray that was both largely supported and closely monitored by the American public. Yet this officially declared war with imperial Spain would, even before the Treaty of Paris went into effect the following April, devolve into an imperialist project that was less universally popular among Americans: the ferocious aggression by U.S. colonial military forces against Philippine nationalist insurrectos fighting for recognition of their newly won independence.

With the end of the Spanish-American War, Philippine nationalists, engaged since 1896 in anticolonial fighting against Spain, now had to wage a revolution against the world power that just months earlier had purported to liberate the archipelago from three hundred years of Spanish tyranny. Philippine anticolonial forces led by Emilio Aguinaldo, with the aid of U.S. military force, had successfully driven out their Spanish colonial oppressors during the Spanish-American War. By mid-June 1898, Aguinaldo (who, as we will see in chapter 3, became an insurgent cause célèbre in popular U.S. consciousness) had declared Philippine independence from Spain. In January 1899, what would later be called the First Philippine Republic was established, with Aguinaldo serving as president. Yet this young Philippine Republic was caught between two competing claims to sovereignty: Aguinaldo's and McKinley's. Despite Philippine nationalists' appeals to the U.S. government and public that the Philippine revolution from Spain was ideologically similar to the United States' own efforts in 1776, the United States refused Philippine demands for recognition. Such refusal took the form of an escalation not just in U.S. exceptionalist rhetoric but also of colonial military attrition warfare.

The fantasy of U.S. democratic exceptionalism in fact supported the reality of colonial surveillance and genocide that occurred during the Philippine-American War. Upon declaring sovereignty over the Philippines in late 1898, McKinley had publicly proclaimed that the U.S. colonial forces were to be seen by the Philippine people—and, indeed, by the rest of the world—"not as invaders or conquerors, but as friends, to protect the natives." Evoking fantasy explicitly, he averred that the military's most "earnest *wish* and paramount aim" was

> to win the confidence, respect, and affection of the inhabitants of the Philippines by assuring them in every possible way that full measure of individual rights and liberties which is the heritage of free peoples, and by proving to them that the mission of the United States is one of benevolent assimilation. . . . In the fulfillment of this high mission . . . there must be sedulously maintained the strong arm of authority, to repress disturbance and to overcome all obstacles to the bestowal of the blessings of the good and stable government upon the people of the Philippine Islands under the free flag of the United States.[78]

In describing the relationship between "benevolent assimilation" and the violence necessary to conduct it, McKinley is missing a "however" here. For McKinley, U.S. imperialism was not, as were those rear-guard European models, decimating or exploitative, despite evidence on the ground; it was a mild hearts-and-minds imperialism, with the evangelical intention ("high mission") to liberate oppressed people and bestow them with the U.S. "heritage" of democracy. As we have seen in every subsequent episode of U.S. imperial aggression against sovereign nations, however, such exceptionalist discourse in the United States' dissemination of modernity, freedom, and care has always gone hand in hand with the imperial military violence to "repress disturbance."[79] Thus, to back up the assertion that Philippine anticolonial revolutionaries were merely "ignorant" of their own "individual rights and liberties," the U.S. Congress legally invented an "insurrection," rendering the status of Philippine anticolonials, as a *New York Times* article put it in 1899, to that of "insurgents against their own Government."[80] The fantasy of U.S. imperial exceptionalism, then, was marked by multiple and mutually enabling disavowals: of its own military colonial aggression, of the Philippine Republic's claims to self-sovereignty, and of the status of "war" itself. This is the condition of McKinley's "wish . . . fulfillment."

The actual combat during the war was improvisational on both sides. Philippine anticolonial forces consisted of a heterogeneous mass of agents that included but were not limited to the *ilustrados* (the Philippine and mestiza/o bourgeois elite, embodying the "offspring par excellence of the Spanish ordering of society");[81] Moro *datus* (chiefs) and their subjects; and an assortment of bandits, farmers, and peasants, many of whom were religiously affiliated.[82] In response to U.S. military escalation, these diverse actors shifted from conventional combat operations to guerrilla warfare tactics throughout many parts of the archipelago. Such tactics, previously unseen by the U.S. military, took on a racial-sexual form against which the imperial military sought to consolidate itself: colonial soldiers saw guerrilla warfare as the inherent mode of combat for the cowardly, savage, degenerate, unmanly race. In response to these strategies of de-territorialist warfare by the insurrectos, the U.S. colonial counterinsurgency was conducted through the evidently more manly and civilized strategies of domination and conquest. Such tactics of conquest, which struggled to reconcile unmitigated brutality with an ethics of colonial care, included a range of modes: hyper-vigilant policing of civilians; colonial state building; the recruitment of Philippine collaborators for colonial state middle management, combat troops, or counterinsurgency fact finding; torture (the simulation of drowning, for example, or waterboarding—what was then known as the "water cure"—was used to extract information and outright punish); point-blank shooting; public executions; and its own brand of guerrilla counter-warfare.[83]

By 1901, the autonomous U.S. colonial military had also established reconcentration camps, whose basic function was attrition: to isolate and starve Philippine insurrectos by relocating peasants who might conspire with them to garrisoned towns and by burning the crops and slaughtering the livestock of the rural economies on which the insurrectos relied.[84] Ironically, this same strategy was copied from Weyler's *reconcentración* playbook for annihilating Cuban insurgents, actions that had so riled popular American acrimony toward Spain. Such irony was not lost on critical U.S. and global publics. The Anti-Imperialist League, the newly formed organization in the northern United States protesting colonialism in the Philippines (composed of such public luminaries as Mark Twain, William Dean Howells, Jane Addams, Andrew Carnegie, Moorfield Storey, William James, and Henry James) publicly decried such violence as antithetical to American ideals of self-sovereignty and isolationism. Even President McKinley recognized the contradiction between such ferocious violence and his doctrine of benevolent assimilation. Upon hearing of the colonial military's "cruel policy of concentration," he admitted in an early message to Congress that, although such tactics may have proved "a necessary measure of war and . . . a means of cutting off supplies from the insurgents," it was not "civilized warfare. . . . It was extermination."[85] The imperial fantasy of benevolence, at least for this moment, failed to protect McKinley from the genocidal violence his phrase enabled.

The U.S. military's scorched earth tactics worked: the reconcentration of Philippine civilians quickly exterminated the Philippine insurgents or forced them into submission; as one general wrote, the military's vicious tactics demonstrated that a "short and severe war" was more effective than "a benevolent war indefinitely prolonged."[86] After the death of some four thousand U.S. soldiers (of the roughly 126,000 that were stationed in the Philippines) and the genocide of between two hundred thousand and one million Philippine civilians,[87] the Philippine-American War officially ended with the surrender of Philippine troops under General Miguel Malvar (who had succeeded the previously captured Aguinaldo) in mid-April 1902. On July 4, 1902, Roosevelt proclaimed the end of a war that had never been officially declared by his predecessor, William McKinley.[88] According to the U.S. Congress's Organic Act of 1902, and building on the infrastructural work done by the two Philippine Commissions that McKinley had previously appointed, a U.S. colonial-backed civil government was soon entrenched both to monitor and fight off ongoing attacks by Moro resistance in the south and to take care of the population with colonial medicine, infrastructure building, bureaucratic governance, and sanitation practices.[89] Fierce combat, especially in the southern Moro or Muslim regions, continued until 1913.[90]

By 1904, as the most ferocious combat in the northern parts of the archipelago was contained to intermittent surges, an estimated ten thousand to twelve thousand U.S. Americans—colonial administrators, public school teachers, scientists, missionaries, business venturers, and physicians, many of whom were men and some of whom were accompanied by their wives—were living in the islands.[91] These agents of imperialist benevolence became the face of the United States' colonial assimilation of the archipelago, while the imperial violence that supported such colonial care became for the U.S. public mere background noise. The U.S. colonial state built new roads, established a communication infrastructure, set up health programs, initiated a vast educational system for the largely illiterate populace, managed policies seeking to liberalize the markets, and granted Philippine subjects access to lower-level bureaucratic government positions.[92] Through these instances of benevolence, whose roots lay in Progressivist goals of social reform, the United States purported to make good on the promise of making the Philippine people fit for self-government. Such paternalism enabled the United States to defer the actualization of Philippine sovereignty until the passage of the Tydings-McDuffie Act in 1934. Although the act demonstrated that the United States eventually did find the Philippine people sufficiently fit for self-government, it simultaneously declared that the same colonial subjects were now no longer "nationals" but "aliens," unfit to cross freely over U.S. national borders.[93] While an examination of this simultaneous independence-giving and immigration-restricting act remains outside of the historical framing of this study, a sustained look at the growth of U.S. state bureaucratic governance during the early period of colonial occupation might explain why Philippine subjects, even after decades of U.S. colonial "modernization," tutelary rule, and political education, would remain so unworthy of full U.S. citizenship.[94]

Archives of Metroimperial Fantasy

Tracking metroimperial intimacies in the Philippines and among its people as they emerge in various forms of state governance and cultural production allows us to understand the specific nature of the United States' supposed colonial care. McKinley sought to cast the United States as a kinder, gentler empire, displaying what Vicente Rafael has called imperialism's "white love" for its "little brown brothers" (another phrase often used by McKinley). Drawing from the rhetoric of the U.S. *Report of the Philippine Commission to the President* (1901), Rafael writes, "Neither exploitative nor enslaving, colonization entailed the cultivation of 'the felicity and perfection of the Philippine people' through the 'uninterrupted devotion' to those 'noble ideals which constitute the higher civilization of mankind.'"[95] Although much of the colonial language Rafael cites here explicitly draws on paternalistic relations—a common trope for pro-imperialists, who saw Philippine peoples as orphans in need of foster care—the reference to imperialism's "uninterrupted devotion" to Philippine civilization, along with the disavowal that the colonial relationship was "neither exploitative nor enslaving," could also be used to describe, say, a late Victorian marriage.

Indeed, many fin-de-siècle U.S. "pro-expansionists," to use the idiom of the day, often cast the U.S.-Philippine colonial relation in marital terms. The pervasive language around Philippine "consent" to U.S. governance intimated a relationship of mutual if hierarchical bonds. Such a trope, which no other colonial power at the time deployed, proves integral to U.S. exceptionalist discourse.[96] One imperialist advocate who held that "God Himself" had united the United States with the Philippines warned ominously, citing Matthew 19:6, the text commonly cited during marriages of the time: "Whom God hath joined together let no man dare to put asunder."[97] Another avowed in *Scribner's Magazine* in 1900: "For better for worse, for richer for poorer, the Philippines have become subject to the jurisdiction of the United States."[98] Such devotion to the form of "white love" might signal the commitment of "intimates who repulse each other [yet] remained coupled when it is no longer fun." To be sure, the pro-expansionist association with the convention of marriage to sanctify colonialism was not merely metaphorical—it was made flesh by the state. By May 1904, the Philippine Commission had "put a premium on matrimony" by raising the salaries of U.S. constabulary officers who married Filipinas; the salary bump, which went toward the commutation of living quarters, was meant to make the islands more inhabitable for potential colonial settlers.[99] The troping of colonial occupation as marriage is especially significant in chapter 4, where I discuss the alleged practice of polygamy by a deviantly racialized Philippine celebrity, and in chapter 5, where I locate in the management of Philippine subjects in the metropole one of the earliest instances of proposed antimiscegenation law that did not target black Americans.

For now, though, we might ask: if colonialism was likened to marriage, even hastened by it, what possible affirmations about sexuality did U.S. colonialism's "white love" for the Philippines make? How would the widespread gendering of the Philippine people as brute male insurrectos, on one hand, and as the passive feminine partner in this marriage, on the other, reconfigure the colonized subjects' racialized sexuality vis-à-vis white hetero-masculine imperial administrators? To the extent that Philippine natives were in need of rule by a "higher civilization of mankind," how was this rule enforced and what uncivilized, perverse racial-sexual truths did civilization have to manage? What else might the euphemism of "benevolence," a word whose etymology ("well wishing") evokes fantasy, obscure?[100] If, as Vicente Rafael, Nerissa Balce, Reynaldo Ileto, Paul Kramer, Alfred McCoy, Benito Vergara, and Julian Go have demonstrated, the project of colonial order was made possible by U.S. military imperial administrators' surveillance of the primitive native's body, and if, as Žižek continually stresses, "there is no reality without its fantasmatic support," then what fantasies about the native Philippine body circulated within the metropole, and what realities did they support in the U.S. colonial imagination?[101] Isn't the relationship between U.S. imperial administrators and their Philippine native wards, after all, sustained by continual performances of love and recognition concealing the fundamental violence and social misrecognitions inherent in colonialism—that is, by role playing, role playing, role playing? These are the questions that the following chapters seek to answer.

White nativists' xenophobic fears escalated when the U.S. federal government, in a show of good faith, granted permission to colonial Philippine subjects to enter into the metropole—an anomaly amid the metropolitan state's exclusionary quotas on Asian immigrants during the late nineteenth century and early twentieth century. Although few Philippine people entered the metropole during the first decade of occupation—pensionadas/os distributed throughout the U.S. mainland and Philippine laborers in Hawai'i made up most of those—the metropolitan public nevertheless panicked around a possible deluge. Under a series of state immigration and citizen laws, Philippine subjects' appearance in the United States necessitated the invention of a new legal term: the noncitizen U.S. "national." The Philippine people's legally and socially ambiguous status as nationals within the metropole was slightly higher than that of Asian migrants, especially Chinese, who, as the constantly renewed immigrant exclusion acts attest, were cast as fundamentally perverse aliens by the state. As nationals, Philippine colonial subjects could travel relatively freely to and within the territory of the U.S. metropole, a privilege to be sure, and their knowledge of and exploitation of loopholes in legislation later enabled them to claim substantive rights before the law.[102] Still, the same status also relegated Philippine noncitizen nationals to the ambiguous, doubly negated legal category, as Allan Isaac puts it, of "noncitizen nonaliens."[103] Indeed, the metroimperial state—influenced by nativist, xenophobic, anti-imperialist U.S. congressmen and other public figures anxious about increased amalgamation resulting from unrestricted immigration—would not grant the island inhabitants U.S. citizenship status en masse or individually. Thus, when in 1904 one Janero Lagdameo, a Philippine student attending Yale University was denied the right to register to vote, he appealed to the U.S. Supreme Court, only to be dismissed once again on the grounds, in the words of the assistant attorney-general of Connecticut, that "the Supreme Court of the United States has held that a Filipino is not a citizen of the United States. Therefore, if the law of Connecticut requires a voter to be a citizen, he must be naturalized."[104] An editorial in Boston's *Globe* spun out the proliferating nomenclature around Lagdameo's status: "the Filipino student who sought registration in New Haven was by birth an alien. The treaty of Paris as construed by the supreme court did not make him a citizen, though it made him a subject. . . . If a Filipino is not an alien, under what statute can he be naturalized and to what country can he forswear allegiance?"[105] The Supreme Court's punting of the case back to legislators in Connecticut, where it eventually fizzled out, was one of many instances of government deferrals around the issue of the naturalization of Philippine subjects. Citizenship for the strange case of the Philippine "national" in fact remained an issue that would have no clear or long-standing resolution, as Rick Baldoz has documented, over the next few decades.[106] In short, the liminal legal status of the Philippines as a territory articulated to but not officially assimilated or incorporated into U.S. empire rendered fuzzy the formal legal status of the Philippine people within the metropole.

Along with the legal status of the Philippine people, Filipina/o "sexuality" was also under construction. To recalibrate Foucault's critique of the "repressive hypothesis," which is usually deployed to talk about the discourse around sexuality, U.S. imperial colonial power not only subjugated Philippine natives but also *incited* U.S. metroimperial administrative and public discourses about racialized Philippine bodies. Yet while the legal status of the Filipina/o remained ambiguous and the categories of sexuality were still under construction, the matter of "Philippine sexuality" for colonial administrators was rarely explicitly addressed. This discursive absence perhaps explains why no scholarly work has examined the governance over sexuality during the first decade of the colonial governance. By 1912, however, as I show in chapters 1 and 2, Philippine sexuality had become a less ambiguous category for colonial administrators. Hence, the bookending of my study with the years 1899 and 1913: the challenge which *Metroimperial Intimacies* takes up is to analyze the epoch before the identity categories that make racial-sexual governance more legible to us now took distinct shape. The benefit of such a study is its window onto the instability of race and sexuality at the moment particular discourses were producing them. Among other things, this temporal window allows us to catch a glimpse not just of the genealogy of the categories we have now but also of how such discourses might have looked otherwise. What does it mean that the racially inferior Philippine subjects were imagined at the same time as—and often in relation to—sexual degenerates? What proliferating modes of discourse would construct Philippine subjects as perverse? And how would such ascribed perversion come to affect other modes of identification and social belonging in the metropole?

While I address these questions in the pages that follow, here is a historically accurate but unsatisfactory answer: in fin-de-siècle U.S. metroimperial culture, the Philippines and Filipinos were always already "queer." Consider the numerous examples from the U.S. press. A story titled "Letter from Manila" in the *Kansas City Journal* in February 1899 labeled that city "a queer old place, filled with queer people."[107] In January 1899, the *San Francisco Call* carried an article titled, "Filipinos Refugees Tell Queer Yarns."[108] In September of that year, the *Salt Lake Herald* and other outposts reported that the military hero Admiral Dewey had said of Filipinos, "These fellow[s] all . . . are a queer lot. . . . Do I think the Filipinos are fit for self-government? Well, no, not just now . . . They are a very queer people—a very queer mixture."[109] Another reporter, taking on a popular point of discussion—Philippine clothing fashions—commented on "how queerly they dress. Many of the men and women are clad in stiff gauze as thin as mosquito netting."[110] Similarly, the author of "Queer Human and Animal Sprigs in Our Philippine Territory" commented on the clothing of "men and boys who go about with their shirts outside their trousers. It seems so queer that you can't get over it." Later, the same writer, describing a "naked brown baby riding on the hip of its half-naked brown mother" and a Manila coachman who used "his toes for candlesticks," claimed that locals in Washington, DC, would never be able to "understand one-tenth of the other queer characters."[111] In April 1902, the *St. Louis Republic* spoke of Filipino Negritos, already regarded by U.S. ethnographers and administrators as the most barbaric of the Philippines' many tribes,[112] as holding "Queer Customs of Religion and Marriage"—indeed, these "Queer Little Natives [were] a Race of Dwarfs."[113] In a bit of hyperbole, a writer for the *Atlanta Constitution* cast Filipinos as "the queerest savages on earth."[114] Even U.S. anti-imperialists were subject to this ascription; as the *New York Times* put it, Grover Cleveland, William Jennings Bryan, George Frisbie Hoar, and Andrew Carnegie's proclamation of "sympathy with . . . Aguinaldo, [Felipe] Agoncillo, and the women of Cavite against the Government of the United States" resulted in a "queer mixture."[115]

These examples of the general attribution of "queerness" onto colonial Philippine peoples do not speak to perverse sexuality per se. Rather than necessarily evoking the early twentieth-century use of the word "queer" by men who had sexual interest in other men, or the mid-century mainstream use of the word to refer derogatorily to sexual perverts or "homosexuals," these examples seem to connote a general understanding of "queer"—as strange, odd, peculiar, deformed, or spoiled.[116] Still, one could contend that the usages of "queer" here spoke to deviant sexual practice more generally, as, for example, in Dewey's description of Philippine peoples as a "queer mixture," which would have evoked racial amalgamation, or in the various articulations of queerness to Philippine fashion styles as barely concealing native nakedness (about which I say more in chapter 3). Relatedly, an article published in the *Des Moines Daily News* declared the Philippine "Sulus" of the South (the subject of chapter 4), notorious already for their perverse practice of polygamy, "a queer lot" for their "mixed blood, with Arabic Predominating."[117] Yet another story rendered Philippine "queerness" closer to how sexual perversion or abnormality would have been understood then. Titled "The Native Filipino a Queer Character: Women More than Men Manage General Affairs," it inverts gender roles: "as to the position of women in the Islands, [Governor Taft] said that the women of the Philippines hold a superior position. They are active managers in general affairs, and the Spanish Archbishop had said to him that if it were to confer any political authority upon the Filipinos, it should be conferred upon the female sex."[118] According to gender conventions of the day, such reversal or "inversion" of gender roles and "positions" might have implied the "degeneration" of Philippine men and women and thus something about their racial-sexual abnormality.[119] Some African American soldiers also found native Filipinas transgressive of Victorian bourgeois gender norms, because they smoked freely in public. Soon, however, the Philippine women would seem, in the words of one black volunteer, "less queer" to the black soldiers, who showed sexual and romantic interest in the Philippine women.[120]

I discuss further the centrality of gender conventions and transgressions in contemporary discourses' production of perversion throughout this book. For now, however, I merely want to note two things about the term "queer" and how it informs the analysis that follows. First, while the word "queer" functioned in the turn-of-the-twentieth-century U.S. metropole as an identificatory code in male same-sex public sites and, later, a *racializing* signifier, it does not necessarily or always signal racial-sexual deviance here.[121] Second, for precisely this reason I will largely refrain from using the term "queer" to refer to transgressive gender performance or deviant sexuality, even as I deploy a queer-of-color critical practice throughout *Metroimperial Intimacies* that seeks to expose the heteronormative logic subtending the U.S. metroimperial management of racialized intimacies. Because the use of "queer" in the metroimperial contexts I consider seems more often attached to Philippine racialization than it does to deviant sexuality or gender-variance, the use of it as a verb, noun, or adjective here does not do the kind of work it might elsewhere. Thus, when I said earlier "in fin-de-siècle U.S. metropolitan culture, the Philippines and Filipinos were always already 'queer,'" I might, at best, not be saying all that much at all. At worst, I risk reproducing, quite faithfully, imperialism's racializing discourse. Since U.S. metroimperial culture regarded Philippine native bodies as strange or even degenerate with the signifier "queer," then retroactively domesticating those bodies with the term as many sexuality studies scholars generally understand it now—as an expression of nonnormative and even liberated sexuality—risks freighting a "queer" reading practice with imperialist baggage. "Queer," to revise an earlier iteration, was not only a "racializing" signifier but also an imperialist one. By not so readily positing "queer," even when I discuss instances of nonnormative gender or sexuality, as there certainly were, I hope that I am contributing, if only negatively, to the robust project of queer-of-color critique seen in the work of Cathy Cohen, Roderick Ferguson, David Eng, José Muñoz, Judith/Jack Halberstam, Gayatri Gopinath, Juana Rodriguez, Chandan Reddy, Martin Manalansan, Martin Joseph Ponce, Jasbir Puar, M. Jacqui Alexander, and Siobhan Somerville, among others. These scholars have insisted, in various ways, on deprivileging sexuality as the primary identity category in queer studies to capture the textures and ranges of abject, nonnormative racialized bodies, relations, and practices more generally.[122] Following their critical lead, *Metroimperial Intimacies* attempts to demonstrate how the "queerness" so often ascribed to early colonial Philippine subjects might or might not have accorded with how we have come to understand that term now.

Any account of U.S. imperial war, whether contemporary or historical, is not only melancholic but also fantasmatic: there are fundamental gaps to knowledge production, even as we try with our scholarly accounts to conceal them, while the modes of accounting used to approach them speak to how knowledge of the event is desired. I put alongside each other colonial state discourse and varied cultural productions as a way to capture what Judith Butler calls the "frames of war." Butler examines how the official, state-directed frame—metonymic of representation more generally—of war might be part of its violence:

> The frame does not simply exhibit reality [of war], but actively participates in a strategy of containment, selectively producing and enforcing what will count as reality. . . . Although framing cannot always contain what it seeks to make visible or readable, it remains structured by the aim of instrumentalizing certain versions of reality. This means that the frame is always throwing away something, always keeping something out, always de-realizing and de-legitimating alternative versions of reality, discarded negatives of the official version. And so when the frame jettisons certain versions of war, it is busily making a rubbish heap whose animated debris provides the potential resources for resistance. When versions of reality are excluded or jettisoned to a domain of reality, then specters are produced that haunt the ratified version of reality, animated and de-ratifying traces.[123]

Metroimperial Intimacies concerns itself with the state's instrumentalized "versions of reality" and also the discarded, "spectral" knowledges that, as the inassimilable remains of the official story, speak different—and often strange—historical realities.

The assembling of the archive offered in this book—just as my reading of it—is a political act. U.S. colonial state governance in the Philippines over same-sex acts or gender-deviant behavior left little archival trace. My scrutiny of a wealth of official and unofficial colonial state records—including administrative orders; colonial constabulary reports; U.S. penal codes, much of which the Department of War adapted from Spanish Penal codes; records of public laws and resolutions passed by the Philippine Commission; administrators' official reviews of the history of criminality in the islands since the start of occupation; reports by the Commissioner of Public Health; memos and private correspondence of colonial officers; and letters by both white and black soldiers—located scant evidence of colonial policing over what would have then been regarded as perversion within the metropole at the same time. By "perversion," I mean same-sex acts, crimes against nature, sodomy, inversion, intimate friendships, male effeminacy, female masculinity, and general gender deviancy. While I do discover evidence of such racial-sexual governance by administrators, what I have come to recognize is that the "truth" produced around the perverse Philippine native body does not wholly remain in the official colonial archives but also *is out there*, in plain sight, in the cultural forms by non-state actors that function as the inassimilable debris of the imperial-colonial fantasy frame. Still, none of these cultural forms reached canonical status—just as no U.S. writers of stature took up the Philippine-American War as their fictional or poetic object. This book, then, following Butler's language, picks through empire's cultural rubbish and puts a few of the scraps side by side. It assembles a minor archive to reilluminate what in contemporary U.S. metroimperial consciousness is already largely seen as a minor event. In doing so, I attend to the charge that Walter Benjamin sets out in "Theses on the Philosophy of History": so that nothing becomes lost for history, we must not distinguish between major and minor events.[124] This is the political—and theoretical—stance on which I assemble an archive that cites the barbaric violence and intimacies of U.S. civilization.[125]

This book's assemblage of cultural production determines its methodological tactics chapter by chapter. My juxtaposition of U.S. imperialism's official records of the first decade of Philippine colonial state building with contemporaneous newspaper pieces, political cartoons, a Broadway spectacular, and published works of Philippine subjects living within the metropole bucks up against an impasse in studies of sexuality and colonialism around the issues posed by interdisciplinarity. Working at the intersection of area studies and queer studies, Anjali Arondekar has characterized this disciplinary impasse as one about archive, genre, and analytical practice. Whereas historians criticize literary scholars for their preoccupation with discourse and lack of critical attention to historical artifacts, Arondekar observes, historians too readily deploy literary sources as self-evident supplements—as example or exception—to the "real" archives they study.[126] The chapters that follow bridge this disciplinary gap by reading the colonial state's archive itself *as also* something of a cultural production—colonial administrators were not, after all, closed to metropolitan social fantasy—and by regarding the other materials' staging of intimacies strictly within the history of the empire's regulatory regimes, however dispersed. Thus, my analytical practices sometimes involve looking for "perversion" in the state and at other times putting together elusive stories spread across multiple archival sites, such as the University of Michigan's Bentley Historical Library in Ann Arbor (which houses perhaps the United States' premiere collection of U.S.-colonial Philippine artifacts); the U.S. National Archives in Washington, DC; the University of California's Bancroft Library in Berkeley; and the Newberry Library in Chicago. They involve locating the various objects I examine within their historical, cultural, and spatial contexts of production, within and beyond the event of the Philippine-American War, and showing how the objects account for intimacies that expose the racial-sexual common sense saturating these metroimperial contexts. Indeed, each object I examine leads to something of a historical surprise, tells us something curious about the past that we would not have known without an examination of metroimperial intimacies.

The first part of the book reconstructs racial-sexual governance by the U.S.-Philippine colonial state during the first decade of occupation. Attending to the development of the colonial administrative state's apprehension of sexually deviant intimacies in the Philippines, chapter 1 shows that during the earliest years of the occupation, there was very little explicit state management of same-sex erotic acts; by the end of the first decade of occupation, however, colonial state administrators were going to greater lengths to locate and punish individuals and populations engaged in same-sex erotic behavior. Chapter 2 narrows the focus to the colonial state's nascent regulation by examining *United States v. Captain Boss Reese* (1911), a hitherto unexamined court-martial trial involving a handful of Philippine Scouts—native Filipinos recruited by the U.S. colonial military—who were abused in varied ways by the defendant. The scandal around the Philippine Scouts bespeaks the limits of the U.S. colonial state's apprehension and management of racial-sexual intimacies in the Philippines, despite the intersecting discourses and policies the state deployed both to apprehend the Philippine insurrecto and to contain deviant sexual and social behavior.

The following chapters move from the colony to imperial metropole, from an examination of state form to what falls outside of the frame, from official records to minor archive. While the colonial state was a formidable executor of racial-sexual management, it was not the only one; cultural production itself, as Stuart Hall among others have taught us, is a key site of sociopolitical contestation. Indeed, the state's complex mode of regulation, as we see in chapters 1 and 2, could be seen as an instance of what Hall refers to as the "condensation" of a range of previous social and cultural practices, which we witness in chapters 3–5.[127] Chapter 3 considers political cartoons that emerged at the beginning of the war, examining how the images attempted to visualize Philippine people. These heterogeneous, ambivalent, and self-contradictory cartoons reveal metroimperial culture's unruly, deviant fantasies about the colonial Philippines and its inhabitants. Chapter 4 examines *The Sultan of Sulu* (1902), a musical comedy about the Philippine-American War by the U.S. Midwestern writer George Ade. In popular discourses, widespread rumors of polygamy surrounded the "real" Sultan of Sulu, attesting to the barbaric sexual practices of the new colonial subjects. Ade's play, however, satirizes metroimperial public discourse with jabs at conventions of compulsory hetero-monogamy. Chapter 5 examines how the earliest pensionadas/os, the Philippine students receiving government scholarships to attend high schools or universities within the metropole, sought to manage their racial self-representation and sexual self-identification within U.S. social life and cultural arena. The students' claims for cosmopolitan modernity and the unlikely prospect of what they call "independence" from the United States required shoring up conventional gender paradigms while disavowing nonnormative sexual desires, however obliquely articulated.

The realities that emerge from these discarded negatives do not always amount to "resources for resistance" to imperial violence, as Butler suggests. As Lisa Lowe has cogently posited, "cultural forms and practices do not offer havens of resolution but are often eloquent descriptions of the ways in which the law, labor, exploitation, racializing and gendering work to prohibit alternatives."[128] While some of the cultural products I examine does attempt to resist the imperial statecraft of war and its attendant racial-sexual ideologies, others clamored for inclusion in the frame, prohibiting alternatives further still. Regardless of the potential for resistance to imperial state violence or to racial-sexual governance these cultural forms might or might not have reached, however, they all attest to intimacies that threatened to exceed the state's unrelenting production of and investment in the normal.

CHAPTER 1

RACIAL-SEXUAL GOVERNANCE AND
THE U.S. COLONIAL STATE IN THE PHILIPPINES

During the first decade or so of the U.S.'s occupation of the Philippines, colonial military officials, trying to quell the anticolonial Philippine insurrection, developed state-of-the-art surveillance, regulatory techniques, and civil reform measures to gather intelligence about and control the racially and geographically heterogeneous Philippine population. But managing sex didn't at first seem to interest colonial administrators that much. While colonial governing involved regulation of some sexual practices considered "moral evils" (such as Philippine women's sex work with U.S. soldiers), it did not often, quite remarkably, target same-sex erotic acts and gender-variant behavior. I say "remarkably" for two reasons. First, both were documented (though not always policed) in the islands during Spanish colonial rule.[1] Second, in the U.S. metropole, there was a "revolutionary expansion" of sodomy laws, which governed over same-sex acts, between 1881 and 1921—an expansion in terms of the varied sex acts that constituted sodomy, the number of states that prosecuted it, and the instances of prosecution.[2]

Imperial expansion into the Philippines did not, however, incorporate the revolutionary expansion of sodomy laws, or, for that matter, the proliferation of anti-cross-dressing laws occurring in the metropole during the late nineteenth century.

In the early years of the U.S. colonial state's consolidation of administrative power in the Philippines, there wasn't so much an explosion of discourse around sexuality as a slow burn. In this chapter, I reconstruct the emergence of U.S. racial-sexual governance in the Philippines during the first decade of colonial state building. As I lay out in the introduction, the U.S. metropolitan state, lacking a clear picture of the "homosexual" developing in sexological discourse, worked toward an inchoate yet capacious understanding of the "degenerate," a term that, evoking a prior evolutionary status, was articulated intimately to contemporaneous racial discourse. At the same time, the U.S. state was producing discourses and knowledges to fix the "Philippine race" on its newly acquired territory an ocean away. Thus, the turn-of-the-century U.S. imperial-colonial state came into form through the racial-sexual governance of a plurality of populations within the metropole, on one hand, and the stabilization of the legal status of the Philippines and its native people, on the other. While several scholars in Philippine and Philippine American studies have recently considered the role of the early U.S. colonial state in the Philippines in regard to continual racial formations, none has studied the state's relationship to what we might now call nonnormative sexuality in the archipelago.[3] The absence of such scholarship is not surprising. Records of same-sex erotic acts or gender variance in the early U.S. colonial state in the Philippines are distinctly scarce. The U.S. colonial state in the Philippines—even while its surveillance techniques within a few years quickly surpassed those in the U.S. metropole[4]—did not yet include same-sex behavior among the objects of its totalizing surveillance.

The claims in this chapter are historical, genealogical. Charting the development of the colonial administrative state's apprehension of illicit sex acts in the Philippines, I argue that during the earliest years of the occupation, there was very little explicit state management of same-sex erotic acts; by the end of the first decade of occupation, however, colonial state administrators were going to great lengths to locate and target individuals and populations alleged to be engaged in same-sex erotic behavior. To track this shift in disciplinary power, this chapter locates both the vague constitution of the *vagrant* and the often unmarked policing of *sodomy* in the archipelago. Colonial administrators in the Philippines imported from the U.S. metropole the capacious crime of vagrancy to regulate, on local and national levels, a range of nonnormative, unproductive, and habitually immoral bodies. Among the habitually immoral bodies, vagrancy laws were then used to prosecute the more elusive crime of sodomy. As many scholars have recounted, "sodomy" in U.S. metropolitan criminal law has historically described a range of perversions not always attached to same-sex erotic acts; non-procreative sex acts between men and women, for example, were prosecuted under sodomy statutes just a few decades earlier. Because of the range of definitions attached to "sodomy" and because criminal legislation has historically treated the behavior with a mixture of severity and tolerance, Foucault called sodomy an "utterly confused category."[5] Still, sodomy in the U.S. metropole by the late 1880s came more and more to refer to anal or oral sex acts between an adult man and a male adolescent, male child, and another male adult.[6] In the U.S. colonial Philippines during the early 1900s, administrators seem to have understood sodomy primarily as a sex act between two adult men. But it took a few years for "sodomy" to arrive as a proper target for the U.S. colonial state in the Philippines at all. Put another way, the discourse of "sodomy" emerged as a shorthand expression of what Slavoj Žižek has called U.S. imperialism's "unknown knowns"—"the disavowed beliefs, suppositions and obscene practices we pretend not to know about, even though they form the background of our public values"—that administrators eventually settled on to make sense of the unmentionable liberties that, to wit, could not have been happening on the empire's new territory (but, in fact, were).[7] Thus, to the extent that this book traces intimacies made possible by and constrained by imperial contact, I consider here how the production of "sodomy" can be regarded as a fantasmatic articulation that makes legally legible the unknown knowns of colonial social life. In tracing the emergence of this category within colonial law and administrative institutions, I show how administrators' utterly confused and culturally informed understanding of the historically unmentionable act saturated the production of its regulation in the archipelago. "Sodomy" might be a behavior, but it is also a cultural production. Moreover, it is a condensation of biopolitical practices regulating immorality that could only have appeared retrospectively—even retroactively—vis-à-vis the more commonly ascribed, though no more precise, category of the "vagrant," another figure associated with habitual immoral behavior. Significantly, administrators sought to brace this regulation of both sodomy and the vagrant against imperial fantasies of the sexually available, disease-carrying, degenerate, and thus perverse figure of the Philippine native. Vis-à-vis the colonial state in the archipelago, the genealogies of the "Philippine subject" and of "sodomy" thus are not that far removed. Both categories—that they are not parallel is no accident—occupy the space of a deadlock in the aspirations to totalizing knowledges of imperial-colonial surveillance and administrative state formation.

The Tentative Character of the U.S. Colonial State in the Philippines

The emergent discursive and legislative attempts within the U.S. metropole to consolidate racial-sexual categories that I lay out in the introduction coincided with the U.S. imperial state's attempts to fix the political status of the colonial Philippines and Philippine subjects.[8] While the U.S. bureaucratic state was, to echo Margot Canaday, merely "maturing" during the time in which knowledges about the sexual deviant or pervert proliferated within U.S. metropolitan consciousness, the U.S. imperial state was far less developed in the area of colonial governance of distant territory and its people.[9] As a prominent scholar of U.S. colonial economic policy would describe in 1905 to anyone interested in studying U.S. colonial state governance in the Philippines, "He is called upon to study a work that is not yet completed; . . . he must examine institutions that to a certain extent may be said to have a tentative character."[10]

This section sketches the "tentative character" of the early U.S. colonial state in the Philippines, focusing on the emergence of its governance of same-sex acts. As several historians have shown, the colonial state was yet immature, but it underwent a tremendous growth spurt during the first decade of occupation in the Philippines.[11] Starting at the beginning of conflict, the U.S. colonial military and civil rule in the Philippines, attempting to stamp out a guerrilla warfare insurrection, mobilized countless techniques and technicians of security, accreting into a bureaucratized surveillance state: a civilian police, typewritten constabulary reports, specialized intelligence units, a centralized phone network, photo-identification systems, fingerprinting, the telegraph, the telephone, the phonograph, the numbered file—not to mention various secret services in the army, constabulary, police, customs, and internal revenue.[12] The formation of an administrative state in the Philippines called for legislative, judicial, and liberal economic systems operating independently from the corresponding institutions in the metropole. In short, while the U.S. state within the conventional borders of the metropole was figuring out how to apprehend and govern increasingly visible racial-sexual individuals and populations, the U.S. state in the colonial Philippines mobilized very early a formidable range of surveillance, security, and finance tactics more generally. Colonial administrators' arguably successful biopolitical management of their subjects in the Philippines—within twenty years, for example, the Metropolitan Police in Manila would compile an astonishing index of alphabetized file cards for 70 percent of that city's entire population[13]—surpassed in a short time the intensity and scope of the regulation of bodies within the U.S. metropolitan arena.

The lack of maturity and tentative character of colonial state governance was conspicuous in 1901, when the U.S. Supreme Court, contemplating what were known as the Insular Cases, sought to determine the legal status of the United States' new island territories under the charge of the War Department's Bureau of Insular Affairs.[14] Not insignificantly, this was the same court that had ruled on *Plessy v. Ferguson* just five years earlier. The Insular Cases, however, did not so much claim to clear up seemingly increasing ambiguities in racial difference vis-à-vis heteronormativity (as I discuss in the introduction) as aspire to resolve legislatively the status of the new territories of the United States vis-à-vis the imperial metropole in Washington, DC. In these cases, the Supreme Court considered the contemporary arguments by pro-expansionist legal scholars and public officials favoring the doctrine of *ex propio vigore*, which held that "by its own force," the U.S. Constitution applied not only to the North American territories but also to the new territories of Hawai'i, Alaska, Cuba, Guam, Puerto Rico, and the Philippines. To put it in the idiom of the day, under *ex propio vigore*, "The Constitution follows the flag." In the cases of Guam, Puerto Rico, and the Philippines, however, the court ruled against the doctrine of *ex propio vigore* and imposed instead a doctrine of incorporation. That doctrine insulated the United States politically from the new territories and left colonial officials to their own discretion when it came to the transmission and application of metropolitan state power. Colonial government bureaucrats in turn decided that the new overseas territories would have the vague and arbitrary status of "unincorporation." This status meant that although the United States would maintain sovereignty over the territories, the territories would only be annexed and would not be immediately incorporated into the union as proper states. The U.S. colonial Philippines, in the end, remained under the sovereignty of the U.S. government but external to its body politic.

In short, if under the doctrine of *ex propio vigore* the "Constitution followed the flag," then under the doctrine of incorporation, the Constitution followed the flag only onto the territories that subsequently would be incorporated into the metropolitan state. Since the Philippines, it was determined, was not such a territory, the Constitution did not then follow the flag into the "unincorporated" archipelago but, rather, tarried indefinitely behind.[15] Colonial administrators, cut loose from Washington, were able to improvise on governmentality in the archipelago. "The U.S. colonial state in the Philippines," as Julian Go and Anne Foster have summarized, "had emerged as a reality on the ground and as an abstraction at home."[16] Such remote and disjointed rule from Washington was supported by the widespread metropolitan fantasy that the Philippine people wanted imperial intervention. As front-page editorials in the *New York Times* and several local newspapers, presuming to project the "desire" of the Philippine people, diagnosed in 1899, "The inhabitants are desirous of American rule."[17]

While the U.S. press presumed to express the desire of Philippine subjects to be ruled, busy colonial administrators did not often concern themselves with Philippine subjects' sexual desire, especially same-sex desire. More specifically, evidence of governance of same-sex or gender-variant acts by the U.S. colonial state in the Philippines, particularly during the years I examine (1899–1912), remains largely elusive. One might assume that the nascent policing of same-sex "perversion" in the U.S. metropole at this time would have also been constitutive of the biopolitical management of racialized colonial subjects in the Philippines. Regulation of, say, cross-dressing, sodomitic Philippine insurgents surely would have justified intervention by reform-minded administrators. My mining of the U.S. colonial archive, however, does not bear out such conjecture. As the U.S. imperial state in the metropole by the fin-de-siècle had an increasing but still nascent idea of the sexual "pervert," the colonial state's legal idea of perversity in the Philippines remained similarly to be determined.

To be sure, colonial administrators did attempt to govern immoral sexual—albeit opposite-sex—acts.[18] Shortly after the arrival of the U.S. colonial forces, for example, as Paul Kramer has recounted, both the U.S. Medical Commission and the Board of Health sought to regulate women's sex work in Manila, especially since many U.S. troops engaged in such commerce, and the troops could not be left vulnerable to disease. The scope of such regulation was unprecedented and formative: the U.S. army's informal program for the venereal inspection of female prostitutes in the Philippines was the broadest program the U.S. military had taken hitherto anywhere and became grounds for the regulation of sex commerce in the military writ large.[19] The administrators' regulation of Philippine women's bodies—regulation that, borrowing largely from Spanish colonial policy, included inspections, the imposition of fees, incarceration, and deportation—received no attention in the U.S. metropolitan press until a prohibitionist journalist, reporting on the dangers of alcohol use in the Philippines, exposed the regulatory practice in June 1900. Once this sexual scandal blew up in the press, a range of social activists were quick to point to how venereal inspection in colonies was itself a symptom of emerging and urgent social and moral diseases resulting from colonial contact.[20] Alcohol consumption, miscegenation, the spread of venereal disease, and the advance of depraved sexual practices in the Philippines all threatened to corrupt not just the U.S. soldiers stationed there but also the U.S. metropolitan public writ large. And colonial administrators, unable to stop the practice, had recourse only to regulating it. It was this notion of regulation of these immoral practices—rather than their outright elimination—to which social reformers most objected.[21] To wit, the sex work of women enabled by colonialism and the tactic of simply containing this work were perverting the republic. Such social panic around the regulation of prostitution was precisely the reason that administrators sought to keep regulatory practices out of the public eye. Imperialism didn't need bad press spoiling claims to benevolent assimilation. In fact, it was this particular "social evil" and "vice"—and not any reports of same-sex erotic acts—that inspired one religious conservative commentator's nominating Manila as a modern incarnation of "the cities of the plain, Sodom and Gomorrah."[22] The colonial state thus did regulate "wicked" sexual practices that, like sodomy, were considered "social evils." Same-sex erotic behaviors just were not often among them.[23]

While the U.S. metropolitan state extended a very small handful of U.S. metropolitan laws managing *race* into the colonial Philippines during early occupation, these laws did not regulate *sexuality*, at least in any explicit way. The colonial state rarely enforced Jim Crow segregation, for example, finding it impractical.[24] And it never imported the antimiscegenation efforts practiced in the metropole, which would have legislated more specifically against "deviant"— because interracial—sex. Deploying the doctrine of *ex propio vigore*, however, the U.S. government did transmit an amended version of the Chinese Exclusion Act of 1882 to the islands in August 1902 to close off loopholes permitting Chinese migrants' entry into the imperial metropole via the colonial archipelago. It is plausible this extension of Sinophobic exclusionary management was influenced by xenophobic fantasies, on both sides of the Pacific, about Chinese people's same-sex proclivities. There is no official documentation saying explicitly that exportation of the 1882 immigration quota to the Philippines resulted from allegations of Chinese perversion; rather, the language around the transmission of Chinese exclusion focused on the threat of Chinese labor.[25] Still, the settler Chinese population in the Philippines did have a centuries-long reputation during Spanish colonial rule for practicing "continual sodomy" in the archipelago and for "communicating" this practice to the autochthonous Philippine subjects—a reputation that some early U.S. colonial administrators and scholars inherited from their Sinophobic Spanish colonial predecessors.[26] Meanwhile, Chinese immigrant men in the United States, suspected by officials for deviant sexual habits in same-sex living quarters in bachelor societies—what Nayan Shah calls "queer domesticities"—threatened white bourgeois heterosexual respectability.[27] In short, while Congress based the extension of the Chinese Exclusion Act on the nativist fantasy of the heathen Chinaman stealing jobs and resources from white laborers—a fantasy that explicitly supported the law—projections of Chinese same-sex degeneracy might have also underwritten the extension. Michael Shoemaker, a celebrated travel writer of the time, expressed precisely this transpacific fantasy in 1899 after a visit to the Philippines, where he claims to have encountered some Philippine political leaders, including the Chinese mestizo President Emilio Aguinaldo. Projecting from his tourist-garnered insider perspective what the Philippines might look like without U.S. rule, Shoemaker wrote, with both dread and delight, "What character of men [Filipinos] are will be more fully understood when it is known that Aguinaldo, in the proclamation of his Constitution, announced that his Government would '*license the Chinese houses of pleasure*.' To the uninitiated this sounds innocent enough, yet through such 'pleasures' came the destruction of Sodom and Gomorrah."[28] Shoemaker's provincializing of the un-cosmopolitan non-world traveler ("the uninitiated")— and, in turn, speculation on how he was initiated—might be fodder for others interested in tracing the "homoerotics of Orientalism" and tourism in a U.S. imperial context.[29] I want to emphasize here, however, that this perhaps ironically apocalyptic warning about the Chinese "pleasures" of Sodom and Gomorrah demonstrates that even as explicit laws governing race, gender, and sexuality did not arrive on the islands *ex propio vigore*, the "force" of metropolitan fantasies about perverse racial others followed the flag.

None of the emergent laws regulating same-sex eroticism or gender-variant embodiment emerging in urban spaces within the imperial metropole were transmitted to the Philippines. Rather, the colonial state conducted governance of same-sex erotic acts in an impromptu and indirect fashion, making evidence of such management scarce. Attempting to locate the fin-de-siècle colonial state's handling of homoerotic or gender-deviant acts, I have examined tens of thousands of pages of the documents likely to mention such behavior. While not exhaustive—a scholar's fantasy of totalizing knowledge to be sure, especially since the documentation of colonial rule in the Philippines is both vast and diffuse—this search is comprehensive. In this glut of colonial documents little evidence remains of the U.S. state's policing of what we would now characterize as transgressive sexual or gender-deviant behavior, acts, or performance: sodomy, same-sex eroticism, inversion, male effeminacy, female masculinity, or general gender deviancy. To put it more precisely, during the first decade of U.S. colonial state building in the Philippines, the state never regulated gender inversion or variance or cross-dressing.[30] The state did, however, govern same-sex acts, though only obliquely.

Given the scarcity of laws explicitly regulating same-sex acts during the first decade of colonial occupation, I offer here a reconstruction of the emergence of the colonial state's apprehension of same-sex erotic acts on the islands. I draw together disparate archival material to tell the story of how the largely informal and implicit regulation of same-sex acts became part of the civilizing apparatus of colonial state governance. While part of this story relies on the positive expression of same-sex governance—in sodomy prosecution, police reports about unnatural crimes, and guidelines for conduct in military law, for example—it also necessitates a queer-of-color reading practice that gets at how such governance emerged in a negative (or even roundabout) yet nonetheless effective form. After all, in a time and place that were devoid of coherent identity categories, the language used to account for same-sex eroticism remained inchoate. I track both in criminal law and military law any signs of the historically "unmentionable crime [of] sodomy." Attending to the production of sodomy in state records, however ephemeral, however implied, furnishes a specific target in the pursuit of the racial-sexual governance of the colonial state. As with the U.S. metropolitan state, the U.S. colonial state in the Philippines took a bit of time to more concretely produce and officially punish the act of sodomy through law, and even then enforcement took longer still to catch up with legislation.[31]

Colonial state regulation affected civilian and military populations differently. Thus, I first lay out the few records in criminal law that attest to the informal (and thus obscured) regulation of same-sex acts by Philippine "native" civilians and U.S. civilians living in the archipelago (a sometimes messy task, as many nonmilitary civilians living on the islands working to establish U.S. imperial sovereignty were former members of the military). Such informal regulation was limited, as apprehension of homoerotic behavior could take place only if the act was performed in public, and the very notion of "public," as I show, was itself being shaped by the colonial state. I finish this exposition by hypothesizing about why such governance of same-sex acts among Philippine civilians emerged in such limited and oblique fashion, despite the proliferation of the regulation of same-sex acts in the U.S. metropole, on one hand, and the widely held perception held by military and medical administrators of the Philippine people as devoid of morals regarding sexual practice, on the other. I next turn to records of military rules of conduct and military law to track how U.S. colonial military administrators attempted to govern same-sex acts among the ranks. Records of the regulation of homoerotic acts in the military are similarly scarce, but the emergence of the clearly defined punitive measures that administrators take make apprehension more tangible. Vis-à-vis civilians on the islands, U.S. colonial soldiers in the Philippines constituted a population that seemed easier to control or more in need of control—or both.

"Necessary to Dismiss"? Sodomy among Civilians

In the U.S. metropole of the late nineteenth century, the utterly confused category of sodomy included bestiality, oral sex performed by both men and women (women for the first time in English-language law, in fact, were intended defendants), and anal penetration by men of either men or women. By the turn of the twentieth century, "sodomy" most often referred to coerced or consensual sex acts between men; in the early U.S. colonial Philippines, it always referred to the same. For reasons that will be made clear later, it is not necessary here to rehearse the historical transformations of sodomy in the U.S. metropole's juridico-discursive institutions.[32] For one, emergent U.S. laws managing sodomy in the late nineteenth century did not follow the flag into the unincorporated archipelago. Indeed, not only did colonial administrators in the Philippines *not* concern themselves with policing sodomy during the very early days of the colonial state, but they also seem to have participated in a tradition of disavowing it. In telling language around a Philippine Supreme Court case in 1908 concerned with the sale of opium between individuals, for example, Justice Adam Carson cites a "learned commentator" of Spanish law, Joaquín Francisco Pacheco, who in the mid-nineteenth century had written, "There may be prosecutions [in the Philippines] which it is necessary to dismiss, as, for example, those for sodomy."[33] Why Pacheco would have found it "necessary to dismiss" prosecutions of sodomy remains unknown: was sodomy among the autochthonous population so pervasive as to be impossible to police? Was evidence of it too elusive? And Carson's reiterating of this particular example of dismissal when discussing a case that had nothing to do with sodomy might seem incidental. Nevertheless, the statement accords with the U.S. colonial state's civilian law of the land, where there was, during the early days of the administrative state, no mention of sodomy.[34]

In 1901, for the sake of efficiently setting up governance of the Philippine civilian population during the political vacuum that U.S. sovereignty had created, the U.S. War Department, the early supervisors of the colonial state, did not import U.S. metropolitan laws into the unincorporated territory. Instead, they translated into English and deployed the Spanish Penal Code in Force in the Philippines of 1870. This document, which Spanish colonial administrators had enforced until the end of Spanish rule in the islands, provided criminal law guidelines from the beginning of U.S. colonial rule well into the 1930s.[35] It thus provided the main guidelines for the management of the sexuality among the civilians during U.S. colonial rule. The U.S.-adapted Penal Code counted among its sexual crimes "adultery," "rape and abuses of chastity," "crimes of public scandal," "abduction," and "seduction and corruption of minors."[36] While same-sex acts certainly could have fallen under these charges, "sodomy," "buggery," "crimes against nature," "unnatural crimes," and "lascivious acts"—legal and common names for same-sex relations in the United States—were not listed. Thus, not only did U.S. colonial administrators find it effective to practice Spanish colonialism's unofficial legal shortcuts in dismissing prosecutions, as Carson's citation of Pacheco suggests, but they also found it expeditious to adapt the official governing techniques of the Spanish colonial state in the form of the Penal Code. Laws against "sodomy," in short, were not on the books during the earliest days of the U.S. colonial state. They were neither inherited from the previous colonial regime nor transmitted formally from the U.S. metropole. Still, even if sodomy was not formally regulated, it was informally policed.

In the absence of official sodomy laws found in the metropole, early U.S. colonial state governance of same-sex acts among civilians occasionally emerged in the enforcement of other laws targeting the poor—for example, laws on vagrancy, indecency, drunkenness, or the corruption of youth. In the U.S. metropole during the late nineteenth century and early twentieth century, antivice societies and metropolitan vice police used such misdemeanor charges as umbrellas to harass and prosecute individuals engaged in same-sex behavior.[37] Similar umbrella charges exploded onto the Philippine colonial scene when the war officially ended in 1902, starting in the densely militarized capital, Manila, and moving outward. In March of that year, the Municipal Board of Manila passed Ordinance 27, which produced and punished the figure of the vagrant. This ordinance described the vagrant as "any person . . . who habitually idly loiters about, or wanders abroad, visiting or staying about hotels, cafés, drinking-saloons, houses of ill repute, gambling houses, railroad depots, wharves, public waiting-rooms, or parks; or who lodges in outhouses, hallways, market-places, sheds, stables, unoccupied houses, lumber yards, or in the open air, not giving a good account of himself; or who habitually accompanies prostitutes or other persons of notoriously bad repute."[38] Manila Ordinance 28, which went into effect in a month later, similarly made it a crime for a person to "be drunk or intoxicated, or behave in a drunken, boisterous, rude, or indecent manner in any public place, or place open to public view."[39]

Reflecting larger U.S. public concerns about temperance, industry, social participation, and illicit sexual relations, these city ordinances' governing of the drunken and "indecent manners" of the vagrant in Manila became part of Philippine law more generally later that year. In November 1902, the U.S. Philippine Commission added to national civil law Act 519, which, like the local ordinances, defined vagrancy in the colonial context and prescribed the appropriate punishment. Act 519 defined the "vagrant" as "every person found loitering about saloons or dramshops or gambling houses . . . every person known to be a pickpocket, thief, burglar, *ladron* . . . and having no visible or lawful means of support when found loitering about any gambling house, cockpit, or in any outlying barrio . . . every idle person who lodges in any barn, shed, outhouse, vessel, or place other than such is kept for lodging purposes. . . . Every lewd or dissolute person who lives in and about houses of ill fame; every common prostitute and common drunkard."[40] Much of this criminalizing language was imported from the metropole. In writing Act 519, for example, colonial legislators drew on late-nineteenth century statutes used to curb vagrancy in some U.S. states, such as California,[41] peppering them with Spanish terms in an effort to speak in the local (albeit elite) idiom. They did not, however, incorporate any of these statutes' language about "sodomy," which by 1897 California legislators had articulated specifically to anal penetration between men.[42] In short, in contrast to what had happened in Puerto Rico, another former Spanish colony, by 1902, U.S. colonial administrators could have readily imported sodomy laws into the Philippines from the imperial metropole but *did not*.[43] Instead, the production of the *vagrant* before the law became a way to regulate nonnormative, immoral behavior while attaching the figure "habitually" exhibiting such behavior to particular public spaces.

Targeting not just Philippine subjects but also U.S. citizens living on the islands, the vagrancy laws over the next few years marked out certain public spaces on local and national levels as either safe or dangerous while casting modes of social contact occurring in those spaces as either moral or immoral, acceptable or abnormal. Municipal governance crafted in and disseminated from Manila within three years would further link immoral relations to particular public spaces. In addition to upholding vagrancy law, administrators instructed municipalities throughout the archipelago to regulate the use of public waterclosets; establish and maintain a police department; punish "mendicants, common prostitutes, or habitual disturbers of the peace"; control alcohol consumption, and quell all disorderly conduct.[44] That specific spaces are named both here and in the vagrancy laws suggests that officials were starting to recognize which public spaces "dissolute" individuals or groups "habitually" frequented.

A Bureau of Health update on Manila water-closets from 1904 reports, for example, that "each public closet is under the direction of a caretaker at all times; this caretaker enforces a set of regulations which prohibit any misuse of closets; the closets are kept scrupulously clean at all times . . . standing on the seats is prohibited, and the prohibition is strictly enforced."[45] Just what kind of "misuse" of the public closet the bureau has in mind and who might habitually do the misusing remain impossible to tell. Philippine natives were known to squat during defecation, and they might have persisted in this practice on the toilet seats. The "strictly enforced" prohibition against standing on the seats, however, seems unlikely to have emerged simply because Philippine natives did not know, as hygiene officials consistently complained, how to shit American-style. Rather, such regulation might attest to the extent to which the water closet, newly installed in the colonial Philippines, was perceived as a space where illicit sexual activity could occur. The water closet, after all, as Lee Edelman writes, historically has been the site of a particular heterosexist fantasmatic anxiety about recognizing what kinds of behavior would constitute "homosexual difference."[46] That the practice of "*standing on the seats*" (as opposed to squatting) seems to the bureau so pervasive a misuse as to warrant not only a caretaker's "prohibition" but also that the prohibition be "strictly enforced" (note the bureau's own emphasis) suggests that administrators regarded the practice as especially "anxiety"-making. While I discuss how the space of the watercloset makes a particular appearance in policing against degeneracy in the next chapter, for now I want to emphasize that certain spaces in urban public areas in the archipelago, as in the U.S. metropole during the late nineteenth century and early twentieth century, became specific targets in the surveillance of civilians' dissolute behavior.

Despite the explosion of vagrancy law, records of individual charges of vagrancy in the Philippines within the colonial archive remain hard to come by, especially when it comes to Philippine subjects, even though one U.S. embassy official claimed as early as 1893 that, in the Philippines, the "uncultivated native is a vagrant by nature and as the result of his surroundings."[47] It therefore remains difficult when considering the colonial archive to determine how frequently this umbrella charge led to more specific prosecutions of sodomy. Such scarcity of records matches the dearth of records of court hearings in cases of alleged sodomy and gross indecency in the metropole.[48] Still, the appearance of these laws in the Philippines remains significant in the state's development of the identification of same-sex acts. Here, even without the specific language of sodomy to signal homo-erotic acts, we find the colonial state approaching a broader construction of sex acts in the production of the "lewd or dissolute person" whose identity remains legally and conceptually articulated to but separate from the feminized figure of the "common prostitute." Under these early ordinances and acts governing morally responsible public conduct and social contact, but not always explicitly governing sex acts, the sexual degenerate was appearing before the state.

To demonstrate how these colonial laws on the municipal and national level prove crucial to the transformation of same-sex governance, I turn to an example concerning a Philippine civilian. In my examination of the colonial archive, I have located a single case in which a Filipino civilian, one Pablo Trinidad, was charged with sodomy.[49] (There are no records of Trinidad's partner—or partners—so we do not know whether the other party was Filipino, white, black, Chinese, military, or civilian.) Manila police originally prosecuted Trinidad not for violating any specific sodomy ordinance but, rather, for violating Manila's Ordinance 28 on vagrancy. Trinidad's conviction of the misdemeanor in 1905 led to a one-month prison sentence and a fine. In his appeals of the conviction, he argued that since the specific act of sodomy did not appear in the language of the vagrancy law, his conviction by the municipal court on the charge of sodomy was invalid. After several abortive appeals, which led to more fines and many more months in prison, Trinidad's case finally went before the Philippine Supreme Court in 1906, which concluded that the charge of sodomy could stick because "it ha[d] not been shown [by the defendant appellant, Trinidad] that the said ordinance was not of a general character, that it [was] not based upon sound principles, or that it [did] not affect all citizens in the same manner."[50] The court's statement, in its vague claims about the capaciousness, sound logic, and universal applicability of the law, reveals how the broad language of the ordinances producing and punishing the vagrant allowed for loose interpretation.[51] Vagrancy was purposefully vague: vagrancy laws in the Philippines enabled a range of umbrella charges to criminalize anyone who threatened social order, and, as Trinidad's case shows, the historically unmentionable act of sodomy fell under these charges. Under vagrancy's capacious cover, sodomy charges against individuals have become all but undetectable in the colonial legal archive.

Importantly, vagrancy laws led to more prosecutions of former members of the U.S. military on the islands than of autochthonous Philippine subjects. By 1902, the year the official end of war was declared, administrators of the Philippine Commission were embarrassed both on the global stage and in front of Philippine elites by the increasing visibility of veterans languishing from drink and lewd behavior on the island—those "dissolute, drunken and lawless Americans [whose] conduct and mode of life . . . [are] not calculated to impress the native with the advantage of American civilization."[52] After charging these U.S. civilians under the vagrancy laws, administrators offered to suspend their sentences if they promised to return home on the government dime and not return for ten years. This provision led to the de facto deportation of 223 veterans from the Philippines in 1906 alone—the same year that the Supreme Court affirmed the legitimacy of Trinidad's sodomy charge.[53] I would suggest that we not regard these two events as merely coincidental and but instead read them "sideways" with each other: they both attest to the colonial state's consolidation of biopower and its production of "dissolute" figures inassimilable to "American civilization."[54] (The Philippine Commission's language to describe the degenerate veterans even anticipates Foucault's language about biopower's drawing "life and its mechanisms into the realm of explicit calculations."[55]) While a scarcity of records makes it difficult to tell whether any of the U.S. deportees faced sodomy allegations under the vagrancy charges, and thus returned home to avoid scandal, public humiliation, or prison time, it is also impossible to rule out such a scenario. Indeed, given the epidemic of blackmailing among administrators at this time, submission to the Philippine Commission's terms would have given the processed vagrants a way out of public disgrace.[56]

I have been suggesting that vagrancy laws led to misdemeanor charges that provided an umbrella for subsequent prosecutions for sodomy—as in the case of Pablo Trinidad—and that vagrancy laws in turn have occluded records of same-sex acts in the colonial archive. Same-sex acts among the native Philippine citizenry, however, were also documented *less* obliquely in the colonial archive. Attorney-General Ignacio Villamor's study *Criminality in the Philippine Islands, 1903–1908* (1909) offered the Philippine Commission a summary of crimes among Philippine natives as reported by provincial fiscals (the title, remaining from Spanish rule, for the attorney or legal adviser of governments of Philippine provinces) throughout the islands. Although it considers factors such as local customs, social environment, superstitions, climate, agricultural production, and politico-economic conditions to account for and predict when certain crimes tended to escalate among which populations, the statistical study nevertheless follows the general colonial fantasy that while criminality of the Philippine native takes a particular social form, it is nevertheless inherent (the "uncultivated native is a vagrant by nature"). As one military expert relayed to the Philippine Commission in 1903, Philippine criminal behavior is "attributable [to] the inborn characteristics of the native to prey upon his neighbor."[57] This attribution of the criminal nature of the native Philippine man affected how administrators regarded sexual crimes, as well.

Although like the Penal Code it never names sodomy or crimes against nature, *Criminality in the Philippine Islands* offers a rare report of homoerotic acts among Philippine men. This report, however, is folded into a list of other morally deviant behaviors. In addition to admitting unequivocally that vagrancy laws in the islands had been established precisely to enable umbrella charges—"Whenever the evidence in a case would not warrant the conviction of the accused," Villamor admits, "he is generally charged with vagrancy and convicted"[58]—*Criminality in the Philippine Islands* lists the crimes violating "public morals." They include adultery, "rape and unchaste practices," abduction, "seduction and corruption of minors," and "bigamy and public scandal."[59] Local fiscals then report the occurrence and motivation of these offenses in their own provinces. The fiscal of the Rizal Province, for example, reports that "crimes against chastity" resulted from "the sexual passions of man unchecked by education, morality, and religion. His sexual appetite once excited, the uncultured man gives way to his passions and makes use of force and violence to gratify his lewd desires."[60] Though the object of the "lewd desire" of the Rizal man is, we're led to presume, the "chaste" woman, there's a sense here that his morally unchecked sexual passions could drive him to indiscriminate mounting. What's more, the Filipino's lewd desire, the fiscal points out, could be roused at any time of the year, having no relation to the seasonal change or local climate. Meanwhile, in the western Visayan province of Occidental Negros, "promiscuous" sleeping arrangements in housing quarters structured to meet the region's agricultural labor demands enabled the crimes violating public morals. These crimes, it turns out, were seasonal, escalating from

> November to April—owing to the fact that during the sugar-cane grinding season a great number of laborers are gathered on the estates with their families who live in crowded and narrow dwellings. . . .
>
> In said dwellings, which would hardly hold 3 or 4 persons, 3 or 4 families live and sleep closely and promiscuously, there being no separation of men from women, of the married from the unmarried, *of old men from young men.* As a result of the immorality growing out of this mode of living, the crimes of adultery, abduction, rape and seduction are committed.[61]

The sleeping quarters of the laborers, putting a range of Philippine bodies into "promiscuous" proximity, made possible multiple combinations of sexual relations. The pairings listed here—men and women, married and unmarried, old men and young men—are treated analogously, and so seem to be treated as parallel constructions in terms of social position. The bodies of women, the "unmarried," and young men are described implicitly as passive objects of the lewd passions of the particularly active Occidental Negros men.[62] While the first two of these pairings most likely presume male-female relations, the third quite explicitly registers same-sex erotic acts. The fiscal's analogy renders all the immoral relations as endangering normative constructions—respectively, women's chastity, conjugal fidelity, and heterosexuality—but it does not cast the same-sex act as any *more* immoral a sexual crime than, say, extramarital sex.

While the same-sex behavior referenced explicitly here is not quite "necessary to dismiss," as Pacheco (and Carson after him) regarded "sodomy," such behavior seems to have been regarded as somewhat commonplace as it emerges rhetorically and without additional comment alongside the other conventionally immoral crimes. Indeed, this rare instance of explicit reference to same-sex erotic relations might explain the rarity of such explicitness more generally: the conspicuous scarcity of documented surveillance of specifically same-sex acts or desire in the Philippine archipelago results from the fantasmatic ascription of inherent perversion onto the primitive Philippine native body in toto. (To be sure, such colonial attribution of perversion would have been directed at only the large lower and working classes and thus more abjectly racialized populations, and not at the ilustrados, or Philippine and mestiza/o elite, who would have been insulted by such an attribution.) To surveil specifically Philippine natives' same-sex perversion, then, would have been redundant—a waste of state time and resources and for that reason necessary to dismiss.

This report by the fiscal underscores another reason that governance of same-sex acts among Philippine citizens leaves so few traces within the early colonial archive. In contrast to the indecent crimes perpetrated in public spaces—crimes that vagrancy laws sought to curb—the "immorality" on which the Occidental Negros fiscal reports materializes in what is ordinarily a domestic, private space: the bedroom. Still, that same-sex relations occurred in the same room where three or four "families" might have slept suggests that the fiscal could have legitimated any allegations of same-sex acts only by relying on eyewitness testimony. This agricultural "mode of living," in other words, blurred the borders between public and private, and thus, for the fiscal, between moral and immoral. Thus, as the vagrancy ordinances and the semipublic nature of the laborers' sleeping quarters both demonstrate, officials, administrators, and the police could detect homoerotic acts only in more or less public spaces. The illicit relation between the old men and young men was a crime against *public* morals, after all.

So why did the U.S. colonial state's management of same-sex acts emerge in this limited and oblique fashion within criminal law? Thus far, I have referred to three practical reasons for the paucity of evidence of state governance of same-sex acts among the civilian population during early colonial occupation: (1) municipal vagrancy ordinances, especially as they enabled umbrella charges, obscured allegations relating explicitly to sodomy; (2) colonial administrators might have regarded same-sex relations as commonplace among what they regarded as the more primitive populations of the

Philippines, as the Occidental Negros fiscal's criminological survey suggests, so reports of such crime would have largely been "necessary to dismiss"; and (3) administrators conducted such policing only within the context of public spaces, even as what constituted "public" was being transformed by the state, so occasions for policing were limited. I would offer four more distinct but related reasons.[63] First, administrators had an evidence problem. Since same-sexual liaisons in public for practical purposes had to be brief, especially given the explosion of vagrancy laws throughout the archipelago, such intimacies would have proved too fleeting even to warrant sustained suspicion or investigation. People engaging in same-sex acts may just have been very good at doing so discreetly; unlike the cohabitation that often came with heterosexual concubinage, such liaisons would have been brief, making them more difficult to detect. Moreover, same-sex acts across racial lines did not incur the risk of conception and racial amalgamation (or *mestizaje*), with progeny whose features would testify to the sexual transgression. Second, the colonial state had a discursive problem. Not only was evidence scarce; how to process it before the law was also difficult. Since U.S. administrators found it more expeditious to retrofit the Spanish Penal Code (which, again, made no mention of "sodomy") than to import U.S. metropolitan tactics policing sodomy and crimes against nature, they were left with no legal apparatus to apprehend same-sex acts, despite knowledge of the natives' "nature."

Third, the colonial state had a public relations problem, both globally and locally. Any state regulation of same-sex acts among civilians had to be performed informally and otherwise kept under wraps. On the global stage, U.S. colonial governance of homoerotic acts would have meant administrators' having to admit publicly that such acts were happening on the archipelago. The scandal in the metropole around the regulation of women's sex work in Manila had already made colonial administrators appear unable to curb the degenerate practices of "Sodom and Gomorrah"; the regulation of what would then have been more popularly regarded as *actual* "sodomy" would have further delegitimized claims to ascendant U.S. imperial exceptionalism. On the local level, U.S. administrators were very concerned about how Philippine ilustrados and other elites regarded the U.S. colonial state and society in the Philippines and felt the need to consolidate and advertise their superior morality as a way to rationalize the occupation.[64] Explicit legislation of sodomy would have risked insulting Philippine elites, attributing to the Philippine people as a whole a perverse and degenerate character or admitting that colonialism engendered, imported, or facilitated unnatural relations, thereby spoiling claims to benevolent assimilation. "Sodomy" could not follow the flag. That administrators deported U.S. civilians charged with vagrancy by the hundreds in 1906 attests to both of these image problems. The colonial state did not just enable U.S. civilians to avoid scandal and humiliation; in disposing of those whose lives were "not calculated to impress the native with the advantage of American civilization," the imperial state also secured its own exceptional character. This public relations problem would explain why the colonial vagrancy laws adapted from California legislation in 1902 did not transmit, *ex propio vigore*, the specific language around sodomy that, as mentioned earlier, had already emerged in that state's own vagrancy laws. While sodomy was a social problem in the metropole, it was not, as colonial administrators would have it, a problem in the Philippines. There was nothing, to wit, unnatural, immoral, or degenerate about U.S. colonial relations. Finally, there was a personnel problem. With an ongoing war against invisible Philippine insurrectos, and given the scattered nature of the U.S. military campaign, colonial administrators would have regarded same-sex acts among the least of its concerns. Deploying governing apparatuses to police homoerotic acts among civilians would have overstretched the empire's already scarce human resources.

"Disqualified for Service as a Result of His Bad Habits": Sodomy within the U.S. Colonial Military

The dearth of records of state surveillance and management of immoral same-sex acts among both civilians and the military throughout the archipelago accords with administrators' practice of colonial care more generally: crimes violating public morals were really troubling only if they affected the military's day-to-day operations. In the case of the aforementioned regulation of sex work, for example, colonial physicians' surveillance of venereal disease shifted in 1901 from an informal practice of examining Philippine sex workers' bodies to a formal policy of inspecting U.S. soldiers' bodies.[65] As Ken De Bevoise summarizes, "The American military was far less concerned with Philippine public health, except as it threatened the army's operation capability, than was the [Spanish] civil administration and therefore kept few records on the subject. Thus the extent to which Filipinos suffered from venereal disease . . . during the war years must be inferred from the health records of American soldiers and their units."[66] When it came to sexually transmitted disease, colonial physicians cared more about—that is, they kept more and better records on—their own. Similarly, colonial administrators supervised soldiers' sexual practices far more intensely than they did the sexual practices of the native Philippine population, often in terms of health but also in terms of contemporary conventions of moral probity.

But because of recruitment shortages, such supervision did not always take the form of intervention. Not only were the U.S. soldiers considered a high-risk population for sexually transmitted diseases (namely, syphilis and gonorrhea) during their tour of duty in the Philippines given the availability of native sex workers, many soldiers had already been discovered to be infected before they were shipped off from the metropole and thus represented a hazard to public health on arrival in the archipelago.[67] The risk the soldiers presented to the Philippine population was often overlooked, however, by military administrators who needed men on the field. Moreover, the source of the risk of venereal disease was projected, fantasmatically, onto the Philippine natives. Administrators grew paranoid, for example, when a rumor circulated in the U.S. Army's Medical Department about a super-strain of syphilis among the Philippine natives. "It is believed," wrote Chief Surgeon Henry Lippincott in July 1898, "that Syphilis of a virulent type exists in these islands and that our men are bound to be affected unless stringent measures are adopted by Commanding Officers to prevent the men visiting houses of ill-fame or associating with lewd women."[68] Thus, the empire's biopolitical care came more in the form of regulation of U.S. military bodies than in the monitoring of the Philippine civilian population.

The surveillance of the bodies of U.S. soldiers for detection of venereal disease quickly became a standard biopolitical technique in the Philippines. As Warwick Anderson and Aaron Belkin have pointed out, military physicians were obsessed with disciplining colonial soldiers' genital cleanliness and hygiene vis-à-vis the wayward filthiness of natives.[69] I examine the discourse around the perpetually dirty Philippine subject in chapter 3, so for now I want to focus on the military administrators' regulation of those in the ranks. The comprehensive and influential thousand-page study *The Theory and Practice of Military Hygiene* (1901), by Captain Edward Munson of the U.S. Army's Medical Department, functioned as a reference book for West Point's Hygiene Department from 1906 to 1914. The study often spoke directly to colonial soldiers' care of their genitals in the Philippines, offering thorough advice to soldiers on how they could keep their genitals clean and should constantly inspect their genitals for variations or abnormalities, especially in tropical climates. In a notable suggestion, Munson emphasized the necessity of keeping any soldiers exhibiting "stricture of the urethra," a telltale symptom of gonorrhea, "excluded from barracks" to avoid the risk of contagion with other men.[70] Adumbrating this warning around the transmission of the sexually transmitted disease is the fantasy of same-sex sexual contact in barracks life. Indeed, Munson's admonition elsewhere against too many men "placed in a single [barracks] room" resonates with the same anxiety the Occidental

Negros Province fiscal expresses about same-sex acts among laborers sleeping in a small space.[71] Recognition of same-sex sexual practices, while only hinted at here, is subsumed under the imperative of regulating the cleanliness of the homosocial space of the soldiers' sleeping quarters. That is, the priority of hygiene officials was not to detect same-sex erotic behavior but, rather, to stave off the transmission of disease among soldiers. In fact, any soldiers suspected of the "moral infirmity" of "sodomy" should already have been rejected during recruitment, as inspection of soldiers' genitalia was specifically part of recruitment protocols. In a section titled "Selection of the Recruit," Munson cautions against admitting men whose criminal records show "conviction of felony," "masturbation," or "sodomy," writing, "The moral character should be scrutinized with care in order that enlistments from the vagrant and criminal classes may be avoided. The recruiting rendezvous is a favorite haunt for these men."[72] Still, that Munson regards the barracks as a space where gonorrhea might be transmitted suggests that such prophylactic measures against the moral infirmity resulting from sodomitic practice—symptomatized here by the vagrant looking to serve the men looking to serve God and country— might have been porous.

The inspection of soldiers' genitalia becomes the grounds later in *Military Hygiene* for a "special word of warning" about the "sexual gratification by new arrivals" onto the colonial scene in the Philippines. Munson suggests that the empire's new tropical possession arouses dangerous erotic impulses for the soldier and offers him opportunity for a broad range of improper sexual liaisons. Immediately following a section endorsing soldiers' moderation of alcohol consumption in the tropics, Munson warns against what such consumption often leads to: immoral sexual behavior. He observes that in the hotter climes, soldiers' "genital function appears to be increased"; when coupled with the lethargy that the tropical climate induces (a soldier in tropical heat is less inclined to "exert physical energy"), the increased genital function swells into a "greatly heightened and exaggerated *nisus generativus*" (or "generative effort") and "excesses in venery." Munson cautions that soldiers typically look to local native women to relieve such "passionate" urges, since among the "native population . . . fornication is not regarded as a moral offence but almost as a legitimate calling." Anticipating the description of the U.S. colonial state we saw earlier, he also attributes to the young U.S. soldier a "largely undeveloped and unstable character" and "animal instincts" when it came to sexual activity.[73] Not unlike the uncivilized Occidental Negros man, then, the young U.S. soldier left to his own devices in the colonial tropics seems primed to mount whatever comes his way. Munson implies as much when he refers to "nisus generativus," a term used by fin-de-siècle biologists and sexologists to describe the sexual instinct or the seemingly blinding physiological compulsion to achieve the "gratification of passion."[74] Though the use of the term "nisus generativus" attaches sexual gratification to some procreative determinism, and so naturalizes hetero-erotic sex, there is also a sense that the "undeveloped and unstable character" of the soldier might lead him to an immature, uninformed, and thus unnatural sexual object choice. The somewhat ambiguous "excesses in venery" may refer not just to sexually transmitted sickness (that is, to *venereal* disease) but also to persons with whom the pursuit of sexual gratification would "exceed" the allegedly innate generative effort.

A similar cautionary diagnosis appears in Colonel Percy Ashburn's *Elements of Military Hygiene* (1909). In this military textbook, the fantasmatic threat of an excessive and therefore "unnatural" sex act takes more definitive shape. Ashburn, who had served on the Philippine Tropical Disease Board three years earlier, often prescribes the standards of sexual behavior necessary for a healthy military life. While he acknowledges that the "sexual organs and sexual desire are placed in man that he may procreate and replenish the race" and that "every normal man has periods of sexual excitement and desire, which constitute one of Nature's powerful influences in the perpetuation of the race," Ashburn calls for the soldier's "self-command" to "enforce a determination that such desire shall not lead to acts that violate the laws of religion and society."[75] The implicit warning here against amalgamation and the allusion to Sodom are not, as we will see, incidental. In a section titled "Sexual Hygiene," he recognizes the soldier's temptations to "gratify passion" vis-à-vis the Philippine natives whose gender is not specified. The heat, sun, exotic locale, and Philippine natives' manner of dress and conduct all "unite to stimulate and excite the sexual desires of the new-comer in the tropics, while his money and the native habits, poverty, and views of morality, constitute a set of circumstances enabling him to gratify them." Yet once the soldier does gratify his excited sexual desires among the morally devoid Philippine natives, so Ashburn's story goes, he soon finds himself with a venereal disease, and his resultant loss of "sexual vigor" leads to grief, "the making of neurasthenia and melancholia."[76] Indeed, "improper sexual habits" in general, such as masturbation and "perversions," produce "a mental state of depression, shame, feeling of unworthiness, fear, and suspicion that others may learn the facts."[77]

Elsewhere, in a chapter devoted to "Venereal Diseases," Ashburn offers a fuller profile of the U.S. soldier in the Philippines who proves

> probably more apt to contract venereal disease than the young civilian, because his associates are practically all males; his topics of conversation are largely such as are only handled in stag gatherings; he is removed from

the restraints of the family and of the public opinion that can most influence him; he may at times find it difficult to obtain access to other female society than that of prostitutes, and these are always to be found. He may also drink a bit to demonstrate his manliness, to relieve his loneliness, to be companionable . . . and then, with judgment perverted and desires inflamed by the alcohol, he forgets danger and seeks intercourse where he can most readily obtain it.[78]

Ashburn's story is somewhat consistent with Munson's cautionary tale: the immature young soldier, marooned in the Philippines without the moral compass of family and U.S. "public opinion," turns to the evils of drink; from there, with "judgment perverted" and "desires inflamed," he looks around him for someone to fuck. What is different here, though, is the more immediate context of the soldier's everyday life. Ashburn does not set the soldier primarily in some Philippine tropical public space, surrounded by the local, native female sex workers or the generally immoral and promiscuous native population waiting for sexual advances that we see in Munson's primer. Rather, the soldier is in a distinctly (even "danger[ously]") homosocial space—in a men-only space (maybe the barracks?) where one must find "conversation," "compan[y]," and even "companion[ship]" amid the continuous "demonstrati[ons]" of "manliness" inhering in "stag" gatherings. Although female prostitutes are everywhere for hire to relieve the soldier's feelings of isolation, there is a sense that such easy commerce eventually and invariably becomes dissatisfactory; the phrase suggesting that "these [prostitutes] are always to be found" itself conveys, tonally, this feeling of staleness. It is perhaps in this homosocial space and state—in the company of other drunk, lonely, horny men with "perverted" judgment—that a soldier pursues "readily" obtainable "intercourse."

While we can only infer the fantasmatic threat of same-sex erotic "intercourse" here, Ashburn a few pages later in the chapter refers to it more directly, if only in passing. When relaying how a syphilis chancre might appear on various body parts, he writes, "If the chancre be on the genitals, it is usually the result of sexual intercourse . . . inside the rectum [as] a result of unnatural practices."[79] Elsewhere the threat of homoerotic behavior among soldiers is only implicitly cautioned against; here it is explicitly identified: the inspection of genitalia leads to the retrospective detection of the kinds of "unnatural" "intercourse" that soldiers may have "readily obtain[ed]." Indeed, the anal inspections referenced here attest to the fact that not only did soldiers find ways to relieve "nisus generativus" with each other, but they also sometimes participated in the even more "unnatural" and perverse practice of passively allowing others to do so with their bodies.

The gradual recognition of same-sex erotic acts among soldiers tracked in these medical administrators' behavior-regulating texts accords with the increased policing against "sodomy" we find in colonial military law. As in criminal law governing civilians in the Philippines, where there was an administrative lag in the apprehension of same-sex erotic acts, it takes half a decade for sodomy to make a formal appearance in colonial military law. (That is not to say, however, that it does not appear in various reports during the earliest days of colonial state building. There is a passing reference, for example, to a colonial military volunteer, one Private Albert A. Widick, facing charges of "sodomy" under umbrella criminal charges in 1901; the general court-martial convening in Mindanao, however, acquitted him.[80]) As I suggested earlier, the year 1906 marked a shift in the apprehension of "sodomy" among the civilian population in the Philippines as the Supreme Court affirmed the prosecution of Pablo Trinidad for this crime. A more dramatic shift occurred in the regulation of the entirety of the U.S. military population just a year later.

Evidence of this shift emerges not in a wealth of military records of sodomy—these might still be out there in the bureaucratic detritus for other scholars to recover—but, rather, in the increased prosecutory measures installed around sodomy. In 1907, the U.S. War Department amended the rarely amended Articles of War, the official regulations of U.S. imperial military conduct as a whole, to account specifically for sodomy, which, it would seem, was emerging more and more frequently in the service. Military administrators appended to Article 62, the article regulating U.S. soldiers' criminal offenses more generally, section C6, which held that those soldiers "charged with sodomy" or "bestial offenses" should either be brought to trial for court-martial if the evidence was strong enough or, in the absence of sufficient evidence, be discharged from the military altogether "for the reason that he has become disqualified for service as a result of his bad habits."[81] Soldiers engaged with sodomy became, in a very different sense from how Pacheco used the phrase, "necessary to dismiss." A year later, the U.S. War Department's *Manual for Courts-Martial* recommended that the punishment for any soldier found guilty of sodomy in a court-martial trial should be dishonorable discharge, forfeiture of all pay and allowances, and confinement at hard labor for five years.[82]

These introductions of the term "sodomy" into the Articles of War and court-martial guidelines, signaling a shift in U.S. military governmentality around the apprehension of homoerotic acts among the military ranks, is significant for several reasons. For one, it preceded the U.S. metropolitan state's recognition of the "homosexual" by almost half a century. The U.S. military was punishing the category of an act but not yet the category of the person, though the sketch of the person was not far away. This management also adumbrates the better-known expulsions en masse of "degenerates" from the U.S. military during the Newport sex scandal (1919–1920) and of "homosexuals" during World War II (starting in 1940).[83] Unlike the former of these military expulsions, which focused on the "unnatural" gender inversion of the same-sex culprits in the military, Article 62 regarded the soldier's "bad habits" of sodomy as constitutive of the soldier himself, a Foucauldian act-to-identity ascription that anticipates the hegemonic categorization of the "homosexual" produced by the U.S. state in the 1940s. In short, the changes to Article 62 of 1907 showed that deviant sexual habits or practices, rather than deviant gender embodiment, indicated one's perversions. Moreover, by establishing the regulation of "bestial offenses," the military now had formal mechanisms to both produce and punish alleged sodomites, techniques that hitherto had been practiced only de facto and with no bureaucratic guidelines.

The amendment to Article 62 had a direct relation to the prosecution of sodomy among U.S. soldiers stationed in the Philippines. While it is unclear whether U.S. soldiers' sexual practices in the Philippines in particular actually inspired amendment C6, the increased numbers around sodomy in the colonial Philippines suggest as much. The Judge Advocate General's Department of the U.S. Army reported that from 1899 to 1917, there were 372 cases of sodomy among the military in the Philippines. An astonishing 308 of these cases—more than 80 percent—were tried after 1911.[84] Put differently, while there were around five sodomy cases in the military per annum during the first decade of U.S. colonial occupation, there were around fifty-one cases per annum in the 1910s, a slightly higher average than that of police arrests for sodomy in New York City (where there were fifty per year) during the same decade.[85] Even though we might not know for sure whether soldiers' actions in the colonial Philippines prompted the more general disciplinary measures, it is important to recall that, even with the establishment of the administrative colonial state, U.S. military combat against anticolonial forces in the Moro south persisted well past the official end of the war, into 1913. Since military and health administrators stationed in the Philippines had such an impact on U.S. soldiers' everyday conduct on a global level, as we have seen, it is not unreasonable to consider that the expulsions of veterans in 1906 and all the warnings against unnatural acts in the barracks, especially as such acts were allegedly primed by colonial tropical conditions, led to the formal disciplining of sodomy that section C6 enacts. What I am suggesting here, in short, is that the apprehension of "unnatural practices" by military administrators, colonial physicians, and military legislators and courts in the Philippines signaled and brought about changes in U.S. military populations' conduct around sodomy in toto. Even before military officials would be concerned that U.S. soldiers serving in Europe would be "contaminated by continental depravity" following the Great War,[86] they were already establishing administrative punishment against the crime against nature in the colonial Philippines within various modes of social life.

The apprehension of "sodomy" by military administrators, colonial physicians, and military legislators and courts in the Philippines led to a shift in U.S. military populations' conduct around sodomy on a global level. This shift, though, was ephemeral. Even as the number of courts-martial around sodomy in the military spiked after 1911—for reasons that I try to account for in the next chapter—sodomy essentially *disappeared* as a crime warranting court-martial under the subsequent version of the Articles of War issued in 1916, which was thoroughly revised as a result of the Great War. In that iteration, only "assault to commit sodomy," and not sodomy itself, was listed as meriting a court-martial. It was not until the version of the Articles of War of 1920 (in Article 93, specifically) that sodomy was again listed as a court-martial offense.[87] This disappearance and reappearance of sodomy in the Articles of War is strange and significant. Historians, social scientists, political scientists, and gay and lesbian activists have consistently cited the Articles of War of 1920 as the founding moment of the government's exclusion of "gays" from the military.[88] Yet as I have shown, sodomy was unequivocally a crime worthy of court-martial in the colonial Philippines more than a decade earlier, taking nothing less than an amendment to the Articles of War to make it so. The production and disciplining of sodomy among the U.S. military personnel in the colonial Philippines, in short, has been overlooked in the history of and protests against the regulation of sexuality in the United States. Such oversight speaks not just to the exceptionalist discourse that underwrites U.S. empire but also to the national disavowal around imperialism in both U.S. gay and lesbian scholarship and activism. While disavowal around imperialism goes unchecked more generally in the United States, it is perhaps worth noting that some historically repressed and reviled people clamoring for inclusion rely on a political genealogy that mislocates its origins in a Great War at the risk of abjuring state violence toward another historically repressed and reviled people clamoring for sovereignty and life during an ignominious one.

In tracing the development of racial-sexual governance conducted by the early U.S. colonial state, this chapter has sought to lay out some of the "empirical" basis for the metroimperial fantasies about the Philippines and its people that I trace in the chapters that follow. The cultural production of U.S. imperialism examined throughout the rest of the book, while not always referencing such racial-sexual management traced here—indeed, much of it, preceding the major changes in the state apprehension of sodomy, could not have done—

might be read as representing differently, "fantasmatically," the so-called realities of governance I uncover. Some of the more important work the chapter does, however, is to show that colonial state governmentality itself, as it emerges around racial-sexual governance, found its support in administrators' collective fantasies about Philippines natives and people engaging in sodomy. The state's aspirational governance of racial-sexual comportment in the Philippines was, after all, *also* a cultural production—an expression of fantasy—and a protection against the impasses of imperialism's life-calculating knowledge project.

CHAPTER 2

UNMENTIONABLE LIBERTIES

A Racial-Sexual Differend in the U.S. Colonial Philippines

"Sensational Developments"

In 1910, the U.S. colonial military in the Philippines conspired to keep from the vigilant U.S. press the details of a scandal that would not only have betrayed President William McKinley's promise of the United States' "benevolent assimilation" of the archipelago but also belied the image of hale, white heterosexual masculinity that the ascendant U.S. empire aspired to convey to itself and the rest of the world. Among the military's top brass, both in Washington and Manila, the crime at the source of the scandal was horrifying and rarely mentioned. Because those same "military authorities at Manila suppressed the case," by the time the few local newspapers in the United States covering the story could recount to the public what had happened, reporters were merely chasing an "investigation of an investigation," able only to relay the U.S. military's disciplinary action rather than the nature of the crime itself.[1] Still, the colonial administrators' suspicious attempt to bury the case in bureaucracy is precisely what drew the attention of the U.S. press. The title of one newspaper story in 1910 captured the ambiguity and titillation around this scandal, which was on the verge of exploding: "May Be Sensational Developments in the Philippines."[2]

Despite the sensational character of the scandal, the U.S. public didn't find out much from the press. What reporters did manage to gather was that the U.S. War Department was bringing Captain Boss Reese, a celebrated twenty-nine-year-old white officer from Carrollton, Georgia, stationed in Puerto Princesa province on the Philippine island of Palawan, and in charge of a colonial military outfit known as the Philippine Scouts, to trial for a court-martial. From the "Army and Navy Gossip" section of the *Washington Post*, we learn that Reese was charged, despite an "excellent record in the field," with "drunkenness, profane language toward subordinates and rough treatment of people under his command."[3] New York's *Evening Post* reported a few months later that Reese was initially dismissed from the military and sentenced to fifteen years of imprisonment and hard labor as a result of the court-martial, but his dismissal and sentencing were later commuted by President William Taft (the former governor-general of the Philippines) to a suspension from rank and command, along with a three-month pay cut.[4] In September 1912, the *Galveston News* reported that Reese, having been convicted in 1911 for "brutal treatment of his enlisted men, neglect of duty, and other offenses" in a second court-martial trial, was dropped from the U.S. Army's payroll altogether.[5] These charges might look bad, but surely drunkenness and verbal abuse toward one's subordinates were common enough and could be overlooked as grounds for a court-martial—at least for a minor military hero with a hitherto "excellent record." So what potentially career-destroying crime could this former military hero have committed, and why would it so alarm the colonial bureaucracy, whose officers were anxious that the scandal remain "entirely hushed up"?[6]

So as not to reproduce this colonial cover-up any longer than I already have, I will put Boss Reese's "crime" as unambiguously as the colonial archive allows me: probably while drunk, Reese actively sodomized several of his military subalterns, most often against their will.[7] A particular "sexual" crime, then, constituted those unspecified "other offenses" with which Reese was charged. How, exactly, Reese accomplished this act might conjure for U.S. wild speculative plot questions: where did he do it? In his captain's quarters? In public? Did he just order his subalterns to line up outside his barracks quarters? Did he tie them up? If so, how did he manage to do *that*? Was it all in one night? Over several nights? Then how did he get away with such repetition without detection? How long had this been going on? Did his subalterns resist at all? Similar questions emerged during the trial. Such questions, though, might not so much make one doubt whether these acts happened as attest to the pru-rient nature of some modes of information gathering in the colonial-military courtroom (or, in my case, among the archival records). Given the particularity of Reese's crime, it is significant that the turn-of-the-twentieth-century U.S. co-lonial military deemed it necessary to suppress knowledge about Reese's "un-natural" sexual acts from the press.[8] I wonder less, though, about *why* this case stirred up so much anxiety among administrators, not to mention the presi-dent himself, and drew "more than ordinary interest" in the U.S. press—the "fallacy of misplaced scale" around "sex" already leads U.S. to an explanation, and indeed such behavior would still scandalize today, more than a hundred years later—than about *how* it came to do these things.[9]

The case of Captain Reese gets messier when we consider the particular-ity of the bodies of Reese's perverse abuse. Reese, as I mention earlier, led a company of the Philippine Scouts, a colonial outfit composed of a few U.S. officers but mostly of allegedly trustworthy native Philippine men recruited by the U.S. military. In October 1901, Theodore Roosevelt activated the first group of native scouts recruited to identify and fight off the allegedly more sav-age anticolonial Philippine combatants, the insurrectos (insurgents).[10] Reese's sexual crime, therefore, was also a racialized and, as we will see shortly, gen-dered one. If, as Ann Stoler, echoing Michel Foucault, writes, "Colonial admin-istrations were prolific producers of social categories," then how might Reese's act speak to the figure of the colonially administered "Filipino" within histo-ries of sexuality—or, for that matter, to the figures of what we might nowadays categorize as "homosexual" or "heterosexual" within the histories of U.S. colo-nialism?[11] What might Reese's case say about knowledges about various bod-ies whose very differentiation and categorization are shored up and governed in direct relation to fundamental impossibilities in U.S. colonialism's fantas-matic project of totalizing knowledge production?

Before the court-martial trials, Reese had built a solid reputation in his military career. He had been promoted quickly among the colonial military ranks (and celebrated twice in the *New York Times*) for his "gallant" heroics during his Philippine Scout company's routing of insurrectos and killing their leader.[12] On a mission in Rizal Province in 1903 to capture or kill the insur-recto Captain San Miguel—whom Governor Taft a year earlier had tried to in-duce to surrender—Reese's company, ambushed by guerrilla fighters, stormed the enemy in a "near-suicidal assault."[13] During the successful charge, Reese, then a lieutenant, was wounded and, one might suspect, earned Taft's esteem. Reese's career as an officer would take off from there, and he was featured in local U.S. papers for his exemplary command. Such a history of masculine valor, duty, and sacrifice (in addition to his current rank as captain) would provide the impetus for the Army's conspiracy to obscure from the press the "other offenses" with which he was charged almost a decade later. Indeed, even before the trial, a court of inquiry conducted between June and October 1910 dismissed the "other offenses" around sexual abuse and recommended that Reese be tried only for drunkenness and disorderly conduct. After the scandalous details of Reese's crime threatened to leak to the U.S. press, however, the military was compelled to conduct the "investigation of an investigation."

Looking at the private discourses colonial officials used to manage their own confusion and disgust around Reese's "perverse" crime reveals the complicated, unstable, and intersecting dynamics of racialized, gendered, and sexualized power relations within the colonial arena of the U.S.-occupied Philippines. Before examining the court-martial records, I turn here to correspondence between high-level colonial officers as examples of discourses used in private. In their letters, Reese's military superiors never ascribe the sexological labels "homosexual" to Reese—nor could they have, since this then pathologizing term had not yet migrated fully from the nineteenth-century scientific discourse of sexology to popular U.S. parlance. Nor did they mention, in these private letters, the more conventional "sodomy" and "crime against nature," terms that emerged consistently during the court-martial trial. Instead, the officers fumbled with late Victorian diction to talk about the historically unmentionable crime. An extraordinary rendering of Reese's "crimes" appears in a typewritten letter from Captain E. M. Joss to Brigadier-General Harry Hill Bandholtz of the Philippine Constabulary in late May 1910: "During the trial evidence was introduced showing Capt. Boss Reese to be guilty of the most revolting of crimes and of drunkenness and brutality towards his men. The court went to the bottom and were convinced beyond a shadow of the doubt that all of the accusations were true. Not less than twelve witnesses, soldiers of the 4th, [sic] and 5th, Co[mpanie]s testified that he had *used them as women* and they were telling the truth if truth was ever told."[14] While the object of our attention is Reese, we learn more here about the letter writer, Captain Joss, and, I would suggest, about U.S. imperialist thought, which Joss metonymically represents.

The Victorian officer Joss is scandalized. In his conspicuous insistence of the "truth," he protests too much. The testimony of the witnesses/victims, "beyond a shadow of the doubt," he avers, "w[as] true"; the soldiers "were telling the truth if truth was ever told." Joss here seems anxious to parry off in advance what he anticipates to be Bandholtz's disbelief of the witnesses' testimony—as if a soldier's admitting his subjection to the "most revolting of crimes" would be so dubious. Yet Joss affirms the "truth" of the matter rather curiously here. First, he seems to presume that the subordinate soldiers must have been "telling the truth," for why else would they attest in court to being so abjectly "used" if it weren't so? After all, in their testimony they have risked subjecting themselves to official and public accusations of perversion and effeminacy, characteristics unbecoming colonial military soldiers—and, in fact, by this time (as I recount in chapter 1) punishable by dishonorable discharge and prison time. Moreover, in averring that these soldiers "were telling the truth if truth was ever told," Joss overemphasizes the "truth" in the soldiers' "telling" about their usage "as women," privileging it rhetorically even over the "truth" of *Reese's actual act.* Joss thereby places the truth in the subordinates' testimony, and thus evidence of their manly duty, on the same ontological level as that of Reese's unbelievable crime. Such an equalization of the two "truths" resolves a cognitive dissonance for Joss, relieving him of the more horrifying, the more "revolting," the more impossible of the two: that Captain Reese would sodomize the soldiers under his command.

If such self-protection isn't surprising, it's because this is precisely how fantasy works. That Joss would insist on and rhetorically privilege the truth in the testimony over the truth of Reese's action suggests that in the hypermasculine, misogynistic domain of the military imaginary there is something fundamentally intolerable about the latter: Reese's "use" of the men "as women," something of an obscene primal scene for Joss, amounts to an un-*man*ning of the soldiers, a horrifying *untruthing* of the subaltern soldiers' masculine bodies. Acknowledging later in the letter such a horrifying possibility, Joss solicits Bandholtz's "best advice" on how to "remov[e] this contemptable [*sic*] cur from the service." Joss's request suggests a lack of precedence. Indeed, to the extent that colonial administrators could punish lower-ranked soldiers for sodomy via revisions to the Articles of War, as I recount in chapter 1, there is no evidence that colonial officers were ever prosecuted. This is perhaps why the knowledge about Reese's actions so vexed military superiors. Captain Reese's "revolting" behavior seemed to have been enabled by—even *resulted* from—his rank within colonial military order. Reese's behavior might thus be regarded as another example of Slavoj Žižek's "unknown knowns" within U.S. imperialism's field of totalizing knowledge.[15] In investigating the horrifying truth about Reese, the military court did indeed get "to the bottom" of the matter, and the unbearable "truths" they encountered there revealed both the incoherence of colonial knowledge making and the fractures of U.S. imperial masculinity.

The colonial administrators' management of the public discourse around the problem of Reese indexes the parameters of racial-sexual governance at the turn of the twentieth century. Only a handful of U.S. colonial government documents, as I demonstrate in chapter 1, referred even obliquely to the recognition or management of same-sex acts in the Philippines. Such scarcity makes the court-martial trial of Reese all the more significant. The relative unavailability of sexual categories and inexperience of administrators in policing same-sex liaisons enabled officers to preserve, however tenuously, the sex-gender "normalcy"—that is, the hetero-masculinity—of Reese in the face of his perverse sexual act. To the extent that Reese's acts of sodomy threatened to define the totality of his being in court, moreover, it is precisely the self-same racial-sexual constitution of the Philippine subaltern that fended off that threat. The attribution of racialized perversion to the Philippine soldiers concealed the "revolting" truth from the white colonial administrators that there might have been a sexual deviant—a "sodomite"—among them. Even if Reese's whiteness did not entirely absolve him of constitutional perversion—he was still court-martialed and found guilty of sodomy after all—it nevertheless afforded him the benefit of the doubt amid ambiguity around his unknowingly known "perversion."

Under the law of the U.S. colonial state in the Philippines, as I also suggest in the first chapter, the genealogies of the "Philippine subject" and of "sodomy" are not that far removed. Both "utterly confused categories," however asymmetrical, occupy the space of a deadlock in the aspirations to totalizing knowledges of imperial-colonial surveillance and administrative state formation. In this chapter, I press this argument further to suggest that the categories of "Philippine subject" and "sodomy" also demarcate the impossibility of articulating a wrong—an injustice—within the existing juridico-discursive system of the U.S. colonial state in the Philippines. I argue that, vis-à-vis the increasingly stable category of sodomy within colonial military law, the "Filipino" constitutes as a particular *differend*, a term that the poststructuralist philosopher Jean-François Lyotard coined to describe a case of conflict that cannot be fairly resolved because the germane rules of judgment or discourse do not apply to all involved.[16] In litigation, an injured party is able to claim grievance or injury under the existing rules of law; in a differend, however, an injured party is divested of the very means of such representation. The claims of the different— that is, the injured party who must present a case of grievance outside of or different from the validated idiom—is, in a case of the differend, "reduced to silence."[17] Such inability to claim or testify makes the injured party in a case of the differend a victim—not just of the original, inexpressible injury but also of the very system that deprives the injured of representation, that reduces the injured to silence. Lyotard's ethical charge is to find some way to articulate the victim's pain, "to give the differend its due."[18] The scandal around *United States v. Boss Reese* involves a normative case of judgment, since the prosecuting U.S. military and defendant Reese are able to present their cases in the same juridical idiom. But it also involves a differend: vis-à-vis the deployment of "sodomy," which in this particular context often proves synonymous with rape, Philippine soldiers are reduced to silence before colonial military law. Such silencing is most salient when colonial officials dismissed from court the Filipino soldiers' claims of having been subjected to Reese's sodomitic act when it came to his prosecution while at the same time dismissed from the military the Filipino soldiers themselves based on the same testimony. This is not just a double-standard but a differend.

In June 1912, the *Washington Post* reported that the court-martial record "in the case of Capt. Reese is a voluminous one."[19] I offer here at times a survey and at times a close reading of this rich and fascinating collection of letters, affidavits, depositions, records of investigation, and court trial transcripts. Despite such "volume," it's significant that none of the sordid details that surfaced during the court-martial trial ever came to light in the U.S. press. Colonial administrators ultimately succeeded in keeping the scandal from becoming the "spectacular development" that the press would have pounced on. Still, though not quite sensational, the Reese trial—*unexamined until now*—was a significant event in the history of U.S. sexuality and the history of the formation of the "Filipino" in metroimperial consciousness. It threatened to spoil the empire's self-image in a way that it could not have necessarily done in a previous time.

"Even His Soldiers"

Let us return briefly to the letters between Reese's administrators. These relatively private relays of discourse—gossipy, even, when read alongside the bureaucratically managed court-martial trial—reveal slightly more candid expressions of anxiety about Reese's actions. The late Victorian language Reese's superiors used unofficially here bespeaks an effort to articulate a long historically "unmentionable" sexual act—a "proliferation," as Foucault famously put it, "of discourse."[20] Reese's military superiors, as we see in the letters, were not just trying to forestall a public scandal by suppressing the details; they themselves were scandalized and baffled and thus grasped at "truths" through a mix of hearsay and official testimony. The language used by the administrators suggests that Reese's actions transgressed not just military comportment but also normative, late nineteenth-century bourgeois propriety more generally: the Victorian impulse to "hush" the chatter about Reese's act itself took on the form of an incitement to discourse among administrators. As Bandholtz reported to another official in May 1910, "There has been a nasty rumor in circulation about Captain Reese. . . . It is understood that he submitted his resignation. . . . These, of course, are only rumors, but a court-martial is now in session . . . and the fact will probably come out."[21] People were talking, and administrators sought to manage how they talked about it. Bandholtz's attention to the rumors (which he's of course spreading in this letter) reveals an acknowledgement that such unofficial discourse as gossip has the capacity to produce "truths" that might exceed the administrators' management. Still, the scant reports of the Reese case within the American press, where it emerged sanitized of all the gritty detail, attest to the great success that military colonial administrators, in collaboration with bureaucrats in Washington, found in retaining U.S. imperialism's public image as an all-knowing, well-governed, hetero-masculine enterprise.

During the thick of the scandal, in a typed memorandum from Bandholtz to Major-General Leonard Wood dated May 1910, Bandholtz conveys that Reese has been "charged with having taken unmentionable liberties with his muchachos and even his soldiers. All this was hushed up."[22] The term "muchachos," an appellation inherited from the recently displaced Spanish colonial forces, conventionally refers to boys, lads, or male servants—in this case, Bandholtz's use of the term referred to the Philippine civilian houseboys attending to the colonial officers and maintaining the mess hall in the barracks. But the term had two other connotations in the colonial context. First, Bandholtz's "muchachos," even as it might have been used as a term of endearment or, at least, familiarity with the help, reaffirmed the imperialist view of the Philippines as a still young nation, a perception that had negated Philippine nationalist claims for self-governance since the turn-of-the-century revolution against U.S. colonialism.[23] Indeed, the colonial Philippines and its people were widely known as the uncivilized, immature wards of the ascendant U.S. empire, the abandoned children of Spain incapable of self-sovereignty and thus unworthy of independence.

Moreover, Bandholtz's use of the infantilizing "muchachos" in this instance, I would suggest, also drew on a late Victorian psychiatric and popular conceptualization of male-male sodomy, which (in keeping with more classical understandings of sodomy) conceives of penetration as affirming a preexisting hierarchy based on age or social status.[24] This is a historically specific point. In accordance with the gender-sexual conventions within the U.S. imperial metropole at the time, especially as informed by late nineteenth-century sexological discourse, Reese's penetration of his subordinates would not necessarily have signaled to his peers and superiors sexual or psychological perversion so much as his subordinates' submission to him (or perceived effeminacy) would.[25] Indeed, in late nineteenth-century and early twentieth-century U.S. sexual culture, a man could engage in a sexual act with another man and still be considered normal (however immoral, "revolting," or "contemptible," as Reese's superiors called him) as long as the man was in the so-called *activo* position of penetrating his *passivo* sexual partner. In such a scenario, the man being penetrated would have been considered the "degenerate" and "feminized" figure, a "pervert" that was reversing—or, to use the medical language of the day, "inverting"—his ascribed sex role. Paraphrasing the work of the sexologist Richard von Krafft-Ebing, whose publication of "Perversion of the Sexual Instinct" in a U.S. medical journal in 1888 introduced his work to the U.S. audiences, David Halperin captures succinctly this gender-sexual dynamic: "if the man who played an 'active' sexual role in sexual intercourse with other males was conventionally masculine in both his appearance and his manner of feeling and acting, if he did not seek to be penetrated by other men, and/or if he also had sexual relations with women, he might not be sick but immoral, not perverted but merely perverse. His penetration of a subordinate male, reprehensible and abominable though it might be, could be reckoned a manifestation of his excessive but otherwise normal male sexual appetite."[26]

The ascription of normalcy and perversion (or masculine and degenerate, respectively) according to a man's position in the sexual act, however, takes on a very particular form in the Philippine-U.S. colonial arena. Reese's penetration of his subordinates seems to have been considered by his superiors—at least at first blush—immoral but not psychologically or sexually abnormal, perverse though not perverted, morally "revolting" but not constitutionally pathological. Reese's normalcy, however, was not entirely self-evident in his penetrating role; rather, it took a collective effort by military administrators to produce and maintain it. Such maintenance required persistently constructing—making self-evident—the gendered and "sexual" abnormality of the "Filipino." Because the muchacho was younger and performed domestic, "feminized" labor—attending to the officers, cleaning the barracks, serving soldiers in the mess hall—he was structurally poised, within this misogynist order, to be "used as" a "woman." The passing differentiation that Bandholtz makes between the soldiers and the muchachos seems to separate the men from the boys: while muchachos might have been regarded as close to the "feminine," the Philippine soldiers, by their virtue of being soldiers, were real men—normal. That Bandholtz emphasizes the distinction of the Philippine soldiers—Reese took liberties with *"even* his soldiers"—suggests that he believed such treatment of soldiers was anomalous. Reese's sexual "liberties" with the Philippine men, however, marks the limits of such exception.

The Filipino Scouts' subordinate social standing, not only in terms of age and military rank but also in terms of *race*, drew them closer to the feminine, marked them as subordinate in regard to metropolitan, normative gender style and sexual role. While Philippine natives were recruited by the U.S. colonial military with the promise of self-determination, there were no mechanisms for their promotion through the ranks—indeed, it would have been inconceivable for a native officer to find himself in charge of a white colonial soldier.[27] Reese's sodomitic act reinscribed this permanent subordination, especially when one considers that he did not use, as far as the records show, any non-Philippine subordinates "as women." Reese's act of sodomy might therefore be seen as performative. His repeated penetration subjectivizes the Philippine soldiers into a subordinate gender-racial-sexual role—namely feminized-muchacho-passivo.[28] Filipinos were indeed more subject to Reese's sexual "liberties" than black or white U.S. soldiers in the Scouts could have been precisely because the Philippine soldiers were closer structurally to the muchachos in terms of racial-gendered character. In short, we find here an odd chiasmus in colonial fantasy: while Bandholtz might have regarded the Filipino Scouts as real men by virtue of their being U.S. soldiers, Reese seems to have regarded them as closer to women by virtue of their being Filipino.

Reese's penetration of his Philippine subalterns, seen in this way, proves not incompatible but, rather, *consistent* with the hegemonically masculine physical and verbal abuse that Reese enacted throughout his career to assert the authority conferred on his rank and race. Recall that Reese's superiors in fact attempted to dismiss—or otherwise "hush up"—the specific charges of sodomy before the court-martial even started for the sake of upholding his longstanding reputation as a colonial officer. Reese's whiteness, it seems, along with his military standing partly explain away—make "unmentionable"—the "liberties" he took with the colonial subjects not yet deemed worthy of their own.

Colonial administrators' concealment of Reese's contemptible and horrifying actions—from the press and from themselves—functioned to protect the colonial military from disgrace, thereby arrogating racial-sexual normalcy. Reese's superiors largely seem to have been tempted to dismiss his aberrant behavior as opportunistic or contingent—a temporary lapse of judgment, perhaps, that resulted from being surrounded largely by native men on the remote archipelago; another symptom of tropical neurasthenia and "severe mental strain"; or a way to relieve his alcohol-exacerbated *nisus generativus*—rather than something that expressed an inherently pathological desire.[29] As one investigator assigned to the case put it, "I felt that whiskey had gotten the better of [Reese] to the extent that he had committed acts immoral in their nature."[30] This persistent normalization of Reese, brought about by his superiors' consistent disavowing of the unbearable "truth" of the act, also necessitated the vague consistency of the more perverse Philippine muchachos and natives. The native Philippine Scouts' subordinate position to the colonial officers, synecdochic of Philippine subjects' roles as wards of U.S. imperial sovereignty in training for their own, determined their racial-sexual degeneracy, attributed to them an inherent perversion and unnatural desire, an intractable proclivity to become not just anticolonial insurgents (an anxious fantasy held by many colonial officers) but also sexual insurrectos.[31] They needed to be governed by a racially superior and more sexually continent race—hence, Reese's sodomitic act merely affirmed the Philippine colonial subjects' degenerate nature. The same reasoning subtended the official court-martial trial.

The Case of *United States v. Boss Reese*

A wide range of colonial military administrators, in protective mode, scrambled to normalize Reese's behavior and protect his reputation—not to mention that of the military more generally—from being sullied in the eyes of local Philippine leaders, the onlooking U.S. public, and the rest of the world. This concealment happened on many levels from the get-go. Reese's resignation from the military, submitted to General John Pershing immediately after his crime was reported, was admittedly "pigeonholed" by his superiors—that is, put aside with the intent of being lost in the colonial military bureaucracy.[32] Pershing, in fact, allowed Reese to tender his resignation in the first place only "with the understanding that the matter was to be dropped."[33] Several white soldiers under Reese's command, meanwhile, suspected him of practicing sodomy but did not confront him about it "for the good," as one put it, "of the service."[34] The two whistleblowers who first reported Reese's acts, moreover, were disciplined or dismissed for their action. The first, Captain Julian de Court of the Philippine Scouts, who "hated having such a superior" as Reese and even threatened to hang himself should Reese ever return to command, was convicted in a court-martial trial for insubordination.[35] The second, First Lieutenant J. I. Thorne, a military physician with the Medical Reserve Corps, was honorably discharged. A court of inquiry conducted between June and October 1910 had Thorne's sodomy charges, "baseless in fact," thrown out in advance of the court-martial trial, despite the fact that Thorne had secured several affidavits offering testimony by the sodomized soldiers.[36] The reasons that the sodomy charges were dismissed included the threat they posed to Reese's "reputation" and "career as an officer and a man" (much testimony and many letters attesting to his "manhood" and his "fondness for women" emerged); a general feeling that the accusers were merely conspiring to tarnish Reese's name as a form of retaliation (Reese was known to be crude, truculent, and abusive, and de Court and Thorne therefore compiled a "black book" of his offenses); and suspicions about the credibility and motivation of the Filipino witnesses attesting to their submission to Reese's act (Filipinos, as a race, were known liars).[37] Accordingly, when Reese first went on court-martial trial on December 1, 1910, the charges concerned only drunkenness and disorderly conduct; he was found guilty on both counts. Not until August 1911 was Reese—faced with increasingly undeniable evidence mounted by Inspector-General J. T. Dickman that "with reference to sodomitic practice . . . actual penetration was effected"—tried by general court-martial for sodomy, as well.[38]

Drawing from the records of the investigation, notations from a court of inquiry, and transcripts from the two court-martial trials concerned with Reese's crimes, I reconstruct in this section both Reese's alleged crimes and the protracted bureaucratic procedures that culminated in a guilty verdict. I reproduce some of the language that the courts, investigators, and witnesses used to talk about Reese's crimes to show how Reese's precarious normalcy was established against presumed Philippine racial perversion. All three charges against Reese of drunkenness, striking his soldiers, and immoral conduct were first raised by Thorne, the colonial physician stationed with Reese in Puerto Princesa. On November 7, 1909, Thorne, who lived in the barracks room adjacent to Reese's—a flimsy partition wall separated their quarters—wrote a letter to Judge Advocate General George Davis, accusing Reese of abusing drink, beating his native subordinates, and acting in a "disgusting manner" with a Philippine Scout, a company musician (trumpeter) named Luis Malonso.[39] The "disgusting" behavior that Thorne refers to here is relatively innocuous, concerned with Reese's "holding the hands of Louis [sic] Malonso and having that soldier sit . . . on Captain Reese's lap."[40] This scene of perceived intimacy occurred on October 31, 1909. Later in the letter, though, Thorne carefully paints a scene that surely disgusted him more. Reminiscent of Munson and Ashburn's cautionary tales about barracks life (see chapter 1), Thorne's scene recounts the actions of November 6, 1909:

> Just before 11:00 I parted company with the Captain at the gateway of the Bachelors quarters. . . . I entered my room (next to the room occupied by Captain Reese) and retired. A few minutes after taps, I saw someone sneak through the dining room and heard *voices* about Captain Reese's bed and voices and groans that made me feel sure that steps should be taken to find out who entered and to stop them coming again. I thought it was a woman and I waited at my door to see if I could identify her as she passed through the dining room. There was a light burning in the dining room and when the person passed through I recognized *it to be* a soldier, and I am *quite*

sure I am safe in saying it was Capt. Reese's striker, Pvt. Sonza, 4th Co. I believe that confession can be had from Pvt. Sonza ... but I am afraid to undertake it alone as Captain Reese has often talked about shooting people for little things he becomes offended over.[41]

Betraying Thorne's titillation, the gothic mode of this narration—note the narrow focalization, the interior domestic space, the indistinct silhouettes, the withholding and revelation of secrets, the impulsive violence of Reese—might have incited the curiosity of administrators. But it was the accusation itself that brought about swift action. By December 8, Inspector-General Dickman had arrived at Puerto Princesa, where Reese was stationed, to conduct an investigation. The interrogations, affidavits, depositions, and trial that followed brought to light several instances involving Reese's "immoral conduct" with several Philippine men under his command, ranging from genital fondling to attempted sodomy, what may have been consensual sex, and sexual violation.

Although evidence emerged that Reese had used Philippine men—indeed, often the same Philippine men—"as women" for years, the specific crimes against nature for which Reese was tried occurred in the last few months of 1909. On August 15, Reese called Sergeant Apolonio Ducut of the Philippine Scouts, who was on guard duty, to his barracks quarters; in Ducut's words, Reese "fucked [him] again!" and sent him back to his post.[42] On October 31, the same night as the hand-holding and lap-sitting incident, Reese walked with Malonso, who had been drinking with Reese at a nearby Spanish canteen on Reese's tab, to a mango tree by the soldiers' camp and possibly sodomized him under the tree. Previously, Reese had tried several times to sodomize Malonso in the barracks water closet.[43] On November 5, under the shade of trees in front of a local schoolhouse, Reese grabbed Corporal Rafael Guevara's hand and placed it on his "privates." The scene described earlier by Thorne regarding Reese's striker or voluntary servant, Private Sonza, visiting Reese's quarters, took place the following day. Two days later, on November 8, Reese ordered Corporal Roman Cortez to his quarters at 3 A.M. and "placed," as the court perhaps euphemistically phrased it, his "penis between [Cortez's] bare legs." Evidently, Reese often engaged in this practice with Cortez, sometimes with and sometimes without Cortez's consent.[44] On November 20 or 21, at around 4 A.M., a drunken Reese crawled into the cot of Andres Calandria, the muchacho who attended to the military quarters, and sodomized him. On November 25, Ducut witnessed "several [Scout] soldiers tied up with ropes" in Reese's room; soldiers who were not tied up had managed to flee, knowing of "Captain Reese's custom of treating soldiers as women."[45] Those soldiers that Reese did tie up, he attempted to sodomize; those who had been tied up and refused Reese beat and threw into the guardhouse. A week later, on December 2, Reese called one of the soldiers put in the guardhouse, Private Tomas Magat, to his quarters and "committed sodomy with" him.[46] On December 6 or 7, Reese chased Ducut into the barracks water closet and tried to sodomize him.[47] Finally, on December 12, Reese having drunk as much as he could of the seven gallons of whiskey he had just acquired during a trip to Manila, pursued and fondled Corporal Guevara and attempted to sodomize him.[48] Although Reese was clearly sadistic in his actions, it is not entirely clear whether any of these incidents transpired with the Scouts' "consent," especially as consent itself in the colonial context was a dubious concept.

In Reese's defense, his lawyers tried to establish that even if he was a hot mess when drunk and was wont to strike his men in disciplinary action, the charges of sodomy leveled against him were simply "incompatible" with—indeed, "at war with"—his history as a "man" and as a U.S. soldier.[49] Reese's lawyers touted his acts of soldierly heroism and record of achievement and called witnesses to the stand who attested to his "sexual interest" in Philippine female prostitutes. The defense also drew on "every author of medical jurisprudence who has written on th[e] subject" of the "grave crime" of sodomy, demonstrating that Reese did not fit their profile. In its closing arguments, the defense claimed that "all of the authorities dealing with this question that a man who is addicted to the practice of sodomy is quiet, gloomy and inclined to be a recluse. . . . He shuns company of any character, especially that of women; that he feels everyone knows that he is guilty of this vile practice, and avoids as much as possible mixing with the world. . . . It is also laid down by the authorities of medical jurisprudence that this practice saps a man's vitality and energy."[50] The medical description of the "addict" of sodomy that the defense cites here, and holds Reese against, accords with Percy Ashburn's profile of the pervert in *The Elements of Military Hygiene* (1909), seen in chapter 1. Reese, the defense argued, proved the antithesis of the addict: "the testimony shows that the accused is a complete antipode of the character as just described. He is shown to be a jolly character, even to boisterousness; that he is general, light-hearted, and very fond of the companionship of both men and women. . . . He is fond of sexual intercourse with women. He is energetic, even to the extent of being strenuous."[51]

In contrast to the lonely, lethargic, and brooding addict of sodomy, Reese not only had sex with women, but he was also sociable and vital, living proof of Theodore Roosevelt's imperialist claim that a "*strenuous* life" builds healthy American men. Moreover, Munson and Ashburn's insistence on examining the genitalia of soldiers came in handy for the defense, who presented to the court the report of a board of medical officers convened to examine Reese in September 1910. Although the physicians had noted "chronic stricture of the posterior urethra, gonorrhoeal in origin,"[52] they found "no signs or symptoms of any tendency to pederasty."[53] Whereas inspection of genitalia for Munson and Ashburn was necessary for locating symptoms of gonorrhea and syphilis, the inspection of Reese's genitalia was also useful in identifying another sexual "infirmity" altogether—the "tendency to pederasty"—for which he somehow tested negative, despite the suspicions that no doubt motivated the inspection in the first place. In the end, the defense claimed in fact that the different charges themselves were contradictory: "they say that *during the very time* that he was carrying on these practices . . . he was beating and striking and kicking these very men with whom he is charged with carrying on these practices! I say it is incomprehensible—it staggers the human imagination—to think that the accused would act in that way!"[54] Demonstrating fantasy's protection from the truth (rather ludicrously here), the defense protested that the coupling of violence and sexual use was simply beyond comprehension.

The prosecution had an easier time building a case of sodomy than Reese's defense team had in countering the charges. Even as the defense insisted that Reese was "fond of women," other witnesses held that he was not "passionate" about them.[55] If the defense claimed that Reese was "fond of sexual intercourse with women," the prosecution showed that even expressions of this fondness were immoral, demonstrating that Reese tried to "have sex" with the wives of the Scouts Ducut and Magat, for example, only when he had failed with the soldiers themselves.[56] (That Reese would attempt such behavior, of course, speaks to the sexual violence against and perceived sexual availability of Philippine women enabled by colonial order.) While the defense argued that Reese's vigor and gregariousness contradicted medical knowledge about sodomy "addicts," the prosecution claimed that there was no consensus among medical authorities that "men who are engaged in practices of this kind [i.e., sodomy] are always weak, anaemic and retiring, shunning the society of their fellows and of women."[57] And as the defense argued that it was "incomprehensible" that Reese would, in seeming contradiction between abuse and desire, strike his men and at the same time sodomize them, the prosecution countered that "the very fact that the story is a remarkable one is some proof of its genuineness."[58]

Once the notion of Reese's perversity was implanted, it would take a lot to redeem him from the charges. Such perversity, in fact, was soon retroactively imposed on Reese when one native witness testified that from August 1904 to January 1907, Reese would "kiss him, and under threats of bringing him to trial, force him to submit to his lust as often as three times a week."[59]

Other witnesses dated Reese's addiction even earlier, to 1901.[60] Still another witness, a white officer, testified that he had in fact recommended that Reese "straighten up." While the officer clarified that he had used this phrase to refer to Reese's habit of "drinking pretty heavy," the prosecutor pressed him on his diction, asking rhetorically, "Was there *any other reason why* you thought he ought to 'straighten up'?"[61] While the use of "straight" to designate heterosexuality did not appear in the U.S. metropolitan vernacular until the early 1940s, the prosecutor clearly uses it in the colonial context here to imply a correction of Reese's notorious degenerate sexual habits.[62] (The officer's use of the phrase "straighten up" and the lawyer's attention to it thus not only bespeak another attempt by officials to make sense of Reese's behavior, but, since it precedes similar usage within the imperial metropole by several decades, it provides another example of how integral the Philippine colonial space is to the histories of U.S. sexuality.) Reese's reputation before the court-martial thus increasingly coincided with his reputation among the ranks.

Other circumstantial evidence emerged to support the truth of Reese's morally depraved character. There was more to the story, for example, that Thorne had introduced about Reese's ordering his subaltern Luis Malonso, for whom he was buying drinks in the canteen, to sit on his lap. Having had several drinks himself, Reese started bragging to the civilian captain of a U.S. trade boat, one A. G. Menz, that the Filipino soldiers under his command were exceptionally disciplined. To demonstrate this, Reese said he could "shave off the moustache of the musician [Malonso] who was there in conversation with Reese . . . and that the musician would let him do it. Then the shaving was done . . . and *then* it was, when Menz appeared to take umbrage— to take offense at the familiarity—that Reese . . . pulled Malon[s]o down on his lap . . . and said he was a good soldier—one of the best of his soldiers."[63] That Reese's proof of military discipline took this form seemed to have been telling to the court-martial. Reese's shaving of Malonso's face effeminized and infantilized the Philippine soldier visually and structurally. Indeed, such hands-on bodily disciplining positioned the already racially and militarily subordinate Malonso all the closer to "women." Might shaving Malonso have also aroused Reese sexually, not just from the visual effect of hairlessness (again, drawing him closer to "women") but also, and especially, from the display of dominance in front of an audience, a kind of "pleasure in showing off, scandalizing"?[64] And might such excitement in turn have led Reese to pull Malonso onto his lap—pulling their genitals in closer proximity? (We already know, after all, a little bit of what transpired under the mango tree moments later.) While it's impossible to reconstruct the entirety of this scene, we see from the bodily coding at work that it is precisely Reese's brazen display of "discipline" that gets him in trouble, since it was the perceived "familiarity"—and thus intimacy—in the act of shaving that so offended Menz, a presumptuousness that Reese, so sure of his gendered status, would flaunt by drawing the Philippine soldier onto his lap. Indeed, in this demonstration of his disciplining of Malonso, Reese also aspired to mastery over his audience, since such immodest "familiarity" suggests that Reese felt that he was man enough to display it before Menz and Thorne with assumed impunity. This redoubled assuredness perhaps emboldened Reese to initiate sex with Malonso immediately afterward in so open a setting.

All of this circumstantial evidence—that Reese shaved Malonso, that Reese had Malonso sit on his lap, that Menz took offense to the apparent familiarity—quickly turned into corroborating evidence of the captain's habit of unnatural practices. Reese had perhaps miscalculated: his excessive masculine dominance became proof of his degeneracy. As a result, it was harder for the adjudicating officials to dismiss his sodomitic behavior as mere aberration, as it looked more and more like a long-standing habit, one with the capacity to pervert all his other actions. Reese was found guilty of the state's charges of brutality, drunkenness, and sodomy on April 18, 1912.

Straightened-Up Reese, Perverted Scouts, and the Colonial Differend

Even after he was found guilty of the charge of sodomy, however, Reese managed to preserve his status as an officer and a "normal" (read, heterosexual and gender-conforming) man. The court-martial's guilty verdict in fact did not stand. President Taft, having already commuted Reese's sentence from the previous court-martial, "disapproved" all charges related to sodomy in this one according to the recommendation of the Judge Advocate General.[65] This benefit of the doubt from military administrators and from the commander-in-chief was supported not only by the defense's attempts to redeem Reese's character, to "straighten up" his reputation, but by colonial officials' projections of inherent perversion onto Philippine subalterns.

Such racial-sexual perversion was attached to the very testimony the native soldiers offered. Despite Joss's insistence of the truth of the subalterns' statements, colonial administrators, both military and civilian, largely suspected the Philippine Scouts' testimony throughout the investigations and trials based on Philippine racial character. Such dismissals of Philippine testimony on the grounds of race resonates with the long-standing practice of abjuring African American testimony of white violence on black bodies, especially black women's bodies, and thereby attest to a transpacific transmission of "white fantasies of racial difference and inferiority."[66] When he heard about Thorne's initial accusations of sodomy, for example, Major T. R. Rivers discredited the "testimony of native witnesses" because they were "uncorroborated in any subst[a]ntial manner by any white man."[67] Similarly, the lead investigator of the charges, Major S. D. Rockenbach, explicitly evoking slavery in the U.S. metropole, wrote, "I know the [S]cout and charges of immorality is a favorite game. . . . I believe [Reese has been] set upon by a pack of curs who needed the lash and boot and are whining and snapping because they got it."[68] The U.S. governor of Palawan province, Edward Miller, claiming a "rather extensive knowledge of, and experience with, the common Filipino," averred that he "would never vote to convict, nor . . . subject to Court-martial, any white man on the statements (sworn or otherwise) of such Filipinos."[69]

In response to these outright dismissals of the Scouts' testimony, the Judge Advocate General deemed that the colonial courts convened in the Reese case "had no jurisdiction of the question of credibility to be attached to the testimony of Filipinos as a race."[70] The subsequent admission of the native Scouts' testimonies into the proceedings expressed a form of liberal governance that was consistent with the project of benevolent assimilation. Nevertheless, Reese's defense hinged on invalidating the Filipinos' testimony. Reese's lawyer, in a flourish of paralipsis—that is, the rhetorical device that invokes a subject by denying that it should be evoked at all—smuggles in the issue of non-credibility in his closing argument: "it is not the purpose of counsel to enter into a discussion of the testimony of the Filipino witnesses in this case, because it is believed that the knowledge of the members of this court of the character of Filipino witnesses would prevent this court from placing any reliance upon their testimony."[71]

The widespread "knowledge" of the inferior racial "character" of the native soldiers in fact made their roles as witnesses/victims in the court-martial a legal impossibility. They were ensnared in a web of legal double binds because of race. The court of inquiry of 1910 deemed that whether or not they were lying about the charges and whether or not Reese would be put on trial for sodomy, the testifying Scouts should be punished:

> With reference to the scouts who have testified that they submitted to Captain Reese's committing unnatural acts with them . . . we are of the opinion that their cases call for action on the part of the War Department, whether Captain Reese is to be brought to trial on charges involving these acts or not. In either case these soldiers are deserving of severe punishment and they should be made an example to all other scouts. If the Department accepts the opinion of the majority of this court that Reese is innocent or if he be brought to trial and acquitted, these witnesses should

be dealt with for false swearing. . . . If however Captain Reese be brought to trial on the charge and convicted, [the Scouts] should be punished and made an example of for submitting to such practices. It should be made known to every Philippine Scout in no uncertain terms that he is not, under any circumstances, of compulsion, threat, or even bodily injury, to submit himself for such acts to any person, officer or other, and that if he does not protect himself, and fails to report the matter at once he shall be declared guilty.[72]

The native Scout as witness/victim/legal subject was in an impossible position before colonial law. The concatenated double binds around the Filipinos' claims constituted a differend—a "case where the plaintiff is divested of the means to argue."[73] If a native Scout had refused to "submit himself" to Reese, he then risked charges of insubordination, which would have been grounds for a court-martial. If the Scout had submitted himself to "such practices" as sodomy and reported the crime, however, he would have been discharged outright from the military for sodomy. If the native Scout submitted to Reese and reported the matter, and if Reese was acquitted, then the Scout would have been dismissed for false swearing (and thus insubordination). If the Scout did submit and reported the charges and Reese was found guilty, however, the Scout would have been found guilty of submitting to the unnatural act and punished by court-martial. Finally—a third double bind—if the Scout submitted to "such acts" and did not report them "at once," then he would have been declared guilty of sodomy. However, if the Scout were to submit to such acts and report them immediately, he would be found guilty for such submission nonetheless. With all of these juridical knots, one of the few options for these scouts, it seems, was to have *not* been an object of Reese's sexual desire/violence in the first place—which, of course, was not their own option at all.

The impossibility of the native Scouts' representation before the law is most starkly laid bare when we consider that even as their testimony was seen as unreliable, and even as it was effectively stricken from the record, it nonetheless became the grounds for the Filipinos' punishment by and dismissal from the colonial military. All of the Scouts who testified to Reese's using them "in a crime against nature" were both summarily discharged from the service after the court of inquiry of 1910 and found guilty in their own court-martial trials for sodomy under Article 62 of the Articles of War, which had recently been revised to account for that crime (see chapter 1).[74] A particular differend emerges here: in regard to Reese, the native soldiers' testimony about his using them "as women" was dismissed without "corrobor[ation] by a white man"; in regard to the native soldiers, however, their testimony itself adduced evidence of such use. In a stunning sleight of hand, Reese's criminal act of sodomy *disappears just as the native soldier submits to it.* The Philippine soldiers were thus found guilty not only of a crime of which they were the victims but also of a crime that did not happen. The net effect of these imbricated conundrums, in other words, is that while there was reasonable doubt among the administrators about Reese's sodomitic habits, there were structural guarantees that the Philippine Scouts were either liars about Reese's sodomitic crime or "degenerates" who submitted to it—or, paradoxically, both. The juridical structure that offered these guarantees found its support not just in military hierarchy but also in colonial racial hierarchy. The mere fact that the Filipinos were testifying to sodomy at all made them guilty of that crime, even if they were the ones who had submitted to it, and even if they were lying about it. Hence, the stakes of the differend: by virtue of their race and rank, if they regarded themselves as having been "used" by Reese, as most of them did, the Filipino soldiers who claimed that Reese had sodomized them had no way to express the violation of rape before the court-martial. Nor, by the same token, did they have any way to express any pleasure in submission or, less likely still, mutuality of desire.

To understand fully the differend of the native Scouts, we might compare it with how Reese's crime was processed. Like the Philippine Scouts, Reese was charged under Article 62 of the Articles of War in his second court-martial trial, but here the article served as a guideline for the charges of brutality—and not for those of sodomy. Instead, the sodomy charge against Reese fell under Article 61, which did not mention sodomy at all. Rather, it concerned "conduct . . . at once disgraceful or disreputable and manifestly unbefitting both an officer of the Army and a gentleman."[75] That administrators would file Reese's sodomy charge under Article 61 might seem strange, given the fact that by 1907 Article 62 explicitly listed sodomy as a court-martial offense. This discrepancy speaks to the range of umbrella charges in military law under which sodomy could have fallen. More important, it offers evidence of the lengths to which his superiors may have gone before the court-martial trial to shield Reese, if he was found guilty, from what they regarded as too severe a punishment. The court-martial's recommended sentence for Reese, once he was found guilty of sodomy, was dismissal from the military and a prison sentence of fifteen years of hard labor.[76] Enoch Crowder, the Judge Advocate General who disapproved this guilty verdict of sodomy, however, recommended reducing the sentence. Crowder pointed out that, unlike other sodomy charges in the military—and, indeed, unlike the sodomy charges on which Reese's native subalterns were found guilty—Reese's "crimes against nature were only laid under the 61st Article of War," so "the sentence of imprisonment [could not] be held to relate to them at all, as under the 61st Article only dismissal can be adjudged."[77] Because Reese was charged under Article 61, in short, the prison sentence he received proved inconsistent with—in excess of—the usual punishment that accorded with that law. In effect, the military administrators convened to conduct the court-martial trial charted, in advance, a way to circumvent the laws they had just installed to apprehend sodomy. Crowder in fact admitted this loophole. Referring to testimonials offered by military brass who regarded Reese "as the *best* Scout officer," Crowder wrote, "Taking into consideration the whole record of this officer . . . it is believed that the interests and the good name of the service call for [Reese's] dismissal"—that is, *just* his dismissal and not, Crowder implies by the conspicuous omission, Reese's imprisonment.[78]

Giving the Colonial Differend Its Due?

I have rehearsed the multiple discursive and legal tactics that U.S. colonial military administrators deployed throughout the protracted scandal around Reese to defend him—and thus U.S. imperialism itself—from charges of same-sex perversion, immorality, and degeneracy. Such tactics, comporting with fantasy's protective function, signal the colonial administrators' self-deception and disavowal about Reese's behavior: the attempted pigeonholing of the unsavory case within the colonial bureaucracy; the discharging of the officers who accused Reese; the management of rumors around him, especially vis-à-vis the U.S. press; the multiple dismissals of the sodomy charges; the refusal to recognize the unknown knowns about same-sex eroticism; the insistence on the incompatibility of the charges of sodomy with Reese's masculine character; the Judge Advocate General's suggestion to reduce Reese's sentence from hard time in prison; the structuring of the charges in advance of the court-martial to allow for a mere dismissal in the face of the laws established specifically to punish sodomy; the presidential disapproval of charges of unnatural crime in the face of a guilty verdict. Such persistent refusal of the truth of Reese's sodomitic behavior sanitized him of perversion. If colonial administrators allowed themselves to consider the horrifying truth of Reese's repeated crime at all, they saw it either as an anomaly—as a blip on his otherwise exemplary record of conduct—or consistent rather than incompatible with his "strenuous" demonstrations of manhood, soldierly conduct, brutal tactics of discipline, and adherence to military hierarchy. Sodomy, to wit, might not have been *their* preferred way of disciplining the Filipino Scouts, but it worked for Reese. Still, in simultaneously foreclosing on the testimony of the Philippine soldiers while at the same time relying on that testimony to prosecute the Philippine soldiers to brace the normalcy of Reese—his military prowess and heterosexual manhood—colonial administrators *reproduced structurally Reese's disciplining violence*, including his sodomitic "use."

As we see in the treatment of the native Scouts' testimony, the colonial administration's tactics of disavowal also necessitated the attribution of inherent perversion to the Philippine "race." Every account of sodomy documented by the court casts the white Reese as the active, penetrating actor, and never as the passive, penetrable, "feminized" receiver. Such a role adhered to the strict hierarchies constitutive not only of military life but also of white supremacy in the colonial scene. The use of transitive verb construction throughout the testimony to account for Reese's "crime" reflects the production of subject and object of the sexual act. Grammatical order, that is, accords with sexual position: Reese sodomized his men; he "used" them "as women"; he placed his "penis between [Cortez's] bare legs"; he grabbed a soldier's hand and put it on his own genitals; he chased soldiers into the water closet; and so on. The testimony given by the Filipinos themselves in their depositions, moreover, reproduce this racialized convention on the grammatical level. We have already seen, for example, Sergeant Ducut protesting, "The son-of-a-bitch, he fucked me again!" Meanwhile, Andres Calandria, the barracks muchacho, claimed, "Two times last night Captain Reese tried to catch my body. . . . I think he want [*sic*] to make a woman out of me."[79] Private Tomas Magat testified, "The Captain had me at his quarters frequently, and committed sodomy with me."[80] Elsewhere, Magat emphasized seriality: "he did me six times like women."[81] The repeated rendering of the sexual relations as something that *Reese did to the Philippine soldiers*—commensurate with the charges of physical assault—naturalized on the level of language the performative reproduction of his sexual authority. The discourse also naturalized the Philippine native soldier's passive sexual position, military inferiority, racial depravity, and status as effeminate object—in a word, "degeneracy."

Still, within the testimony in the court-martial trial we might locate an alternative to this racial-sexual governance that renders impossible the legal subjectivity of the native Scout vis-à-vis Reese's acts of sodomy. I suggested earlier that by virtue of their race, the Filipino soldiers had no way to express either a violation before the court-martial if they regarded themselves as having been "used" in this way or any pleasure in submission or mutuality of desire. This silencing constitutes the differend for the Filipino soldiers. In thinking about the differend, however, it is not enough for us to locate a case in which a victim is divested of representation before the law. One must also aspire, as Lyotard puts it, to "institute new addressees, new addressors, new signification, and new referents in order for the wrong to find an expression and for the plaintiff to cease being a victim"—to "give," in short, "the differend its due."[82]

But what would attending to this ethical call look like in this context? Part of this task would involve recovering, as I have been doing piecemeal throughout this chapter, the testimony of the Scouts as it is recorded in the colonial archive. To be sure, all of the testimony by the Filipinos concerning the immoral act were subject to—and often affirmed—the differend. But at least one of the natives' statements implies something like *pleasure*, which for Foucault proves an experience that might remain irreducible to discursive modes of regulation. Indeed, pleasure is the typical Foucauldian answer to power and subjection. Distinguishing pleasure from "desire," which has been used "as a grid of intelligibility" and thus a regulatory apparatus determining the pathological and abnormal, Foucault writes, "There is no 'pathology' of pleasure, no 'abnormal' pleasure. It is an event 'outside the subject,' or at the limit of the subject . . . in short, a notion neither assigned nor assignable."[83] Would pleasure, which for Foucault exceeds discourse yet is intelligible only within it, offer a new mode of expression to the juridically unrepresentable wrong? Corporal Cortez of the Philippine Scouts, using language similar to Calandria's, admitted to experiencing pleasure when he said, "Captain Reese has used me as a woman very often, and sometimes when I did not like it the Captain would catch me and force me to submit."[84] While Cortes repeats the grammatical convention of being "used" by Reese, of his body being caught, of sometimes being "force[d] to submit," he also perhaps unwittingly confesses, by saying that "sometimes" he "did not like" being sodomized by Reese, that he at times *did* in fact "like" it. Is it possible that pleasure, even if expressed only in the negative, as it is here, emerged elsewhere in the native Scouts' testimony? Would locating such pleasure give the differend its due? Is pleasure the site of habilitating an otherwise impossible justice?

In pursuit of another such expression, I return to the testimony of the Philippine Scout Luis Malonso, the native soldier who so "disgusted" Thorne and so "offended" the civilian Captain Menz by sitting on Reese's lap at the Spanish canteen. Malonso's statement about what happened after the lap-sitting scene is the lengthiest instance of the native subalterns' speaking before the law in this case. The trumpet-playing scout never testified during the court-martial, but he did offer testimony both in an affidavit and before the court of inquiry of 1910 (testimony that was, again, eventually dismissed on the premise of Philippine racial character).[85] In his statement before the court, Malonso responded to Captain Rockenbach's questioning this way:

Q. Tell me all that you know about anything that occurred between you and Captain Reese on the 31st day of October?

A. The first time that Captain Reese—he was in the canteen and I went inside the canteen and I got permission from Captain Reese if we could drink a little whisky in that canteen, and Captain Reese told me, Yes, so I and the other men went down to the table and we told the Spaniard to give us a couple of glasses of whisky, little glasses. And after we had the drink of whisky Captain Reese called me over to his chair, and I went down, and the captain on the boat, I couldn't remember his name, asked me how many years I know Captain Reese. I told him I know Captain Reese about seven years. So Captain Reese after that called me near him and told me to sit down on his knees . . . and afterwards I stood up and Captain Reese went outside after that he told me to go along with him, and I went along with him, and he was holding me by the arm, by my hand, and he took me on the road, and I told him, "Captain, I am going back to the canteen and I am going to pay [*sic*] my drink." Captain Reese told me, "Never mind, I am going to pay for your drink." After that Captain Reese held me by my hand again and went down the road, and we met the other road. We went down that road, and Captain Reese saw a mango tree and he took me in there and told me to go and lay down under the tree, and after that Captain Reese tried to open my pants, and I told him, "No, don't open my pants," but I don't know how to drink, and I am a little drunk, and Captain Reese tried to open my pants and I couldn't help it, because he was stronger than me. He opened my pants and he wanted to try to make me a woman, and he tried to go on top of me, and I rolled on the grass so he couldn't do it what he wanted to do with me. So after that Captain Reese never bothered me anymore. I went to sleep after that time, and when I woke up Captain Reese is not near my side or near me anymore. I don't know where he went to, and after that the soldiers saw me under the mango tree and they took me home and I went to sleep on my bed. That is all I can say.[86]

I render Malonso's testimony in full here to demonstrate how difficult it must have been for the Filipino subaltern to express a wrong done to him before the colonial military court. One detects here Malonso's pains to speak English, which just three years earlier became the mandatory official language of the court system in the Philippines.[87] In this sense, Malonso's statement accords literally with Lyotard's description of the differend: "a case of the differend between two parties takes place when the 'regulation' of the conflict that opposes them is done in the idiom of one of the parties while the wrong suffered by the other is not signified in the idiom."[88] The continual repetition in the testimony (e.g., "he was in the canteen and I went inside the canteen and I got permission from Captain Reese if we could drink a little whisky in that canteen"), along with what might be perceived as narrative inefficiency ("after that he told me to go along with him, and I went along with him, and he was holding me by the arm, by my hand, and he took me on the road . . . and went down the road, and we met the other road. We went down that road"), bespeak further linguistic difficulties. Not only do Malonso's repetition and rhetorical stuttering attest to a labored effort to give an account of himself before colonial law, but they also speak to his assiduity in moving past the repetition-compulsion symptomatizing the trauma of his (near?) violation. All of these efforts to work through Malonso's linguistic limitations demonstrate his recognition of and faith in the authority of colonial military "regulation"—an institution that, of course, would shortly refuse to recognize him at all. In short, I quote at length here to show how profoundly heartbreaking Malonso's testimony is, both for its content and for the conditions of its impossibility.

Still, does Malonso express pleasure in this testimony? The answer is a very qualified yes. It is distinctly a pleasure in intimacy. Malonso at times seems to "like" the fact he and Reese were drinking whisky together in the canteen. Indeed, this shared drink is all the more significant if we consider both that the bartender (a "Spaniard") serving the native Malonso has been reduced to a vestige of the previous colonial power and that some bars in the Philippines that catered to U.S. officers refused to serve Philippine natives. For this brief moment, in this public space, Malonso might have felt he was Reese's structural if not social equal. Malonso finds it notable that Reese has bought his drink, signaling for Malonso perhaps a gesture toward friendship, one that might have been in the making (as Malonso implied to Menz) for several years. The native does not seem to mind, moreover, that he and Reese are holding hands while they walk, making no unequivocal reference in his testimony to wanting to break this intimate gesture. It is as if Malonso shared, here, in the "pleasure in showing off" that Reese had felt when he flouted military propriety before Menz.

Malonso's consistent use of the subjective "I" reasserts agency in the testimony; he is no longer always the object of Reese's action and the transitive verbs used to describe them. We could note, for example, Malonso's immediately cutting off and amending his initial response to Rockenbach's question ("The first time that Captain Reese—he was in the canteen and I went inside the canteen"); the correction conveys a recuperation of equal social standing. Further, during the most narratively interstitial and therefore perhaps power-neutral moments in his testimony, Malonso uses the plural "we" ("we could drink a little whisky," "we met the other road," "we went down that road") to demonstrate mutuality, some shared subjective experience. Malonso thus seems to want to extract some homosocial pleasure from the fleeting moments of Reese's seeming recognition of and perhaps respect for him, which might have signified for the Filipino a brief leave from the racial and rank hierarchies instituted by the colonial military structure. Malonso's pleasure inheres precisely in the perceived flashes of mutuality, friendship, equality, and recognition, in the perceived intimacy with his captain.

Such pleasure, though, isn't free of the regulatory techniques of military structure in the imperial colonial arena but constitutive of them. We must not separate Malonso's narrative from the mise-en-scène from which it picks up—that of Reese's shaving Malonso in the bar in front of Menz and calling the native "one of the best of his soldiers" as a marker of his humiliating mastery. Seen in this way, Malonso's narrative, already a pathetic display of naiveté and the abuse of power, becomes even more heartbreaking when we recognize that the mutuality and friendship Malonso seems to have found pleasure in was not only manufactured by Reese to disarm and charm him but also perceptible at all only because of the backdrop of Reese's consistent abuse. To the abused, flashes of nonviolence perceived against continual domination feel like care. (Fantasy, once again, protects from a horrifying truth.) Whatever recognition, mutuality, or kindness Malonso might have felt from Reese, and might retain in his testimony, was merely a demonstration of his captain's desire, roused by the act of publicly dominating the Philippine Scout just moments earlier. Still, it is also impossible to ignore the fact that throughout Malonso's testimony, he demonstrates a distinct respect for, and deference to, his superior. Note, for example, Malonso's neutral, objective tone; his wanting to see recognition where there was none; his passing remark that Reese was "stronger"; his continual use of the title and proper name "Captain Reese"; and, perhaps most distressing, his stopping short of accusing Reese of sodomizing him ("That is all I can say"). Despite Malonso's account of Reese's betrayal, he still protects his Captain Reese's "reputation" and "career as an officer and a man." Significantly, of the nine separate counts of sodomy under the general charge, this incident remained the only one in which Reese was found "not guilty."[89] Malonso's method of evading Reese under the mango tree matched his method of avoiding having to testify against him: he merely rolled away from the scene. In this sense, whatever "pleasure" Malonso extracted from this scenario, pleasure that was possible only because of the strict hierarchies of colonial military power, and pleasure that he in turn wished would last by not saying too much, was precisely what enabled the differend before sodomy law.

Locating pleasure does not lead to a satisfactory response to the wrong done by Reese and the colonial court; pleasure in homosocial intimacy might well have offered Malonso a momentary leave from the colonial military's "assign[ment]" of his abject racial-sexual-gendered-militarized subjecthood, but identifying this pleasure does not produce new expressions of the wrong done to him by Reese and the military. Malonso does not cease to be a victim before the differend. Moving beyond attempting to locate what might be understood as subaltern pleasure, then, I recover a "new referent" in the archive around the Reese scandal, one that exceeds not just the U.S. colonial "idioms" of race, gender, and sexuality, but also, in productive fashion, our own present attempts at retroactive understanding. Indeed, in what follows, I reproduce self-consciously both the language used by the court-martial and, as I have done throughout this chapter, some of the taxonomies that administrators seem to have been familiar with to emphasize the conceptual limitations inhering in turn-of-the-twentieth-century colonial idioms. To be sure, like the task of locating pleasure in Malonso's testimony, this recovery does not give the differend its due by imagining some kind of just outcome for the native subalterns in the face of Reese's and the colonial court's injuries. It does, however, attempt to frame "new signification" outside the colonial grid of intelligibility that might negotiate knowledge-power differently.

In early 1909, when briefly stationed in Pasay, outside Manila, Reese frequented a seedy dancehall. One night, after several drinks, Reese ordered his striker, Private Sonza, one of the soldiers he would later be accused of sodomizing in his barracks, to, in the words of the prosecution, "*buscar*" (Spanish for "look for") the "female character . . . who was called—nicknamed— '[M]orphodite'."[90] Although the court-marital records refer to Morphodite several times, we do not know much about her, apart from the fact that Reese referred to her as "hot stuff" and sought her out because of her reputation (and perhaps his experience with her) as a "cocksucker."[91] Despite her evident on-the-ground notoriety, Morphodite remains an ephemeral, mysterious figure, not just a minor "character" in this archive, appearing a mere five times in some one thousand pages of trial transcription, but also, therefore, off the empire's grid of discursive intelligibility.

At one point, the court slips into referring to the person known as Morphodite as a "hermaphrodite"—and, indeed, the word "morphodite" was at the time a slang alteration of the much older term.[92] This ascription, however, does not so much illuminate for us the social identity of Morphodite as expose a gap between contemporary sexological and psychiatric discourse and U.S. colonial discourse, despite any continuum we have seen hitherto, especially when it came to the colonial underworld. It is possible that Morphodite was an actual hermaphrodite—that is, what we might now regard as an intersex person.[93] Given the lack of a record of inspection of Morphodite's genitalia or morphological description, though, and the relative rarity of "true" hermaphrodites,[94] it is more likely that Morphodite was closer to what would have been known in contemporaneous sexological and medical discourses as an "invert" or in psychological discourse and U.S. vernacular as a "fairy," both of which signaled effeminate men.

More likely still, the court's deployment of the term "hermaphrodite" might have resulted from the imprecise translation at some point of the untranslatable Tagalog or Philippine word *bakla*. Within the local idiom, "bakla" referred (and still sometimes refers) to an effeminate, cross-dressing figure born male, bearing a *pusong babae* (woman's heart) and tending to be sexually attracted to normatively masculine (cisgender) men.[95] The figures of the bakla, the hermaphrodite, and the invert would have been "utterly confused" by colonial administrators. With so scant a trace of Morphodite in the records, some speculation is necessary here. Perhaps when Reese was first introduced to her, she might have been referred to (or referred to herself) as a "hermaphrodite," which would have been the imprecise English translation of "bakla." Or perhaps Morphodite herself appropriated and restyled an earlier mistranslation to express and brand her persona within Pasay's social and commercial underworld. In any event, in identifying Morphodite as a hermaphrodite, the court made no attempt to grasp the social or cultural specificity of the person it surely understood as a degenerate or pervert. Rather, Morphodite simply indexed Reese's alleged perversity in the trial. While the fact that Reese may have sought oral sex from a bakla—and my retroactive ascription exemplifies what Jack/Judith Halberstam has called "perverse presentism," to be sure[96]—complicates any understanding of the orientation of Reese's desire, the prosecution took his seeking out of a supposed female-presenting hermaphrodite as consistent with his apparent habit of sodomizing Philippine men.[97]

Morphodite, in short, was perhaps not an actual hermaphrodite, as the court hastily presumed, but a figure who evoked something like "psychic hermaphrodism."[98] Morphodite's fleeting appearance in Reese's record is significant, as it is the only reference I have found—and, indeed, to my knowledge, that anyone has found—of the early U.S. colonial state's apprehension, however vague and imprecise, of gender variance (maybe even *kabaklaan* [bakla-ness]) in the Philippines.[99] For this reason, Morphodite's appearance provides for me a satisfactory way to address the differend. This address does not so much enable a mode of redressing the pain or grievance of the native Scouts as identify a sociality that remains irreducible to the racial-sexual governance that has rendered impossible the legal subjectivity of the native scouts vis-à-vis Reese's act of sodomy. Morphodite's ephemeral appearance in the colonial archive presents a "new expression" of Philippine natives' social worlds, of the immoral publics loitering at the borderlands of the colonial state's policing. She has extracted an "unmentionable liberty" of a radically different sort. In remaining fundamentally inassimilable to the U.S. colonial state's discursive modes of surveillance and knowledge production, Morphodite in effect mobilized something of a differend for the U.S. colonial state itself. Precisely because of its inability to grasp Morphodite in her own colonial Philippine underworld "idiom," the state could not make the charge of any social "crime" (e.g., a charge of the "crime against public morals" for being an alleged "cocksucker"). The colonial state was divested of the means to address her action let alone prosecute her. To attribute to Morphodite this capacity to elude capture by the state neither romanticizes her as occupying some prediscursive body that colonial state biopower merely disfigures nor orientalizes her agency by articulating to it some precolonial "Philippine" past. Rather, Morphodite's unassimilability is constitutive of a gender-deviant performance with historical specificity and cultural density, dating from pre-Spanish culture and modified variously by Spanish and U.S. colonial rule, evolutions in forms of commercial exchange, upheavals in family structure, transformations in religious and spiritual practices, and the emergence of U.S. vagrancy laws and other modes of the colonial state's apprehension of degeneracy. In short, her gender variance was neither prediscursive nor precolonial; it was a modern perversity, an instance of a perverse Philippine modernity. That the court officials were able to understand Morphodite only through Reese's "sodomitic" ways exposes the conceptual limitations of the U.S. state's racial-sexual governance, which is unable to think past a naturalized binary gender framework. The figure of Morphodite in this already obscure colonial archival object thus does not merely expose the blind spots of colonial knowledge formations but subverts the hierarchy they assert: as a quintessentially modern racial-sexual-gendered form navigating a colonially occupied Philippines, Morphodite provincializes the U.S. colonial state.[100] Her fleeting presence offers a glimpse of a vibrant, adaptive subaltern social world—one, we might imagine, whose evasive racialized gender performances and sexual practices make empire's will to knowledge-power, with its legal (if not affective) attachment to "sodomy," look, for all its panoptic apparatuses, rather myopic.

The Reese Effect: Looking Ahead, Looking Back

I suggested earlier that the Reese trial in 1911 was a significant event that threatened to spoil empire's self-image in a way that it could not necessarily have done in a previous time. To conclude this chapter, I suggest ways to map this event onto the histories that followed and preceded it. My reading of the scandal draws on what Foucault has called "eventalization," which he describes as "a breach of self-evidence": "[eventalization] means making visible a *singularity* at places where there is a temptation to invoke a historical constant, an immediate anthropological trait, or an obviousness which imposes itself uniformly on all. . . . Eventalization means rediscovering the connections, encounters, supports, blockages, plays of forces, strategies and so on which at a given moment establish what counts as being self-evident, universal, and necessary. . . . [It] means analyzing an event according to the multiple processes which constitute it."[101] According with Foucault's genealogical method, eventalization involves showing how contemporary knowledge formation around an event is not destined to take the form that it does but, rather, results from a more or less arbitrary accretion of established knowledge-producing techniques. These techniques, in turn, might feel natural—that is, "self-evident, universal, and necessary"—but are actually an aggregate of sanctioned practices of power and discipline.

It is not self-evident that the act of sodomy should mark Reese, the entirety of his being, as "degenerate," as it surely would at a later time or place. Even as Reese "used" his Philippine subalterns "as women," I have no interest in labeling him "homosexual" or his behavior "queer," as one might be tempted to do today. Nor should we understand his "revolting" sodomitic act as a "singularity" within everyday life in the colonies, a "reasonless break in an inert continuum," as his superiors sometimes sought to code it.[102] Rather, we ought to see his actions as an expression of desire, pleasure, power, and intimacy, primed and conditioned by colonialism's regulation of social relations and its attendant fantasies. Examining the military discourse and policies that attempted to understand and contain the scandal around Reese's actions has revealed the extent to which the optimization of white imperial heteromasculinity—in a word, "colonianormativity"—itself was not a social "obviousness." By "colonianormativity," I mean the sometimes coercive, sometimes mild regulation of bodies, populations, identities, comportment, acts, behavior, affects, attachments, and desires into modern racial, sexual, and gendered conventions that accorded with the optimization of compulsory heterosexuality, white supremacy, and overseas colonial expansion. Colonianormativity was an implantation that continually had to be disciplined and maintained ("straighten[e]d up") over against imperial-colonial fantasies of the "self-evident" racial-sexual inferiority of the Philippine natives—scenes composed of "connections, encounters, supports, blockages, plays of forces, strategies" I have attempted to recover here.

Did the event of the Reese scandal affect sexual governance by the military? I think so, although the change was imperceptible by design. The colonial military administrators' success in suppressing the scandal around Reese had something of an inverse effect on policy: it seems to have led to increased surveillance of sodomy among the military stationed in the colonial Philippines. As I showed in the previous chapter, not long after military administrators mobilized the category of sodomy in the revised Articles of War of 1907, the number of court-martial trials around the crime spiked in the early 1910s. More specifically, from 1899 to 1917 a total of 372 cases of sodomy were recorded among the military in the Philippines; more than 80 percent of these cases were tried *after* 1911, the year of Reese's trial. I would argue that the scandal around Reese is precisely the event that provoked this amped-up policing of sodomy. After *United States v. Boss Reese*, that is, colonial administrators, anxious that U.S. empire might no longer wield the moral authority locally and globally that had justified occupation hitherto, increased the surveillance and punishment of the "crime against nature" in the ranks.

As Reese's trial shows, colonial fantasies of Philippine racial-sexual deviance did a lot of work to consolidate U.S. imperial colonialism's ideal of white hetero-masculinity. Such a shoring up of U.S. empire's idealized self-image manifested not only within the colonial Philippine arena but also on the U.S. domestic scene back home. Indeed, Reese's embodiment as a metroimperial ideal was staged in the Midwestern United States a few years before his sodomitic crime became grounds for an investigation and court-martial trial in the Philippines. We in fact find Reese—who died and was buried as a "civilian" in the Philippines six months after his dismissal—amid another far more "spectacular" event in the U.S. public imagination.[103]

In 1904, as a reward for his heroic feats in the colonial Philippines, Lieutenant Boss Reese was put in charge of the "Native Scouts" exhibition at the infamous spectacle of U.S. imperial ascendancy within the colonial metropole, the St. Louis World's Fair. There, in a forty-seven acre "reservation," various Philippine tribes were displayed within their so-called natural, primitive habitats.[104] The display was a study and spectacle of racial anachronism, purporting to demonstrate the different stages of Philippine evolution—starting with the mostly naked, allegedly dog-eating Negritos and Igorots, moving through the "semi-civilized . . . Moros," and culminating in the "civilized and cultured" Philippine Constabulary Band, Philippine Scouts, and pensionados.[105] This attraction was by far the fair's most popular (and, for current Philippine and Philippine American scholars, the most notorious), as it promised to make visible the *past*, embodied by the United States' new overseas wards, of which a vast majority of the American public had only read or seen images. The fair's living diorama of the "Philippines," engineered by the U.S. Philippine Commission's staff of physicians, ethnologists, and educators, microcosmically captured a version of Krafft-Ebing's ethnocentric vision of the world as staging, in different national spaces, "the evolution of human culture." On the "primitive ground" of non-Western nations, the influential Victorian sexologist argued, "the satisfaction of the sexual appetite of man seems like that of the animal." Projecting the racial-sexual fantasies of U.S. imperialism abroad *avant la lettre*, Krafft-Ebing propped the most civilized nations' societies with the "highest virtues" up against those he imagined as sexually unrepressed, uninhibited, and thus uncivilized. Among that group, Krafft-Ebing argues, were the always "naked," sexually incontinent "savages" of the "Phillipines [*sic*]."[106]

We might speculate—or even one day uncover in some other archive— whether or not Reese was as captivated with the dog-eating Igorots as the American public or whether the pensionados (the subject of chapter 5) were among the Filipina/os that met Reese in Saint Louis. What we can safely assume, though, is that against the gestalt of the mostly naked Philippine bodies, on one hand, and the military-uniformed Philippine Scouts, on the other, Reese's soldierly command and self-discipline must have positively gleamed, must have modeled an aspirational white hetero-masculinity, the apex of human evolution. Reese's performance in fact surely screened from the onlooking U.S. public the unknown knowns about the cross-racial same-sex desire on which, as would be alleged during his trial seven years later, he was already acting in 1904 and of which, because of his repeated performances of strenuous white masculinity, he would eventually be absolved.[107]

CHAPTER 3

MENACING RECEPTIVITY

Philippine Insurrectos and the Sublime Object
of Metroimperial Visual Culture

By the second half of their first decade of rule, I have been arguing,
U.S. colonial administrators in the Philippines found it necessary to
incorporate tactics of governance of same-sex intimacies into imperial statecraft. Here, I begin considering how metroimperial culture
had already implanted such an idea—a "perverse implantation," for
sure—years earlier.[1] This chapter initiates a shift that the rest of this book
makes, both in time and in objects. It moves from 1911, the year that
sodomy prosecutions began to explode in the Philippines, back to the
beginning of the war in 1899—before colonial administrators started policing deviant sexuality under vagrancy and sodomy legislation, before
the Philippine Scouts were dismissed from the military for being used
"as women," before the elusive figure known as "Morphodite" was tenuously apprehended by court-martial testimony. The chapter also marks
a turn to examining how popular and middlebrow cultural production relayed metroimperial fantasies about the colonial Philippine native. To the extent that the story I tell in the previous chapters about

the development of racial-sexual governance by the U.S. colonial state in the Philippines—about the co-constitutive construction of the perverse autochthonous Philippine subject and the white, colonial, heterosexual male subject before the law—amounts to something of a sjuzet, the remaining chapters amount to the fabula, a chronicle of colonianormativity foretold.

While U.S. colonial administrators took a few years to confirm Philippine subjects' deviant racial-sexual form within the law, metropolitan culture did not hesitate to hypothesize. I don't mean to imply a simple cause-effect relationship between culture and the law. Rather, I mean to recall (as I do in the introduction) Michel Foucault's warning that the state is not the primary site of power and Stuart Hall's and Lisa Lowe's provocations that culture is a key site of ideological contestations. This chapter attends to how U.S. *visual* culture in particular proleptically inscribed colonialism's racial-sexual governance of intimacy. As Sumathi Ramaswamy has argued, it is an "undeniable fact that visual technologies and practices frequently underwrote colonial governance and power."[2] Visual technologies also, I would add, underwrote metroimperial governance of racial-sexual form. The specific examples of visual culture I examine in this chapter, political cartoons, offer a range of intimacies in which the Philippine body was imagined to have participated—or, if not intimacies per se, then a range of how the Philippine body intimated intimacy by virtue of its represented relation to or metonymic association with other "deviant" bodies. Through these political cartoons we see how the previously unimagined Philippine body was paradoxically regulated within the U.S. public imagination as racially and sexually unmanageable.

In the previous chapters, we saw the U.S. colonial state in the Philippines struggling to make sense of the "utterly confused" category of the "Filipino" vis-à-vis the production and enforcement of vagrancy and sodomy law in colonial legislation; in this chapter, we see a genealogical strand of that confusion emerging within the regime of the visual. Indeed, to the extent that we might interpret the sodomizing of several Philippine Scouts by a white U.S. military officer as an expression of desire, pleasure, intimacy, and power primed and conditioned by colonialism's attendant fantasies, for example, as I suggested in chapter 2, we find here how such actions were adumbrated by those depicted in political cartoons, how such an expression first found articulation in visual form. Captain Reese's sodomitic acts, more specifically, were prefigured in some cartoons' depictions of imperial discipline as sadistic anal punishment, the latter of which I show later. Again, this is not to claim that reception of these images somehow led to Reese's sodomitic actions. Clearly, his behavior was aberrant, at least judging by the absence of similar cases within the colonial archives. Rather, I suggest that the conjoining of punishment and desire in his actions was not unforeseen and that there is some consistency in metroimperial fantasy and the perverse "truths" against which it protects.

In what follows, I offer a synchronic reading of various political cartoons that emerged at the beginning of the Philippine-American War, examining how these often politically disparate and varied drawings sought to shape metropolitan public perceptions of Philippine people. While largely popularly forgotten, the cartoons I examine would have been "discarded" as "frames of war" had they not been collected and compiled by the Philippine activists and historians Abe Ignacio, Enrique de le Cruz, Jorge Emmanuel, and Helen Toribio in *The Forbidden Book: The Philippine-American War in Political Cartoons* (2004).[3] This collection, which draws its title from a *Chicago Chronicle* cartoon with the same name showing President William McKinley locking up a book titled "True History of the War in the Philippines," brought to light many images stored in private collections, lost in antiquarian bookstores, or otherwise "pigeon-holed" in history. Thanks to these editors' work, I am able track the ways in which these cartoons belied the metroimperial fantasies about the colonial Philippines, its inhabitants, and imperial power itself. Part of the method in examining these fantasmatic images involves not attending to the individual cartoonists who produced the drawings I examine, even as some political caricaturists of the time, such as Thomas Nast and Eugene Zimmerman, achieved minor fame for their renderings. This choice is less an exercise of recognizing the "death of the author" than it is about recognizing the extent to which these cartoons not only attempted to shape but also purported to reflect collective fantasy, to mediate the fundamental impossibility in collective knowledge-formation.[4]

The Spanish-American-Cuban-Philippine wars gave political cartoonists fodder, reason, and license to conceive of and disseminate the image of U.S. empire's far-off and "new" racial others, to "picture the invisible."[5] Before these concatenated fin-de-siècle wars, such a range of racialized figures was not frequently featured in editorial political cartoons, which journalistic outposts deployed to educate and sway the U.S. public on matters of local, federal, and international state policy. Rather, racial difference was more often worked out in what Roger Fischer calls "ethnic filler pieces," which periodicals and magazines used to rehearse, expose, or fuel racial antagonism through humor. Newspaper and magazine editors valued ethnic filler pieces—cartoons that proliferated after the Civil War and whose punchlines relied on overdetermined racial stereotypes—for the "empty white space" on the page they filled.[6] Indeed, these cartoons regularly contradicted the ideological or political values of a given publication. One found in the magazine *Judge*, which often appealed to African American voters in the South to support the liberal Republican

Party, for example, the "most outrageously white supremacist filler art of any periodical of the time."[7] Meanwhile, in several of his drawings for *Harper's Weekly* the famous illustrator Thomas Nast would denounce the brutalities against Chinese immigrants even as the magazine itself would print editorials demanding stricter restrictions on immigration from Asia.[8] In addition to being at odds with the political convictions of the rest of the periodical in which they were found, moreover, late nineteenth-century ethnic filler pieces relied on and repeated racial stereotypes with no regard to historical context or the unstable dynamics of post-Reconstruction racial politics. As Fischer recaps, "Ethnic filler art represented not so much an outpost of editorial journalism as a sort of visual vaudeville or minstrelsy."[9] Nevertheless, even if the racial stereotypes that these cartoons reproduced did not attend faithfully to changing racial politics, the cartoons affected the lived realities of ethnic peoples directly as softer apparatuses of biopolitical control and as justifications for state and civic abuse, regulation, or neglect.[10] Indeed, late nineteenth-century political cartoons were integral to the white supremacist ideologies that shaped both metropolitan life and U.S. foreign policy.[11] Margo Machida has put the relation between stereotyping iconography around Asians, more specifically, and its effects on the everyday more strongly: "because [such images] are convenient and constantly repeated, they quickly become normalized, absorbed into popular consciousness, and read back into the texture of life."[12]

Images of the peoples from the Spanish-ruled territories of Guam, Puerto Rico, Cuba, and the Philippines rarely needed to be imagined for ethnic filler pieces, in contrast to the repeatedly caricatured images of, say, African Americans, Native Americans, and immigrants from Asia and Ireland. The spoils of overseas imperial war, however, compelled cartoonists based in the United States to conceive of largely unseen racial others in the new colonies. Indeed, as the rise of Hearst's and Pulitzer's yellow press at the onset of the Spanish and Cuban wars attests, because political cartoons by the late nineteenth century had come increasingly to share the ideological convictions of the newspapers in which they were printed, racial caricature shaped much of the visual culture in the United States of the reported colonial wars abroad.[13] The cartoon renderings of the new colonial subjects were thus distinctly hybrid, an assemblage of interpretations of widely circulated photographs of natives in so-called colonial life; common tropes found in ethnic filler pieces; and images found in editorial political cartoons, whose caricatures' "creative exaggeration and droll absurdities" of political luminaries depended "on a certain reality of context."[14] This new hybridized image would not only come to draw from "a certain reality of context"; they would also fill in that context—the "empty white space" of the national imaginary, as it were—with a certain distortion of reality.

Put another way, as imperialism provided political cartoonists with the concatenated wars, the wars in turn infused racial caricatures that emerged, however absurd and decontextualized, with a vague sense of political immediacy, of historicity. Racial caricatures, even if the public knew they were ridiculous and exaggerated, now also felt historical. What's more, because the mostly white (Anglo-American and Western European immigrant) publishers and caricaturists often fancied themselves as cosmopolitan flaneurs, wandering about the cities and visually chronicling life's realities and whimsies, they were able to project an aura of now-ness and specificity in their depictions of political and social worlds.[15] Political cartoons thus often succeeded in influencing bourgeois public opinion through its use of widely and instantly understood symbols, slogans, and referents—which by the turn of the twentieth century included the scheming but imbecilic African American, the noble but savage American Indian, the plucky but simianized Irishman, the industrious but duplicitous Chinese "coolie," and the well-dressed but effeminate dandy.[16]

The fantasmatic invention of the "Philippine native" in these cartoons in fact drew frequently from these commonly and instantly recognizable, if contradictory, racial and sexual tropes. Thus, even as the images of Filipinas and Filipinos in these cartoons similarly contradicted each other—natives were docile yet ferocious, everywhere yet elusive, uncivilized yet cunning, penetrable but menacing—they affirmed U.S. mass culture's knowledge about the new colonial others' racial inferiority. These cartoons were in fact often popular precisely because they presumed (and were presumed) to reflect widespread sentiments about the "Filipino." Indeed, that both pro-imperialist and anti-imperialist publications deployed many of the same tropes of the Philippine native suggests that there was an inchoate consistency in this figure's racial form, despite the particularities and disparities of each rendering. Whether the cartoon was Republican and pro-expansionist, and so generally saw Philippine autochthonous subjects as barbaric and in need of rule, or Democratic and anti-expansionist, and so generally saw colonization as a prelude to an invasion by even more brown and black bodies into the United States, the Philippine subject caricatured was almost always male, stupid, shorter than whites, savage, demonstrative of some deviant desire, and subject to discipline or punishment.

In an effort to manage these disparate renderings, while still attending to contradictions, this chapter homes in on a few of the recurring tropes of the autochthonous Philippine body in turn-of-the-century political cartoons. The first section attends to some of the peculiar fashion signs in the drawings.

The particular forms taken by imperial culture's dressing and styling of the otherwise naked Philippine natives reveal metroimperial anxieties about white U.S. hetero-masculinity. Such anxiety is both announced and disavowed by the ways in which the cartoons render the assimilating "Americanization" of the Filipinos—a racializing project enacted by way of what we might now know as the fashion makeover. More specifically, I argue, the uncivilized Philippine subject is made over into what would then have been deemed racially and sexually "degenerate"—and thus socially threatening—figures: the black dandy and the invert. The second section examines the frequent figurations of violence in these cartoons, theorizing how the relationship between metroimperial visual culture and the distinctly sadistic violence it evokes produces the Philippine body as the "sublime object" of U.S. imperialism, its unconscious and unbearable fantasy object. The third section extends the examination of violence in the cartoons, fleshing out the terms of imperialism's sadistic punishment: imperialist figures' seemingly endless capacity for the misuse of the male native's buttocks bespeaks a non-dialectical relation between the sadistic tormentor and its victim. The fourth section considers how the evident fixation of imperial administrators, as these cartoons suggest, on Philippine men's buttocks reveals a truth that belies the liberal process of the assimilation of Philippine subjects into the metropole: Filipinos' bottoms terrorize the public.

Black Dandies, Fairies, Degenerates: Visualizing Philippine Racial-Sexual Form

By the middle of the first decade of colonial occupation, just as colonial administrators in the Philippines had started with increased frequency to use vagrancy law as a way to govern intimacies, U.S. metropolitan culture often indexed the barbaric nature of Philippine natives by their seemingly incurable lack of clothing. Philippine natives' perceived inability to dress themselves (regarded by reporters, as I point out earlier, as "queer") confirmed their inability to govern themselves.[17] The ever present G-strings donned by the Philippine "primitives," captured in countless photographs taken by both administrators and civilians in the colonial Philippines, at once scandalized and titillated the U.S. mass public.[18] No wonder that the Philippine Exhibition at the St. Louis World's Fair in 1904 gathered the most spectators. One reporter from the fair sardonically appraised the topless fashions of the native "Igorrotes," referring to an ethnic group from the highlands of Luzon, as "extremely décolleté."[19] However effective the fair was in staging and disseminating the image of the naked native, smaller traveling "Wild East" shows conveyed this image to a larger American audience. Asterio Favis, one of the first pensionados, decries the story of a former colonial administrator who had smuggled "fifty Igorots" into the United States in 1904, and, having put the people on display throughout the country, capitalized on having "satisfied the curiosity of the inhabitants of more than fifty cities and towns who saw these . . . 'naked people.'"[20]

The sartorial difference that marked the distinction between barbarism and civilization was so pervasive that it led to cognitive dissonance when the white U.S. public encountered the earliest Philippine nationals living in the metropole, most of whom were upper middle class and fully dressed pensionados. Indeed, a pensionado is most likely the "metropoli[tan]" Philippine figure referred to in this description of the World's Fair from the *Wichita Daily Eagle*: "every tribe will be represented. The non-Christian tribes of the wild interior will be seen. The dainty, dandy Filipino of the metropolis, Manila, will be there in his gladdest garb."[21] We'll see more of the urbane Filipino figure as a "dainty dandy" later, but for now I wish simply to point to this reporter's attention to the "gladdest garb," a phrase that leaves the reader's imagination to decide whether the reference is to uninhibited (and thus freeing) nakedness or modern (and thus glad-making) finery. Pensionados, exemplifying W. E. B. Du Bois's fin-de-siècle notion of "double-consciousness," were very aware of how often they were subjected to this scrutiny of their mode of dress.[22] A serial section of the *Filipino Students' Magazine* (which I discuss at length in chapter 5) titled "United States Queries" compiled the surveying questions the Philippine students were asked by Americans in the metropole daily. Along with "What 'tribe' do you belong [to]?," "Do you eat dog meat up there?," and "Are you married?," one of the questions most frequently posited to the Filipina and Filipino students was "How do you like to wear clothes?"[23] Although relatively innocuous, and perhaps coming from a place of genuine curiosity, this last question, implying that nakedness was the pensionados' preferred (or, at least, default) mode of dress, exemplifies the sometimes dull force of racial-sexual fantasies supporting metropolitan forms of social recognition. The U.S. metroimperial public seems wont to disavow partially the attire of the fully dressed Filipina and Filipino students to fortify white, bourgeois propriety. The nakedness underneath the clothing of the Philippine students seems somehow not only more conspicuous, moreover, but perhaps also more deviant and perverse than that of the mass white public. Yet this seemingly more perverse nakedness is also a fetishistic site charged with curiosity and interest as the very mode of the address to the pensionados (the "query") attests. Thus, while the pensionados' responses to these microaggressive "queries" might in turn have been met with fascination, interest, or incredulity, they could have done little to displace the public's deep association of the Philippines with barbarity, an association that the natives' seemingly unmanageable nakedness signified.

Such attention to the clothing of the Philippine colonial body in public culture and social life indexed what Mimi Nguyen calls U.S. imperialism's "biopolitics of fashion."[24] U.S. public interest and investment in the Philippine people's fashion sense were perhaps all the keener since the U.S. government had, in accordance with the liberal policy of benevolent assimilation, allowed colonial Philippine subjects to enter the metropole—an anomaly in state governance vis-à-vis the severe federal quotas on Asian immigrants. The Philippine colonial subjects' immunity from the state's immigration restrictions, however, tested dominant white nativist sensibilities. Attention to Philippine dress, in this context, thus proved one way for the U.S. public to both imagine and manage, via normative codes of style, the racial-sexual form of colonial newcomers in the metropole. Conspicuous nakedness became something of a dense transfer point within metroimperial culture: colonial Philippine subjects' allegedly recalcitrant nakedness within the metropole signified, as I show, a racialized sexual availability.

The U.S. public's "curiosity" and anxiety about the dress of its colonial subjects during the middle of the decade was first indexed by various political cartoons' continual attention to sartorial details at the beginning of the Philippine-American War. Although the attention to Philippine dress signaled concerns about native propriety, the particular outfits that imperialism has the Filipino natives try out in these cartoons betray anxieties about white hetero-masculine integrity. More specifically, the United States' new colonial subjects in the Philippines, through their very assimilation into the nation, guaranteed the revitalization of U.S. white heterosexual masculinity by embodying its negative, pathological character. The cartoons put this revitalization into relief.[25]

As the cartoons' attempt to capture the newly encountered otherness of Filipinos drew in part on the commonly held stereotypes of recognizable racial others in the United States, then one way to make Filipinos if not "American" then at least legible to Americans was to remake them in the image of the most familiar racial other in the metropole: African Americans. The cartoons' rendering of Filipinos-qua-Americans, however, likens them not to "real" African Americans but, rather, displays them as a parody of a particular racial-sexual style: the black dandy. For example, in one cartoon from *Judge*, Uncle Sam plays a barber, holding long shears whose blades are each labeled "Education" and "Civilization" (figure 3.1).[26] His shop is filled with the kitschy accoutrements of U.S. modernity and imperial style—the star-spangled barber's chair, the perfume bottle of "Dewey's Manila Bay Rum," the bullet-shaped dispenser of

FIG. 3.1 "Uncle Sam to Filipinos—'You're Next.'" (*Judge*, 1899; artist, Eugene Zimmerman)

"Sampson Complexion Powder," and the advertisement in the background for "3. R.R.R.'s [*sic*] Tonic" (i.e., "Roosevelt's Rough Rider Tonic"). By Uncle Sam's feet we see piles of shorn hair spelling out "Porto Rico," "Hawaii," and "Cuba." Behind him, his evidently satisfied clients appraise and primp themselves before a mirror; these two men, though still simianized, have been transformed into dandified monkeys in blackface. Turning to the gruesomely wild, mostly naked "Filipino" sitting in the waiting chair behind him, Uncle Sam calls, "You're next."

A similar trope appeared on the front page of Boston's *Sunday Globe* in March 1899.[27] Not unlike advertisements for, say, diet pills, ab sculpting machines, and acne ointments that one might find in magazines nowadays, the cartoon spread, as the headline "Expansion, Before and After" claims, offers a series of before-and-after graphics of Filipinos (figure 3.2). One sketch, for example, posits a "before" scene showing one mostly naked Filipino silhouette chasing another with a spiked club against an "after" scene of Filipinos in blackface with exaggeratedly big lips playing baseball. The caption reads, "He could exchange the war club for the baseball bat readily." Another sketch contrasts an image of a grass-skirted, long-haired Filipino shaking a primitive shield and spear with another showing a neatly shorn and exceedingly natty dandy in blackface, complete with a cane, pink suit, and top hat, flouncing before an audience of similarly blackfaced Filipinas donning stars and stripes. The caption, "From the war dance to the cake walk is but a step," suggests that the distance between the primitive Filipino "Negroes" and genteel

A Magazine
Humor and Stories

The Boston Sunday Globe.

A Magazine
Humor and Stories

VOL. LV. NO. 64.   BOSTON, SUNDAY MORNING, MARCH 5, 1899.   PRICE FIVE CENTS.

EXPANSION, BEFORE AND AFTER.

He could exchange the war club for the baseball bat readily.

His old habit of running amuck will aid greatly on the football field.

THE FILIPINO BEFORE EXPANSION.

His water buffalos ought to go well in tandem.

THE FILIPINO AFTER EXPANSION.

From the war dance to the cake walk is but a step.

FIG. 3.2 "Expansion, Before and After." (*Sunday Globe* [Boston], 1899; artist unknown)

American "Negroes" could be bridged by snappy dance moves, a haircut, and a gaudy suit. The center cartoon bears the largest before-and-after scenario—juxtaposed there is a wild, skirt-wearing native wielding a bow, arrows, and a spear with an ingratiatingly smiling, dandified, and ostentatiously dressed figure in a top hat, suit jacket, high-collared shirt, and tie fashioned into a Windsor knot fastened with a bejeweled tiepin. Uncle Sam's styling of colonial subjects in the *Judge* cartoon and the social Darwinist evolutionary narratives sped up in the *Globe* spread not only plays on the widespread discursive designation, especially by U.S. troops stationed in the archipelago, of native Filipinos as newly found "blacks" or "niggers."[28] It also manages public perception about an ambiguously racialized people through the conventions of derision of a more familiar one.

The cartoons' makeover of the uncivilized Filipino into a preposterous black dandy marks a specific historical moment in which dominant nativist whites' growing fear of Filipinos' entrance and subsequent integration into the U.S. metropole converged with the long-standing terror of a growing African American petite bourgeoisie. Monica Miller has traced the evolving political significance of the black dandy, arguing that the black dandy's interpretation (rather than mere imitation) of European and white U.S. high style throughout the nineteenth century should be read as "a fabulous appropriation and revision of fancy clothes [and] a highly readable performative text" challenging dominant fashions.[29] With the rise of the increasingly visible postbellum, well-dressed black men in the North, however, came the increased popularity of minstrel performance and its star character, the dandy. Describing minstrel tropes akin to those shown in these political cartoons about Philippine subjects, Miller argues that minstrel shows' derision of dandies at once governed race, gender, sexual, and class difference: "the minstrel show's dandy was used to riff on Northern blacks who were thought to be overstepping the bounds of their newly won or imminent freedom. . . . Often on stage delivering mock speeches about 'ebucation,' dressed ostentatiously in plaid tuxedos, accessorized with top hats, gloves, and canes, effeminate in both senses of the word (hyper-sexual and womanly, illustrated by their attention to appearance), these dandies were designed to ridicule the small, but seemingly dangerous, black middle-class."[30] The hypersexual black man, now well dressed and middle class, troubled the dominant white gaze; the parodic figure of the effeminate, overdressed black dandy in minstrel performance, however, eased that trouble. Seeing well-dressed middle-class African Americans in public spaces elicited both anxiety and hilarity for white onlookers; this coupling of feelings led to dominant white culture's "minstrel joke."[31] The prospect of imperialism's new racial subjects' entrance into and mobility within the borders of the metropole thus intensified those feelings, and these cartoons tried to get the U.S. public to laugh them off.

The made-over "Filipino" in these cartoons, in short, is also the butt of white U.S. culture's minstrel joke. Rendering Philippine subjects' assimilation into the metropole as a makeover into a black dandy, thereby casting Philippine emergence into racial recognition as socially ludicrous according to contemporary fashion norms and effeminate according to emergent gender conventions, these cartoons style Philippine subjects after images found in a post-Reconstruction cultural form that attempted to consolidate racial boundaries by mocking a stylish black bourgeoisie.[32] This new blackened figure of the Filipino, like its predecessor of minstrelsy, would feed public millennial fears about miscegenation and portend President Theodore Roosevelt's famous warning against Anglo-Saxon race suicide, both of which were signs of racial/sexual excess and degeneration. Indeed, to the extent that white minstrel culture's staging of a widespread anxiety of miscegenation indicated a panicked "white male attraction to and repulsion from the black penis," as Eric Lott suggests,[33] then the cartoons' transformation of the Filipino into the minstrel dandy similarly betrays racial-sexual anxieties haunting the collective white gaze. The difference, though, as I discuss later, is that what becomes the object of anxious discourse and surveillance is not the concealed Filipino penis but, rather, the open secret of the perverse Filipino bottom. In the figure of the Filipino-as-black dandy, the Filipino is the butt, indeed.

The exaggerated blackface disparagement of African American masculinity that the Filipino's makeover assumes in these cartoons relieves the cultural anxiety resulting from imagined Filipino arrival into the metropole by attributing to the Philippine native a nonnormative gendered and sexual embodiment. The decadent "effeminacy" expressed in these cartoons by the ostentatious dress and flamboyant behavior of the Filipino blackfaced dandy ascribes to the autochthonous subject a deviant, excessive sexual nature. Male effeminacy, embodied most significantly by the figure of the "fairy," was by the turn of the century a sign of perversion, of one's interest in same-sex erotic acts. It in fact signaled what would later be understood as "homosexual" identity and behavior at the post–Oscar Wilde fin de siècle more clearly, perhaps, than it could have in any earlier moment in the American public imagination.[34] The makeover of the Filipino into the black dandy, therefore, does not just transform the monstrous native into the more recognizable racial body of the black American. It also articulates the assimilated native to another menacing identity under increasing surveillance within medical and police discourse within the imperial metropole by the 1890s: that of the invert or fairy.

The Filipino-as-black dandy in these cartoons marks the colonial native as both "decadent" and "degenerate," two terms that at the turn of the twentieth century marked deviant racial, sexual, and gendered form. How these terms came to signal racial-sexual-gender deviance was knotty, so a brief discussion of decadence and degeneracy is necessary here. As Jennifer Terry, Siobhan Somerville, and Margot Canaday have stunningly traced, "degeneracy" signaled racial inferiority of non–Western European peoples in mid-nineteenth-century scientific discourses. By the late nineteenth century European and U.S. sexologists, drawing on evolutionary theory, began to use the term as an index of the racial regression of some *white* individuals, particularly those who displayed "contrary sexual instinct," effeminacy, or inversion. Ideologies of race and gender were deployed, that is, to construct early figurations of "homosexuality"—the invert, the fairy, the dandy—as degenerate. While some physicians and scientists regarded such biological and moral degeneracy as inborn, others conjectured that, especially for white people showing contrary sexual instinct, it resulted from either "modern stress and contaminations" or overindulgence and consumption—all indicators of social decadence.[35] Inherent degeneracy, for sexologists and, eventually, state administrators, was characteristic of lower racial status.[36] The degeneracy that allegedly resulted from luxury, idleness, and leisure, in contrast, was a marker of aristocratic and bourgeois decadence within white populations. Public anxiety about the latter etiology of manly decadence within the U.S. metropole, incidentally, resulted in the perceived need for the revitalization of national masculinity, a recuperative work that, as mentioned earlier, fin-de-siécle empire building promised to provide.[37]

In U.S. public consciousness, the tropes of degeneracy and decadence converged in the figure of the dandy, who was deemed "effeminate" in misogynist late nineteenth-century U.S. culture especially because of his perceived attention to, exaggeration of, and innovations in style; his excessive consumption; and his lack of strenuous activity, all of which were enabled by industrialization. The dandy's alleged softness was seen as an indicator of his proximity to women on an evolutionary scale; indeed, the dandy's supposed desire to be like women occluded the possibility of any sexual desire for women. The (white) dandy thus posed a threat to Anglo-Saxon supremacy, embodying at once the vestige of an earlier racial type within an evolutionary schema (i.e., degeneracy) and a harbinger of the race's imminent failure to reproduce (i.e., decadence).[38] In this sense, Neville Hoad argues, the dandy occupies the same space—"same sequential position"—on a developmental continuum as the colonial "primitive."[39] The dandy and the primitive were equally out of joint; both marked the evolution of whiteness and threatened its extinction.

The caricature of the primitive Filipino-as-black dandy redoubles the racial-sexual degeneration of the native as he is assimilated into metropolitan modes of racial recognition. To make intelligible the racial form of the population threatening to encroach on metropolitan space, U.S. mass culture drew on a more legible racial-sexual degenerate. The dressed "Filipino" thus figures in U.S. popular and middlebrow consciousness as a cathected point of particular fin-de-siècle imperial-national anxieties about white heterosexual masculinity, as an assemblage of the concomitant fin-de-siècle fears about African American advancement and mobility, decadence, the degeneration of the white masculine body, immigration, cross-racial affiliation, imperial incorporation, miscegenation, and assimilation. Indeed, this early articulation of the Filipino as the derided black dandy—these images appeared in 1899, at the beginning of the war—was integral to the production of the Filipino native in visual culture more generally as a racial-sexual degenerate.

This latter trope would take on several incarnations. Concurrent cartoons, for example, depict Emilio Aguinaldo—the president of the short-lived, interregnum Philippine Republic and notorious leader of the anti-U.S. insurrecto movement—keeping intimate company with white U.S. anti-imperialist men, or "antis." Pro-expansionists often deployed the term "antis" because of its homonymic correlative ("aunties") as an effort to deride anti-imperialist sentiment as sentimental, weak, and cowardly, thereby feminizing anti-imperialists. In these cartoons, Aguinaldo plays the desirable dandy, the "Idol of the Aunties"

FIG. 3.3 "The Idol of the Aunties." (*Puck*, May 10, 1899; artist, Louis Dalrymple)

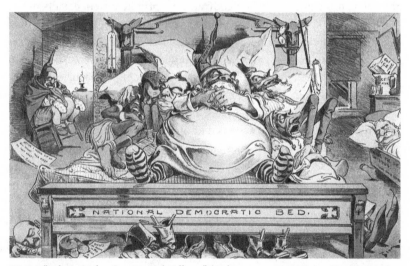

FIG. 3.4 "Politics Makes Strange Bed-Fellows." (*Judge*, 1900; artist, Eugene Zimmerman)

(figure 3.3); he cuddles in bed with antis (figure 3.4); and he dances in a dress with those same figures (figure 3.5).[40] The cartoons thus deride the Northern antis' sympathy for Filipinos as the white men's desire for Aguinaldo. As in concurrent, misogynist political discourse, in each of these cartoons, while the white male politicians could assume various relations to manhood in relation to each other, "femininity" is figured as the index only of the ineffectual, silly, or sentimental. The surest way to discipline the Northern anti-

FIG. 3.5 "'Judge' Forsees [*sic*] the Democratic Inauguration Ball if Bryan Should Be Elected." (*Judge*, 1900; artist, Eugene Zimmerman)

imperialists and to demonstrate their lack of political authority, then, was to effeminize them—to cast them "as women."[41]

Yet I am more interested here in how Aguinaldo is made over vis-à-vis these antis: on one hand, as a rakish dandy in his own right, and on the other, as a figure deemed even more racially-sexually degenerate, as an invert. Affirming the political leanings of the pro-expansionist *Judge* (published from 1881 to 1939) and *Puck* (published form 1877 to 1918), these cartoons accord with the widespread attributions of racialized effeminacy—and therefore of perversion or degeneracy—to Aguinaldo in contemporary mass discourse. That one newspaper correspondent would call his own ability to prove that "Aguinaldo *certainly* has a wife, and he is very fond of her," a journalistic "coup" suggests that there was plenty of public speculation about the Philippine leader's gender-sexual normalcy or his possible bachelor status.[42] What's more, both the U.S. colonial state and the popular press claimed that Aguinaldo had given the "strange order" to his Philippine *insurrecto* soldiers in 1900 to "dress as [women]" in order to infiltrate U.S. colonial defenses.[43] In "The Idol of the Aunties" (see figure 3.3), set vaguely in the Philippine tropics, various anti-imperialist political figures in dresses, including George Frisbee Hoar and William Lloyd Garrison, swoon at the feet of a dandified Aguinaldo. Yet even as the antis, on their knees, passively pine and pray for Aguinaldo's attention, the cartoon's Americanizing dandification of Aguinaldo ascribes to him a more perverse decadence and degeneracy. His ostentatious military uniform, his seemingly painted face (seen clearly in the original color image), his red socks, and his white gloves in particular symptomatized what at the time would have been seen as an excessive, "feminine" attention to fashion.[44] Aguinaldo's famous golden whistle, here attached to his blue sash, was elsewhere mocked in the press as an attempt "to put on style."[45] Indeed, according to an editorial published in February 1899, "It [was] the desire of Aguinaldo [to don] a pair of old pants and a spiked tailed coat so that he [could] go into society."[46] (The insurrecto general's alleged desire here is to be not just a dandy but a black dandy.) Aguinaldo's posture, moreover, evokes turn-of-the-century stereotypes of fairies: his limp wrist resting on his sword; his mannered fingers (and not whole hand) melodramatically pressed to his chest, feigning a "Dear Me!" coyness to the antis' idolatry; his head cocked to one side; his arched eyebrows; his knowing, expressive eyes; his demure but flirtatious smile.[47] Indeed, against this more decadent Filipino dandy, the white antis in dresses might not read as effeminate at all. They just look like white men wearing dresses.

The cartoons published in *Judge* in 1900 mark Aguinaldo's racial-sexual degeneracy more explicitly. In "Politics Makes Strange Bed-Fellows" (see figure 3.4), Aguinaldo, figured as a savage native with a skirt on—and so "dress[ed] as a woman"—lies in bed with prominent anti-imperialists, so his relation with white men is not as a hostile but as an intimate.[48] Aguinaldo sleeps in fetal position, with his head nestled in the crook of the presidential hopeful William Jenning Bryan's arm. The intimacy between these two, represented here by cuddling in private, appears differently in the other *Judge* cartoon, where we find them cutting a rug in public. In that cartoon (see figure 3.5), Aguinaldo, again an effeminate savage in a skirt, is Bryan's dance partner at Bryan's would-be presidential inauguration. In *Judge*'s hysterical (not just in the funny sense) rendering of what might happen if the anti-imperialist court jester Bryan won the presidency, we are led to imagine that Aguinaldo would join in the celebration, since a victory for Bryan would mean Philippine independence. By casting Aguinaldo as the feminized, skirt-wearing partner in bed and on the dance floor, these cartoons ascribe a degeneracy to the insurrecto president; more specifically, the cartoons produce him as invert or fairy. While understood nowadays as constitutive figures within the genealogy of "homosexuality," these terms at the turn of the twentieth century referred not to a person's "sexuality" directly but, rather, to gender reversal or inversion and, thus, abnormality.[49] Even in the absence of any "sexual" act, the effeminacy of the insurrecto leader—exceeding that ascribed to the onlooking antis, and so even they look over their shoulders at the first couple in curiosity—indexes his alleged perversion.

It is significant that the cartoons imagine the intimacy between Aguinaldo and Bryan emerging not just in the boudoir but also in a public space. Within the U.S. metropolitan context of 1899, the illustrated scene of an inverted Aguinaldo dancing with Bryan—amid a sea of same-sex, cross-dressing (but still all-white) pairings—perhaps drew on and called to mind a range of contemporary public spaces known for enabling degenerate intimacies and gender transgressions. For example, the fantasmatic scene might have conjured for U.S. metropolitan readers New York City's Paresis Hall, the infamous "principal resort in New York for degenerates." Paresis Hall, which gained infamy throughout the 1890s for the subculture of flamboyant fairies who convened there, by 1899 had established the dominant public image of male sexual abnormality.[50] Apart from evoking Paresis Hall's perversions, the cartoon also visualizes the fantasmatic picture we have already seen: that "Aguinaldo, in the proclamation of his Constitution . . . would 'license the Chinese houses of pleasure,'" and from such pleasures "came the destruction of Sodom and Gomorrah."[51] Similarly, the cartoon warns, Aguinaldo would bring these sodomitic "houses of pleasure" to the United States. Such an ominous and thrilling scenario of degenerate natives invading the metropole and gaining intimacy with a white public might in fact have already been capitalized on. In April 1899, another "vulgar" little Paresis Hall–like dance club in New York City was slowly becoming notorious for a few police arrests of fairies, or "male degenerates." According to vice reports, one could also spy a "ragtime and a kiky."[52] "Ragtime" refers to a less than "moral dance," because of its perceived amalgamation of black and white traditions, and "kiky" possibly alludes, as Audre Lorde would remind us almost a century later, to gender-nonconforming, black "gay-girls" who sometimes slept with men.[53] This decadent and degenerate Bowery neighborhood dance club, which was patronized by black and white folks alike (though surely for different reasons), was called, not incidentally, the "Manila."

Ultimately, the racial form that the colonial "Filipino" assumes in these various caricatured makeovers is marked by articulations to bodies known for gendered-racial-sexual degeneracy and perversion. Although the cartoons may have presumed to render the Filipino more familiar or intelligible to a U.S. metropolitan public—to make over is a biopolitical project, after all, meant to "rescue and modernize persons whose aesthetic sensibilities or taste competencies are deemed temporally or socially inappropriate"—the assimilated Filipino body proves all the more unmanageable as a result.[54] Such unmanageability is more than a matter of contradiction. It results from a degeneracy that remains out of joint with the evolutionary narrative on which sexological and medical discourses relied and whose completion was being realized by the body of the white hetero-masculine ideal venturing off for U.S. empire. Yet it is through this makeover of the recalcitrant Philippine male body—a metroimperial attempt at signification and subjection—that U.S.

state and culture attempt to shore up gendered, racial, and sexual order in the face of the anarchy of empire. In the attribution of racial-sexual degeneracy to the "Filipino," as the cartoons dramatize, U.S. metroimperial culture aspires to fortify white hetero-masculine virility and safeguard the de jure racial segregation and hierarchies that *Plessy v. Ferguson* instantiated and that the project of imperialism, by expanding and loosening its borders, threatened to dissolve.[55]

The Philippine Native as the Sublime Object of Imperialism

As the United States' new colonial others jeopardized American racial order, political cartoons both represented and enacted modes of transpacific border patrol. Some of these cartoons rendered the autochthonous Philippine subject knowable—albeit unmanageable—by way of a fashion makeover. Other cartoons used more violent tropes to represent the management of unruly Philippine natives. These tropes most often took a paternalistic form: cartoons produced Filipinos' immaturity by casting them as monstrous children who deserved corporal punishment. Representing the supposed youth of the Philippines vis-à-vis its recent unyoking of centuries-long Spanish rule, caricatures of the United States' new colonial people frequently rendered them as newly found, very nearly naked, and unruly toddlers—or, if not as toddlers, then as grossly exaggerated miniatures vis-à-vis the adult white colonial administrators.[56] The depictions of Filipino orphans perhaps meant to elicit two main affective responses. On one hand, in anti-imperialist publications such as *Life* magazine they represent Philippine natives as pitiable, naïve waifs whose helplessness vis-à-vis a dominating empire might move the sympathies of the U.S. public.[57] On the other hand, in pro-expansionist journalistic outposts, the native orphan toddlers become a justification for colonial occupation—they have become the unexpected burden of empire, the baby at the doorstep in need of adoption by a benevolent parent.[58] Numerous cartoons, pro- and anti-imperialist alike, rehearse variations on these two basic configurations of the diminutive foundling as either enslaved and helpless urchin or unexpected but manageable obligation. Some combined features of both. In neither trope, however, even when mingled with the other, are the white man's burdens capable of social, political, or historical maturity—hence, the paternalistic punishment that disciplines the native child. White love was tough love.[59]

Punishment of the unruly, childlike Filipino in these cartoons, however, often takes the form of the sadistic violence. There was something of an incitement to discourse about sadism in the United States during the last quarter of the nineteenth century, particularly since, along with "homosexuality" and other perversions, sadism was increasingly attached to moral, legal, and social panics. Sexologists' theories of sadism, which at the time was not always understood as intertwined with masochism, typically characterized it—like degeneracy—as an atavistic perversion.[60] Demonstrating Siobhan Somerville's claim that sexology drew on evolutionary theories about race, turn-of-the-century conjecture on sadism, and algophilia (sexual pleasure received from inflicting or receiving pain) more generally, progressed from the psychiatrist Shobal Vail Clevenger's hypothesis in 1881 that sadistic desire originated in primitive hunger (an amoeba had "cannibalistic" habits "that were reminiscent of copulation when they enveloped smaller bacteria"), through Edward Spitzka's hypothesis that there was a "confusion between the sexual and hunger desires and that blood drinking and cannibalism had a sexual etiology," to Clevenger's revised hypothesis of 1903 that sadism was "the atavistic development toward animals that employed violent means in copulation."[61]

Yet it was not these Darwinian-inspired, racialized theories but Krafft-Ebing's less explicitly evolutionary definition in the 1893 edition of *Psychopathia Sexualis* that would come to be the most influential. Krafft-Ebing, who gave this perversion its name after the libertine Marquis de Sade, characterizes it as "the impulse to cruel and violent treatment of the opposite sex, and the coloring of the idea of such acts with lustful feeling."[62] Drawing from and exploring the sexologists' discourse, and especially from Krafft-Ebing's definition, Freud would reserve the term, as he does in *Three Essays on the Theory of Sexuality* (1905), "for cases where there is an association between sexuality and violence used against others."[63] Concurrent with early U.S. colonial rule in the Philippines, this proliferation of discourse in sexology and medicine around sadism matched the U.S. public's fascination with it. Indeed, by 1914, a description of a trip to the "queer" Philippine region of Jolo (also known as Sulu) in the *Tensas Gazette* of St. Joseph, Louisiana, characterizes the "unsubdued and piratical tribe of Moros" as "handy with all sorts of weapons" and "hav[ing] no weak antipathy to blood."[64] Another story on the same page talks about the "exciting career" of a "six-year-old 'Jack the Ripper,'" whom a "psychopathic laboratory of the municipal court" in Oak Park, Louisiana, called "a perfect specimen of sadist." (Alienists and neurologists concluded that the boy's having been adopted eight times might have drawn out his sociopathic behavior, which included killing cats and attempting to kill a baby.[65]) What we find on the same page of this local newspaper from the colonial metropole, in other words, is paratactic evidence of how the notion of the "Filipino"— particularly the unsubdued, bloodlusting "Moro," whom we see more of in the next chapter—and the "sadist" have become so entrenched within metroimperial consciousness that one might immediately recognize a "perfect specimen" of each.

Yet why might these political cartoons come to figure imperial discipline as the crossing of "cruel and violent treatment" and "lustful feeling"? The cartoons' articulation of the popular tropes of infantilization to those around sexual violence draws out imperial sadism and public panic. Numerous pro-imperialist cartoons dramatize the empire's might over infantilized Philippine men's bodies in openly phallic ways. One cartoon, which appeared on the cover of *Judge*, showed Uncle Sam pointing a rifle, waist high, at the chest of a fearful, mostly naked, adult, dark-skinned Filipino native. Hanging on the end of the rifle's bayonet was a punctured note marked "Liberty and Civilization." The caption posited this note as a hitherto failed message to the native: "He wouldn't take it any other way."[66] Yet another cartoon, from *Puck*, showed two strapping white U.S. soldiers holding down a colonial fort, both brandish long weapons. In the background, diminutive white antis try to tug down the fort's thick, erect flagpole, which is marked "Philippines" and bears the U.S. flag. The caption emphasized the shank's phallic potency: "It won't come down."[67] Such examples demonstrate visually what Theodore Roosevelt would profess in 1902 about American manhood: "we of America . . . the sons of a nation in the pride of its lusty youth . . . know that the future is ours if we have in us the manhood to grasp it, and we enter the new century girding our loins for the contest before us, rejoicing in the struggle."[68] The cartoons here evince a quiet confidence in American white sons' capacity to grasp the future looming on the horizon, if not also a quiet pleasure in grasping their "manhood" and girding their loins in the effort.

The cartoons in the pro-expansionist *Puck* and *Judge* employed overdetermined phallic tropes to demonstrate the hale and virtuous masculinity of white colonial administrators and foot-soldiers of empire. The cartoons in the anti-expansionist *Life* did so to render the violence of imperial masculinity as unrestrained and excessive. A cartoon published in *Life* in July 1899 bearing the caption "The Harvest in the Philippines" showed the profile of a smug Uncle Sam standing upright, while the horizontal barrel of a large cannon behind him unambiguously projects his "manhood." Yet beyond him, in the background, lay fully clothed corpses of Filipino soldiers, lined up as if a harvested field—Uncle Sam's shadow on the ground, moreover, bears no trace of the barrel.[69] *Life* was thus disclosing Uncle Sam's phallic overkill. Elsewhere *Life* likened imperialism's phallic violence, somewhat explicitly, to anal rape. In a cartoon published in February 1901, a wizened, frail Uncle Sam aims a spear-ended flagpole bearing the Star-Spangled Banner toward the buttocks of an infantilized Emilio Aguinaldo, who is pinned down by Uncle Sam's boot (figure 3.6).[70]

FIG. 3.6 "Victory at Last. The Final Filipino." (*Life*, February 28, 1901; artist, Joe Scheuerle)

Here, again, the figure of Aguinaldo functions as the cathected metonymy of the unruly Philippines. (Indeed, paired with his being rendered as a dandy and fairy, "Aguinaldo" proves something of an assemblage, what Jasbir Puar and Amit Rai call a "monster-terrorist-fag."[71]) The cartoon, whose caption reads "Victory at Last. The Final Filipino," discloses the real consequence of benevolent assimilation: the utter annihilation of a racialized people in the name of caring imperialism. Yet it also implies the futility—the impossible finality—of the war, recognizing the unlikelihood that the "Final Filipino" could ever be located over against the Philippine insurrectos' deterritorializing guerrilla tactics. What the cartoon cynically mocks, in other words, is the very notion of "Victory," the task of finding and killing the "Final Filipino," of eradicating all of the insurrectos. Uncle Sam's action and frailty—especially in contrast to the hale musculature that typically characterized him in contemporaneous visual cultural products—suggest that the U.S. imperialist endeavors might be impotent and, to borrow from Roosevelt, forever "grasping": impotent in the face of the insurgents' successful deterritorialist tactics and therefore grasping in imagining phallic "Victory" in the exaggerated form of anal penetration. Yet how would imperial administrative "victory," in this satire, come to take the form of anal punishment of Philippine men/boys in metropolitan visual culture?

The *Life* cartoon posits Aguinaldo as a potential martyr: his death, brought about by anal penetration, would not in fact lead to "Victory at Last" over anticolonial nationalism. Instead, it would infuse his body, like that of the venerated Philippine nationalist hero José Rizal (who would later be called "The *First* Filipino" by Leon Ma Guerrero and Benedict Anderson) with a certain charisma—an indestructibility and abstraction that would reemerge later in the seemingly limitless bodies of the insurgent Filipino other. The effect of the indestructibility and abstraction of the insurgent enemy's body through death need not, though, be accomplished by the figural death of a recognizable leader—Aguinaldo's body, however widely familiar, is one of many that would suffer such violence. Indeed, the seemingly infinite reproducibility of the Filipino colonial and alien body is precisely what makes possible its abstraction, and its menace, within the metroimperial imaginary.[72]

One astonishing cartoon in particular depicts allegorically how the native body becomes abstract in visual culture (figure 3.7). In "The First Black Bored in the Philippines," a drawing that appeared in 1899 in *Collier's Weekly* of New York City,[73] a partially dressed, simianized Filipino native is shot at from behind by a white soldier who is still aiming his bayonet in the background.[74] Leaving his hiding spot among the rocks to retreat from combat, the escaping insurrecto has dropped his sword, which signifies the previously imminent threat (sometimes now called "probable cause") that has now been contained. As if to demonstrate that the U.S. soldier has hit his mark, the cartoon fantastically depicts the bullet, which has passed clear through the native's torso, as flying ahead of him. Here, the Philippine native, in wide-eyed shock, looks and grasps at his chest, which bears a hole. Yet in figuring the bullet as piercing and flying ahead of the native, the cartoon does more than emphasize the good aim of the colonial soldier. It casts the autochthonous Philippine subject as, in part, indestructible. The cartoon fixes the insurgent native between two deaths—between the native's fatal wounding in the scene and its body's belated

FIG. 3.7 "The First Black Bored in the Philippines." (*Collier's Weekly*, 1899; artist, Grant Wallace)

recognition of fatality. It is as if the insurrecto, in seeing the fatal wound—and despite seeing the fatal wound—has not yet remembered to die.[75]

Slavoj Žižek discusses a similar moment to demonstrate the Sadeian victim's possession of two bodies. In Žižek's scenes, one of these bodies takes material form, "part of the natural cycle of generation and corruption"; the other, however, is "composed of some other substance, one excepted from the vital cycle—a sublime body."[76] These two bodies—one natural and one sublime—have two corresponding forms of death:

> natural death, which is part of the natural cycle of generation and corruption, of nature's continual transformation, and absolute death—the destruction, the eradication, of the cycle itself, which then liberates nature from its own laws and opens the way for the creation of new forms of life *ex nihilo*. [The sadist's] victim is, in a certain sense, indestructible: she can be endlessly tortured and can survive it; she can endure any torment and still retain her beauty.

Today, we find this same fantasy at work in various products of "mass culture," for example in animated cartoons. Consider Tom and Jerry, cat and mouse. Each is subjected to frightful misadventures: the cat is stabbed, dynamite goes off in his pocket, he is run over by a steamroller and his body is flattened into a ribbon, and so forth; but in the next scene he appears with his normal body and the game begins again—it is as though he possessed another indestructible body.[77]

Sadistic violence—a violence from which the sadist extracts sexual enjoyment—endows the victim with two bodies: one that takes abuse and humiliation and another that emerges from the sadistic act unscathed. This second body Žižek calls the "sublime body," the thing inassimilable to symbolization or historicization and, paradoxically, retroactively composed by—at the limits of—that symbolization or historicization. Although the Collier's Weekly cartoon doesn't have a next scene—one in which the native might "appear with his normal [bullet hole-less] body"—the native body emerges, fully intact, time and again in other cartoons, "and the game begins again." Indeed, projecting U.S. colonial administrators' fantasies that guerrilla insurrectos were everywhere, this cartoon seems to set up what might happen next in the scene. Behind the white colonial soldier is one who looks just like him; following the gaze of this second soldier, we find a tropical bush whose shadowy form doubles that of the penetrated native's hair, as if this silhouette might morph into, or be revealed as, the "second" insurrecto, ready to pick up the previously dropped sword. The U.S. imperial soldier's enemy, once killed, seems able to re-spawn immediately and, to echo Žižek, ex nihilo. Such seeming unstoppability of the insurrecto's murderous desire, which is characterized by a primitive sword (and, thus, a barbaric phallus), is precisely what legitimates imperial necropolitics—in the form of military attrition, concentration camps, and scorched earth techniques. The attribution of pathological desires to the other justifies one's own; as Saidiya Hartman has argued, "Fantasies about the other's enjoyment are ways for us to organize our own enjoyment."[78]

In effect, the Collier's Weekly cartoon dramatizes the emergence of the native's indestructible, sublime body, which appears over and over in other cartoons and elsewhere in public visual culture as the renascent victim of sadistic, colonial violence. It might be tempting here to account for cartoons' rendering of the native body as the sublime object of imperial knowledge, to answer "why" the abused native stands in as the sublime object of imperial significance. To the extent that the U.S. colonial military in the Philippines, for example, found the insurrecto bodies to be seemingly limitless and therefore indestructible—if it reluctantly, even unconsciously, conceded the impossibility of achieving the death of the "Final Filipino" because of the insurrectos' deterritorializing guerrilla tactics—then imperial power, rendered impotent in the face of this sublime body, could only take the compensatory form of phallic violence, a kind of impotent acting out, of grasping. Yet this reason is not entirely satisfactory, since the sublime object of the network of imperial knowledge and desire remains by its nature radically autonomous, recalcitrant to symbolization. The very diversity of the cartoon figures, not to mention their unintelligible relation to each other, signals not only the unruly, autonomous nature of the insurrecto within the metroimperial public imagination but also how the insurrecto other becomes signified, made intelligible. To suggest that imperialism's response to the sublime object of its knowledge must take the form of phallic, sadistic violence merely begs the question. Rather, we might instead consider a temporal inversion of these terms: sadistic colonial violence—a particularly phallic violence—inflicted time and again on the body of the insurgent native retroactively casts the Philippine native body as sublime.

This is what this cartoon allegorizes: the very process of the abstraction of the Philippine native within the visual culture of the U.S. metropole. The cartoon's persistent rendering of the "Filipino's" desire—murderous or perverse—might itself be understood as enacting a sadistic violence that endows that figure with two bodies: a manifest Philippine body, in that representational modes signify or otherwise make intelligible Philippine racial-sexual form, and the sublime Philippine body, one that is somewhere "out there," exceeding metropolitan representational forms, eluding U.S. imperial-colonial governance, unintelligible except as an unknown known, bearing a perverse desire that is "sensed but always missed."[79] Fundamentally disjointed—assembled from photographs, journalistic coverage, official colonial discourse, the individual artist's imagination, and incongruent fragments of preexisting stereotypes of disparate racialized and sexualized bodies, yet backed by the force of historical events—the Philippine insurrecto body is retroactively rendered in these cartoons into imperialism's sublime object ("an incarnation of [empire's] impossible *jouissance*") within the U.S. cultural imagination.[80] The autochthonous figure in these cartoons occupies the gap between U.S. imperialism's attempt to acquire totalizing knowledges about the "Filipino"—metropolitan, colonial, racial, and sexual—and such a project's inevitable failure. In short, the Philippine body in these cartoons belies and holds together metroimperial cultural fantasy (especially if we recall fantasy's function of protecting one from a horrific truth, from the impossibility at the heart of knowledge production). The Filipino body is "sublime" precisely because the particular fantasy form it assumes mystifies and occludes, even as it threatens to render visible, the terrifying impossibility—the "absolute death"—of U.S. colonial knowledge-making systems.[81] The abused Philippine body in these cartoons bespeaks the limits of U.S. imperialist knowledge, power, and desire and alludes to the unknowable object of its terror and desire.

FIG. 3.8 "Incorrigible." (*Washington Post*, March 28, 1899; artist, Clifford Berryman)

A Filipino Is Being Beaten

For its intractability, both representational and real, the Philippine native must be punished. A cartoon from *Puck* that was published in March 1899 shows a hobgoblin-like Aguinaldo being smashed down by an enormous hand decorated with the U.S. flag onto a child's hobby horse labeled "Dictatorship."[82] In another cartoon, from the *Washington Post*, Uncle Sam holds a hideous Filipino, belly-down, over his knee (a conventional spanking-session position), taking aim at the Filipino's buttocks with a bunch of reeds.[83] The caption reads

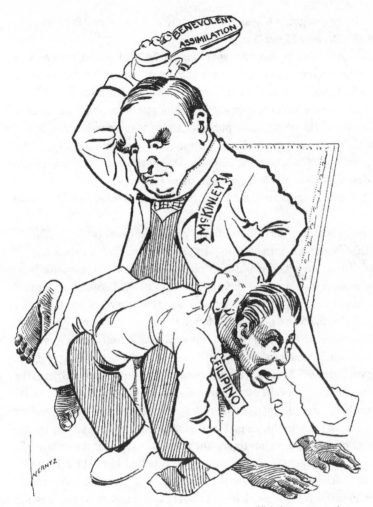

FIG. 3.9 "Popular Song Illustrated—'Because I Love You.'" (*Chicago Record*, November 28, 1899; artist, Carl Werntz)

"Incorrigible" (figure 3.8).[84] Still another cartoon, found in a May 1902 issue of the *Pioneer Press* (St. Paul, Minnesota), repeated this scene, although instead of the reeds Uncle Sam holds a boot marked "U.S. Army." The caption professed the toughness of Uncle Sam's white love: "This isn't my trade, but if you think you can't get along without it, I guess I can fix you."[85] A cartoon published in the *Chicago Record* in November 1899 employs a similar scenario, although this time it is McKinley holding a simianized Filipino, dressed in an ill-fitting suit, over his knee, while the shoe he readies to spank the Filipino monkey's bottom is marked "Benevolent Assimilation" (figure 3.9). The caption again conveys the begrudging obligation to the duty of white love: "Popular Song Illustrated—'Because I Love You.'"[86]

This cartoon, which casts the spanking by McKinley as a paternalistic "this-is-going-to-hurt-me-more-than-it-hurts-you" scenario, belies imperial discipline's claims of identification with the "little brown brothers," its projection that colonial violence is really an affront to U.S. exceptionalist values and character. [87] The paternalistic punisher, the cartoon reveals, never in fact identifies with the victim; his abuse is not founded on some dialectical relationship or mutual recognition. To presume that the sadist metonymically might identify with its victim's pain is to share U.S. imperialism's liberal fantasy of "loving" recognition—that is, benevolent assimilation—of its colonial other.

This point is more clearly illustrated in another cartoon from the *Chicago Record* that figures the intractability of the Philippine native (figure 3.10).[88] In it, the distinction between anti-imperialist sympathy and imperialist punishment is represented as the difference, respectively, between a teaching practice that rewards good behavior and one that punishes disobedience. Standing in for the former, and at the left in the scene, is the anti-imperialist Republican Senator George Frisbie Hoar of Massachusetts, who, rendered elderly and portly, wears a skirt-like apron over his schoolmaster's garb (thus evoking the "auntie"); he is also holding out a stick of candy. At the right of the scene, representing imperial discipline, stands a young, fit Democratic Senator Albert Beveridge of Indiana, who rolls up the sleeve of his cane-wielding arm not only to show off his ripped musculature but also to get ready for the dirty work of spanking he has to do. The caption reads, "Mr. Beveridge (To the Rival School Teacher)—'The trouble is you petted him. What he needs is the rod.'" Beveridge's face is stern and unflappable compared with Hoar's shadowy profile, his "rod" much longer than Hoar's candy cane. Between the two schoolteachers, in the middle of the scene, is Emilio Aguinaldo—this time a chronically disobedient schoolboy in shorts, standing with eyebrows raised and a finger in his open mouth, perhaps in compensation for the rod of candy he has not yet received or as an expression of shock about the imminent beating.

The cartoon's schoolroom context is an apposite backdrop for apprehending the terms of imperial sadism. Although many cartoons of the time mocked the benevolent project of educating Philippine subjects into modernity and civilization (and, indeed, U.S. colonial public schooling became metonymic of this project) as a questionable proposition, this caricature's setting reveals such tutelage's impersonal, ideological function of violence.

FIG. 3.10 "Mr. Beveridge (to the Rival School Teacher)—'The Trouble Is You Petted Him. What He Needs Is the Rod.'" (*Chicago Record*, 1900; artist, Clyde Newman)

In a fitting metaphor, Gilles Deleuze has characterized the sadist's show of reasoning as impersonal instruction:

> The [sadist] may put on an act of trying to convince and persuade. . . . But the intention to convince is merely apparent, for nothing is in fact more alien to the sadist than the wish to convince, to persuade, in short to educate. He is interested in something quite different, namely to demonstrate that reasoning itself is a form of violence, and that he is on the side of violence, however calm and logical he may be. He is not even attempting to prove anything to anyone, but to perform a demonstration related essentially to the solitude and omnipotence of its author. The point of the exercise is to show that the demonstration is identical to violence. . . . In every respect . . . the sadistic "instructor" stands in contrast to the masochistic "educator."[89]

Evocative of the canteen in which Boss Reese commanded the Philippine Scout Luis Malonso to submit to being shaved (see chapter 2), the schoolhouse setting illustrates a distinction between what Deleuze might have characterized as the sadistic "instruction" and the caring "education" of colonial rule. The United States' "intention to convince" the Filipino of its care, the cartoon exposes, is "an act"; empire's demonstration of benevolence merely sustains "the solitude and omnipotence" of imperial rule. The cartoon depicts Beveridge's rhetoric of paternalistic duty (the caption alludes to the puritanical adage "Spare the rod; spoil the child") while simultaneously unmasking his didactic role as one "identical to violence."

Beveridge's teaching philosophy is maximal discipline, his rod an "instrument for [the] elimination," as Sara Ahmed has recently described, of the "willful subject's" willfulness.[90] The relation of the Indiana senator to his audience, whether the effeminized Hoar, the childlike Aguinaldo, or the mass U.S. public, is, like his flexed arm, merely "demonstrative" of his capacity for cold, cruel force. He is actually unconcerned with preventing the child's spoiling; such an objective presupposes at least some dialectical relation with his victim. Instead, his version of imperialism is fascinated with the "hermetic circle" of its own rule.[91] This caricature cohered with Senator Beveridge's white supremacist, pro-expansionist worldview; as Meg Wesling puts it, Beveridge "offered an exemplary model of imperialist excitement . . . that melded racialized fears about the erosion of white dominance in the face of Asian immigration and African American enfranchisement with opportunistic reams of new markets and U.S. global power, all articulated through the religious and moral discourse of the divine supremacy of 'Anglo-Saxon civilization.'"[92] Indeed, when Beveridge urged fellow Americans in a speech to take up their rightful place as "master organizers of the world," he claimed a particular racial right to conquest, claiming that Anglo-Saxons alone possessed the rightful "blood of government."[93] Accordingly, the "calm and logical" profile of Beveridge in the cartoon obscures a significant part of a segmented map of the world in the schoolroom background. Where one would expect to see the "Eastern" hemisphere and the Philippines, one finds the robust, disproportionately large head—the inflated imperial ego—of the disciplinarian, a substitutive cartography evoking what Krafft-Ebing identified as "a pronounced form of sadism operating to a great extent in geographical and mathematical patterns."[94] Moreover, the cartoon's play of overdetermined phallic tropes—the long stick of candy; the longer caning rod; the image of either "petting" or thrashing the schoolboy Aguinaldo, whose finger (tinier still compared with the stick of candy or rod) doesn't nearly fill his wide-open mouth—bespeak something of a sexual, even pederastic, enjoyment in imperialist domination.[95] Sucking one's fingers in public at the turn of the century, for some in the know, would have signaled fellatio.[96] Significantly, Aguinaldo's schoolboy shorts betray his arousal around these rival teachers; by his left hand there seems to be what can only be described as a bulge, and it points to Beveridge. The cartoon thus stages a more revealing version of the *New York Times*'s "truth," as cited in chapter 1, about what the Filipino wants: "the inhabitants are desirous of American rule."

Punishing the Filipino Bottom

A later cartoon, published in 1906 in *Puck*, affixes the imperial sadist's flexed arm on the shining example and champion of fin-de-siècle virile U.S. masculinity, President Theodore Roosevelt (figure 3.11).[97] Here again, imperialism's

FIG. 3.11 "Trouble ahead for the Trainer." (*Puck*, 1906; artist, John S. Pughe)

role is instructive, concerned only with the display of power over the unruly native. A fit Roosevelt, dressed in a skin-tight, sleeveless shirt and thigh-revealing shorts, shows off quite a bit of skin. Brandishing a conspicuously angled training whip, the president manages a throng of unwieldy creatures representing colonial holdings and policy interests, one of which is a monstrous, semi-naked, and muscular native man whose grass skirt is held up with a belt marked "Philippines." Roosevelt domesticates these wild, wayward creatures with a set of ropes, the ends of which are tied to the harnesses around the necks of the creatures; as the president leans backward to offset their collective weight, his legs, torso, and arms flex into a "demonstration" of tension and strength, of "solitude and omnipotence." Emphasizing the spectacular nature of the scene is the circus tent surrounding the domesticated figures and the caption, "Trouble ahead for the trainer."

Despite the strenuous task Roosevelt faces, however, his face, like school-master Beveridge's or McKinley's when spanking his monkey ("Because I Love You"), is impassive. Any recognition of trouble in the task at hand is expressed only by a look of calm focus. Yet it is the object of his focused, stern gaze that reveals what "trouble" he may find "ahead." As if a guide for the audience's gaze, a taut rope draws a line from Roosevelt's eyes to the body and returned gaze of the monstrous Filipino. Seemingly accustomed to assuming this position of restraint, the smiling native, sitting on the ground and holding himself up with muscular arms on each side of him, has raised his heels. In this semi-recumbent position, suggestive of the missionary variety, the coyly grinning native seems to be exposing the barbaric promiscuity underneath his thick grass skirt to the penetrating look of the imperialist. The "trouble ahead" for Roosevelt, then, seems to be the monstrous Filipino bottom.[98]

So why the *bottom*? The images of the punishment or containment of the troubling Filipino buttocks derives, at least in part, from the practices of racialized surveillance and bodily control throughout many parts of the archipelago during American colonial rule. As Warwick Anderson's remarkable *Colonial Pathologies* (2006) shows, disease- and germ-phobic U.S. physicians in the Philippines sought to manage imperial medical care—and thereby establish colonial governmentality—by inspecting and regulating the bodily comportment and sanitary practices of the native population. More specifically, Anderson traces how American doctors fixated on containing what Captain Edward L. Munson, adviser to the Bureau of Health in the Philippines, called the natives' "promiscuous defecation."[99] (Munson also argued, as we saw in chapter 1, that among the "native population . . . fornication is not regarded as a moral offence but almost as a legitimate calling." To wit, Filipinos are thus a slutty people with slutty shit.) For American doctors in the Philippines, Anderson argues, "Waste practices became a potent means of organizing a heretofore diffusely threatening foreign population. That is, the colonial state came to be delineated on racial bodies (Filipino or white) and behaviors (promiscuous or retentive); it was intimately reduced to orifices (open or closed) and dejecta (visible or invisible). . . . [American doctors] imagined Filipinos inadvertently subverting their hygienic abstractions and defecating regardless. Such promiscuous defecation seemed potentially to mock and transgress colonial boundaries at the same time as it confirmed the necessity and value of such demarcations." U.S. tropical medicine attempted, in short, to discipline a native people feared to be vaguely hostile to colonial order—a "diffusely threatening foreign population"—by obsessively controlling their rectums.[100]

Within the allegedly pristine space of the U.S. colonial laboratory that was the Philippines, natives' promiscuous defecation may have proved tantamount to insurrection. Even as Filipinos often "confessed" their sanitary "rottenness" to "make themselves available for hygienic salvation" and to be "admitted to a sort of probationary citizenship,"[101] colonial physicians might have also imagined (in a fantasy redolent of Sade) the natives' willful "promiscuity." As Anderson argues, colonial administrators were often paranoid: "all the fauna in the archipelago, whether human or nonhuman, seemed increasingly duplicitous, ready at any moment to come into focus, to sting, to infect, to shoot."[102]

Such an image of paranoia accords with the cartoon of the Philippine native being shot, where the tropical bush in the background might morph into another insurrecto agent. In a sense, native excrement—an insurrection of abject bodily matter—was, in the eyes colonial administrators, representative of the promiscuous insurrecto movement writ large. Both, indeed, had to be disciplined by white colonial administrators. Attempting to secure their own bodily "sublimity" vis-à-vis the promiscuous filth and filthy promiscuity of the autochthonous Philippine body, Americans would be "obliged to perform a transcendence of their lower bodily stratum, to act as though they inhabited a more formal, expressive body."[103] U.S. colonial transcendence was thus supported by scatological symbolism. On one level, the former would involve not only the management of Philippine native waste but also the denial of its own abject matter; on another, it would necessitate the disavowal of any recognition of the insurrectos' claims to sovereignty, to self-rule. As Anderson puts the conflation, "The anus was a synecdoche for the medicalized Filipino body."[104] Thus, as an "open or closed"—indeed, naked or clothed—orifice, the promiscuous Filipino bottom seemed also to "trouble" American physicians, colonial toilet "trainers" after all.

The anus has always been in dominant (i.e., homophobic) culture a synecdoche for the sodomite, the transhistorical location of same-sex acts between men. The anus proves time and again, as D. A. Miller renders it, the "popularly privileged site of gay male sex, the orifice whose sexual use general opinion considers (whatever happens to be the state of sexual practices among gay men and however it may vary according to time and place) the least dispensable element in defining the true homosexual."[105] Such an essentialized association has also fantasmatically linked "gay male sex" with feces; as Tim Dean speculates, "Homosexuality's being branded 'the love that dare not speak its name' must have been a consequence primarily of its association with . . . the anal object"—that is, excrement.[106] A reticulation for so many deviant, promiscuous practices at the fin-de-siècle, then, the Filipino bottom proves the abject sine qua non in the fortification of homophobic colonianormativity. In the imperial endeavor to uphold the "American sublime"[107] within the white colonianormative body, U.S. colonial officials would have to manage a body all the more sublime, albeit inversely—all the more "troubling" because of its perceived proximity to the socially and symbolically abject, bodily waste.[108] Hence, disciplining punishment by racializing, imperial care would take a peculiar form in these cartoons, be it of the "incorrigible" insurrecto, the "Final Filipino," the undisciplined schoolboy, or "trouble"-some native. Sadistic violence at once renders the Philippine insurrecto body sublime and, further, attributes to the insurrecto body, even reduces it to, a mortifying, promiscuous, and intolerable asshole—a sublime bottom.

This chapter has ventured quite a way from examining cartoons' attention to Philippine clothing styles and the claim that the fashion makeovers of the autochthonous Philippine subject into a black dandy, invert, and fairy indicate attempt within the cultural imagination to manage, to make intelligible, Philippine racial-sexual form. As a way to conclude, I want to make explicit the link across these images articulating the Philippine native to other figures of racial-sexual deviance, on one hand, and to the concurrent cartoons portraying sadistic punishment, on the other. Both visual forms bespeak a metroimperial public anxiety about a promiscuous proximity to or even perverse intimacy with the colonial Philippine sublime body. Extrapolating from the cartoon depicting the native who has been shot from behind, I suggested earlier that these cartoons' varied representations of the desiring autochthonous Philippine figure can be seen as effecting a sadistic violence that endows that figure with two bodies: a figural body attempting to capture visually Philippine racial-sexual form and the sublime Philippine body unassimilable to metroimperial representational modes. The cartoons' attention to the Philippine subject's clothing, in this sense, even when not necessarily depicting violence toward the Philippine body (but especially when doing so), signifies the extent to which these representational technologies might not be "identical to" but certainly integral to "violence." The various cartoons' makeovers, in signaling the degenerate desires of the Philippine native, "perform a demonstration related essentially to the solitude and omnipotence of [their] author[s]." As Saidiya Hartman has said about other scenes of racial subjection, "Representing power was essential to reproducing domination."[109] In the effort to capture, to make knowable, the racial character of the unassimilable Philippine insurrecto in visual form by articulating to more popularly recognizable racially and sexually deviant bodies, these cartoons purport to "demonstrate" the perverse sexual and gender-abnormal desires of the colonial native to the metroimperial public, thereby unwittingly exposing those of the latter.

With the logic and force of a sadist, these cartoons in aggregate produce the sublime body of the autochthonous Philippine subject. The Philippine native body's sublimity in the cartoons, however, is referenced less by Romanticist ideas of the beautiful than by a wild, barbaric, and threatening monstrosity. In one cartoon from the April 1899 issue of *The Herald* of Salt Lake City, Aguinaldo was figured as a demon-faced hobgoblin charging at the reader, talons and toes outstretched; behind him followed the menacing hordes of replicated Aguinaldo-faced gremlins.[110] The caption read, "Press Dispatch: 'Aguinaldo led his forces in person.'" While the background, which was occupied with U.S. soldiers raising their swords in victory, suggested that Aguinaldo was leading his regiment's retreat from U.S. military forces into the Philippine tropics, his bearing of his claws toward the reader implied that he was coming for *you*, activating the xenophobic fears about so many Filipino monsters entering the United States, the metroimperial fantasy of a brown invasion that would swell among white nativist pro- and anti-imperialists over the next thirty years or so.[111] To the extent that Aguinaldo was concurrently depicted as a racial-sexual-gender deviant threat—as a black dandy; as the fey, dandified idol of the antis/aunties; as a general who would instruct his soldiers to dress as women to infiltrate U.S. military camps; as a fairy; as one who wanted punishment or petting by a rod; as one who would liberate pleasures that would bring about the "destruction of Sodom and Gomorrah"—it is not a stretch to say that whatever public panics a horde of Aguinaldos or Filipinos would have triggered were not just about their racial difference but also about their gendered-sexual menace. That's not just Aguinaldo coming after you, America; it is also a promiscuous insurrecto rectum wanting to be punished.

The visual and discursive scenes of Aguinaldo's alleged perversity listed here accord with both the other cartoons' rendering of the autochthonous Philippine body receiving punishment by colonial administrators and the colonial doctor's attempts to manage the promiscuously defecating natives: all figure the Philippine bottom, the quintessentially sublime object of metroimperial governance, as a *penetrable* but simultaneously *encroaching* threat. The position and character of Aguinaldo and other Philippine male insurrectos in each of these scenes draw him closer to what would have been understood in misogynist culture as the "feminine" (and thus abnormal), not just because of the effeminate decadence of the dandy and the rumors about cross-dressing ("as woman"), for example, but also because of these figures' attributed assumption of the penetrated position (the bottom) in the sexual and sexually violent act. Yet being positioned thus works quite differently here from how we saw it earlier. What bottomhood evokes is not so much the subjugated *passivo* position when it comes to penetration (e.g., as with the Philippine Scouts vis-à-vis Reese) but rather, like the muscular, coyly smiling native exhibiting himself to Roosevelt (figure 3.11) or the schoolboy Aguinaldo (figure 3.10), the *actively receptive* position.[112] To the extent that the passive position in penetration, both in the sexual sense and within banal conventions of imperialist tropes, would typically have signaled domination, the persistence of Philippine anticolonial insurrection, especially one that within metroimperial fantasy might claw its way to the metropole, has foreclosed the possibility of a totalizing passivity. It is as if the insurrecto's bottom, in being open to penetration, and despite being open, has not yet remembered to be subjugated.[113] As a target for punishment, the sublime bottom is sensed but always missed. What the Philippine sublime body elicited, and was paradoxically constitutive of, then, was the metroimperial public's obsession with and terror about an alluring brown bottom, the dread desire for the undoing—the uncivilizing—of a disciplined white hetero-masculinity, its absolute death.

These political cartoons accord with how this book has understood what metroimperial fantasy does—that is, it protects the metroimperial public from the impossibility of totalizing knowledge of the Philippine subject and stages, in its varied content, metroimperial desire, even as such content mediates the impossibility. The extent to which fantasy of the Philippine bottom's posing a menacing receptivity in metroimperial visual culture might have influenced U.S. colonial administrators in the archipelago cannot be measured. Yet the subsequent explosion of vagrancy and sodomy law, the naturalized ascription of same-sex behavior to the autochthonous Philippine subject, the demonstrations of racial-sexual subjugation by Reese, the differend around the Philippine Scouts' victimization, the alleged promiscuity of native defecation, and so on, attest to inassimilable consistency in what troubles—and attracts—imperial trainers. Still, the Philippine subject's bottom is unstable as the sublime object of metroimperial management of racialized intimacies. As other forms of U.S. cultural production would purport to demonstrate to the metropolitan public the unruly, uncivilized enjoyment of the new native subjects, so, too, would the impossible object of metroimperial knowledge/desire find, ex nihilo, a new body, one that would both promise—and terrorize with—the possibility of intimacy.

CHAPTER 4

THE SULTAN OF SULU'S
EPIDEMIC OF INTIMACIES

President Theodore Roosevelt's proclamation ending the United States' genocidal war with the Philippine insurrectos on the Fourth of July 1902 was upended at the end of that year by an unlikely cultural form: a musical comedy.[1] The Midwestern writer George Ade's *The Sultan of Sulu*, an operetta that premiered at Wallack's Theater on Broadway on December 29, staged the fictional encounter between the U.S. colonial military and Ki-Ram, the title character. The historical Sultan of Sulu ruled over the Muslim Sulu region of the southern part of the archipelago, a region that even during three hundred years of previous Spanish occupation largely resisted colonization because of the region's tradition of notoriously fierce martial institutions, which were autonomous from Manila's. In the effort to avoid war with the unassimilable Muslim population in the southern Philippines, President William McKinley had ordered the U.S. military to negotiate a treaty with Sultan Hadji Mohammad Jamalul Kiram. Declaring sovereignty over the sultanate, the U.S. colonizing forces, continuing one of many inherited Spanish practices in the region, offered a salary of $760 per month to the sultan for his assistance with U.S. commerce and settlement in the region. The agreement, brokered by Brigadier-General John C. Bates, became known as the Bates Treaty.

None of this might sound like musical comedy material. Indeed, the Sulu archipelago might not have been on the radar of Ade, or most folks in the United States, at all, if not for the public's horrifying discovery that slavery and polygamy were being practiced in Sulu. That these "twin relics of barbarism," as they were deemed by the Republican Party's inaugural platform in 1856, were discovered in the new U.S. colony now, during the United States' allegedly "modern" practice of exceptional imperialism, shocked many Americans. The fifth issue of the *Anti-Imperialist* bore an unsubtle headline on its cover: "Slavery and Polygamy Reestablished under the Jurisdiction of the United States So Far as Can Be Done by Authority of William McKinley, in Carrying on this Effort to Deprive the People of the Philippine Islands Their Liberty."[2] Meanwhile, political cartoons reinforced the public's fascination and disgust with the supposed immorality of the polygamous "Moro" people, a racializing designation the U.S. empire inherited from Catholic Spanish colonization. In one cartoon published in the generally anti-imperialist *Life* in May 1900, several grotesque, troll-like, and (again) mostly naked Moro Philippine people are shown lounging around and gossiping. In reference to a man pleading with a coy woman, one Philippine figure asks another, "Is he a bachelor?" "Comparitively [sic]," is the response. "He has only twelve wives" (figure 4.1). In two other cartoons from that year, published in *Life* and the *Times-Democrat* of New Orleans, the sultan is rendered not only as a polygamist, but also as a curly shoed "Muslim."[3] In the first cartoon, the black-faced "sultan" dons an ornate turban, while in the latter he wears a fez and smokes from a hookah, his Turkish cigarettes strewn on the floor and his throng of wives in the background (figures 4.2–4.3).

Perverse sexuality defined the totality of this colonial subject's social identity. While Emilio Aguinaldo (metonymic for "the Filipino") was a dandy and an invert (see chapter 3), the sultan (metonymic for the "Moro") was an Oriental polygamist. However scandalous, the discovery of the decidedly un-American practice of polygamy in the colonial Philippines provided Ade with fodder for what would prove to be one of the 1902–1903 Broadway season's biggest and most influential hits. Titillated, perhaps, by the prospect of seeing the exotic Philippines—especially harems of "Moro" women—live and on the stage, the middle classes flocked to his opéra bouffe. While audiences may have gotten such a spectacle, they also witnessed the staging of unexpected intimacies particular to Ade's anti-imperialist fantasy of the Philippines. Ade himself admits that the play is *his* fantasy, writing in the liner

FIG. 4.1 "In Sulu Society." "Is he a bachelor?" "Comparitively [*sic*]. He has only twelve wives."
(*Life*, May 10, 1900; artist, T. S. Sullivant)

FIG. 4.2 "The Allied Emperors." "SULTAN OF SULU: 'Certainly; your flag shall flutter beside mine at $1,000 per flutter.'" (*Times Democrat* [New Orleans], October 1900; artist's name illegible)

FIG. 4.3 "The Sultan of Sulu." (*Life*, June 21, 1900; artist unknown)

notes to the original program that *The Sultan of Sulu* does not "attempt to show what . . . happened, but merely what might have happened."[4]

In keeping with the shift made in chapter 3, this chapter continues to examine metroimperial cultural production, other "frames of war," to show how non-state actors imagined intimacies in the archipelago that "might have happened." In chapter 3, I showed how fin-de-siècle political cartoons made the Philippine insurrecto's body legible by linking it to more recognizable figures of sexual-racial deviance; here, I demonstrate how the racialization of the United States' Philippine colonial subjects in the Sulu region was rendered through the unassimilable form of polygamy. As Michael Salman has already examined at length colonial administrators' discovery of slavery in Sulu and the controversy it stoked among the post-Reconstruction U.S. public, this chapter focuses on the other relic of barbarism. Widespread rumors of polygamy surrounded the "real" Sultan of Sulu, attesting, in quite a different way from what we have seen thus far, to the barbaric sexual practices of the new colonial subjects. This confirmation of the autochthonous Philippine subject's excessive sexuality in toto—in this case, the Moros exhibited a perversion not only sanctioned, according to a scandalized public, but also funded by the United States—bolstered both sides of pro- and anti-imperialist debate. On one hand, the apparent persistence of polygamy in the archipelago authorized the muscular Christian imperialism of McKinley and Roosevelt to manage the excessively sexualized Filipinos. On the other, prolonged contact with polygamous Moros of the south threatened to further corrupt the already waning morality of colonial foot soldiers, while payment of the sultan suggested the U.S. government's condoning of his perverse ways. In Ade's play, however, the sexual iniquity conjured by polygamy—informed, as I show later, by turn-of-the-twentieth-century racializing discourses around "Muslim," Native American, Chinese, and Mormon practices—is supplanted both by the sultan's attraction to Colonel Budd, the operetta's version of Bates, and by the jabs at compulsory hetero-monogamy that the various characters consistently throw.[5] Indeed, one of these jabs, in which Colonel Budd diagnoses an "epidemic of marriages" (116) in the region, refers not to Sultan Ki-Ram's exorbitant eight wives but, rather, to the pathological proliferation of "normal"—that is, hetero-monogamous—marriages between the play's U.S. Navy volunteers and local Filipina women (a proliferation, as I showed in the introduction, that would be managed by colonial administrators). What's more, both polygamy and the epidemic of marriages that threatens the ostensibly normal or proper modes of colonial intimacies serve as something of obverse socialities to Ade's social identity as a "bachelor."

Retrieving part of Ade's corpus, which has all but lost any critical attention, despite the "admiration" of Mark Twain, famed anti-imperialist and Ade's literary hero, this chapter reads Ade's treatment of the Moro practices of plural marriage against his own adamant decision never to marry.[6] I am not interested in proving that Ade, a corn-fed white man from small-town Indiana transplanted to Chicago, was a "homosexual." Although it appeared in sexologists' writing and psychiatric practice in the late nineteenth century, the term "homosexual," as I have already shown, did not in fact register as an identity in U.S. public culture until decades later into the twentieth century. In an effort to be historically precise—and, more important, to remain faithful to Ade's own self-identification—I examine instead how Ade was known in his day and how he saw himself: as a bachelor. Michael Warner has argued that by the early part of the nineteenth century, "bachelorhood" in the United States was "consistently regarded as anomalous, problematic, and probably immoral."[7] As Eve Sedgwick, Nayan Shah, and Howard Chudacoff have demonstrated in varied contexts, the bachelor came to be integral to the genealogy of late nineteenth-century and early twentieth-century taxonomies around the "homosexual."[8] The few critics who have attempted throughout the twentieth century to revalue Ade's corpus have focused on only one of these two concerns: either that Ade is more significant and influential than he is traditionally given credit for or that his "bachelorhood" remains a puzzle. Concerning the latter, for example, his biographer Fred Kelly finds it a "natural . . . curiosity [that] one of the most sought-after men of his time, who seemed instinctively a family man, should have contrived to remain a bachelor all his life."[9] Ade's "contrived" bachelorhood was unnatural, Kelly unwittingly implies, and contradictory to his perceived reproductive "instinct[s]." One critic puts the question of Ade's bachelorhood within the terms of his literary legacy: "why Ade never married must ever remain one of the curious mysteries of American letters."[10] Presuming not to find Ade's bachelorhood a "mystery," I would suggest that these two gaps in critical inquiry about Ade might have served to hollow each other out. While Ade's exclusion from the American literary canon is as debatable as it is uninteresting, it is telling that biographers and editors of collected works attempting to recuperate his corpus do not directly address his continual companionships with other white men.[11]

This chapter proceeds in five sections. The first examines the contemporary racialization of the Moro Philippine subjects, on one hand, and the practice of polygamy, on the other, demonstrating how both categories were regarded, in the diction of the time, as "queer" for their gendered and sexual excesses. The second section shows how Ade came to find in these discourses a prime target for his anti-imperialist, satirical humor, while the third lays out the topsy-turvy plot of the cheekily Orientalist *The Sultan of Sulu*. The fourth section turns briefly to the official transcription of the actual Bates Treaty, highlighting the awkward (and unintentionally funny) nature of colonial formalities, to frame Ade's rendering of the intimacies that "might have happened." At the end of the chapter, I suggest how both polygamy and the topsy-turvy modes of contagious or "epidemic" relationality in *The Sultan of Sulu* might have functioned for the bachelor Ade as a transposition of romanticized, racialized relays of alternative belonging and affiliation. Ultimately, while Ade's satire of the sultan's alleged polygamy was hilarious (though I'm often in the terribly unfunny position here of having to talk about its punchlines), it was also a searing critique of pro-expansionist sentiment, of the public discourses around race and polygamy, and of excessive or "epidemic" compulsory heterosexuality. Indeed, not only was the ascendancy of whiteness within metroimperial culture attached to the normalization of heterosexuality, but metropolitan bachelorhood itself, I would argue, took a detour through fantasies about the perversely racialized colonial subject in the Philippines.

Racialized Polygamy

The rumors circulating in the United States that the Sultan of Sulu and the male Moros within his sultanate practiced polygamy were built on obscure details. Upon the arrival of the Twenty-third Infantry at a Spanish colonial fort established within Jolo, an island in the Sulu archipelago, one Captain E. B. Pratt wrote a memorandum to Military Governor Elwell Stephen Otis mentioning that the sultan was "30 years of age, and ha[d] 1 wife, 13 concubines, and many slaves."[12] Although Pratt noted the sultan's many female sexual companions, his report indicated that he was actually married to only one of them. What's more, in the fifteen-article treaty established between the sultan and Bates, of the American occupation forces, there is not a single mention of marriage practices, multiple or otherwise.[13] And in the 111 page, single-spaced report that accompanied the publication of the Bates Treaty, which included official correspondence and transcriptions of meetings, there was also no mention of the practice of plural marriage; of the "twin relics of barbarism," only slavery was discussed beyond Pratt's original report.[14] The American public, however, seems to have latched on to the detail of the sultan's "13 concubines" and conflated it with polygamy.

Polygamy quickly became shorthand for the sultan's, and the Moro Sulu people's, racial-sexual excess. The U.S. colonial state's governance over the Moros was markedly different from that of the Hispanicized Catholic majority of the population. The majority, being partly "civilized" by Spain, was administered by U.S. political institutions that were preparing it for self-government, while the Moros, categorized among other "Non-Christian Tribes" and so marked as especially savage and tribal, while still "semi-civilized," were governed without the right to vote by U.S. political-military administrators.[15] I show how polygamy came to be attached to Moro racialized sexuality later, but first I demonstrate how the social deviance of the Moro Sulu people within the metroimperial imagination was indicated not just by their practice of multiple marriage but also by their expressions of gender transgression, on one hand, and gendered excess, on the other. As in the cartoons shown here and those depicting Philippine subjects more generally (chapter 3), Philippine Moros also allured and repulsed the metroimperial public with their conspicuous clothing or lack thereof. Explicitly rendering Moros as "Oriental," these images resonate with Theodore William Noyes's descriptions of a trip to the Philippine "Moroland," which were published in *Oriental America and Its Problems* (1903). Observing the fishing village of Bus-Bus in Jolo, Noyes observes, "The Bus-Busites swarmed about us in every condition of dress and undress. There were many samples of the characteristic native costumes, with the sarong and jabul for the women and the tight-fitting trousers, small jacket and voluminous sash for the men, but the most frequent costume of all showed as its dominating characteristic the brown skin of the native unadorned."[16] Even as Noyes here might notice the "tight-fitting trousers" of the men of "Moroland," he admits that the "brown skin of the native unadorned . . . dominat[es]" his visual field, attesting to the colonial titillation around the Moro's sexually available body.

Other reporters focused on Moro fashion as aberrant—even "queer." As I suggested in the introduction, "queer" was often a colonial, racializing classification in U.S. metroimperial culture. In the instances that follow, we see how the racial term also signaled (as it does more generally nowadays) modes of gender transgression and nonnormative sexuality, though in very particular ways. In a letter printed in the *Princeton Union*, Irvin Reems, a U.S. colonial soldier stationed in Sulu, reported on a dance performed during a "Mahommedan" festival, comparing it with "Indian dances" he had seen back home: "This is a little more tame than the Indian dances but the costumes are so queer. The women wear trousers with a large waist band, and they twist this into a knot. Then they have a tight fitting waist. The men have besides this a loose sort of skirt they twist around themselves. . . . The dress is made from highly colored cotton goods, the more gaudy the color the better they like it."[17] Reems's reference to the Moros' costumes as "so queer" evokes abnormality, but in a very distinct way. Abnormality or perversion within the fin-de-siècle U.S. metropole, as I recalled in the previous chapters, was indexed most often by gender-deviant behaviors; the "hideous" spectacle of women wearing trousers and of men wearing a "loose sort of skirt" thus codes such "costume" as perverse. The use of "queer" in this context proves a derogatory marker of *racial-gender* transgression, perhaps one that was all the more offensive to Reems because of its "gaudy" nature. The ascription of "queer" thus also seems to be attached to the Moros' evident flouting of gender norms. Other writers use this understanding of "queer" as a colonial marker of gender deviance elsewhere in the Sulu context. In keeping with the U.S. public's attention to "Oriental" fashion,[18] for example, the white feminist Marilla Weaver's article "The Women of Sulu: The Oppressed Sex in the Philippines," published in the *Wichita Daily Eagle* in July 1901, considered how "the Sulu women dress."[19] Observing, like Reems, that Moro women wore "baggy trousers gathered in at the ankle," she continued, "Some of them wear on their heads the same style of queer hat that men do. . . . They are a queer lot—as uncivilized and barbarous as a people can be." Such sentiments resonate with the nineteenth-century U.S. public's anxiety about gender-deviant practices, an anxiety the resulted in U.S. cross-dressing laws that, as Clare Sears has traced, marked a widespread "regulatory approach toward gender transgressions, and . . . attempted to draw and fix the boundaries of normative gender during a period of rapid social change."[20] Yet, both Reems's and Weaver's accounts attribute the Moros' gender-deviant modes of dress to their "uncivilized and barbarous" ways. To wit, Philippine Moros were "queer" in part because they were not yet regulated by boundaries of normative, civilized gender. Indeed, as if such "queerness" were contagious, Weaver recounted that at one point she grew so disgusted during one of her meetings with a Moro woman "dressed in her best" that she "got up and walked away" because she "simply could not stand it." What renders the Moros' dress—and, as Weaver makes explicit, the Moro women and men themselves—queer is not just the transgression of gender norms but also how these transgressions express premodern, unregulated life. Moros were disparaged as "queer" because their perceived barbaric gender-inverting practices persisted in the face of U.S. civilization and modernization.

The ascription of "queerness" was in fact used to discipline a range of Moro practices of gendered excess, including colonial hyper-masculinity: Moro men were known to be "powerful men and religious fanatics, who care nothing for death."[21] In "Philippine Customs and Oddities," drawing from Spanish reports and published in April 1899, Margherita Hamm claimed that Moro leaders often primed their male youth to be assassins (*juramentados*) and that Moro men apparently had the habit of "running 'amuck' or 'amok'" as a result of "some physical and mental fever."[22] Hamm offers this account of the war-bent Moro—who is "taught that his self-sacrifice will insure him a perpetual paradise, and that the greater the destruction he inflicts upon the infidels the higher will be his happiness in the other world"—even as she confesses that "of this nothing authentic is known," that the Sulu ways remain "an enigma of the darkest kind."[23] Though Hamm admits to knowing "nothing" about "enigma[tic]" Moro cultural and religious practices, she nevertheless presents a terrifying (and, for us, familiar) portrait of the berserk, religious-extremist Muslim. An article in the *Red Cloud Chief* of Red Cloud, Nebraska, that appeared exactly a year later corroborated Hamm's admitted fantasy with a visual rendering (figure 4.4), along with the panic-inducing headline, "Running Amuck in the Philippines: A Queer Form of Insanity to Which the Natives are Sometimes Subject."[24]

RUNNING AMUCK IN THE PHILIPPINES.

A Queer Form of Insanity to Which the Natives are Sometimes Subject.

Much attention has been called to the number of men in the army serving in the Philippines who have gone insane. The government has sent a special commission out there to investigate the matter, and there has been talk of a mysterious disease called the "Soudanese Fever." It is believed by some that this disease is peculiar to East Indian and African tropics; that it was this which caused Dr. Peters to get into trouble for killing Africans, and made the French officers in the interior of Africa recently slay other officers sent to their relief, is one theory. Everybody has heard of the Malay who runs amuck and, frenzied, kills right and left until he himself is killed. The word "amuck" is a corruption of the Javanese word "amoak," to kill. There seems to be no doubt that the Malay occasionally goes crazy through the overindulgence in opium or hasheesh and, springing from his "shack," runs through the streets of his village, killing all whom he may meet. When in a Malay village the cry "Amuck" is raised, it is like the cry of "Mad dog!" in an American village, and the populace turn out with long bamboo spears and kill the man as soon as they can. But the "Soudanese fever," if it exists, is another thing apparently. It may be that the disease which has afflicted white men in the Philippines and in equatorial Africa, is only a variation of apoplexy, brought on by indulgence in heating and stimulating foods.

Dr. Louis Livingston Seaman, who has visited the Philippines, and was with General Bates when the general made his treaty with the Sultan of Sulu, is inclined to doubt the existence of any such thing as the "Soudanese Fever." He says: "I believe the army ration is the cause of the spread of insanity among our troops serving in the Philippines. The ration is perfectly unscientific. It might do well for temperate or arctic climates, but to feed men on so much heating food as is given to the soldiers out there is absurd.

"We hear a great deal about natives of the Philippines running amuck, especially those who live on the Sulu Islands. I do not believe that those wild outbreaks of murderous passion are brought about by any peculiar physical disease. It is religious frenzy, usually fostered for political reasons, which causes the natives to run amuck. I investigated the subject somewhat while I was in the Sulu Islands, where the natives have been given most to this sort of thing, and found that in every case which I could come at the murderous insanity of the men had

on with favor by this government, and somebody might be held responsible. The result is that there has not been a case of running amuck in the Sulu

shouted to Lecturer Rollins: "Look out, the elephant's going to sneeze!" All the attendants deserted their posts and ran to look. Jolly had drawn up

But the effect on that individual was unexpected. He gave one horrified glance, and then rushed at the old surgeon and seized him by the throat. "You infamous scoundrel!" he yelled, "you have broken my poor darling's jaw!" At that stage of affairs I beat a retreat. I never did learn exactly what the husband thought had happened or what sort of explanation was offered."—New Orleans Times-Democrat.

Cowboy Blacksmithing.

"Up at my camp near the Four

A VICTIM OF PHILIPPINE ISLAND INSANITY RUNNING AMUCK.

FIG. 4.4 "Running Amuck in the Philippines." "A Queer Form of Insanity to Which the Natives are Sometimes Subject." (*Red Cloud Chief* [Red Cloud, Nebraska], April 6, 1900, 2; artist unknown)

The attribution of "queer" to the Moro figure in this headline corresponds not with gender-inversion but with something of its opposite, as the accompanying cartoon makes clear: a Moro excess of racialized masculinity, a lack of civilizing restraint, indexed by indiscriminate killing and naked musculature. The article suggested that this particular "disease"—that is, the "mental fever" that drives one to "murderous insanity"—resulted from Muslim "religious feeling" and practices of the "Mahometan tribes." The piece then quoted at length one Dr. Louis Livingston Seaman, who, having accompanied General Bates during his negotiations with the sultan, was regarded as an expert on "running amuck." Seaman observed that "with promises of seven wives in the seventh heaven" in his head, the previously selected and primed juramentado would then go on a wild killing spree. The promise of a polygamous afterlife, in other words, made up the etiology of this "queer form of insanity."

While the connection is only implicit in Seaman's diagnosis, the press also used "queer" to refer to polygamy as another symptom of the excesses of Moro masculinity. For example, in June 1900, the *Evening Star* of Washington, DC, decried the Moros as participating in "Queer Marriage Customs."[25] By striking a deal with the sultan, according to the press, colonial administrators effectively supported the "queer" custom of polygamy among the Moros. One writer for *Harper's Weekly*, for example, warned that in the Sulu region, "polygamy is . . . deeply rooted and will only disappear when Islam succumbs to the superior race."[26] While the juramentado symptomatized a "queer" excess of Moro masculinity, a violent barbarism that threatened Christian colonialism's civilizing mission, polygamy symptomatized a "queer" excess of Moro sexuality, constitutive of racial and religious savagery. As the Philippine Moro on a berserk killing spree proved unstoppable (indeed, like one of the cartoons described in the previous chapter, the illustration here suggests he is coming after *you*), so the practice of polygamy, according to colonial administrators, was beyond regulation. Moro polygamy in the Philippines was queer, in short, because it was marriage run amok.

The hysterical discourse around Moro polygamy in the turn-of-the-twentieth-century metropole was also informed by regulatory measures around race, sex, and gender, embodied by late nineteenth-century U.S. antipolygamy laws, particularly as they intersected with immigrant exclusion acts, American Indian management, Christian moral order, and the ascendancy of U.S. empire. By 1852, the open practice of polygamy, or "celestial marriage," by Mormons in the Territory of Utah stirred public panic about this white religious group, even marking its members as "Asiatic."[27] In his study of Mormon polygamy, Bruce Burgett has shown the "ways in which discourses of sex and race are produced and reproduced through the conjuncture in the mid-nineteenth century of the deployment of monogamous conjugal norms on the one hand, and the imperial consolidation of the nation-state on the other."[28] Examining the writing of the prominent mid-nineteenth-century political scholar, racial theorist, and anti-polygamist Francis Lieber, Burgett shows how polygamy in fact indexed racial distinctions: "the difference between monogamy and polygamy [according to Lieber] is 'one of the elementary distinctions—historical and actual—between European and Asiatic humanity.' "[29] White Mormon settlers in the Territory of Utah, in Lieber's view, were ethnically inferior to Anglo-Saxon settlers of the expanding republic. Indeed, Mormons threatened to prize open a U.S. future overrun with Asiatic and African ways of life; in Lieber's xenophobic nightmare, the nation then would soon "become so filled with Chinese, that the whites [would be] absorbed," and some states might become "*bona fide* Africanized."[30] U.S. whiteness is braced here against the apocalyptic threat of encroaching foreigners lurking at the gates of a "contiguous" space, poised to take the country over—an ironic nightmare, to be sure, given U.S. settler expansion.

Lieber was not the only one to topple down this slippery slope. White female literary producers also stirred public anxiety about polygamy. Nancy Bentley has deemed the highly popular genre of the domestic novel "probably the most important force" in the grassroots movement against polygamy. In domestic novels by white women, Bentley observes, "almost all women in polygamous unions are coerced into marriage in one way or another, forced to reconstitute on American soil the 'harems' of 'Oriental concubines, in which the women were near-slaves.'"[31] Moreover, as Nancy Cott has argued, the immigration-restricting Page Act of 1875 branded "Oriental" immigrant women in particular as both potential agents of prostitution and potential victims of "coolie" slavery. The widely held belief about Chinese women, Cott shows, was that they "were not Christians; their inherited culture accepted polygamy; their livelihoods showed them to be the enemies of the civilization embraced by the American nation."[32] Federal immigrant-exclusion laws targeting "Asiatics" substantiated this swirl of national hysteria, in which non-Christians, immigrants, and polygamists were figured as threats to Anglo-Saxon manifest supremacy. The practice of monogamy, then, created good U.S. citizens and maintained the racial order of things. As Bentley describes this convergence of legal restriction and antipolygamy sentiment, "By joining 'legal structure to emotional structure,' antipolygamy law endowed the state with the power to enforce the fantasy of a homogenous sphere of moral feeling."[33] By the end of the nineteenth century, it was simply contrary to the nature or instincts of white Christian Americans to participate in anything but hetero-monogamy, so much so that polygamy (now having a status similar to miscegenation) was tantamount to perpetrating treason. As an article published in the *Washington Post* in December 1898 put it, in conspicuously militaristic terms, "Race instincts in this country [are] arrayed against polygamy."[34] This fantasmatic "homogenization of moral feeling" against plural marriage became so naturalized that there was little public resistance when a new federal clause in 1907 considered the question of whether all Muslims from other countries had to be excluded from entry into the U.S. metropole because their religion tolerated polygamy.[35]

It is against this backdrop of governance over celestial marriage in the metro-imperial arena, on one hand, and racialized Mormons, Asiatics, Africans, and Muslims, on the other, that we should consider the contemporary discourse around the Sultan of Sulu's "queer" practice of polygamy—and Ade's satirical treatment of it. The metropolitan press in fact frequently compared the Sultan of Sulu's case with that of Mormons and native peoples in the United States. In October 1900, the *Dubuque Daily Herald* of Dubuque, Iowa, for example, protested, "The McKinley policy is a queer thing. . . . Mormonism is prohibited in Utah by law, while in the Sulu islands . . . polygamy is sanctioned by a treaty bearing William McKinley's signature."[36] (The sultan's "marriage custom" was so "queer," evidently, that it seems to have contaminated McKinley's liberal-ist policy sanctioning it.) Other stories in the press identified the Democratic politician and Mormon leader Brigham Roberts, who was denied his elected office in Congress in 1898 because he practiced polygamy. In December 1899, the *Washington Post*, after reporting that the "Mohammedans of to-day [and] all the native tribes of Africa practice polygamy," claimed that Roberts was "out of harmony with the spirit of the [civilized] age," thereby placing Roberts (as did Weaver's piece about the Moros) in a barbaric time.[37] In the same editorial, the author wonders "what our Congress would do if a polyandrous husband should show up some day as a delegate from some remote corner of our lately acquired possessions in the Orient," thereby expressing, in the reference to the sultan, another version of the xenophobic fears we have seen about colonial Philippine subjects entering into the metropole, perversions and all. Under-scoring this comparison between Roberts and the sultan, an editorialist for the *Hornellsville Weekly Tribune* of Hornellsville, New York, wrote hyperbolically, "It is all right to go against Mormon Roberts for having three wives, but how about . . . coming under our jurisdiction of the Sultan of Sulu, with his three hundred wives . . . Are our people going to strain at such a little gnat as Roberts and swallow a camel like the Sultan?"[38] Finally, an article titled "Rank Discrim-ination" in the *Virginian Pilot* criticized the double standard in anti-polygamy law in relation to the Sultan of Sulu and Chief Narjo, an Apache leader who was restricted by anti-polygamy law to "hav[ing] one wife only": "now, wherefore, one law for the potentate of Jolo and another for Apache Narjo. . . . Narjo and all his tribe should emigrate . . . and take to the islands of the sea, where the more wives the potentate has, the bigger salary he gets from a fatherly govern-ment!"[39] Here, we see a racist fantasy that American Indians as sexually exces-sive racial others might be managed by the state not, as immigrants were, by barring via immigration laws them from U.S. metropolitan space but, rather, in a perverse twist, by compelling them to deport themselves to the colonial Phil-ippines, where they might even be subsidized for their polygamous practices.

In sum, what these examples from the press demonstrate is the extent to which polygamy at the turn of the century, as Mark Rifkin argues, "is a discursive site at which undisciplined 'lust,' domestic chaos, unnatural sexual drives, evolutionary (dis)order, and geopolitical confusion are condensed and signify each other; it sits at the crossroads of jurisdiction, race, ethnology, and sexology, operating as a dense transfer point among them in which their tensions and contradictions resolve around the image of a violated nuclear norm."[40] Given his often irreverent sense of humor, his anti-imperialist politics, and the modes of social policing to which he was subjected for being a bachelor, it's no wonder that Ade would find in the discourse around the polygamous Sultan of Sulu plenty to work with for his musical comedy.

"All the Ingredients of a Comic Opera"

Ade's subject matter was typically concerned with everyday civic life in the U.S. Midwest. The colonization of the Philippines and, more significant, the assimilation of the Filipinos struck him as antidemocratizing, however, as seen in his writing immediately after the commencement of war. Ade's satirical writing about the new Philippine colony began with the sixteen-part weekly serial "Stories of Benevolent Assimilation" (1899) in the *Chicago Record*. Ade was already garnering a fair amount of both critical praise (most notably, from Mark Twain and William Dean Howells) and commercial success for his serial column "Stories of the Streets and of the Towns" (1893–1900) in the *Chicago Record*; his nationally syndicated series "Fables in Slang" (1897); and two novels, *Artie* (1896) and *Pink Marsh* (1897).[41] He was able to use the "Stories of Benevolent Assimilation" as a platform to satirize on a large scale McKinley's and other pro-expansionists' allegedly new, evangelically inspired, caring imperialism. Suspicious of such political spin, Ade's fictional "Stories of Benevolent Assimilation" recount the exploits of the cynically and allegorically named Washington Conner, a missionary sent by the McKinley administration to convince a native Philippine family, the Kakyaks, to adopt the American lifestyle and ideals—or, as the "conner" from Washington puts it, to impose "the instruction of you islanders in all the details of our American civilization."[42] Conner cautions the Kakyak family, "Those who don't want to be assimilated had better take to the jungle. This isn't the first time that we've tried this benevolent assimilation. We've assimilated Indians, Mexicans, and Chinamen, to say nothing of several million of negroes, and when any of them hung back, I'll tell you, it went hard with him."[43] Many of the stories were reprinted in pamphlets by the Anti-Imperialist League (though Ade himself never joined the league), but what made them popular was not just their wide dissemination in the mainstream press but also the slang and down-home U.S. vernacular used to mobilize the subtle critique—a rhetorical technique that the Anti-Imperialist League, with its often academically pitched civic prose, failed to employ. Ade's vernacular, peppered with bits of knowledge about the Philippines he gleaned from the dispatches of his longtime friend John T. McCutcheon, then a reporter and cartoonist for the *Chicago Record* assigned to the islands, allowed the "Stories" to win the sympathy of many American readers for Philippine people.

Despite his interest in the Philippines and the critical and popular recognition his anti-imperialist writing had drawn, Ade did not first consider the colony a suitable topic when he was approached in July 1900 by a nineteen-year-old British musician, Alfred Wathall, to write a "book" for music he had written for light opera.[44] Initially declining Wathall's proposition to collaborate, Ade traveled by steamer to the Philippines, staying in Manila with McCutcheon and other press correspondents, all of whom were reporting on the "insurrection" led by Aguinaldo. During this visit, the correspondents recounted stories about the notorious sultan. Ade was intrigued, later noting, in particular, that "the situation in Sulu had all the ingredients of comic opera and I believed that a good satirical musical play could be built around the efforts of our American civilizers to play ball with the little brown brother."[45] When he returned from the colony, Ade began working with Wathall on fitting together his verses with the composer's melodies, as well as with McCutcheon on costume design.

Ade's comic opera (his first of several) made its world premiere at Chicago's Studebaker Theater on March 11, 1902. Critics in Chicago (who had also seen the U.S. debut of Gilbert and Sullivan's Orientalist comedic opera *The Mikado* in that city in 1885) praised the production, especially the libretto. Yet Henry W. Savage, the producing manager, often quarreled with Ade, arguing that the play had not pandered to its audience with sufficient slang and insisted on continual revisions. Despite Ade's efforts to avoid writing in the style that found him earlier success—he came to regard writing in slang as gimmicky, following Howells's critique that it was a waste of his talent—he capitulated to Savage's editorial notes.[46] Ade did well to heed the advice of Savage, who had commercial success in several Orientalist productions, including an interpretation of *The Mikado* in 1895 and, later, the U.S. premiere of Giacomo Puccini's *Madama Butterfly* (1906). From Chicago, the show toured various parts of the Midwest, getting rave reviews. One critic in St. Louis called Ade's "excruciatingly funny" play "the best thing we've gotten out Philippines yet. . . . It almost reconciles one to the $20,000,000 we blew in for the archipelago."[47] *The Sultan of Sulu* would soon have a Broadway run of 192 sold-out performances—an extremely rare success for a production born in the Midwest—and a national tour followed.[48] Although a critic from New York's *Sun* found Wathall's score "poor," he attested to the "continuous roar of laughter and applause" for Ade's "queer and original humor."[49]

Plotting *Sultan*

The hyperkinetic, convoluted plot of *The Sultan of Sulu* requires navigation. From the start, polygamy on the island is naturalized and introduced casually. Act 1 begins with a roll call of the Sultan's eight wives, most of whom he captured from his enemy, "Datto Mandi," a *datu* (chief) from a neighboring area. The roll call is interrupted by the arrival of an all-white U.S. military troupe and a troupe of all-white female public school teachers, singing in chorus about the virtues of assimilation and public education for the sake of increased commerce: "though we come in warlike guise/All battle-font arrayed,/It's all a business enterprise;/We're seeking foreign trade" (11). Following this chorus number, in preparation for the arrival of Sultan Ki-Ram, the company's officer, Colonel Budd—again, the play's version of the historical figure of Brigadier-General Bates—orders his outfit to maintain a characteristically American military (phallic) posture: "for the first time you are about to stand in the presence of royalty. Stiffen yourselves for the ordeal, and remember, no deference, for each of you is a sovereign in his own right" (20–21). When Ki-Ram arrives on the scene, the colonel apprises him of the soldiers' administrative duty; as with most scenes involving Ki-Ram, this one ends in one of his punchlines:

> BUDD. We are your friends. We have come to take possession of the island and teach your benighted people the advantages of free government. We hold that all government derives its just powers from the consent of the governed. . . . Now, the question is, do you consent to this benevolent plan? (*The soldiers bring their guns to "charge bayonets." KI-RAM looks right and left and finds himself walled in by threatening weapons. He hesitates.*)
> KI-RAM. Are the guns loaded?
> BUDD. They *are*.
> KI-RAM. I consent. (25–26)[50]

Throughout the subsequent process of Sulu Americanization, the men of the U.S. military unit and the seemingly unmarried women of Sulu begin to commingle. Any threat of miscegenation, however, is temporarily deferred, both by the soldiers' realization that the women are already married to the sultan and by the more acceptable intraracial marriage engagement between Henrietta, Colonel Budd's daughter, and Lieutenant Hardy, a white military regular. The two male protagonists, Ki-Ram and Colonel Budd, also fraternize intimately. Budd, in a further effort to assimilate the sultan, introduces him to alcohol. "The constitution and the cocktail," Budd instructs Ki-Ram, "follow . . . the flag" (46). While Ade plays here with the popular shorthand for the policy of *ex propio vigore* and public concern about the abuse of alcohol among soldiers stationed in the Philippines (see chapters 1 and 2), Ade also attests to the use of alcohol as a social lubricant between men. Indeed, Ki-Ram and Budd frequently run off-stage, to the "life-saving station," throughout the rest of the play to have a "cocktail." Once while inebriated, Ki-Ram proposes to Pamela Jackson, a shrill judge advocate accompanying the soldiers and female schoolteachers. When Pamela realizes that Ki-Ram actually means for her to join his "harem," she storms off, humiliated at his "monumental effrontery" (49), and returns later with the announcement of a new Sulu law coming from Washington: "a man [is allowed] but one wife" (53). The first act ends with the inauguration of Ki-Ram as the "governor" of Sulu and the renewed threat of marriage between the military volunteers and the soon-to-be-single-again native women of Sulu.

The second act of the musical proves even more convoluted than the first, involving the constant machinations of the comical Ki-Ram to avoid paying alimony to his now ex-wives and to stay out of jail for failing to do so. Finalizing her revenge for Ki-Ram's audacity, Pamela declares that she has granted divorces to seven of the sultan's eight current wives. Seeming not to have learned his lesson, however, Ki-Ram soon proposes marriage to Henrietta, Budd's daughter, who must politely decline because, in her words, she has already become "engaged—in a sort of way" (73) to Lieutenant Hardy. Nevertheless, Ki-Ram serenades Henrietta with the show's most memorable song, "Since I First Met You," whose melody and refrain, to Ki-Ram's dismay, are soon taken up by each member of the ensemble to woo his or her love interest, leaving Ki-Ram alone. When Pamela then appears on the stage, she clinches the terms of her revenge, as she declares, according to the incorporation of "Arkansaw" state law into Sulu law, that "each of your eight wives is entitled to one-half of your total income," and if the alimony is not paid by five o'clock that afternoon, Ki-Ram will be imprisoned. Ki-Ram explains his paradoxical straits to his assistant, Hadji:

KI-RAM. Say my income is ten thousand pesos a month. Each wife is entitled to one-half that, or five thousand pesos. Eight wives—forty thousand pesos. In order to keep out of jail, I must raise forty thousand pesos.

HADJI. That's right.

KI-RAM. But look here. The moment I increase my income to forty thousand pesos, each wife is entitled to twenty thousand. Eight wives, one hundred and sixty thousand pesos. If by any miracle of finance I could get hold of that much money, then each of the eight would be entitled to eighty thousand. Eight times eight is eighty-eight—eight times eighty-eight is eight hundred and eighty-eighty eight thousand, and—Oh, what's the use? I'm broke! And the more money I get, the worse I'm broke. (*Collapses.*) (80–81)

In the vein of a topsy-turvy scenario concocted by W. S. Gilbert (of Gilbert and Sullivan fame), Ade (who was inspired by a performance of *The Mikado* during his undergraduate days at Purdue University[51]) underscores here the arbitrary nature of colonial law, vis-à-vis polygamy in particular.[52] Ki-Ram then takes on a series of abortive schemes to get out of jail, including conspiring with his ex-wives' original "master" to kidnap them and the establishment of an ad hoc business as a "matrimonial agent," since the nuptials of his ex-wives to the bachelor military volunteers—the prospect of which Colonel Budd laments as "an epidemic of marriages"—would relieve Ki-Ram of having to pay alimony. Despite his failed plotting, however, Ki-Ram ultimately resumes his rule in Sulu in the play's parting send-up of benevolent assimilation's laissez-faire policy. Satirizing the Bates Treaty's attempt to forestall conflict with the Moro societies by imposing indirect colonial rule, the play offsets its topsy-turvydom with U.S. metroimperial written law's arrival as a deus ex machina:

> BUDD. (*Looking at paper.*) Aha! This is important. (*Reads.*) "The Supreme Court decides that the constitution follows the flag on Mondays, Wednesdays, and Fridays only. This being the case, you are instructed to preserve order in Sulu, but not to interfere with any of the local laws or customs.["] (*To soldiers.*) Release him! He is no longer convict number forty-seven. He is—the Sultan! (126)

Evidently it was an off day for the constitution, and so the play ends with Ki-Ram "resum[ing] operations as the Sultan of Sulu." ("I wasn't ready to say good-bye," he sings, "and I'm glad that I didn't have to die.") Then the full cast serenades the audience in a choral reprisal of "Since We First Met You."

The operetta's fantasmatic staging of the Philippines participated in a tradition of Orientalist productions in the United States, but with a difference. Although it was preceded on the stage by *The Mikado*, Tin Pan Alley songs, and performances that were set in either China or Chinatown, as well as by David Belasco's tragic *Madame Butterfly* in 1900 (Puccini later adopted Belasco's script for the libretto for his opera),[53] *The Sultan of Sulu* turned out to be the first of several U.S. musical comedies with a variation on the same denouement: American civilization, typically represented by the U.S. Navy, arrives just in time to bring order to a far-off, utopian, tropical isle hitherto ruled by "an outlandish clown of a king."[54] Ade's successful satire of imperial occupation was in fact mimicked by a flurry of musical comedies. None of these orientalist imitators, however, had the same critical impetus as *The Sultan of Sulu* toward U.S. imperialist intervention.[55] What's more, the play was something of an outlier in its refusal to deploy some of the Orientalist techniques that had flourished in theater at the time.

Following Edward Said's influential critique of European Orientalism, Helen Jun has recently offered a succinct definition of the nineteenth-century U.S. version: "a discursive formation that was determined by and determining of U.S. economic and political engagements with East Asia and the Pacific and that provided the ideological structure for producing and managing Asian racial difference in the United States."[56] While *The Sultan of Sulu* remains unequivocally "Orientalist," its satirical modes set it apart from the subsequent musical comedies that would uncritically reproduce widespread nineteenth-century fantasies of the "Orient."[57] (Indeed, by the middle of the twentieth century, as Christina Klein has argued, Orientalist musical theater productions would be integral to consolidating a "national identity for the United States as a global power" in Southeast Asia.[58]) Before Colonel Budd can assure a terrified Ki-Ram that he will not be killed but, rather, will be *assimilated*, the sultan sings in Act 1 "what he believes to be his swan-song" (22), a tune praising the virtues of his "Smiling Isle":

We have no stocks and tickers,
No Scotch imported liquors,
To start us on the downward path and some day land us broke;
We've not a single college
Where youth may get a knowledge
Of Chorus girls and cigarettes, of poker and the like;
No janitors to sass us,
No bell-boys to harass us,
And we've never known the pleasure of a labor-union strike. . . .

REFRAIN
And that is why, you'll understand,
I love my own, my native land,
My little isle of Sulu.
(Chorus.) Sulu!
Smiling isle of Sulu!
(Chorus.) Sulu!
I'm not ready to say good-bye,
I'm mighty sorry that I have to die.
[VERSE]
We have no short-haired ladies

FIG. 4.5 "'The Constitution and the Cocktail Follow the Flag': Mr. Moulan as Ki-Ram," from *The Sultan of Sulu: An Original Satire in Two Acts* (New York: R. H. Russell, 1903), n.p.

> Who are always raising Hades
> With their finical and funny old reformatory fads;
> No ten-cent publications,
> Sold at all the railway stations,
> With a page or two of reading and a hundred stuffed with "ads." . . .
>
> REFRAIN
> And that is why, etc. (22–24)

FIG. 4.6 "'In Early Morn, at Break-Fast Time': Six of Ki-Ram's Wives," from *The Sultan of Sulu: An Original Satire in Two Acts* (New York: R. H. Russell, 1903), n.p.

The song scoffs at the quotidian stuff of modern U.S. life that Ade himself found entertaining—as one sees throughout his Midwest-set "Fables"—and sometimes "harass[ing]": highly abstracted capital, imported hard liquor, the culture of higher education, the tasks of service workers, those workers' alienation from their labor, first-wave feminist reformers, and ad-driven magazines without content. The list reiterates the fantasy of Ade's Philippine smiling island *as* fantasy through a satirical portrait of what it is not: distinctly American, with "modernized" American ways. In this sense, Ade's description of his operetta is not quite accurate; he depicts not what "might have happened" but, rather, what *could not* have happened. Described only by way of negativity, by the sundry inconveniences it lacks, the "Philippines" is revealed as merely a facile representation of the "Orient."

Moreover, although the figure of Ki-Ram is rendered as a comical racialized figure, he is not played in any recognizable form of yellow face or brown face (figure 4.5), even though the technique had been all but perfected by the 1880s and the actor Frank Moulan, who played Ki-Ram on Broadway, had previously starred in several blackface musicals.[59] (As part of his makeup, Moulan did "obliterate his eyebrows, making two smaller but heavier ones high up, that slanted Malay fashion," though I cannot say how this alteration might read "Malay."[60]) None of the actresses playing Ki-Ram's wives seem to have browned it up for the performances or press releases, either (figure 4.6). This non-commitment to phenotypical "accuracy"—along with a conspicuous lack of actual "Philippine" or "Moro" objects in the production, objects that perhaps would have authenticated its Filipino-ness—attests to how little the notion of verisimilitude mattered to Ade in the portrayal of Philippine Moros.[61] As one critic put it in 1903, "The piece will scarcely satisfy the student of Philippine affairs. . . . The manners and customs of the people have been manufactured for farcical purposes."[62] Thus, like Ki-Ram's image in the press photo, the play's Orientalist and racializing techniques, thus laid bare, were deployed with a wink. The target of the satire proves to be not the actual figure of the sultan, polygamy, the Moros, or the Philippines. Rather, it is the panicked, Orientalist discourse around these tropes itself.

Satire of a Colonial Encounter

The Sultan of Sulu, as Salman describes it, "followed the spirit of Karl Marx's dictum about history repeating itself as farce."[63] Salman here refers to Ade's exaggeration of the United States' exceptionalist assumption that other forms of sovereignty would uncritically accede to U.S. rule of law—or, as Ade put it, "the efforts of our American civilizers to play ball with the little brown brother." As ridiculous and campy as this satire's dialogue is, it proves far more elegant than the actual dialogue among the colonial administrators, the Sulu administrators, and the sultan. The play was a farce of an already absurd exchange.

In February 1900, the U.S. Senate released a publication of the *Treaty with the Sultan of Sulu*, which Ade would have had access to or knowledge of during his trip to the Philippines later that year. The published treaty includes transcriptions of meetings among the colonial administrators and the Sulu officials in a form that closely resembles a script or libretto. Ade's assertion that the "situation in Sulu had all the ingredients of comic opera" may in fact have been based on these amusing, and amusingly transcribed, dialogic exchanges. Colonel Budd's declaration at the end of the play, for example, that the U.S. constitution only "follows the flag on Mondays, Wednesdays, and Fridays" might correspond to the transcription's record of how difficult it was for Bates to set up a meeting with the sultan in person:

> GENERAL BATES. About what date can the Sultan be here? I would like to see him, and all his counselors and chiefs he would like to bring with him.
>
> SECRETARY [speaking for Sultan]. He thinks it will be Sunday or Monday before the Sultan comes here, but he will send over a letter and let you know.
>
> GENERAL BATES. I would like to have it as early as possible. I came down here just to do this and then go back again to our governor-general.

SECRETARY. He says festivities are to-morrow and day after tomorrow. It is to go on day and night, and they would want one day's rest.

GENERAL BATES. I would like it to be Sunday for sure.

SECRETARY. He says they will have to arrange with the Sultan, but thinks pretty sure it will be Sunday or Monday.

GENERAL BATES. I would like it as early as possible.[64]

While in the play the fiat declaring that the rule of U.S. law only obtains on every other weekday underscores what Ade saw as the arbitrariness of the execution of the U.S. Constitution in the Philippines, here the transcribed dialogue reveals the very inanity of mundane bureaucracy. Even everyday colonial life— recorded in Bates's grumbling that he "came down here just to do this" and in the sultan's expressed plans to attend the all-day "festivities" and to recover from them—gets in the way of the empire's attempts to administer time.

This inelegance of imperial business meetings appears throughout the transcriptions. Here is another somewhat absurd exchange between the sultan's proxy ("Secretary") and Bates:

SECRETARY. The Sultan sends his greetings, and begs to be excused, because he has got a boil on his neck and another underneath his arm, and can not [*sic*] even put a coat on.

GENERAL BATES. I am sorry to hear that, and I trust he will soon be better. . . .

SECRETARY. The Sultan sends you word that he will recognize the protection of the United States, and that he will hoist the American flag; at the same time he asks of the United States the favor that alongside of the American flag he be allowed to hoist his own flag.

GENERAL BATES. The American flag must be higher—must be supreme. There is no objection to having his own flag (a lower flag) [*sic*], but the American flag is to be the flag of the nation.

SECRETARY. . . . They say that they recognize the United States flag, . . . but at the same time they ask again the favor to let the flags be hoisted side by side.

GENERAL BATES. No, they are not equal at all. The flag of the United States is the sovereign of the islands; it owns them all; but we do not want to detract anything from the authority of the Sultan or his advisers. (33)

The attempt to articulate the terms of an international trade treaty with England and Germany (the lofty objective of this particular meeting) gets postponed by—of all things—a boil on the sultan's neck. If he read the transcripts at all, Ade must have found this ghastly detail delicious. Moreover, the conversation gets derailed by conversations about the protocols of flag flying: if, as proponents of *ex propio vigore* insist, "the constitution follows the flag," then this succinct rule proves utterly useless, if the very matter of where, how, and under what terms the flag might fly remains moot. Further, what is exposed here is not only the seemingly arbitrary nature of U.S. constitutional law's execution on the archipelago, but also the basic difficulty administrators had in negotiating the U.S. liberalist ethos (you can fly whatever flag you like; you have authority) with imperial sovereignty (but our flag has to be on top; actually we are in charge).

Ade's rendering of the encounters between Bates and the sultan retains some of the social awkwardness seen here, although the formal nature of the conversation is supplanted by a peculiar familiarity. Indeed, *The Sultan of Sulu* challenges and supplements the official colonial archive in *The Treaty* by both inscribing intimacies that "might have happened" between the colonel and the sultan and modulating its formalities into a campy key. (Ade's attention to commodities, labor, and resistance in the metropole might recall Andrew Ross's argument that camp culture is the "re-creation of surplus value from for-gotten forms of labor," which might, in this case, be that concerned with colonial bureaucratic niceties.[65]) In Act 1, after Colonel Budd proclaims Ki-Ram the next governor of Sulu, offering lavish platitudes, "that valiant leader, that incorrupt-ible statesman, that splendid type of perfect manhood" (29), Ki-Ram, in turn, confesses his assessment of Budd:

> KI-RAM. Colonel, I want to thank you. It [your speech] was great! . . . Say where did you learn that kind of talk?
> BUDD. You mustn't mind that. I'm in politics. I say that about every one. . . .
> (GALULA *comes from behind the palace carrying a large, long-handled fan of Oriental pattern. . . . She timorously approaches* KI-RAM *and begins fanning him from behind.*)
> KI-RAM. Colonel, you'll excuse me for mentioning it, but you are one of the handsomest men I ever saw. I–I–(*He pauses with an expression of alarm growing on his countenance.* GALULA *continues to fan him.*) Col-onel, do you feel a draft? (*Turns and sees* GALULA.) Oh-h-h! Galula, I know you love me, and I don't blame you, but you want to remember one thing, "Absence makes the heart grow fonder." (29–31)

Ki-ram's professed admiration for Budd may be read as a mimetic form of the political civility we see in the official *Treaty*: Budd hails Ki-Ram as a "splendid type of perfect manhood," and Ki-Ram returns the acclaim by calling Budd "one of the handsomest men" he has ever seen.[66] Yet the difference in return is significant. Colonel Budd's praise is, as he points out, public, a "politician['s]" display; Ki-Ram's admiration is private, a bashful confession between two men. As such, the latter's tongue-tied appreciation of the American's "handsomeness" not only rings more sincere in its articulation despite—or perhaps out of—his discomfiture; it also escapes what Foucault calls the "public interest" in sexual discourse.[67] Ki-Ram's stage-directed "pause," coupled with the "expression of alarm growing on his countenance," denotes, perhaps, not so much his noticing the "draft" that Galula's hitherto unnoticed fanning emits but, rather, that his newly recognized attraction for the colonel might have engendered a startling bodily response. The soon-to-be-governor's stuttering "I–I–bespeaks the unexpected desire of a subject beside himself with shock. Ki-Ram is perhaps too turned on to speak. The "draft" might in this sense also thus refer to a militarized call to heteronormativity: Galula, Ki-Ram's first wife, interrupts the scene of intimacy between the two men, reminding the sultan that he has already been drafted into hetero-erotic contract, albeit several times over.

The Sultan of Sulu's staging of the "alarm[ing]" attraction between the U.S. colonial representative and the native Moro sultan displaces, however fleetingly, the spectacle of the sultan's polygamous relationships. Ki-Ram's dismissal of Galula reflects what may be the beginning of his increasing ambivalence toward plural marriage, on one hand, and his increasing attraction to Colonel Budd, on the other. When in Act 2 Ki-Ram, in his first act as governor, reviews the new imperial guard appointed to "protect" Sulu territory, he is once again taken off guard by the colonial administrator's good looks:

> KI-RAM. Good morning troops! (*Sees* BUDD *and is staggered by the glory of his apparel. In the meantime* PAMELA, *very much on her official dignity, has entered from the right.* KI-RAM *addresses* BUDD.) My! My! Colonel, you are without a doubt the handsomest man I– (PAMELA *interrupts.*)
> PAMELA. Governor Ki-Ram!
> KI-RAM. Oh-h! Here she is again. I don't believe I'm going to like her very well.
> PAMELA. I have granted divorce to seven of your wives.
> KI-RAM. Oh, very well! (70)

Ki-Ram's second appraisal of Budd's apparently overwhelming or staggering handsomeness is again marked by stuttering. Here, "I–I–" becomes "My! My!" reiterating the precariousness of Ki-Ram's desire vis-à-vis Budd's fine form. What's more, his appraisal is again cut off—this time by Pamela, expressing the half-century-long antipolygamy "state of feeling" Bentley identifies. Pamela acts as the state-authorized arbiter of "official dignity," not only in her normalizing imposition of divorce onto Ki-Ram and his multiple wives but also in her interpellating disruption ("Governor Ki-Ram!") of his potential flirtation with Budd. Functioning as the embodiment of the U.S. rule of law in the operetta, Pamela, in her effort to eliminate both perversions, demonstrates that hetero-monogamy also follows the flag. Further, Ki-Ram's enthusiastic concession to Pamela's injunction ("Oh, very well!") marks, perhaps, an admission that one perverse desire has replaced another. That Ki-Ram's remarks about Colonel Budd's "handsomeness" occurs once more in the play (94) bespeaks the persistent unmanageability of Ki-Ram's affection.

Beyond these appraisals, the sultan's feelings for Budd find their most erotic expression in the scenes concerned with alcoholic drink. That Ade would stage intimacy between the native and the colonial administrator through drink is unsurprising, given the evident frequency of "immoral" behavior that the consumption of alcohol led to in the archipelago. Despite Ki-Ram's perpetual hangover, he continually escapes off-stage with Budd to partake of more "cocktails" at the "lifesaving station." Yet alcohol functions as more than a buffer for homosocial relationality in the play; Ki-Ram's description of its consumption evokes sexual awakening. Here he tells Pamela about his first experience of drinking with Budd:

> KI-RAM. When the Colonel took me aside in there he said he was going to make me acquainted with one of the first blessings of civilization. He told me that the constitution and the cocktail followed the flag. Then he gave me an amber-colored beverage with a roguish little cherry nestling at the bottom. And, oh, little friend, when I felt that delicious liquid trickle down the corridors of my inmost being, all the incandescent lights were turned on and the birds began to sing. I felt myself bursting into full bloom, like a timid little flower kissed by the morning sunlight. So I ordered two more. (47)

Ki-Ram is indeed "turned on." This pleasurable recollection is expressed not with phallic imagery (which, as I discussed in chapter 3, often corresponded within the metroimperial imaginary to fantasies of anal penetration and discipline) but, instead, in adherence to turn-of-the-century conventions, with more "feminine" sexual tropes ("liquid trickl[ing] down corridors of my inmost being" and "bursting into full bloom"). In fact, in an earlier draft of the libretto, Ki-Ram sings during the same scene about being "full of the oil of joy," a line that seems to have been rejected by Savage, who, in Ade's words, found the line "too subtle or too frivolous or too *something*."[68] While the phrase "oil of joy" alludes to a biblical verse (Isaiah 61:3), Savage has perhaps edited out, as Ade insinuates with his deliberate vagueness here, what the manager might have seen as Ki-Ram's (and Ade's) excessive, feminine *jouissance*.

The play activates, I am suggesting, a discourse of gender-sexual desire by transposing it into a campy critique of the concurrent reformist warnings about the dangers of alcohol in the Philippines—"Three cheers for the W. C. T. U!" (23) sings Ki-Ram in his protest song to hangovers, "R-E-M-O-R-S-E." Recounting in the same song that he "hoisted twenty-three/of those arrangements into me"— and that he was "pickled, primed" (63) by that "little friend," the cocktail—the sultan finds himself "acquainted" with a new pleasure: the pleasure in being a bottom. Ki-Ram sings of this different kind of pleasure while drunk: "the world was one kaleidoscope/Of purple bliss." This last phrase, "purple bliss," referring perhaps to the sky just before sunrise, not only evoked insipid "romantic" love poetry of the time but was also used a few years later by a newspaper writer to describe a heterosexual "friendship [that] ripened into love."[69] Pickled, primed, and filled up with Budd's cocktails, the sultan is also full of romantic ripening. The sultan's description of his first drink with Budd also anticipates the language of a scene in Carlos Bulosan's canonical novel *America Is in the Heart* (1946). Bulosan's narrator recounts his first sexual experience with a woman: "it was like spring in an unknown land. There were roses everywhere, opening to a kind sun. I heard the sudden beating waves upon rocks, the gentle fall of rain among palm leaves. Was this eternity? Was this the source of creation?"[70] Whereas Bulosan's narrator, not insignificantly evoking the solipsism of hetero-erotic, masculinist reproduction ("Was this the source of creation?"), places himself *among* the roses "opening to a kind sun," Ki-Ram likens *himself* to a "timid little flower." The sultan's participation in the romantic act, again in accordance with gendered conventions of the time, thus proves one of "feminine" reception rather than "masculine" penetration.

Complicating George Chauncey's description of the "centrality of effeminacy" in the fin-de-siècle designation of the abnormal figure of the "homosexual," Ki-Ram confesses here not his adopting a feminine position or self-presentation per se but, rather, his feeling "feminized" within his "inmost being." On one hand, Ki-Ram's articulation of his desire draws from the conventions of late nineteenth-century sexological discourse around the "invert," largely understood as a figure that reverses his or her sex role; on the other, Ki-Ram's language bespeaks his gender identification, in the language of the time, as bisexual. Chauncey describes how the latter term was then understood: "at the turn of the century . . . *bisexual* referred to individuals who combined the physical and/or psychic attributes of both men and women. A bisexual was not *attracted* to both males and females: a bisexual *was* both male and female."[71] While there is nothing to suggest that Ade was familiar with contemporary sexological taxonomy, it is significant that he imagines the sultan's unstable sexual attraction for Budd along a spectrum of U.S. metroimperial conventions of gender style and their inversion. His musical comedy thus offers a particularly intimate rearrangement of the colonial sociality recorded in the *Treaty*: the famous Moro's racialized, deviant sexuality in *The Sultan of Sulu* is marked not by his alleged barbaric polygamous practices but by a cross-racial homoerotic attraction and intimacy that "might have happened."

The Savage Bachelor; or, the Racial Obverse of Polygamy

The perversion attached to Moro polygamy in metroimperial discourse is displaced in *The Sultan of Sulu* not just by Ki-Ram's "alarming" attraction to the colonial officer, but also in Ki-Ram's attempted orchestration of his newly divorced wives' post-polygamous marriages to the colonial military volunteers. After learning that "Arkansaw state law" declares that "when a divorced woman becomes desperate and remarries, then the first victim doesn't have to pay any more alimony" (107), Ki-Ram concocts a business scheme with his secretary: "Ki-Ram and Hadji, matrimonial agents" (108–9). As result of the sultan's plotting, Budd becomes engaged to one of Ki-Ram's ex-wives, Chiquita, and approves the engagement of his daughter, Henrietta, to Lieutenant Hardy. In turn, all of the other "nice soldiers" are matched up with each of Chiquita's "sisters" (117). Budd "cordially" calls this proliferation of engagements an "epidemic of marriages." Yet such an appraisal is something of an outlier among the rest of the play's views on marriage. Even as Ki-Ram advertises his "matrimonial agency," for example, he contradicts his campaign sotto voce: "our object in life is to make people happy, it being a well known fact that all married people *are* happy. (*Aside.*) Heaven help me!" (114). Moreover, when Henrietta and Hardy become "engaged in a sort of way," they devote an entire number not to extolling marriage but to lamenting it:

> HARDY. Sweetheart, doubt my love no more;
> Believe me, I'm sincere.
> I love no other on this tropic shore;
> You're the only girl that's here. . . .
> HENRIETTA. Marriage is a doubtful state.
> I think of it with dread.
> Still, an engagement need not indicate
> That we really mean to wed (42–43).

At the risk of stripping these lines of their humor: seen either as a compulsory duty (despite the scarcity of proper sexual object choices, i.e., white women) or as a state to be doubted and dreaded, marriage is regarded as something a reasonable person should steer clear of. In this satirical comedy billed as a critique of the racialized perversion of "polygamy," Ade skewers instead the nation's "fantasy of a homogenous sphere of moral feeling," the unchanging affective life symptomatized by and upholding the epidemic practice of that which renders "celestial marriage" perverse within, and even "treasonous" to, U.S. nationhood: hetero-monogamy. Indeed, Ade's supplanting of polygamy by the threat of a more (for him) vexing epidemic of hetero-monogamous contracts adumbrates his own life of "single blessedness," as he himself would later describe his bachelor status.[1]

Sultan Ki-Ram's scandalizing, "queer" practice of plural marriage, I am arguing, is the inverted image of Ade's "perverse" (i.e., "anomalous, problematic, and probably immoral") practice of non-marriage. At the turn of the twentieth century, the figure of the bachelor, like the polygamist, was often regarded as something of a racialized other threatening the invented integrity of the American nuclear family. The typically white bachelor was pathologized for his alleged renunciation of the domestic scene and for seeking kinship in other spaces. As Howard Chudacoff puts it in his book about turn-of-the-century U.S. bachelor subcultures, "Bachelors who rented rooms in supposedly isolated and asocial boarding houses created relationships that approximated those they would have experienced in a family setting."[72] As an example of this new kinship, Chudacoff cites the bachelor lives of Ade and his longtime friend, John McCutcheon; the two bachelors, living their twenties in Chicago at the end of the so-called Gay Nineties, "spent almost every spare hour together, sharing adventures out on the streets and coming back to their boardinghouse as little as possible."[73] Threatened by such perceived prodigal intimacies of single men, moral reformers such as Jane Addams regarded bachelors as "the vanguards of social breakdown, threatening the presumed stability of family and community."[74] Despite being a "bachelor maid" herself, as Scott Herring has pointed out,[75] Addams cautioned against bachelor sociality at the fin-de-siècle, saying, "The social relationships in a modern city are so highly made and often so superficial, that the human restraints of public opinion, long sustained in smaller communities, have also broken down. Freed from the benevolent restraints of the small town, thousands of young men and women in every great city have received none of the lessons in self-control which even savage tribes imparted to their appetites as well as their emotions."[76] Drawing from the characteristics of racialized others wanting self-control, and so evocative of both metroimperial and anti-polygamist rhetoric, Addams here compares the bachelor in the modern city to "savage tribes." Her reference to city dwellers unfettered from the "*benevolent* restraints of the small town" moreover, conjures the concurrent rhetoric of the imperial project about assimilation of the Philippine archipelago. For Addams, then, metropolitan space undomesticates—uncivilizes—the bachelor, who has lost the ability to control his appetite.

Against this backdrop, Ade's character of Ki-Ram would function—in the words of the late queer-of-color scholar José Muñoz—as a "disidentificatory" figure: by disidentifying with a racialized Ki-Ram, the bachelor Ade participates in a "disempowered politics or positionality that has been rendered unthinkable by the dominant culture."[77] Ade himself was a member of the household-threatening subculture to which Addams alludes—indeed, his intimacy with his lifelong friend and, at the time, fellow bachelor McCutcheon provides the backdrop for his composition of *The Sultan of Sulu*. In 1890, after graduating from Purdue, Ade moved to Chicago and lived in various boardinghouses. By the time he was contemplating the libretto for *The Sultan of Sulu* and collaborating with Wathall, he was residing among "Room Number Six," an inner circle of bachelors who occupied the first floor of the Chicago Athletic Club, which was well known as a place where men could have sexual relations with other men.[78] As Fred Kelly recounts, not long after McCutcheon returned to Chicago from the Philippines in late 1900, he developed a "serious lung infection" from the "variety of germs" he had picked up in his travels.[79] McCutcheon's physician advised Ade that he transport his friend at once to Asheville, North Carolina, to convalesce. Ade arranged for a highly expensive special Pullman car to move his infected friend and himself to the remote site, justifying the cost by saying, "Won't it seem a mere trifle if it saves John's life?"[80] During the subsequent three months of bedside care that Ade would offer McCutcheon, he began writing his first Broadway hit, which was set in the Philippines. The rest, as they say, was farce. Ade's "wandering" bachelor life, disposable income, and leisure time to tend to his sick companion, in short, provided him with the opportunity to imagine the sultan's polygamous Moro life.

In the figure of Ki-Ram, the racialized discourses around polygamy and bachelorhood converge. Indeed, I would argue as a way to conclude this chapter that Ade's inverted disidentification with the sultan assumes a racializing appropriation: through the polygamous Ki-Ram, the bachelor Ade might have fancied himself a perverse racial other. Ki-Ram, after all, imagines himself as something of a bachelor. In *The Sultan of Sulu*'s satirically sentimental showstopper—"Since I First Met You"—Ki-Ram presents his marriage proposal to Henrietta:

I am a dashing gay Lothario;
I've a reputation as a gallant beau;
Courting girls is a habit hard to break;

I'm a bold coquette and rather reckless rake.
I've told my love to many a girl,
But never a word was true,
For my passion intense, it was a mere pretense
Until I encountered you. (74)

Ki-Ram confesses to Henrietta—and the audience—that his wooing of her might simply be the force of habit, his "passion intense" around girls a "mere pretense." Although he is a practicing polygamist, the "reckless rake" Ki-Ram comes off as something of a bachelor, with all the connotations that word carried. His campy self-description as a "gay Lothario" and a "bold coquette," figures that connote careless sexual excess and gender inversion, respectively, attest to the "dynamic, interactive, and contested process" of emergent identificatory codes in sexual subcultures.[81] Ki-Ram thus confesses an "open secret," to borrow D. A. Miller's famous term, about some real passion (perhaps, at this point in the play, for Colonel Budd).

Ki-Ram in fact bespeaks the open secret about George Ade's "reputation." Such tongue-in-cheek, campy *dissembling in plain sight* was, after all, often Ade's modus operandus. George was a known practical joker among his Broadway friends. Once during a theater-business literary event to which he was invited to read his work, for example, he did not respond when the announcer called him to the stage. Instead, the event's organizers were handed one of his "Fables"— one that was not intended for general circulation—along with a note of regret. Yet Ade was hiding among the audience, and when he could not stop giggling during a proxy's reading of his evidently bawdy fable, a "companion" had to poke him in the ribs and warn, "Not so loud, George, or you'll queer the whole thing."[82] Open secrets, with a select audience in on the gag, was "Just George Ade's Way."

Ki-Ram's confession to Henrietta, in other words, would come to characterize Ade. As Kelly would make a point of emphasizing throughout his biography of the very private satirist, Ade had a "reputation as a gallant beau," a "dashing gay Lothario." Yet when asked why "one of the most sought-after men of his time" never married—as if marriage would have dissipated the evident rumors circulating around the confirmed bachelor—Ade would generally give flippant, self-deprecating answers. One such response recalls Addams's comparison of bachelors to a "savage tribe": "at a time when I might have contemplated marriage, a license cost $2 and I never had the money. . . . I suppose I lived in a hall bedroom and became *thoroughly undomesticated*. On top of that maybe no woman would have had me."[83] Other times Ade would suggest that he had merely missed his boat. Referring to Lillian Howard, a woman he was associated with before he moved to Chicago, he claimed, "I didn't marry because another man married my girl."[84] He might have been a reckless rake but he was also a known bachelor. So when a newspaper article profiling Ade in 1902 sported the subheading "Popular with the Women," it quickly clarified, "Mr. Ade is especially popular with feminine *readers*."

Like Ade here, Ki-Ram conjectures as to why he has failed in social life—although, of course, Ki-Ram's "failure" is not that he did not get married but that he could not help but do so. Lamenting the topsy-turvy financial, marital, and governing straits he is in toward the end of the operetta, the sultan offers a campy but poignant admission to Colonel Budd: "I have a feeling . . . that I loved not wisely, but too often" (83–84). This pithy, pitiable epiphany—echoing that of another white playwright's fantasmatic Moor, Othello—resonates with how Ade conceived of his bachelorhood in his later years.[85] In a piece ironically called "The Joys of Single Blessedness" (1922), Ade describes the alienation that comes with being a bachelor:

> The bachelor is held up to contempt because he has evaded the draft. He is a slacker. He has side-stepped a plain duty. If he lives in the small town he is fifty per cent. joke and fifty per cent. object of pity. If he lives in a city, he can hide away with others of his kind, and find courage in numbers; but even in the crowded metropolis he has the hunted look of one who knows that the world knows something about him. He is led to believe that babies mistrust him. Young wives begin to warn their husbands when his name is mentioned. He is a chicken hawk in a world that was intended for turtle doves.[86]

Here and throughout this essay, Ade describes the social estrangement and affective remoteness of the bachelor in terms both funny and sad. Although "he trie[s] to be a good citizen" (7), the bachelor is regarded as a "slacker," one who has neglected his "plain duty" to the hetero-monogamous injunction of the nation, who has (recalling the scene with Galula's fanning) "evaded the *draft*" into the military-like service that is marriage. I get the sense, though, that Ade was probably OK with the continuous suspicion about and social criminalization of the bachelor (who "slowly slumps in public esteem until he becomes classified with those granite-faced criminals who loot orphan asylums" [3]), that he had a sense of humor about his own alleged "unregenerate" (4) betrayal of hetero-reproductivity, laughing it off with the joke that even "babies mistrust him." Later in the essay, after all, Ade alludes to "fellow travelers" (20), "others of his kind" in the cities or in "stag boarding-house[s]" (6) in whom one might "find courage in numbers." Indeed, exemplifying what queer studies scholars have described as the early twentieth-century white gay or lesbian subject's longing for queer others in ethnic terms, Ade here imagines himself among a "selfish tribe" of bachelors.[87] His appropriation of this racialized term, though problematic in many respects, also suggests an anti-imperialist critique of those who have "hunted" him for his anti-normative social life. He perhaps saw himself besieged by "the vast army" (2) of colonial agents (like Pamela), subject to a kind of imperial assimilation into hetero-monogamy.

Yet failing to find this imagined "tribal" formation, Ade warns, might lead to loneliness, to a "state of ostracized isolation" (3). "The more you camp by yourself," he wrote, "the more you shrivel" (19). Fortunately for Ade, however, in addition to having McCutcheon in his life as a longtime companion,[88] he also found one in Orson Collins Wells, a millionaire businessman with whom he traveled the world in 1910.[89] In an oil-painting caricature of the couple by Ade's friend William Schmedtgen (figure 4.7), the intimates are shown touring the Pyramids, with Ade, signifying bottom status, wearing a dress and carrying a suitcase marked "Fables in Slang" in one hand and a parasol in the other. Wells, quite the literal "fellow traveler" to whom Ade alludes, wears the red tie (seen more clearly in the original color painting) of the "selfish tribe" and holds a lollypop bearing the insignia of the Chicago Athletic Club.[90] The painting hung for years in the men-only Chapin and Gore bars in downtown Chicago and thus confessed Ade's open secret, a joke in plain sight, to those in the know.[91]

In 1905, when the Hoosier-at-heart Ade moved back to Indiana, within fifteen miles of his hometown of Kentland—while still keeping his room at the Chicago Athletic Club—he would refer to himself as "a blanket Indian who had returned to the reservation," suggesting that even Chicago's subcultural bachelor life had never quite fully suited him.[92] Ade's racializing self-ascription here during his retreat from city life returns us, in turn, to the title character of *The Sultan of Sulu*. Ki-Ram could be seen as exhibiting what Anne Cheng has called the "pathological euphoria" intrinsic to the musical comedy form. In her discussion of Rogers and Hammerstein's "Chinatown" musical *Flower Drum Song* (1958), Cheng attributes this "condition" to the racialized subject, who must stage a euphoric "double identity" to "alleviate the pains of exclusion," to "conceal . . . the pain of dividedness."[93] While Ki-Ram as a colonial subject is not directly subjected to U.S. metropolitan forms of racial-sexual management and exclusion, the U.S. military does manage to impose, through various colonial agents, punishing modes of regulation for his racialized practices of polygamy, for his having loved too often. That Ade, as I have been arguing, would come to understand his bachelorhood in the imperial metropole through the sultan's "queer marriage practices" in the colonial Philippines, and that Ade would soon leave the "crowded metropolis" of Chicago for small-town life in Indiana, suggests that he perhaps recognized

FIG. 4.7 Caricature of George Ade and Orson Collins Wells, 1912 (oil on canvas; artist, William Herman Schmedtgen)

an affinity, vis-à-vis the modern city, between life in the remote "smiling isle" and life on the farm.[94] With this Philippine Moro figure—that "queer potentate of the east"—whose loves and intimacies are subjected to racial-sexual governance and who frequently had to hide behind camp and punchlines to alleviate his punishment, Ade found kinship in the face of the metropolitan public's militarized draft into hetero-monogamy, locating, perhaps, a fellow traveler in whom he might have concealed, in plain sight, the joys *and* pains of single blessedness.[95]

CHAPTER 5

CERTAIN PECULIAR TEMPTATIONS

Little Brown Students and Racial-Sexual
Governance in the Metropole

How would a Philippine subject living in the U.S. metropole during the early years of occupation come retrospectively to imagine
the Philippine-American War as an occasion for same-sex intimacy?
Consider this scene from "On the Battlefield," a short story written in
1905 by Pacifico Laygo, a Philippine student given a government pen-
sion to study at the University of Missouri.[1] Set two months into the
Philippine-American War, in August 1899, on the outskirts of Payapa, a
small village in Luzon, the story locates two dying soldiers, a "Yankee"
and a "native," after a skirmish won by the Philippine insurrectos. The
"American" soldier, whose "paleness of countenance" both "show[s]"
that he was one of the wounded soldiers" and alludes to his whiteness,
is left for dead by his defeated battalion, when "the moans of another
wounded lying but a few yards from him turn[s] him back to life."
Initially fearful, the American soldier recognizes "by the few words
he had learned of the native tongue, that the other wounded [is] asking for water" and "roll[s]" toward the Filipino, who grabs his knife.

"Some way," however, "the looks and the expression of sympathy from the eyes of the American quieted him down." When the dying American offers the dying insurrecto water (*tubig*) from his canteen, whispering in Spanish, Tagalog, and English, "Mi no combati, mi amigo. Tubig! Tubig! Here," the Filipino reflects:

> What a kind of Providence was that above. And the foe was the providence itself, at least before the eyes of the wounded. And it was real, real water, somewhat warm, though. He drank in a big draught of the refreshing liquid until completely satisfied. Then he handed the canteen back to the other, who made a finish of the rest.
>
> A sense of gratitude moved the soul of the native, and extending his hand, he shook hands with the foe. The dagger was previously thrown away. The wan face of the American reddened with joy. With an effort he drew close to him and weakly shouted "Hurrah for the Filipinos!" The native answered him with a "Viva America!" And the two men, representing the fighting sides of the battle of the morning, hugged each other. And the two enemies were clasped in a dear embrace on that battlefield.
>
> Meanwhile the heat became almost suffocating, and the two wounded began to bleed profusely. Gradually they weakened and saw their ends coming. But in their dying whispers they spoke of their homes; of the loving mammas who were waiting for them; of the little sweethearts who brightened their hopes; of all those who were dear to them; and prayed that the end of that struggle might come—a struggle where a mighty people were fighting another of less age, experience and strength, but rich with patriotism and enthusiasm.[2]

Amid the alienating effects of war and violence of colonial conflict, an intimacy is in "some way" roused, exchanged between whispers. That the title of the story finds its refrain in the same sentence as the "dear embrace" underscores the importance of the latter image. The multiple moments of bodily exchange in this scene—the initial "expression of sympathy," the sharing of the canteen, the handshake, the "dear embrace," the mirrored and contiguous wounds, the presumable commingling of racialized blood—double the more implausible verbal exchange of stories of home, of their "loving mammas," and of the "little sweethearts who brightened their hopes." While the stories traded here are typical of those sustaining and defining homosocial (presumably nonerotic) relationships, the language barrier—indicated by the clumsy code-switching across English, Tagalog, and Spanish—must surely delimit their transmission. Thus, although the trafficked memories of the "little sweethearts" might otherwise safeguard against the eroticism that threatens the presumably nonsexual embrace of the two men, the "dying whispers" amount to something like pillow talk (albeit on a deathbed).

It is remarkable to me that a Philippine student living in the U.S. metropole would come to imagine such an intimate reconciliation in the thick of racial, imperial violence. "On the Battlefield" appears among a significant but largely unknown body of writing by the pensionada/os, Philippine students who received government scholarships to study in the U.S. metropole during colonial occupation.[3] Laygo's story, I admit, is an aberration within the already small corpus of writing by this population—aberrant both because nonfiction essays far outnumber literary production of any kind and, more so, because such homosocial intimacy is so rarely expressed in the archive they have left behind. This chapter attempts, in part, to make sense of the anomalous appearance of this story by surveying two concurrent publications offered by the first generation of pensionada/os: the *Filipino Students' Magazine*, first published in Berkeley in April 1905, and later renamed the *Philippine Review*, and *The Filipino*, first published in Washington, DC, in January 1906.[4] Few scholars have examined at length this particular body of writing by some of the first Philippine nationals.[5] Although different ideologically and politically—*The Filipino* was more socially and politically conservative than the *Filipino Students' Magazine*—both journals made claims for Philippine modernity and nationhood, and, on occasion, even for Philippine sovereignty or decolonization. The journals offered their pensionada/o and American audiences short essays on Philippine civic duty; photo essays documenting infrastructural "progress" in the Philippines under U.S. tutelage in the wake of the war; news briefs on the successes of Filipinos and Filipinas "at home" and in the U.S. metropole; photographic portraits of prominent political figures, pensionados, and pensionadas; polemical essays written by prominent anti-imperialists; and, occasionally, short stories, poetry, and bits of humor. While most of the entries were written by the Philippine students themselves, a number were written by somewhat prominent U.S. figures, such as David Barrows, Erving Winslow, Benjamin Ide Wheeler, Moorfield Storey, and William Lloyd Garrison, as well as by other, less prominent North Americans, many of whom were white women commenting on their pleasant experiences with young Filipinas/os, both in the United States and abroad, cheering on their good behavior and academic and civic success.[6]

In the previous chapters I examined U.S. colonial state modes of governance over and metroimperial culture's representations of Filipinas/os. This final chapter considers how Philippine subjects themselves, through these publications, sought to manage at once their racial self-representation and their sexual self-identification in the face of such state and cultural management within the metropole, in the face of metroimperial fantasy. Scholars have previously examined the early migration wave of mostly male Philippine workers who were recruited to fill U.S. labor needs, but none have considered how this handful of Philippine subjects within the colonial metropole at the turn of the twentieth century responded directly to metroimperial representation and racial-sexual management.[7] To be sure, class distinctions made the experiences of these two populations of noncitizen nationals starkly different—indeed, the pensionada/os' access to print culture attests to how many of them came from wealthy or privileged backgrounds. Despite their relative privilege, however, the students' precarious positions as colonial subjects within the space of the metropole's educational system led to vexed responses to both dominant discourses around the occupation of the Philippines and the racial-sexual management attending to U.S. imperialism, both in the metropole and in the archipelago. Such compromises often emerged directly out of editorial constraints. The pensionada/os writing for *The Filipino* out of Washington, DC, for example, had the official ward of the Pensionado Program, William Sutherland, at the editorial helm. Meanwhile, the slightly more autonomous editors and writers for the *Filipino Students' Magazine* out of Berkeley had University of California administrators to wrestle with. When the staff of the *Filipino Students' Magazine* tested the waters of national politics in their writing, they were quickly checked. As the *San Francisco Call* reported in March 1906, Benjamin Ide Wheeler, then the president of the University of California, wrote a letter to Ponciano Reyes, the magazine's editor, congratulating him on the publication's one year anniversary while at the same time issuing a cautionary statement: "I cannot believe that supreme attention to politics in the other and more common sense of agitation is the best field for the Filipino students of today. I should be glad to see their principal interest associating itself rather with economic and social questions."[8] In writing about "politics," rather than "economic and social questions"—evidently mutually exclusive matters—the "agitat[ed]" Philippine students were crossing a line. In October, the *San Francisco Call* followed up on Wheeler's editing notes, reporting that that university president's "hints apparently have been unheeded" by the unruly pensionada/os.[9]

This chapter is concerned with how these earliest colonial subjects in the metropole registered the dominant modes of their colonially inflected racialization—a racialization that, as I have demonstrated throughout this book, was constituted through their imagined deviant sexualization. Susan Koshy has read the literary work of the canonical, mid-twentieth-century Filipino American writer Carlos Bulosan as representing "Filipino Americans' resistance to state control over their intimate lives [as] a political response to the penetration of their lives by biopower."[10] While Koshy situates Bulosan's bildungsroman *America Is in the Heart* (1946) as responding to almost half a century's worth of state and social prohibitions—most notably, antimiscegenation laws, the first of which targeted Filipinos in 1933—I track here how these undergraduate Philippine students indexed the very *emergence* of such biopolitical expression within the metropole at the turn of the century. By surveying this early archive, a cultural production that preceded the legal and social racial-sexual governance over Philippine noncitizen nationals (e.g., antimiscegenation laws, immigration restrictions, and lynching), this chapter examines the biopolitics—the "calculated management of life"—of benevolent assimilation, whose force, despite genocide in the colonial Philippines, these colonial students might have felt as more diffuse.[11] Such an analysis furnishes insight into how these Philippine colonial subjects, whose relative autonomy and agency within the U.S. metropole during these early years gave them a "unique sociolegal status," negotiated everyday racial-sexual management before the U.S. state would shore up that management by rule of law.[12]

By the last two decades of the nineteenth century, Michel Foucault has argued, "an entire social practice, which took the exasperated but coherent form of a state-directed racism, furnished the technology of sex with a formidable power and far reaching consequences."[13] While attending to this claim, I also advance in this chapter something of its inversion: that the inchoate management of sex by the U.S. metroimperial state furnished the technologies of race with a formidable power over the local, over individuals' interiorities and intimate lives. I contend that in the students' attempts to manage their racial self-representation within the U.S. imperial metropole, a project of social respectability undertaken to prove their capabilities for Philippine sovereignty, they simultaneously reinforced and reshaped increasingly visible fin-de-siècle regulatory norms of gender and sexuality. This chapter builds this claim in five sections. The first offers a background of the Pensionado Program of 1903, as well as a snapshot of how the pensionada/os were received in the metropole, where they were seen as a potential racial-sexual menace. The second shows how in the journals the pensionada/os sought to manage their self-representation in the face of such reception by setting themselves apart from those who were, they claimed, racially inferior. Section three focuses on how the pensionadas (the female Philippine students) were situated and situated themselves within the largely hetero-masculinist discourses of their peers: whereas the pensionados took it upon themselves to speak to the project of modernizing Philippine national public space, often through discourses around hygiene and sanitation, the pensionadas emphasized how such cleaning up projects should begin at home, in the domestic space, for the sake of securing maternal futures. The fourth section examines the precariousness of such discourse, focusing on one pensionado's essay that attempts to manage his peers' behavior against moral evils in the metropole and another pensionado's tale that, hinting at a longing for male-male intimacy, exceeds such administering. The concluding section returns to "On the Battlefield," showing how its imagined homosocial intimacy does not counter but rather affirms benevolent assimilation.

The pensionada/o journals do not furnish a proliferation of expressions of illicit desire or gender troubling.[14] Rather, what I have discovered is that the pensionada/os' shoring up of seemingly transparent gender paradigms and, thus, their claims for and evidence of modern subjecthood required the conspicuous disavowal of unassimilable desires and the rejection of deviant figures with whom they might be associated, however obliquely rendered. Moreover, the self-management by the largely male—and, indeed, masculinist—student population involved both their own acts of comparative racialization, as they set themselves apart from African Americans, American Indians, and the allegedly "true" primitives of the Philippines, and modes of discipline over the female students who, as budding feminists, were seen as threatening the gendered order of things. In these moments of *conspicuously* performing prescribed gender and sexual norms, the students disclose the invention of their racialized heterosexuality within the colonial metropole.

Promising Education

The U.S.-Philippine colonial state's criteria for selection for the Pensionado Program of 1903 marked shifts in the scale of surveillance in turn-of-the-twentieth-century U.S. colonial rule, imperial education, and immigration, moving from the management of populations to the ethnographic policing of individual bodies.[15] These criteria would come to inflect, however unevenly, the pensionada/os' printed responses to colonial management in the journals. A direct consequence of benevolent assimilation and an apparatus of colonial education, the Pensionado Program, initiated by the U.S. Philippine Commission's Act 854 of 1903, allowed for the probationary admission of high school and college students of "good moral character" and "sound physical condition" into schools throughout the United States. Administrators of the program sought out U.S. high schools and universities that would help with cost sharing; universities were asked to waive tuition, while the colonial government covered transportation and housing costs.[16] The first crop of institutional locations covered a range, from high schools in Meriden, Connecticut, and Parkersburg, West Virginia, and normal schools in Westchester, Pennsylvania, and Dekalb, Illinois, to universities such as the Massachusetts Institute of Technology; the Drexel Institute (now Drexel University); Oberlin College; the University of Michigan, Ann Arbor; Indiana University, Bloomington; Cornell University; and the University of California, Berkeley. The program was cast as a mode of preparing Philippine students for modernization and nation-building back home. Most of the 104 students chosen in the first year of the program were compelled by their governmental patrons to study agriculture, engineering, education, law, medicine, and other industrial fields that would modernize the Philippine nation's already existing but underdeveloped infrastructure.

Particular bodies were necessary for the modernizing project of nation building. As the Philippine Commission's Act 854, also known as the "Pensionado Act," prescribes, each prospective student had to undergo a physical examination by a state-designated physician. What's more, at the same time that a pensionado had to sign the official agreement that "he [would] conform to all the regulations, rules, and laws of said institution [i.e., the school or university attended] and such other regulations as may be prescribed by the Department of Public Instruction; that he [would] diligently, studiously, and faithfully pursue the established course of studies," he also had to "take the oath of allegiance to the Government of the United States."[17] Body and mind, in other words, had to be submitted to U.S. empire. In addition to these abstracted forms of subjecthood, which coded the Philippine Student as male, the very material attributes of health and privilege factored explicitly into the nomination of those who received the title "pensionado." As Sutherland, the program's first supervisor and ward of male students in the United States, would later recount, "In the telegram of instructions prepared for Governor [William] Taft to sign was written, 'Each student must be of unquestionable moral and physical qualifications, no weight being given to social status.' The Governor, more realistic than I, scratched out the word 'no' before the word 'weight.'"[18] Social capital secured the students' cultural capital.[19] Indeed, in June 1902 Philippine Secretary of Foreign Affairs Felipe Buencamino, regarded by a *San Francisco Call* reporter as "one of the most prominent Filipinos on the islands,"[20] had proposed to U.S. Secretary of War Elihu Root that Filipino students be sent to the U.S. metropole.[21] His son, Felipe Buencamino Jr., not only appeared among the first class of students in the Pensionado Program studying at Berkeley but also served as editor of the *Filipino Students' Magazine*, while securing the magazine's start-up finances.[22] Taft's allegedly penciled-in revision thus appealed to the skeptical ilustrado, or bourgeois and enlightened elite of the Philippines, as selectivity in membership promised to reproduce older markers and mechanisms of distinction that the Philippine oligarchy found attractive.[23] Indeed, most students in the earlier years of the program, like Buencamino, came from the elite landowning class or expanding middle classes in the provinces.[24] Benedict Anderson's story of the persistence of late nineteenth-century "cacique democracy" and privilege of the ilustrado elite in the Philippines, then, can be tracked in the impetus for the civil and political education of many of these early pensionados.[25]

The U.S. public, however, was not impressed with the Philippine students' distinction. Newspaper reports show that another reputation altogether preceded the pensionada/os: that of insurrectionist natives. For example, not long after the students arrived in the metropole, in August 1904, a headline in the *Arizona Republican* read, "Captured by Filipinos: A Hundred of Them Held Phoenix for an Hour Last Night."[26] Although the accompanying story went on to report amicably on the "one hundred bright faced, well mannered, and neatly dressed Filipino youths"—that is, the newly arrived pensionada/os—at the Phoenix train station, the headline must have been terrifying. A profile in another newspaper assessed Philippine students at "various grades of intelligence," reporting that they could not pass through school hallways without alerting the attention of others, even though the well-behaved Philippine students were "not a bit suggestive of the 'new caught sullen peoples' of Kipling's verse."[27] The article "suggest[s]," here, even when saying it ought not to, a comparison to the pathetic image in "The White Man's Burden." The profile concluded with a description of two pensionadas who were "very small, although they dress and act like full-grown women. . . . As they wander through the corridors of Drexel they look like the dark-eyed, swarthy pygmies beside the strapping American girls." Such colonial discourse persisted in the press, even after the students demonstrated their capabilities. "What an inferior race the Filipinos are," one editorial jeered, "is shown by the fact that two of the honor prizes at Yale this year were taken by Filipino students: one was cum laude and the other was cum laude magna. Mollycoddles!"[28] With a defensive joke, the nativist editorial disparages the pensionados' achievements by attributing to their "inferior race" an overly domesticated effeminacy—the pensionados' good grades adduced decadence. What's more, not only did the press often undercut the students' academic achievements with colonial, racializing discourse, but it also disparaged their extracurricular athletic victories. As an editorial published in 1906 in the *Omaha Daily Bee* opined, "That Filipino students are showing well as runners in college athletic events is not surprising to those who remember the good races won by the followers of Aguinaldo during the insurrection."[29] For the metroimperial public, pensionada/os might as well have been the progeny of insurrectos.

Such racializing discourse had logistical consequences, as pensionadas and pensionados, meeting the U.S. color line head on, were deemed ineligible to attend southern U.S. schools. In 1904, for example, the state educational board of Kentucky debarred from matriculation four Philippine students set to study agriculture in Louisville. The exclusion, which evidently resulted from "the prejudice of the Southern student bodies,"[30] held that such segregationist practice was legal because "the word 'colored' applied to negroes, Indians, and other brown races."[31] The staff of the *San Francisco Call* had anticipated far worse from Kentucky a year earlier. On the same page where one editorial held that "all Filipinos look alike," another entry reflected on the newly arrived Philippine students: "it is to be hoped that the young men will not be permitted to know that Kentucky is on the map. Armed with a six-shooter and Kentuckian morality a single Filipino could keep the islands indefinitely in an uproar."[32] Regionalist stereotypes notwithstanding, such accounts made it clear to the young Filipina/o students that they had to conduct themselves in a fashion that would not threaten the evidently besieged U.S. public.

The U.S. public also regarded the male Philippine students in particular as a racial-sexual threat in need of state intervention. Not long after the pensionada/os began their studies in the metropole, wedding announcements of Filipino students and white U.S. women started appearing in newspapers' social pages. The pensionado Antonio C. Torres, the son of a first justice of the Philippine Court, and Eunice Miller James, a "member of the prominent James family of Virginia," for example, were married in July 1905.[33] A sixteen-year-old "Berkeley girl," Lillian Newell, and James Charles Araneta, "the dashing young scion of a wealthy Filipino family" and "the most brilliant Filipino student . . . sent from the Orient," tied the knot in February 1906.[34] The law student Ignacio Rosario, a "full-blood Filipino of the Tagalog tribe," "wooed" and married Margaret Alberta Cruthers of Poughkeepsie, New York, during the summer of 1906.[35] Although not frequent, these interracial marriages seem to have provoked significant anxiety. Rosario and Cruthers in fact kept their nuptials secret for a year; it was only during his funeral in April 1907, which the newly widowed Margaret attended, that the family and friends, including his fellow pensionados, learned of the marriage. Such secrecy implies recognition by the couple of an inchoate moral panic against this particular form of pairing, even as exploitative marriages between white soldiers and Filipina women in the archipelago proliferated with impunity.

This moral panic took a range of forms. One "little American girl," for example, who was recently married to one of the Filipino students, faced "danger of being ostracized socially by some of the American women" in her social circle.[36] In Indiana, legislators sought to create what would have been the first antimiscegenation law between Filipinos and whites. In February 1905, State Senator Davis of Indiana's Monroe and Greene counties introduced a bill, evocative of the one-drop rule, to prevent whites from marrying "persons having more than one eighth Filipino blood."[37] News stories with titles that put the proposed legislation in ballistic terms ("Aimed at Filipino Students"; "Hits Filipino Lovers") or that likened the pensionados to blacks ("Indiana Parents Want No Dusky Sons-in-Law") recounted that Davis's proposed legislation resulted from "a situation at Bloomington, where Filipino students [at Indiana University were] flirting with white girls . . . Parents of these girls [were] fearful of marriages." Sutherland, the pensionados' first ward, gives a different account of the origins of the Indiana bill, contending that a middle-aged, white lawyer from Bloomington who was interested in a university "co-ed" was incensed that the young white woman had broken a date with him to go out with the pensionado José Valdez. The humiliated lawyer then coaxed his friend Davis to introduce the bill.[38] Regardless of the impetus behind the proposed legislation, which in the end did not pass, the ideological motivation is clear: the male Philippine students threatened to contaminate white American girls' sexual purity and, in turn, white blood. This instance of miscegenationist fantasy precedes by decades those circulating around Filipino immigrant laborers who arrived in the metropole during the 1920s and 1930s, as Leti Volpp, Linda España-Maram, and Ruby Tapia have discussed.[39] What these earlier representations tell us is that there was not so much a historical shift, to use Tapia's provoking language, in the image of the "Filipino" from "short, docile, low-to-the-ground, ideal farm laborers" to that of "hypersexual, slick-mannered" men "out to get white women and stain America's future brown."[40] Rather, these earlier reports convey that these images, however seemingly incongruous, existed simultaneously. While pensionados at the University of Michigan, Ann Arbor, did protest Davis's bill publicly—Frederic Unson, a Philippine student there, in fact pointed to the double standard, saying, "We know very well that in the Philippines, Americans can enter into legal matrimony with our girls at any time, therefore why should not the Filipinos be allowed to marry American girls?"[41]—they never did so in the journals they published. Instead, as I show see in the following section, pensionados attempted to establish implicitly their eligibility to marry white women by explicitly disparaging the sexual incontinence and threat of black U.S. soldiers stationed in the Philippines and by reproducing colonial distinctions that set them apart from other Philippine ethnic formations.[42] They sought to be regarded as model minorities in love.

Model Minorities in the Imperial Metropole

In the inaugural edition of the *Filipino Students' Magazine*, the editors Ponciano Reyes, H. R. Luzuriaga, Jaime Araneta, A. M. Taizon, José Reyes, and Felipe Buenamino Jr., asserted that, although "it is almost unavoidable to let race feeling enter when one's people are unjustly criticized," they would attempt to suppress such feelings and "confine [their] subjects to Literature, Science and Arts."[43] Nevertheless, "race feeling" seems to saturate each essay and literary entry. Indeed, many of the magazine's articles attempted to demystify what the pensionados regarded as popular presumptions about the new colonial wards: that they were premodern, uncivilized, childlike, unruly, unindustrious, naked, sexually inassimilable, dog-eating savages. In challenging these preconceptions, the writers often took a serious, polemical tone: "all of these [stereotypes] we can without hesitancy state are caused by ignorance, led by pessimistic ideas and lack of more mature judgment."[44] Troping the colonial perception of the Filipinos, the pensionados suggested that it was the general U.S. public that needed "matur[ing]."

Throughout the journals, the Philippine students wrote about the prospect of modernizing, cleaning up, and sterilizing the physical space of the Philippine nation. The rhetoric of hygiene and sanitation demonstrates that their oblique criticism of U.S. imperialism was often tethered to colonial, racializing ideologies. Contributors to the *Filipino Students' Magazine* often touted mechanized irrigation, industrialized textiles, urban planning, the safeguarding of hygiene, and effective sanitation management. In doing so, the pensionados would come to compose, and traffic back into the Philippines, part of what Warwick Anderson has called the "American poetics of pollution in the colonial Philippines, a racializing of germ theories that conventionally contrasted a clean, ascetic American body with an open, polluting Filipino body."[45] The pensionado J. P. Katigbak lamented in April 1905, "The sewage [in the archipelago] is disposed of in a *primitive* and dangerous way. Hence, when cholera, small-pox and fever attack a few and circumstances favor, plague soon follows and the havoc becomes appalling."[46] Just a few months after writing about the dear embrace of soldiers and their commingling of saliva and blood in "On the Battlefield," Pacifico Laygo (who later, as a physician, would serve as a medical inspector in Manila) wrote the less gripping nonfiction essay "Municipal Sanitation in the Philippines" (1905).[47] What Katigbak and Laygo demonstrate here is an unquestioned deployment of the racializing poetics of colonial surveillance.

At times, a critique of popular conceptions—and, indeed, the project of benevolent assimilation—took something of an allegorical form in the *Filipino Students' Magazine*:

Unto a little nigger,
A swimming in the Nile,
Appeared, quite unexpectedly,
A hungry crocodile,
Who, with that chill politeness
That makes the warm blood freeze,
Remarked, "I'll take some dark meat
Without dressing, if you please!"[48]

The poem, untitled and facile, is also anonymous—it was in fact not written by a Philippine student at all, having appeared earlier, in 1891, in *The Tech*, a journal written by students at the Massachusetts Institute of Technology.[49] Despite its lack of historical specificity, which is at least promised by the matter of authorship, the very placement of the poem in the *Filipino Students' Magazine* gives it another historical context altogether. The poem immediately follows, though without any direct reference to, the pensionado Lorenzo Onrubia's brief essay "Education in the Philippine Islands."[50] Onrubia's essay concludes with two sentences commending the Pensionado Program: "there are now over two hundred students in the United States[,]of which one hundred and forty-four are sent by the government. Under American guidance, it is not too much to hope that Philippine Islands are sure to make a [*sic*] rapid progress."[51] I read the juxtaposition of the two pieces as significant—specifically, the diegetic structure of the poem repeats the one found in the final sentences of the preceding essay. The "little nigger" might, in other words, stand in for the pensionados and pensionadas (or Filipinos more generally), while the "quite unexpected . . . hungry crocodile" whose "chill politeness [or benevolence] makes the warm blood freeze" might stand in for the Pensionado Program (or the paternalistic empire more generally). In this sense, and with this alternative historical specificity, the poem functions as a mode of what José Esteban Muñoz has called a "disidentification," a performance of "a disempowered politics or positionality that has been rendered unthinkable by the dominant culture."[52] By imagining themselves, "unthinkabl[y]," as the hyperbolically abject, alienated figure of a black American—the "little nigger" in a perilous environment—the pensionado editors obscure their anti-imperialist, antiracist critique via seemingly insignificant paratactic juxtaposition and juvenile allegory.[53] This is guerrilla politics in written form: the "chill politeness" of imperialism is met with a sneak-attack joke.

Such disidentification on the part of the pensionada/os was rare. Lisa Lowe has revived Franz Fanon's call to imagine a "third term" of decolonization—that is, to conceive of a way to engage anti-imperialist politics, produce cultural national forms, and allocate resources that would neither capitulate to nativist essentialism nor reproduce the hierarchies that colonialism engendered.[54] Unfortunately, it often seems inconceivable for the pensionados to imagine such a politics. Although there is scant effort in these publications to retrieve a precolonial "Filipino" history, the students do reproduce U.S. colonial modes of power, not only in terms of class distinction, but also within the unstable processes of racialization and sexual identification. Although critical of the ways in which they themselves are racialized, both by popular and print culture and by encounters in everyday life, they also uncritically uphold the increasingly fortified color line and its demarcation in the Philippines.

Indeed, they position themselves as early twentieth-century model minorities. Thus, for instance, in an issue of the newly renamed *Philippine Review* dated July 1907, the editors C. M. Alcazar and B. Palmares admonish the Roosevelt administration for its deployment of "Negro Troops" throughout the archipelago:

> The first of Negro Soldiers sent by the United States to the Philippines proved to be a failure. Rapes, murders, stealing, etc., were reported to have occurred in the localities where they were stationed. Their presence did not prove to be an assurance of peace. Oh, they were "nice and straight" when they were "under the officer's nose", but . . . we would suggest that Uncle Sam give up the idea of negro-soldiering in the islands. Even the white soldiers, which we prefer for the islands, commit the same things the blacks are accused of, but the former's eccentricities are very few—few indeed—compared with those of the latter, and we choose the lightest burden.[55]

Despite the numerous letters by African American soldiers published in the black press empathizing with the Filipinos; despite a few black soldiers even switching sides to fight alongside the insurrectos; despite the black press's widespread anti-imperialist, antiracist linking of the "Negro Problem" with the "Filipino Problem"; and despite even the pensionados' disidentification within the metropole with the "little nigger" of the poem, these pensionados predicted and at once confirmed the "negro" soldiers' moral degeneracy rather than feeling their shared racial domination.[56] The pensionados either inherited or mimicked metroimperial fears about black men, especially in regard to the safety of Philippine women. Hence, when alluding to Kipling's poem when talking about colonial soldiers, the pensionados claimed, in reference to skin color, to "choose the lightest burden." The pensionados also referred here to the ways in which black American soldiers might have negotiated their double-consciousness before the white officers' military disciplining gaze, commenting on the black soldiers' "nice and *straight*" conduct when "under the officer's nose." The pensionado editors seem to have bought wholesale the image of the black rapist that metroimperial culture, including the American-controlled press in the Philippines, continuously portrayed.[57] While "straight" was used to connote heteronormativity in the Philippine colonial context (see chapter 2), my drawing attention here to the use of the word is not meant to posit retroactively a sly heterosexuality, in which the African American soldier is merely staging something of a minstrel show of sexual continence for the gaze of heterosexist administrators, only to elsewhere act on more illicit, same-sex desire. Rather, I mean to underscore the pensionados' presumption—their fantasy—of the incontinent, unmanly "negro" soldier defined against the erroneously imagined better-behaved—not to mention, sexually self-possessed—white colonial officers. Such metroimperial fantasy persisted even as black soldiers in the Philippines made up a much smaller fraction of the colonial U.S. military compared with white soldiers and so could be blamed less often for rape.[58] As a result, the pensionados brandished something of a model minority status vis-à-vis the sexually criminal black soldiers: the Philippine noncitizen nationals not only *acted* "nice and straight" before their educational wards and the U.S. public writ large but also actually *were* so in their everyday conduct. The Philippine students were not, to wit, the incontinent sexual predators that the hysterical white U.S. public might have thought them to be.

In their attempts to manage their own racialization, the mostly elite and largely male Philippine students set themselves apart not only from the sexually unmanageable African American soldiers but also from the still more unruly Philippine Igorots—the unconquered highland animists of Luzon, whose naked, savage image often figured metonymically as the typical "Filipino" within U.S. metroimperial fantasy. At times the pensionados decried the exploitation of Igorots, who were often imported as exotic spectacles of the U.S. empire's new colonial possessions. The pensionados even took Sutherland to task for attempting, in 1906, to round up "another band of Igorots, Moro[s], and Filipinos" for the upcoming Jamestown Exhibition. In the December 1906 issue, the editors of the *Filipino Students' Magazine* reprinted an editorial from the *Manila Times* that condemned Sutherland's "contemptible traffic in naked human flesh."[59] More often, however, the modern, cosmopolitan pensionados set themselves apart from what they regarded as the barbaric natives. The Philippine students grounded this evolutionary schema, as did the empire itself, in what Richard Drinnon has called a "metaphysics of Indian hating." One pensionado writer attempted to disabuse popularly "Wrong Ideas about Filipinos," that had already been long tainted by "scenes showing groups of naked savages, igorrotes [*sic*] eating dog meat and other such things not to be seen in the more civilized parts of the Islands." He asked, "What in the name of conscience would you call the Indian tribes in America? How would it sound to Americans if others were to represent the bulk of the American people as savage Indians?"[60] Though appearing to rail against the injustice of the practice of stealing and smuggling Igorots into the United States as part of expositions— such as the St. Louis World's Fair and various traveling "Wild East" shows—the students nevertheless seemed less concerned with the inhumane treatment by the smuggling curators than with the impression the expositions would invariably leave on the U.S. metropolitan imagination. Asterio Favis, a pensionado writing for *The Filipino*, recounted a tale of misconduct by a sub-provincial colonial administrator named William Hunt, who had duplicitously trafficked in "a band of Igorots" to display in a traveling fair.[61] After lamenting the tale of the "terrorized" and abused Filipinos, Favis collected himself "to come back to the subject," the real point of his reportage: to debunk Hunt's advertisements of "'Filipino dog-eaters,' 'Igorot savages,' 'naked people,' and other names and misnomers," images that drew from political cartoons:

> Those who saw these people [in Hunt's traveling fair] and who had no right idea and did not possess true knowledge of the real Filipino, and whose idea was only got from ridiculous, degrading, and malicious cartoons representing the Filipinos in the state of savagery and barbarism, were more than ever convinced of the incapacity of the Filipino branded by his enemies. Americans who know the Filipino people—and when we speak of the Filipino people we mean the seven million Christians who represent the Philippines politically, intellectually, socially, and religiously, and not the Negritos, Igorots, and Moros who are to us what the most savage Indians are to the civilized Americans—may . . . regard it as absurd.[62]

While Favis did at the end of the essay "protest most vigorously" against the collecting and trafficking of unsuspecting Igorots into the United States for the gratification of a popular white gaze, he did so in an effort to control the representation—"the true knowledge of"—the "real Filipino" in the popular imagination. Only through such management of self-representation could "real" Filipinos, and not the minority Negritos, Igorots, and Moros who constituted what colonial rule designated "Non-Christian Tribes," make legitimate demands for self-governance on behalf of all the islanders.

Elsewhere, to shore up these elitist distinctions, pensionada/os deployed the biopolitical apparatus of colonialism par excellence: the U.S. census of the Philippines. As Vicente Rafael has argued, the colonial census, which commenced in 1903 and finished in 1905, functioned as an exercise "in character building": "not only would the census provide the empirical grounds for shaping the direction of colonial legislation and facilitating the influx of U.S. capital investments in the archipelago; as with the colonial legislature, it would also function as a stage on which Filipinos were to be represented as well as represent themselves as subjects of a colonial order: disciplined agents actively assuming their role in their own subjugation and maturation."[63] While Rafael traces how colonial administrators mobilized "disciplined" Philippine subjects to gather the data on the native population, in the journals we see how these subjects themselves deployed the racial statistics to discipline the means of their own representation in the metropole. Commenting on the numerous advertisements for Igorot and Philippine headhunter traveling shows, the editors of the *Filipino Students' Magazine* resisted their "first impulse . . . to tear the paper[s] into thousands of pieces and let the waste basket be its final fate." A "sense of responsibility seize[d]" them, they wrote, "and good, truthful information to our readers seems to be better suited for the occasion":

> The Igorrotes are from the Philippines, it is true, but they by no means make up the bulk of the population. The last census records:

Total Population of the Philippines	7,635,426
Civilized	6,987,686
Wild	647,740
Among the wild tribes the Igorrotes make up	211,520

> Therefore by saying that the Igorrotes are savages one could not infer that the Filipinos are savages. The inference must be from a whole to a part, not from a part to a whole. [The Igorrotes'] relationship to the civilized people is similar to the relationship between the Indians and the whites in the United States. The civilized people live on the plains, the Igorrotes up on the mountains and in the wilderness. No social contact seems to exist between the two.[64]

The same statistics are repeated several issues later in the editorial "Truth versus Falsehood" (March 1907) to contest a contemporary article in the *Chicago Evening Post* that asked, "Could anything be more primitive, more savage [than a Filipino]?"[65] In these Darwinian distinctions made by the Tagalog student, where synecdochic logic is refused as a mode of legitimate knowledge ("inference must be from a whole to a part, not part to a whole"), the "civilized" Filipinos are contrasted with the overly determined Igorrotes, and the latter, in turn, are contrasted with a population that was "Wild[er]" still.

Such insistence that a minority could not represent the entirety of a population, of course, contradicted the editors' arguments against "Negro Troops in the Philippines," where the allegations against a few black soldiers rendered the entirety of that "race" culpable. What's more, the students surely would not have minded if the "civilized" population of the Philippines was the "part" that the U.S. public regarded as the "whole." The failure of the pensionada/os' reasoning here, however, lies less in its logical inconsistency than in its mimicry of colonial knowledges. Fanon cautions in *The Wretched of the Earth* (1961) that regional separatisms, or "micro-nationalisms," such as those shown in the pensionada/os' distinctions, are legacies of the territorializing strategy of colonialism. Following Fanon, Lowe argues that "a nationalist politics of racial or tribal separatism may be quite congruent with the divide-and-conquer logics of colonial domination."[66] The students' census-citing essays reanimate, thus, the results of colonialism's supposedly panoptic "logics of colonial domination" to inscribe proleptically this tribal separatism in an attempt both to stave off the synecdochic association of "Filipinos" with barbaric "Indians" and to "conquer" the pervasive image of the wilder tribes. In the end, in attempting to secure the so-called accurate representation within the metropole of "real" Filipina/o character—a kind of cultural battle that Igorots, Negritos, and Moros, because of their lack of access to social and cultural capital, could not wage—the elitist pensionados unwittingly affirmed U.S. justification for imperial intervention.

Pensionadas and Domestic Injunctions

The Pensionado Program also expressed its own divide-and-conquer-logics along gender lines by separating the pensionadas from the pensionados. As superintendent Sutherland recounts, the first group of male students fell under his charge, and the eight female students fell under that of his wife.[67] The division of the students along these gendered, heteronormative lines led, on one hand, to the cultivation of the male students for Philippine national civic life and political participation and, on the other, to training in the "domestic sciences" for the female students, who were more interested, they profess in the journals, in making the home in which future good citizens of the Philippines would be raised and after which that nation would be modeled. Although the essays discussed later in the chapter might seem overdetermined vis-à-vis a conventional division of labor according to fin-de-siècle gender paradigms, what subtends the pensionadas' petitions is an obscured heteronormative division of labor attempting to negotiate the turn-of-the-twentieth-century "New Woman's" place in the Philippines. The ethos of "manifest domesticity" evinced by the female Philippine students is perhaps meant to have been safeguarded by Mrs. Sutherland's guidance, however much or little counseling she might actually have given during their course of study.

Vexing the conventions of heterosexual femininity, the fin-de-siècle figure of the New Woman, especially as a potential model for pensionada femininity, was scrutinized in the journals, not only by male and female Philippine students, but also by white women and a Japanese American man. What echoes throughout the discursive policing of feminine propriety is the implicit yet powerful injunction to the woman on behalf of, and for the good of, Philippine nationhood: *reproduce!* In an article titled "Feminism in the Philippines," the male editors of the *Filipino Students' Magazine* discussed the "interesting point" of appropriate "feminine behavior":

> The restrictions of the past . . . are loosening rapidly and surely under the parental influence of the great American nation.
>
> The Filipino girl no longer confines herself to household duties, her education no longer limited to what the "colegios" [schools] created by religious communities could give her; now she comes to take her place by the side of her husband, also interested in the progress of her country. . . .
>
> But how the morality of the woman is to be understood . . . whether our girls should enjoy the almost masculine freedom of their sisters in this country or should they be confined and chaperoned as nowadays, is a question that encites [*sic*] a vivid interest.[68]

The pensionados' benevolent assimilation into the U.S. fold engenders benevolent sexism: the slippage in topic, from the "Filipino girl's" education to the "morality of the woman"—marked by an attendant slippage in age and, thus, reproductive capacities—denotes a particular anxiety about the duties and childbearing imperative of the pensionada. The possibility that the Filipina might "enjoy [an] almost masculine freedom"—a punitive gender-inverting rendering of the agency to pursue her own desires unchaperoned—threatens the heteronormative logic of the nation, which was imagined by many of the pensionados to be the real end for women's education, if not women's desire, after all.

The New Filipino seemed to want nothing to do with the New Woman. Pensionado politics in the metropole thus repeated "the overwhelmingly masculine construction of colonial order." As Vicente Rafael puts it, "Colonial politics was conceived of as a homosocial affair involving the tutelary bonding between white fathers and their male native-mestizo apprentices. To be coded female . . . was, in effect, to be consigned to a marginal position in the public sphere of colonial society."[69] For the pensionado editors, such marginalization involved punishment. In "The American Girl," an essay published in 1907 in the *Philippine Review*, the white feminist author Nellie L. Pritchard compared "American girls [of] fifty years ago" to contemporary "girls."[70] The former, according to Pritchard, were misguided, "brought up with the idea that the chief object of their existence was to marry and raise a family," while the latter eventually "awoke to the realization that all women do not marry" and thus "rebell[ed] against the prescribed order of things, essayed to 'make her own way.'"[71] Yet something of the old-fashioned American girl persisted "in some measure" in the contemporary Filipino girl.[72] Thus, when regarding the "new-fashioned" American girl, Pritchard wrote, "her little Filipino sister looks at her dubiously. Fain would she, to acquire knowledge, be independent; but the 'free and easy' manner of the American girl, her 'compania' with her fellow-students of the opposite sex, so different from her own almost cloistered condition, is a little bewildering. She does not understand it, is a little shocked." The nun-like Filipina's "shock" at changing gender conventions in the metropole was expressed elsewhere by scandalized women from the Philippines who wrote to the male editors of the *Philippine Review*, chastising their fellow pensionada Genoveva Llamas for having aspired to personal "independence." In defensive response to her colleagues' criticism, Llamas later retracted, writing, "You must not think that as we are in America we are adopting that excessive freedom of the young girls in the country."[73] Thus, while the pensionados might write about Philippine national independence, in defiance of colonial administrators, they still, alongside Philippine women, disciplined the pensionadas for claiming "independence" and "freedom." Philippine self-sovereignty, as they imagined it, seemed incompatible with Philippine women's self-sovereignty.

This resistance to liberal feminism was consistently attached to retroactive inventions of a Philippine national identity defined against the far too modern metropole. In a speech before a "ladies' society" in Maine—the speech would later appear in print in October 1906—J. P. Katigbak set out to educate his audiences about "The Filipino Woman." As the essentialist title already suggests, the speech professed to profile "one of the most picturesque types of women in the Far East."[74] After describing the Philippine woman's convention of leaving the house only when accompanied by chaperones and praising her innate "artistic proclivities," Katigbak—who, as we saw earlier, preached about proper sewage disposal—wrote, "The ethics of the Filipinos . . . are based on a certa[i]n definite principle, namely to bring up the girl in such a way as to make of her later a good wife and a good mother. . . . To be a good mother is the ideal of the Filipino woman. . . . The result of such procedure is most gratifying. To it is to be attributed the increase of our population, the healthy growth of our families, the perfect harmony between wives and husbands and the happiness of the home."[75] Echoing the masculinist ethos of so many nationalist movements, Katigbak's "Filipino woman" here acts as—is "brought up" to be—a good mother not just to an individual but to an entire population. This sentiment was echoed in the *Filipino Students' Magazine* by William Ju Sabro Iwami, a Japanese American student whose essay pit the "gross method [of] revolt"—performed by early turn-of-the-century suffragists and divorced women, for example—against the "delicate" ways of "Japanese women":

> Our women in Japan rank morally high. To Japanese women the idea of divorce is strange. The Japanese woman . . . stands as a woman simple and pure, with absolute delicacy of breeding, and innate refinement of manner. She never seeks for business or official career in offices, but leads good motherhood. She never insists upon woman's suffrage, law-giving, or vote-rolls, but respects her husband as a head of the family and intrusts [sic] to him the whole of business and politics. . . . Change, of course, must come toward improvement, but not through a gross method such as revolt, by which American woman gained her social standing as the equal of man, even above the man, at the sacrifice of sweetness of disposition and delicacy of taste. It is too strenuous for a daughter of Japan.[76]

Iwami's critique of liberal feminist "revolt" in the United States consists of lamenting the "American woman['s]" sacrifice of decent motherhood for more dubious prospects. Any desire expressed by the Japanese woman outside the realm of her household would mark her as "almost masculine" and certainly not capable of "lead[ing] good motherhood." The appearance of Iwami's essay in the male-edited journal is telling. Despite the pensionados' distaste for being mistaken for Japanese in the streets because of their physiognomically "Oriental" features,[77] and despite the pensionados' "dread" of a Japanese imperialist "supremacy over the Philippines,"[78] here they seem to have identified with Iwami in his rebuking of the "revol[utionary]," white "New Woman" and his condescending praise of the submissive, old-fashioned, "Oriental" woman. The male Philippine students' printing of Iwami's contrast of these figures helped to remind the pensionadas of their duty to the domestic and moral space of the nation. The pensionados' capitulation to benevolent assimilation involved a cross-racial solidarity that deployed benevolent sexism.

But what did the pensionadas themselves imagine as "domestic" in these journals? "Nature has destined the woman to be the governess of the house," advised Llamas, who after retracting her previous promotion of women's "independence," was given the reins to co-edit the special "Ladies' Number" issue of the *Philippine Review* in December 1907. "Two inseparable things (cooking and cleaning) are needed," she wrote in an article titled "Domestic Sciences," "followed by repairing, renewing, serving, and nursing. In order to perform these industries properly, a knowledge of the chemistry of foods and of cleaning processes . . . is required. . . . Hygiene and general sanitation go hand in hand with both."[79] Toward the end of her article, Llamas expressed outrage over the failure of Filipina child rearing. "How many people died in our community because of ignorance and lack of care of their own people," she asked. "How many helpless infants perished because of the improper raising of their ignorant mothers[?]"[80] In a similar essay titled "From Our Girls," published a year earlier in the more socially conservative *The Filipino*, N. M. Lisos, another pensionada, urged her "beloved sisters in the Philippines" to "obtain a higher education" but cautioned them not to "forget that it is woman's duty . . . to look after the household affairs, that is, she must take heed that the house is . . . equipped with all sanitary and hygienic appliances and conveniences."[81] Such attention to the dangers of filth—or, rather, the transcendence of filth through "sanitary and hygienic appliances"—echoes not just the racializing discourse of U.S. colonialism's tropical medicine, as Anderson has traced, but also the discoures of Llamas's and Lisos's male counterparts throughout the journals. As Amy Kaplan has famously argued, the sphere of domesticity among white women in nineteenth-century U.S. culture remained intertwined with the imperialist ideology of Manifest Destiny.[82] The admonition and counsel offered by the female colonial students here on the necessity of learning the empire's "domestic sciences" marks the naturalization and internalization of this inseparability, of "manifest domesticity," by colonial subjects. Philippine women's juxtapolitical participation in projected national *bildung*—a participation that, like national sovereignty itself, must in fact always be projected, oriented toward futurity—necessitates the affective and material investment in the "modernizing" technologies that were developed to mark racial distinction in the archipelago in the first place.

The pensionadas' education in the "industry" of nursing, moreover, presumes, with the hope of ensuring, their heterosexual reproductive "destiny" in the nation. Lisos made this performative enactment of normative gender and sexuality according to the socially sanctioned codes of the Philippine nationhood quite explicit: "the woman, in her home, generally is the governess of the children. The children are the future of a nation. Hence, poorly trained children mean a poor future for the nation."[83] In this succinct proof of the need for education for Philippine women, Lisos explicitly endorsed a gendered division of labor and enforced the heteronormative reproduction of both bodies and national culture. This injunction to hetero-erotic reproduction for the nation has a history. In her provocative reading of the U.S. Naturalization Act of 1790, which limited the right to naturalized citizenship to free white people of "good moral character"—a phrase repeated in the Pensionado Act of 1903—Siobhan Somerville has argued that "the seemingly abstract citizen invoked is actually one who is also delineated through his/her (sexually) reproductive capacity, a capacity that, like the racial prerequisite, curiously re-embodies this seemingly abstract national subject."[84] The right to U.S. citizenry is offered only to the white, hetero-erotically reproductive applicant. Although these Philippine students, like all of the other immigrant subjects of U.S. empire, could not become its naturalized citizens at the time, they nonetheless had to demonstrate their proper subjecthood within metropolitan space, according to long-standing, naturalized standardizations of the abstract good citizen. Thus, even with no prospect of gaining U.S. citizenship, the pensionadas within the space of the metropole nevertheless had to embody—indeed, were compulsorily *educated* in—a good citizen's appropriate gender inscription by way of correct, heteronormative citizen formation. Indeed, one's "sexually reproductive capacity" became a criterion for Philippine national legitimacy. Like the seemingly portable accouterment of hygiene, this compulsorily heterosexual ideology, clad in progressivist rhetoric of the New Woman, was expected to be transported from the empire's metropole to its archipelago as an apparatus of the "social engineering" of the Philippines.[85]

The attention given to personal and public "hygiene" by the female students within the context of nation-building was significant: the young pensionadas' insistence that Filipinas maintain "hygiene and general sanitation" at home further destabilized the boundaries between the private and the public, between the domestic and the foreign. To the extent that the pensionados' study of sanitation and waste management participated in a racializing discourse of germs that would be imported "back" into the Philippines, as seen earlier, the pensionadas' duty to maintain standards of hygiene and good housekeeping would similarly inscribe, and traffic in, the same poetics of racial pollution. Yet the pensionadas' practice of manifest domesticity did not merely supplement their male counterparts' deployment of colonial logic; it enacted the same *particularly in the service of their reproductive destiny*. In urging other Philippine "ladies" to maintain standards of personal and public hygiene and sanitation, they also marked the standards of proper childbearing and child raising—of national social welfare. What Foucault identifies as the theory of "degenerescence," the late nineteenth-century merging of the biomedical and sexological discourses around perversions with the emergent programs of eugenics, operates here. The theory of degenerescence "explained how a heredity that was burdened with various maladies . . . ended by producing a sexual pervert . . . , [and] it went on to explain how a sexual perversion resulted in the depletion of one's line of descent."[86] As Hubert Dreyfus and Paul Rabinow succinctly have rephrased Foucault's observation, "Appeals to the very fate of the race and of the nation seemed to turn in large part on its sexual practices."[87] The pensionados' and pensionadas' anxiety about "primitive" modes of waste disposal and the maintenance of hygiene thus converged with their concern with the representation of "real" Filipinos within the space of the metropole. Both can be encroached on and polluted by some abject, perverse, foreign agents, be they germs and disease, barbarically hypersexual Igorots and Moros, sexually incontinent African Americans, or even unhygienic—and thus bad—mothers. The pensionados, tasked with imagining the future of a healthy and independent Philippines first needed to sanitize their space.

"Certain Peculiar Temptations"

Indeed, the pensionados seemed to dream of a Philippine nationhood free of "sexual perverts." Their bourgeois nationalist repetition of the racialized structures of colonial hegemony inflected, and was shaped by, emergent and unstable *sexual* categorizations within the colonial metropole. The Philippine students' efforts at self-racialization in the journals, as I have been arguing, involved their own tactics of playing it "nice and straight," in contrast to the seemingly transparent—in fact, overdetermined—racial dissipation of Igorots, Negritos, Moros, African American soldiers, and American Indians. Moreover, the students' management of what we might understand as their *sexual* identities, behavior, and practices was similarly structured against the same foreign bodies. Indeed, the pensionados' nationalist repetition of the logics of racial hegemony was braced by the constant rearticulation of the terms of their colonial heterosexuality and normative gender propriety, both of which had to be characterized by somatic and psychic restraint.

The serial column "United States Queries" in the *Filipino Students' Magazine*, assembled and written collectively by the pensionados under the name PGS, for Philippine Government Students, purported to list the questions asked most frequently of Philippine students in the U.S. metropole. It revealed similar panoptic tactics to those used on the Philippine natives across the Pacific. Here, however, the Filipino self-staging that Rafael locates in the U.S. colonial state's census projects surfaces only obliquely in the seemingly unadorned rearticulation of the questions themselves:

"How do you eat fish?"

"Do you like our girls?"

"How do you find the climate?" . . . [sic]

"Are you going back to the Philippines?" . . .

"What do your girls, [sic] do?"

"Are they pretty, too?"

"Would you rather marry an American girl or your own?" . . .

"Do you have schools up there?"

"How do your girls dress?"

"What are your girls' favorite colors?"

"Are they older than you?" . . .

"Do they marry young up there?"

"Are you married[?]"

"I suppose you feel lonesome once in a while?"

"How many girls have you?"

"How long does it take to go from here to the Philippines?"

"How much does it cost to go to the Philippines?"

"Would your sister answer if I write to her?"

"Give me her address."

Et cetera, et cetera.[88]

As seen from this list of "queries," in which the interrogator and the interpellated seem to be men, the face-to-face questions enact what Foucault calls a "proximity that serves as surveillance procedures."[89] Among the more innocuous queries concerned with the weather in the Philippines, or among the provincial and bizarre queries presuming familial relations with the notorious Philippine insurrecto Emilio Aguinaldo, the questions excerpted here function as technologies of racial-sexual surveillance of the pensionados' relationships with their sisters, their marriage practices with their "girls," their desire for "our [white] girls," the availability of "their [Filipina] girls." Indeed, such questions prefigure those in the U.S. Public Health Service's *Manual for the Mental Examinations of Aliens* (1918), which not only tested the general intelligence of would-be immigrants into the United States but posed questions about their intimate lives, such as, "Are you married? Do you want to marry? Do you care for the opposite sex? Have you acquaintances of the opposite sex? Are you in love? Have you had any love affairs?"[90] The "United States Queries" column, like the state's imminent monitoring practices, incorporated surveillance and governance of social intimacy. The queries to the students braced the arrangement of proper homosocial relationality, which ensured, via the triangulation made possible by the presumed female object of desire—or, at least, via the trope of "marriage"—an appropriate amount of buffering distance in the "proximity." Thus, the pensionados' very desire—a presumed heterosexual one—was monitored by the same heteronormative "queries" that, at first blush, might have appeared only to seek to make sense of racial difference in the metroimperial space.

The collective PGS's point in repeating these social interrogations was to underscore the multiple, incessant, and even banal ways in which the pensionados were racialized under the paranoid, metroimperial gaze. The punchline, "Et cetera, et cetera," finishing each of these columns attests to the pensionados' increasing annoyance with the FAQs and a smirking awareness of their absurdity. The paratactic form rends the queries from their immediate social context: the very act of listing the questions abstracts them from their origins of inquiry, thereby rendering them insipid stereotypes, exchangeable and inert metonymies of racialization. The editors' arrangement of the queries, in other words, attempts to flout and destabilize the calculated will-to-knowledge thrust behind them, flattening out and diffusing the relays of biopower supporting, and supported by, the metroimperial gaze.

Yet as should be unsurprising by now, the pensionados also constantly policed one another through the lens of that gaze. In moments of such policing, we see the rare recognition of unbecoming intimacies. In the apocalyptically titled essay "The Dangers of College Life," which appeared in the December 1906 issue of *The Filipino*, the pensionado Gervasio Santos warned his fellow students against the profligacy that threatened the relations of the male college student. Note the shady characters:

> Perhaps there are no stronger temptations for a young man to overcome than those that surround him during his college life, when he is away from his parents, when he has free disposal of the money he gets from home, and when comrades of all sorts can hang about him.
>
> The very day he enters college, he takes a step into an entirely different phase of life. A strong will power, a strong and firm character, a power to resist temptations, sound moral principles, *self-possession, and full control of himself are requisites to make his college life a success....*
>
> There is no place in the world where higher ideals are set before young men ... but it is also true that in college there are *certain peculiar temptations.* Whenever hundreds of thousands of young men are together ... vice is almost thrown at them. In a modern college, moreover, a student has much more freedom as to his time than at home or at school.

Temptations of pleasure, or other, are so influential that they may prevent him from seeing the relation between industry now and success in later life.

A student who would succeed in college must fight persistently all temptations that naturally come along his way. There are [sic] what we may call *bad associations* which cause, perhaps, the *greatest harm among the evils in college. Once in company of this kind, a young student is, very likely, to be like his associate. We should help him away from this sort of fellow as much as possible.*

Another danger that may lead to vice and misery during college life, is the awful loneliness of a boy far from home. The boy who is used to girls at home, and who knows in his new surrounding no such girls as he knew at home . . . , is only too likely to scrape an easy acquaintance with a kind of girls who have but little education and no refinement.[91]

Dangers, indeed. College life in the metropole here sounds a lot like colonial barracks life in the Philippines (see chapters 1 and 2). Of the many "temptations" the Philippine male college student might face—on his own in the metropole for the first time and left to his own devices with a bit of spending money— I am most interested in the unqualified "bad associations" Santos warns against here. The caution to the "young student" against keeping the "company" of "this sort of fellow" seems the most ominous warning—indeed, the fellow poses nothing less than the "greatest harm among the evils in college"—even as, if not precisely because, it is the most vague. Just what kind of "certain peculiar . . . [t]emptations of pleasure, or other" this "bad association" might offer to the "lonel[y]" student—or, for that matter, just how "*peculiar*" those temptations might be—remains unsaid. Significantly, the "bad associations" are rhetorically juxtaposed with—and set in contradistinction to—the "easy acquaintance" of unfamiliar, poorly educated, and unrefined *girls*. Santos's particularly elitist and misogynist judgment notwithstanding, that the lurking "bad associations" are defined against the objects of immoral heterosexuality intimates that the former "sort of fellow" might also "lead to vice."

I am suggesting that the phobic typology around this evil and harmful "sort of fellow," this "bad association," sketches the outline of a figure that would only decades later become more popularly known as the "homosexual" (perhaps even a "wolf" preying on susceptible young Philippine student "punks").[92] It is impossible to tell whether the pensionados ever participated in same-sex sexual acts or intimacies with other men or among themselves in the metropole because explicit admissions of such intimacies seem not to exist in the archives; nor have I discovered any vice reports or trial notes involving pensionados. But as Ann Stoler has argued in her discussion of another colonial context, finding evidence of "actual" sexual deviance neither resolves nor dispels our uncertainties: "the question is not whether these were real dangers. . . . The task is rather to identify the regimes of truth that underwrote such a political discourse and a politics that made a racially coded notion of who could be intimate with whom—and in what way—a primary concern in colonial policy."[93] What we gather here in Santos's "racially coded notion of who could be intimate with whom—and in what way," in other words, is evidence not that the pensionados participated in same-sex intimacies but, rather, that such "evil" was imagined to be a "temptation" among the pensionado population in the metropole. Santos issues his own metroimperial policy.

Santos implicitly introduces a racial differentiation within turn-of-the-twentieth-century practices of same-sex sociability. Nayan Shah has discussed a similar context of early twentieth-century male migrants and their "dangerous encounters" and intimacies in public places: "male migrant sociability was entangled into the culture and mobility of the streets. The geography of the rapidly urbanizing town and city provided the settings and spaces for casual, fortuitous, and dangerous encounters between men and boys of different ethnicities, classes, and ages. Migrant males encountered each other on the streets, alleys, parks, at the train and stage depots and other public spaces where men congregated."[94] Urban public spaces became sites where men could engage, however precariously, in erotic intimacies that were otherwise relegated to (and protected by the notion of) the private. Although Shah notes a correlation between these early twentieth-century encounters and the contemporary event of gay cruising, he criticizes how some critical discussions of cruising do not attend to racialized differentiations that might vex the "pleasure of belonging in a sexual world" that cruising provides—differentiations that, I suggest, result precisely from the forms of submission such sexual contact would demand and that might even produce different modes of enjoyment altogether. Santos's warning does seem to take these differential factors into consideration as he attempts to warn his fellow pensionados—the racialized objects and *subjects* of metroimperial surveillance—of what is at stake ("the greatest harm") should they be caught with such a nefarious figure: "a young student is, very likely, to be like his associate." To participate in such an illicit association, according to Santos, entails more than "belonging in a sexual world."[95] It means expulsion from the dream of participating in metroimperial civic life. Worse still, Santos implies, it would lead to disfranchisement from an institution for which the industry of "college life" and metropolitan education are merely means: Philippine nationhood. The pensionado's expressed lack of "self-possession" or "full control of himself" within the metropole threatens not only to signify but also to forestall the Philippine nation's prospects for self-possession.

Given the metroimperial social world's quotidian and, as the PGS's column demonstrates, tiresome policing of Philippine students and attempts to identify their desires and social relations, representations of "certain peculiar" associations took oblique forms. Here, I turn to Andres Aguilar's narrative, "A Vision That Was Not Altogether a Vision," published in the inaugural issue of *The Filipino* (January 1906), as such an instance.[96] Aguilar's plot centers on the certain peculiar "friendship" between two men—a white U.S. army sergeant, Charles Turling, and a pensionado narrator, perhaps Aguilar himself. "A Vision" is divided into four diegetic parts: an introduction and three numbered movements. In the introduction, Aguilar's narrator relates how the milieu he and his "companion," Turling, find themselves in prompts a story from Turling. Turling's short, bizarre tale then co-opts the rest of Aguilar's narrative space, beginning with an interracial romance and ending in a popular fantasmatic scene of the U.S. imperial army's fending off a nighttime attack by insurrectos.[97] In part 1, Sergeant Charles Turling, stationed in the Philippines during the war in 1900, falls in love with Francisca, the "attractive" daughter of a local storeowner. Her "pretty face, dark as that of a native of the tropical country, but with a smooth skin and a small mouth," and her returned love "[drives] away [his] homesickness." In part 2, after attending a Christmas eve dance at the house of Francisca's father, Turling walks back to his quarters, falls asleep, and has a "tender dream" of Francisca, who, "drawing his face close, kisse[s] him passionately." In part 3, Turling wakes up abruptly to a "burning kiss," which turns out to be not from his "sweetheart" but from "his faithful watch-dog Yankee." His waking comes "not a moment too soon," Turling narrates; it is just in time to fend off an attack on the camp by "Aguinaldo's scouts." The story concludes with a description of how Turling's subconscious and dutiful sidekick aided his regiment: "the insurgents were driven back, and the dream of Francisca and the good dog Yankee had conspired to save the camp."

Because we never return to Aguilar's introductory framing of the story, we are left to wonder what to make of Turling's somewhat peculiar story and why Aguilar would recount it in the first place. Following Turling's interpretive lead, we might consider his dream. His interpretation suggests that he conjured the dream's hetero-erotic content to prolong his sleep, which the outside stimulus of the dog's cautionary kisses threatened to cut short. Yankee's kisses, though folded into the dream as hetero-erotic passion, soon become so insistent and irritating that Turling is compelled to wake up, thereby losing the object of his fantasy, the "vision" of his dream, Francisca. In this reading prompted by Turling, then, the titular "vision that was not altogether a vision" refers directly to the dream kiss from Francisca, which turns out not to be a dream kiss but, in fact, a very "real" kiss from his dog.

As Slavoj Žižek might put it, however, when it comes to reading dreams, "the logic is quite different."[98] In his reading of Freud's account of the father who in his guilt has nightmares about his burning child, Žižek, following Jacques Lacan, offers another way to read the relation between the external stimulation and the dream content:

> The subject does not awake himself when the external irritation becomes too strong; the logic is quite different. First he constructs a dream, a story which enables him to prolong his sleep, to avoid awakening into reality. But the thing he encounters in his dream, the reality of his desire . . . is more terrifying than so-called reality itself, and that is why he awakens: to escape the Real of his desire, which announces itself in the terrifying dream. He escapes into so-called reality to be able to continue to sleep, to maintain his blindness, to elude awakening into the real of his desire.[99]

Žižek's inverted reading of the dream and the external irritation accords with how I have understood fantasy through this book: the state of awakedness (or "so-called reality") in this case is the space of fantasy, which enables the avoidance of, a blind spot around, a scenario that is far too traumatic. Perhaps Sergeant Turling wakes up not because of Yankee's warning kisses but because he can no longer bear, and so must escape from, the terrifying "reality of his desire," the impossible, unassimilable object of his fantasy made manifest in his dream. In such an interpretation, then, the terrifying desire, the object he cannot bear, is Francisca's tellingly (and, apropos of Freud's story, uncanny) "burning" kiss. Indeed, such an interpretation would locate a rare instance of transgressive desire in this archive: what Turling really wants, what really "maintain[s] his blindness" from the awful image he encounters in his hetero-romantic dream of Francisca, is not normatively "pleasur[able]" (Francisca's kiss) but, rather, something else ("or other"). He desires, perhaps, the homosocial and potentially homoerotic confines of his barracks, the potential penetration and "fierce assault" of the camp by Aguinaldo's scouts, or maybe even a face-to-face confrontation with the fabled Emilio Aguinaldo, who was often dandified or effeminized in popular culture (see chapter 3).

While this interpretation of Turling's dream extracts a fantasy of nonnormative, same-sex intimacy from the archive, it is clearly asinine. Instead of following Turling's misdirection, then, I would suggest stepping back to review the formal features of Aguilar's story. Indeed, I would suggest that the story is not about Turling's desire at all but, rather, about the Philippine pensionado narrator's. While Turling's tale is set in 1900, "A Vision That Was Not Altogether a Vision" opens in 1903, after the official end of the Philippine-American War and thus during the early days of U.S. colonial occupation:

> It was in the year 1903 that I gained the friendship of a young American, who was a sergeant in the U.S. Army in the Philippines at the time, and he told me this true story. Charles Turling, which was his name, and I, were walking one day in the old Walled City of Manila. The sun was pouring mercilessly down upon those stone streets, the burning pavements sent it up again, the walls reflected it, and no breeze found its way in to tell of cooler things. My companion observed that it seemed the delirium of a lunatic even to imagine the jingling of sleigh-bells, or a December east-wind off New York Bay.
>
> As we left the Walled City and walked toward the Luneta, along the Malecon drive, we found a breeze that hinted of a pleasanter land.
>
> The Luneta is the most charming and popular place in the Philippines, with its spacious and picturesque rectangular ground and its rows of seats in the form of a half-moon, which in Spanish is *luneta*, its two band-strands in the center and the very high flagpole, with the red, white, and blue banner of Uncle Sam.
>
> We sat down near the beach, facing Manila Bay, which forms one side of the Luneta, and while the beautiful strains of Englemann's "The Melody of Love," played by the splendid Philippine Constabulary Band, were wafted across the sea, my companion started his narration.[100]

While Turling only sparsely describes the details of his courtship with Francisca, Aguilar's narrator offers quite a bit of detail in recounting this short-lived moment with his "companion" Turling, whom he refers to later, in his third-person, internally focalized narration of Turling's story, as "Sergeant Carlos." Turling and Aguilar "escape" from the claustrophobic space of the Intramuros ("Walled City of Manila") and into the more "charming" and, indeed, more romantic Luneta, whose breeze "hint[s]," *for them both* (or so Aguilar imagines) "of a pleasanter land"—perhaps even a land to pursue "certain peculiar temptations." Remarkably, even as Aguilar conceives of Luneta as a utopian but clearly U.S. *colonial* space, it is still a space, perhaps, slightly beyond the panoptic gaze (embodied by the description of the inescapable "burning" sun) that monitors the "old Walled city." The two men manage (conjuring what might be considered a quintessential, even cliché, romantic diversion) to take a long walk on the beach, while a soundtrack—"the beautiful strains of Englemann's 'The Melody of Love'"—"wafted across the sea."

It is at this moment of intimacy, of perceived mutuality, that Turling begins his story—his daydream—and, more significant, that Aguilar's narrator interrupts his own. Žižek's description of awakening from the dream, leading us astray earlier, is useful here: "[Aguilar's narrator] escapes into so-called reality to be able to continue to sleep, to maintain his blindness, to elude awakening into the real of his desire." A facile interpretation might suggest that the narrator defers to—"escapes into"—Turling's proper and hetero-erotic plot to escape the "terrifying" nature of his homoerotic desire. That is, in an attempt to deflect the unassimilable desire expressed in his own story of intimacy, Aguilar's narrator mobilizes Turling's story of colonial hetero-romance to "maintain his blindness" to the more dangerous temptation. Yet I would offer a different reading: the "real" of the narrator's desire, the unbearable object of his fantasy, is *not* his "friendship" with Sergeant Carlos—this friendship is, in fact, unmistakably pleasurable. Rather, what is unbearable is the painful recognition that the "charming" day they spend together at the Luneta is *only a recollection*, perhaps one to which Turling, in the present day, might not cling with such fondness, if he even remembers it at all. The "vision that was not altogether a vision" in this sense corresponds to the narrator's loving reminiscence, which turns out not to be one he wishes to dwell on in the end. The "so-called reality," then, that he "escapes into" is the heteronormative love story that Turling does recall so lovingly. In something of a masochistic gesture, Aguilar must "maintain his blindness" *in* Turling's narration, while the narrator's pleasure in homosocial intimacy (save the persistence of his endearing nickname "Sergeant Carlos") all but disappears, to keep from awakening into the "real of his desire": the aching, "deliri[ous]," even "lunatic" memory of his lost "friendship" in Luneta, a "companionship" that in a "pleasanter" land could have been much more.[101]

The fact that it is not clear whether "A Vision That Was Not Altogether a Vision" is a memoir or fiction makes this story—which seems to be about one thing (Turling's romance with his Philippine "sweetheart" Francisca) but is in fact about something else altogether (the Philippine narrator's fleeting moment of mutual intimacy with Sergeant Carlos)—more poignant than it might seem at first blush. I suspect Aguilar's story is at least part memoir: there was a historical figure named Charles H. Thurling, who, like Aguilar's character, was from New York City and served as a sergeant in the U.S. military during the Philippine-American War.[102] Moreover, given the publication date of "A Vision," Aguilar might have written his own "true story," rather sadly, during Christmastime, while in New York, where he was studying through the Pensionado Program and where Turling's (the character's) recollection of home were set. It is even possible that the holiday season's "jingling of sleigh-bells, or a December east-wind off New York Bay" conjured for Aguilar that day he spent with his American friend on the Luneta. Aguilar's writing around Christmastime from New York—a "pleasanter land," where one would have found more opportunity for clandestine erotic intimacies between men and, indeed, the place to which Thurling returned after his tour in the Philippines—perhaps drew him to escape into his reverie of Sergeant Carlos, although the reverie turned out to be not altogether just that.

The toggling back and forth in "A Vision That Was Altogether Not a Vision" between "real" and "imagined" space, between memory and prescience, between memoir and fiction, between "heterosexual" and same-sex intimacy, between the subject and object of desire, between the fantasized and the horrifying—this seemingly unstable thematic and diegetic shifting is nonetheless tethered to the space of U.S. empire, whether in the metropole or in the archipelago. The setting that Aguilar and Turling escape into, away from the burning heat of Manila and the Spanish colonial legacy with which its modernity is imprinted, and the metropolitan "pleasanter land" it evokes, remains an imperially occupied space with "the very high flagpole, with the red, white, and blue banner of Uncle Sam." The unmistakable (and banally phallic) marker of U.S. imperial sovereignty casts its shadow, *ex propio vigore*, over this recollected vision of obscured romantic friendship. On one hand, then, perhaps Aguilar cannot yet envision a space unstamped by imperialism and so cannot yet articulate an anticolonial critique of the various "proximit[ies] that serve . . . as surveillance procedures," proximities that colonial occupation itself has made possible. On the other, Aguilar seems to imagine a kind of "cruising utopia," some pleasanter space at a future moment that might give men the opportunity to give way to certain peculiar temptations that empire, and its benevolent project of modernization, might offer.[103] (By the 1970s, postcolonial Luneta would in fact become famous as a gay cruising spot.) Of course, these are not mutually exclusive readings. The first implies surrender to permanent colonization; the second, assimilation into it. That Aguilar's story also features one side plot concerning Turling's defeat of Aguinaldo in battle and another concerning a racialized hetero-erotic courtship involving a white male soldier and native Filipina conducted with impunity attests to the extent to which the violence of imperial war, and the uneven gender-sexual relations that result from it, simultaneously haunt and become seemingly incidental to Aguilar's fantasy of male-male intimacy. The promise of utopia follows the flag. What Aguilar's story demonstrates is how the pensionado, as a colonial subject within the metropole—where racial-sexual-gender surveillance, including that conducted by fellow pensionados, burns from all sides—both imagines same-sex intimacy and must simultaneously regulate its expression not only for the sake of demonstrating his own "good moral character" but also for the sake of fending off a melancholic "delirium." This, in short, is another kind of sanitizing altogether.

Imperium in Memoriam

I return by way of conclusion to Pacifico Laygo's short story "On the Battle-field," which opens this chapter and might now, given the constant polic-ing and *self*-policing of the pensionadas/os within the metropole, seem all the more exceptional within this pensionado/o archive. I suggested earlier that the story about the dying white soldier and dying anticolonial insurrecto offers rec-onciliation around racial, imperial violence in the form of same-sex intimacy. I want to examine here how such intimacy becomes absorbed by the narration into grander discourses of race, empire, and nation. The tension between the gritty modes of intimacy of the scene (recall the exchange of warm canteen water, the "dear embrace," the contiguous mortal wounds) and the increas-ing immateriality of the soldiers' individual subjectivities (played out, on one hand, by the shifts in narrative focalization from that of the Yankee soldier to that of the Filipino insurrecto to that of their union and, on the other, by the narrative slippage from their "struggle" to that of the two countries at war) is preserved at the end of the story:

> On the evening of the same day a party of natives who were burying the killed and carrying off the wounded, found the corpses of the two men, just exactly in the same place where they had met and breathed their last. They found the corpses embracing each other, with the empty canteen lying between them. A tint of satisfaction and friendship glorified their rigid fea-tures. And the men understood what it meant.
>
> A grave was dug for the soldiers. And the empty canteen accompanied them in their final resting place. . . . The story of how the corpses were found after the battle has been told and retold among those plain and simple country folk. . . .
>
> People of Payapa, and occasional visitors to the place, stop by that mound whenever they pass. . . . May their example wipe out forever the ill feelings and prejudices between the Americans and Filipinos, which shaped their minds during that wicked war. Gallant enemies they have been! What power on earth would keep the two races from being sincere friends after that struggle?[104]

The intimate scene is clearly fantasmatic, romantic: the "sincere friends" die in each other's arms. While the soldiers' private, ecstatic embrace ("[a] tint of satisfaction and friendship glorified their rigid features") becomes a public site of shared signs among the male villagers—"And the men understood what it meant"—it proves a moment of critical ambiguity for us. On one hand, this phrase posits the scene as a picture of possible resolution between the "two races," of the homosocial recognition of the hostile other in the face of war. On the other, it allows for the possibility of reading the intimate embrace not as exceptional during wartime but as a normal, if occasional, affair, suggesting that such same-sex intimacy might even have been expected—already "understood"—by the local "natives." Given the local people's elegy for the soldiers ("May the example of those boys who died for their country . . . help to bring the two races to a better understanding"), the former, heteronormative reading seems the intended one, though the latter cannot be easily discounted. That the repositioning of the drained canteen, the spent vessel, is so conspicuous—first it is found between the "two boys," then it is buried with them in their shared grave—attests to this alternative "underst[anding]."

The symbolic value of the canteen for both the villagers and the narrator is significant. In 1913, the colonial administrator Dean Worcester recalled that, when he first witnessed the carnage of war in Manila in 1899, he had noted that "every wounded Insurgent whom we found had a United States canteen of water at his side, obviously left by some kindly American soldiers."[105] Before Worcester's fantasy of colonial kindliness, however, it turns out that the trope of the shared canteen had been a symbol within U.S. military culture of male-male intimacy for several decades—one that dated back at least to the U.S. Civil War. In fact, the Civil War-era male-bonding poem "We've Drank from the Same Canteen," which was attributed to Private Miles O'Reilly and appeared in print several times at the end of the nineteenth century, shows just how integral this trope is to soldiers' "manly love."[106] Not only does the poem (whose title is also the refrain that ends each stanza) begin by claiming that the "bond" forged by a shared kiss between "the girl and the boy" pales to that forged by two men who have shared a canteen, but it also ends on the battlefield, where the two men have previously "shared [their] blankets": "when I wounded lay on the outer slope,/With my blood flowing fast,/Oh, then I remember you crawled to my side,/And, bleeding so fast it seemed both must have died,/We drank from the same canteen." That Laygo's story so closely echoes this sentimental picture of soldierly intimacy, of the "manly love of comrades," may be accidental, but it is not incidental: both posit the canteen as a memento of unparalleled physical closeness of soldiers, of an intense intimacy between men just before death.

By fantasizing about a cross-racial romantic friendship in the face of colonial violence, here, Laygo projects a scene of mutuality, of recognition. Indeed, the very appearance of the canteen attests to how Laygo shares in U.S. military culture's tropological convention. While the canteen was not so much symbolic of same-sex intimacy as representative of exceptional imperial benevolence for Worcester, Laygo's short story blends these two referents. By sharing in the metaphor of the canteen, "On the Battlefield" not only represents reconciliation across racial, colonial, and enemy lines; in its benediction, it makes an appeal for it. To the extent, then, that Laygo buries the intimacy of the scene, he buries it in a shallow grave, "in a way left to lie fallow."[107] And it is precisely the possibility of that intimacy's eventual resurfacing that fuels Laygo's naïve fantasy that such "sincere friendship" might outlive the racial-sexual management that, as I have been arguing in these pages, is integral to empire itself.

While "The Dangers of College Life," "A Vision That Was Not Altogether a Vision," and "On the Battlefield" all gestured, in very different fashions, to same-sex male intimacies, they did so, in accordance with the overall projects of the *Filipino Students' Magazine* and *The Filipino*, in the interest of forwarding a politics of recognition, inclusion, and *assimilation*, as opposed to "a transformative one, of changing the demography of the hegemonic group rather than reconfiguring the coordinates of power."[108] As cross-racial, same-sex sexual associations and intimate friendships were warned against, longed for, or memorialized, such expressions must be regarded within the pensionados' nationalist discourse that both affirmed U.S. metroimperial racial hierarchies and punished Philippine women for not committing at all times to a hetero-reproductive, domestic futurity. In this sense, it is possible that Aguilar and Laygo regarded the same-sex male intimacies imagined in their stories not as antithetical to the journals' project of racialized respectability within the metropole—a project marked by gender-sexual normative constraints—but as permissible. Indeed, precisely because of the journals' continual proofs of racial, sexual, and gendered distinction and restraint, not to mention the anticolonial insurrectos' victory over the U.S. troops in Laygo's story, such fantasies of same-sex intimacy, which proleptically envision a cross-racial, masculinist mutuality in some vague future, did not detract from the claims to Philippine "self-possession"—bodily and national—but, in these pensionados' minds, gave evidence for them.

Despite the Philippine students' aspirations to bourgeois respectability (if not to the ascendancy of hetero-patriarchal whiteness within the metropole), many were met with the kind of distrust at which Santos hints in "The Dangers of College Life" when they returned to the Philippines.[109] In "The First

Pensionados" (1950), her master's thesis for the University of the Philippines, Filipina Celia Bocobo Olivar documents how their "countrymen" regarded the members of this group with a certain peculiar suspicion: "the Filipino Pensionados of course brought back with them customs and practices which they had learned in the United States. . . . All the new things they did appeared queer and artificial. They were looked upon with distrust, even to the extent of ridicule. They were mockingly referred to as 'Americanized' or 'American Boys.' The mode of dressing appeared queer."[110] It is impossible to determine the extent to which Olivar's mid-twentieth-century ascription of "queer" to the male pensionados in the Philippine context would have connoted what it surely would have in the United States at the same time—namely, and derogatorily, "homosexual." That "queer" is articulated here as contrivance, over-civilization, and conspicuous self-styling suggests that we should not divorce it from its metroimperial and, by this point, postcolonial context—the returning pensionados were to their evidently hetero-sexist compatriots something like mollycoddles, dandies, or individuals who might have given in to "certain peculiar temptations" while abroad. Such reception is all the more ironic given that Olivar's father, Jorge Bocobo, was among the pensionados at Indiana University who were targeted by prospective antimiscegenationist legislation. It would seem that in their collective efforts to accord with hetero-masculine bourgeois propriety in the metropole, to prove their civilization and thus their capacity for sovereignty—or, at least, marriage with white women—the students somehow missed, or exceeded, their marks.

Pensionado Pacifico Laygo's image of native Philippine people memo-
rializing the intimacy between a U.S. soldier and a Philippine anticolonial insurrecto that closed chapter 5 resonates with Michel Foucault's
tropes of how critical knowledge production can emerge out of archival
matter in the face of institutionalized epistemologies. The cross-racial,
same-sex intimacy between these soldiers was buried, I have suggested,
in a shallow grave; their "deep embrace," put in the ground but "left to
lie fallow," was meant to be recovered at a future time, and perhaps, as
in our case, from some other place. In his *"Society Must Be Defended"*
lectures of 1976, Foucault describes his genealogical method as apprehending "the insurrection of subjugated knowledges." By "subjugated
knowledges," Foucault means "historical contents that have been *buried*
or masked in functional coherences or formal systemizations" and, quite
differently, "knowledges that have been disqualified as nonconceptual
knowledges . . . knowledge[s] that [are] local, regional, or differential."[1]
What Foucault points to here are, on one hand, historical matters that

get "buried" under other institutionalized truths and epistemologies, and, on the other, "local memories"—that is, "what people know." Laygo's image of the soldiers being buried in a "deep embrace" functions both as an instance of the insurrection of subjugated metroimperial knowledge and as an allegory for how such knowledge might be made, by us, to revolt. That is, the story's "historical content" of same-sex soldierly love across racial lines has been "buried" beneath the imperial "tyranny of overall discourses"—discourses that shored up and often disavowed U.S. imperial sovereignty—and beneath the heteronormative, racist Philippine nationalist discourse that makes up the rest of the pensionada/os' journals.[2] More, as a work of fiction, "On the Battlefield" itself is buried beneath the teleological Philippine nation-building discourses—the specialized scientific, biomedical, engineering, and agricultural knowledges—that surround it. Yet as if anticipating such interment, Laygo also confers a "local" knowledge on the Philippine native population. When they saw the "satisfaction" on the dead soldiers' faces, the people "understood what it meant." What local or "differential" meaning such bodily expression could have had for the Philippine "plain and simple country folk" in Laygo's imagination remains elusive. More important, though, Laygo's projection of a knowledge that might be apprehended by *someone else eventually* ("occasional visitors") speaks to what Martin Joseph Ponce refers to as the "politics of address" in a Philippine diasporic literary context, a politics that "pivots on inferring and positing differently located audiences."[3] As students, scholars, and activists working—and living—at the convergences of sexuality, gender, race, and U.S. imperialism, *we* are perhaps the differently located "occasional visitors" to the scene of intimacy that Laygo, despite his forward-looking projections, could never have imagined but nevertheless addressed.

Throughout this book, I have been unearthing an archive composed by and concerned with various racial-sexual insurrectos that has been subjugated. Indeed, this book has deployed an "insurrectional method."[4] The material I recover has either been "pigeonholed" (to borrow administrators' language in the case of Boss Reese in chapter 2) within colonialism's vast administrative state documents and metroimperial culture's other frames of war, or otherwise disqualified as naïve and hierarchically inferior. There are in fact manifold and concatenated forms of subjugation at work. Beyond the catchall term of "vagrancy" that may have "masked" records of the policing of sexual deviance (chapter 1) and the widespread, systematic "straightening up" of Reese's violent sodomitic acts (chapter 2), for example, we have seen political cartoons concerned with U.S. imperialism that have only recently emerged out of obscurity (if not "forbidden" status), thanks to scholar-activists (chapter 3); a play that perhaps lost popular favor because it was critical of and, later, a reminder of U.S. imperial racializing governance (chapter 4); and published writing by Philippine colonial youths that, perhaps because they did not accord with and actively resisted popular stereotypes about racially and sexually deviant Philippine natives, never had the chance for reception by a mass audience (chapter 5). Beyond these local constraints, these flashes of metroimperial intimacy have also been subjugated in toto for the sake of maintaining a persistent and ongoing U.S. metropolitan cultural amnesia about its own imperial status and, paradoxically, its sexual exceptionalism. That is, the intimacies that stage their insurrection in this book adduce U.S. imperial-colonial violence and the perverse implantations that attend to imperial conquest.

Part of the challenge (and payoff) in conducting this study involved having to locate the Philippine subject against the emergent discourses of sexuality in a time before the identificatory categories of "homosexual" and "heterosexual" were common ascriptions, well before they would come to be, as Chauncey has pointed out, "hegemonic."[5] In doing so, I have shown how the Philippine subject was fantasmatically articulated to—shared something of an intimate genealogy with—a range of differently perverse or abject figures in the idiom of the time: the sodomite, the vagrant, the woman, the hermaphrodite, the bakla, the dandy, the black dandy, the degenerate, the anus, the Oriental, the bachelor, the polygamist, the invert, the bisexual, the mollycoddle, the punk, and so on. In these concluding pages, I turn very briefly to yet one more deviant figure, one that affirms and interrupts the archival knowledges staging their insurrection here. This historical agent also shows modes of participating in metroimperial fantasies quite differently from the varied figures I have tracked and, indeed, from how I have done so.

I consider here what we might only refer to now, in another perversely presentist gesture, as a trans* figure or, more specifically, a transman, although that term does not fully capture the ways in which he straddled gender boundaries—hence, my apprehensive, tactical use of masculine pronouns in what follows. Jack Bee Garland, also known to Northern California locals as Babe Bean or Beebe Bean, was born Elvira Virginia Mugarrieta in San Francisco in 1869, a daughter of the former Mexican Army officer and San Francisco's first Mexican consul, José Marcos Mugarrieta, and Eliza Garland. After a "happy" childhood, during which Elvira was a "regular tomboy," and a brief marriage as a teenager to a man (which enabled Elvira to escape domestic duties as an oldest daughter in San Francisco), Elvira began living as a man in Stockton, California. This involved hiding his past, telling people he was from Southern California, for example, and hiding his voice. He never spoke, instead writing all communication on an ever present notepad. By his early twenties, he was known by locals as "Babe Bean," as Stockton's *Evening Mail* would put it in 1897, "a woman in town masquerading in male attire."[6] Bean explains in an interview conducted by the *Evening Mail*, "For two very good reasons I am attired 'thusly'—for protection and for convenience."[7] The *Evening Mail*, impressed with his writing during the interview, would soon hire Bean as a reporter. Bean's sex-gender ambiguity seems to have been accepted by the locals, but it still piqued the curiosity of newspapers and the police. As Bean and other journalists reported, he was rather idiosyncratic, living on an "ark" (i.e., houseboat) among other "ark-dweller" men on McLeod Lake, frequenting bars alone and ordering "soda lemonades," showing little sympathy for the "New Woman," and sleeping all day while going out only at night. Because of his minor celebrity status, Bean was invited as an honorary member of Stockton's Naomi Bachelor Club, whose membership consisted exclusively of "young men committed to bachelorhood and not actively interested in women or marriage."[8] When visiting the club, Bean welcomed the bachelors' fawning and flirtation. (He was also impressed with their musical entertainment. "Even savages are fond of their own peculiar style of music," he wrote for the *Evening Gazette*, reminiscent of the language about bachelors we saw in chapter 4, "so it is not astonishing to learn that all the members are great lovers of music."[9]) Bean saw in the bachelors' hospitality and flirtatious advances recognition of his manhood—in his words, "proof of brotherly love."[10] Indeed, Bean continually sought out other forms of such "love" when he roamed the streets at night. Bean forged intimacies with male "hoboes" and "tramps" (i.e., *vagrants*, the figure traced in chapter 1), who took him into their company as a "punk" and a "gay cat"—the former referring to a physically slight male youth who let himself be sexually penetrated by an older man in exchange for protection or money, and the latter turn-of-the-century slang for a "tramp's younger, homosexual companion."[11]

While several histories of female-to-male cross-dressers—in the effort to document lesbian, feminist, and butch figures living in the late nineteenth-century United States—have narrated how cross-dressing figures (including Bean) used the protective cloaking provided by men's clothing to pursue relationships with women in relative safety, this was not Bean's motivation.[12] As Bean would muse, "Many have thought it strange that I do not care to mingle with women of my own age, and seem partial to men's company. Well, is it not natural that I should prefer the companionship of men? I am never happy nor contented unless with a few of the 'boys.'"[13] As Louis Sullivan, whose biography of Garland/Bean I have been drawing from here, would discover, Bean's effort was not that of a butch lesbian but rather that "of a man craving the company of other men."[14] Bean was perhaps something of—to be *vulgarly* perversely presentist—a gay mixed-race Chicano transman.

In 1899, Bean also sought intimacy with other men by stowing away on a military personnel transport ship, the *City of Para*, docked in San Francisco and headed for the Philippines, whose people had just started an "insurrection" against U.S. invaders. As Bean put it (in a manner that vexes all retroactive gender ascriptions), "A newspaper woman and the daughter of an army officer, all my ambition and interest and inclination naturally gave me the fever to go to Manila when things were at their liveliest there. . . . My purpose in going to Manila was to see war from the soldier's point of view, with a woman's eyes."[15] After a physically taxing voyage across the Pacific, during which Bean hid, ate, and worked among the cabin boys (who called him "Benny"), and that included a layover in Honolulu, which had recently been colonized by the United States, the military transport arrived in Manila.[16] Upon securing housing just north of Manila in the municipality of Caloocan, dressed in a U.S. soldier's blue shirt and khaki pants, Bean presented himself before colonial military administrators and convinced them that he should stay on as an embedded reporter among the troops. Justifying his wearing of men's clothes, Bean suggested that since there was no law in California forbidding women to wear masculine clothing (which we now know was not entirely true, as San Francisco had passed such a law in 1863), there was no such prohibition in Manila, either (which we can now corroborate).[17]

With military approval, Bean—who was increasingly preferring to use the name Jack—joined the Twenty-ninth Infantry on treacherous hikes, acting as a buyer of supplies, an interpreter (Jack's Spanish-speaking skills were particularly useful), and a nurse. In addition to bonding with the U.S. soldiers on the battlefield, Jack had a few interactions with local Philippine people, who referred to him endearingly as "Picanniny Captain" or "Little Captain."[18] At one point, Sullivan narrates, Jack "leaped from a window and saved the life of an unarmed soldier who was about to be murdered by two natives."[19] Sullivan's portrait does not document how Bean fended off the "natives," but it is hard to imagine that violence was not involved. Bean seems to have been pretty good with a revolver, after all, having shot a U.S. soldier who was harassing him in the leg.[20] Moreover, Sullivan notes that Jack "had been a soldier with the best of them, known in the regiment as 'Lieutenant Jack' . . . on the firing line whenever there was a firing line."[21] In the Philippines, Jack found the company he craved. The soldiers of the Twenty-ninth Infantry, in a show of respect for Jack's patriotic and manly spirit, pooled $200 to forge a gold medal for him and presented it during a small ceremony. Before leaving the Philippines after a ten-month tour, at thirty, Jack got an elaborate tattoo on his arm that bore the word "MANILA," the year "1899," the American flag, a drawing of crossed guns, and his new name, "Jack." After returning stateside, Jack Garland, as he came to be known, spent most of the rest of his life in poverty in San Francisco, working as an accredited male nurse for the Red Cross, advocating for and befriending the homeless youths finding their way to the city, and frequenting the city's notorious underworlds. He died in 1936 at sixty-six.

I offer this sketch of Garland to underscore the historical disjuncture, alluded to in the "Introduction," between LGBTQ studies, on one hand, and critical race studies, U.S. imperial studies, and ethnic studies, on the other—and to suggest briefly just one area where future studies at the crossings of these fields might go. Originally recuperated among feminist, gay, and lesbian scholars as part of the genealogy of "lesbian" political and social identity in the 1970s, Garland in the late 1980s was reclaimed by Sullivan as "a female-to-male transsexual, even though such luxuries as modern-day male hormone therapy and sex reassignment surgeries were not available options during his lifetime."[22] Allan Bérubé, who introduced Sullivan to Garland's story in 1979 during a slideshow presentation titled "Lesbian Masquerade: Some Lesbians in Early San Francisco Who Passed as Men," hailed Garland as "a pioneer explorer who ventured across gender boundaries to invent his own life."[23] While Bérubé rightly points out the transgressive nature of Garland's cross-dressing, his celebratory metaphor, recalling Frederick Jackson Turner and the settler-colonial spirit of Manifest Destiny, now sounds off-putting, given Garland's participation in overseas colonialism. Gesturing to a similar critique in 1997, Nan Boyd, in turn, reframed Sullivan's biographical portrait of Garland within the turn-of-the-twentieth-century rise of white supremacy, U.S. exceptionalist discourse, and overseas colonization. Boyd points to Garland's continual adoption of Anglo names, despite his patrilineal Mexican descent, and suggests the possibility that "while his silence in Stockton masked, most obviously, the feminine tenor of his voice, it also hid any Spanish language affects that would have destabilized his ethnic and national crossings."[24] Boyd then attaches Garland's gender and *racial* passing to his "participation in the Spanish-American War" and military service, arguing that together they "wrapped a cloak of national allegiance around his political subjectivity, highlighting both his masculinity and American-ness."[25]

What this historiography around Garland shows, in short, is how different times have their own "functional coherences," by which the same "historical contents" can be reformulated, reframed. As Boyd writes, "the story of Babe Bean/Jack Garland exceeds a singularly recuperative narrative."[26] While Boyd's reframing is largely cogent, it's significant that she locates Garland's military service in the "Spanish-American War" rather than the related but distinct Philippine-American War. A similar elision also marks Sullivan's exceptionalist account, which, in addition to praising Jack's military toughness, somewhat bizarrely describes the Philippine insurgency as a "revolt against the treaty [of Paris]" rather than against U.S. imperial colonialism.[27] These omissions bury and mask. What Garland had a "fever" for, after all—what inscribed his status as both American and "Jack," as was emblazoned on his arm—was the *fantasy* of "MANILA." It was not just "*national* allegiance" that secured Garland's whiteness and masculinity but, rather, his *metroimperial* subjectivation. The historiographic inattention to Garland's participation in colonial conquest glosses over the fact that Garland served the same U.S. imperial, settler-colonial force that his Mexican Army father had fought against some fifty years earlier, during the Mexican-American War (1846–1848).[28] It also obviates historical inquiry into possible cross-racial violence, or even homosocial or homoerotic intimacies, that Garland might have engaged in or sought out in the Philippines. In short, it misses the force of colonianormativity—how it would come to operate on different bodies differently. What I am getting at here is how particular U.S.-based historiographies of gender-sexual dissidence, in an effort to recuperate transgressive figures and "pioneers" from the past, have tended to overlook the conditions of persistent, white supremacist settler-colonial expansion that have enabled these figures' existence and their emergence in the archive—or *shaped the nature of their very transgression*. To elide U.S. imperial-colonialism is to miss the full distribution of biopolitics, its management over what constitutes and constrains intimacy. Such a slip is perhaps why, around the same time that the first volume of *The History of Sexuality* was published, Foucault insisted in his "*Society Must Be Defended*" lectures on recognizing the state's optimization of life—the ways in which biopower acts diffusely on subjects in times of perceived security—as a function of war: "beneath the omissions, the illusions, and the lies of those who would have us believe in the necessities of nature or the functional requirements of order, we have to discover war: war is the cipher of peace."[29]

When Foucault identified the insurrection of subjugated knowledges in his lectures, he was describing what was emerging not just in his genealogical work but also in epistemological transformations that had been occurring in discursive critique over the past fifteen years.[30] He was providing both an analytic of the archive and a reflection on the scholarly present. I hope to have demonstrated, at least implicitly, how this book attempts to do the same. The recent convergences of minoritarian discourses—sexuality studies, gender studies, ethnic studies, and U.S. empire studies—have enabled the most generative means of conducting the most "meticulous rediscovery of struggles and the raw memory of fights" that took place in the Philippine-U.S. metroimperial arena.[31] Queer-of-color scholarship and the critical attention to U.S. imperialism, in short, have led the charge in this insurrection.[32] In its examination of racial-sexual governance at the turn of the twentieth century, this book has demonstrated how the calculated management of life in the Philippines was conducted by the colonial state's gradual folding in of sexual discourse, how the simultaneous explosion of discourse around sexuality within the metropole both muddled and consolidated the governance, including the self-governance, of the autochthonous Philippine subject. It has shown, in other words, how racialized violence can be the cipher of intimacies. Looking forward, I anticipate that the historical contents of the metroimperial archive will continue to be reframed, reformulated, through different functional coherences. Especially as I write at a time that the U.S. empire persists in aspiring to a totalizing global dominance—in the form of neoimperialist, capitalist hegemony; permanent war; securitization; police and state terrorism; and even neoliberal, exceptionalist flexibility around some acceptably "queer" bodies (though not others)—I hope that this book will serve as a prompt, an incitement, to further insurrections.

INTRODUCTION

1. John D'Emilio, "Capitalism and Gay Identity," in *The Lesbian and Gay Studies Reader*, ed. Henry Abelove, Michèle Aina Barale, and David Halperin (New York: Routledge, 1993), 467–76; Vladimir Lenin, *Imperialism, the Highest Stage of Capitalism: A Popular Outline* (1916), repr. ed. (New York: International Publishers, 1969).

2. To be clear, many scholars whose work I draw from and to whom I owe *utang ng loob* (Filipino for a "debt of gratitude") have considered nonnormative gender-sexuality in a Philippine colonial and postcolonial context. However, they all examine later time periods: see, e.g., Kale Fajardo, *Filipino Crosscurrents: Oceanographies of Seafaring, Masculinities, and Globalization* (Minneapolis: University of Minnesota Press, 2011); Martin Manalansan, *Global Divas: Filipino Gay Men in the Diaspora* (Durham, NC: Duke University Press, 2003); Martin Joseph Ponce, *Beyond the Nation: Diasporic Filipino Literature and Queer Reading* (New York: New York University Press, 2012); Neferti Tadiar, *Fantasy Production: Sexual Economies and other Philippine Consequences for the New World Order* (Hong Kong: Hong Kong University Press, 2006). J. Neil Garcia's monograph, *Philippine Gay Culture: Binibae to Bakla, Sihalis to MSM* (1996), repr. ed. (Quezon City: University of the Philippines Press, 2009), which impressively examines a range of gender-sexual acts and identities in the Philippines from the pre-Spanish colonial period to the 1990s, does not cover the early U.S. colonial era.

3. Ann Stoler, *Along the Archival Grain: Epistemic Anxieties and Colonial Common Sense* (Princeton, NJ: Princeton University Press, 2009), 1.

4. M. Jacqui Alexander, *Pedagogies of Crossing: Meditations on Feminism, Sexual Politics, Memory, and the Sacred* (Durham, NC: Duke University Press, 2005), 70. Many Philippine and Philippine American scholars have called attention to U.S. historical forgetting around colonialism in the Philippines: see, e.g., Oscar Campomanes's groundbreaking essay "Filipinos in the United States and Their Literature of Exile," in *Reading the Literatures of Asian America*, ed. Shirley

Geok-lin Lim and Amy Ling (Philadelphia, PA: Temple University Press, 1992), 49–78. Allan Punzalan Isaac, in contrast, casts the condition as aphasia in *American Tropics: Articulating Filipino America* (Minneapolis: University of Minnesota Press, 2006).

5. Kandice Chuh, *Imagine Otherwise: On Asian Americanist Critique* (Durham, NC: Duke University Press, 2003), 35.

6. Siobhan Somerville, *Queering the Color Line: Race and the Invention of Homosexuality in American Culture* (Durham, NC: Duke University Press, 2000), 3.

7. W. E. B. Du Bois, "Present Outlook for the Darker Races of Mankind" (1900), in *The Oxford W. E. B. Du Bois Reader*, ed. Eric J. Sundquist (New York: Oxford University Press, 1996), 40.

8. Du Bois, "Present Outlook for the Darker Races of Mankind."

9. Louis Althusser, "Ideology and Ideological State Apparatuses," in *Lenin and Philosophy and Other Essays*, trans. Ben Brewster (London: New Left Books, 1969), 165. My understanding of fantasy accords with the understanding of fantasy's relation to the Philippine nation-state in Tadiar, *Fantasy Production*, 3–11.

10. More concurrently, in 1897 Freud pointed to this function of fantasy, whose scenes are "protective fictions" enabling one to escape repressed memories: see Sigmund Freud, *The Origins of Psychoanalysis: Letters to Wilhelm Fliess, Drafts and Notes, 1887–1902*, ed. Marie Bonaparte, Anna Freud, Ernst Kris (New York: Basic Books, 1954).

11. I use "Filipina/o" and "pensionada/o" throughout the book to steer clear of the Hispanicized masculine gendering of these terms.

12. I draw the phrase "sex/gender system" from Gayle Rubin, "The Traffic in Women: Notes on the 'Political Economy' of Sex" (1975), in *The Second Wave: A Reader in Feminist Theory*, ed. Linda Nicholson (New York: Routledge, 1997), 27–62. "Racial hegemony" comes from the description of the post–Civil War United States in Michael Omi and Howard Winant, *Racial Formation in the United States: From the 1960s to the 1990s*, 2nd ed. (New York: Routledge, 1994). In Lacanian terms, the "organizing system" is called the "symbolic order" or "the Other."

13. Lacan, revising the Freudian understanding of the unconscious, would come to call this excessive something the "Real," the "domain of whatever subsists outside symbolization": quoted in Dylan Evans, *An Introductory Dictionary to Lacanian Psychoanalysis* (London: Routledge, 1996), 159.

14. That is, fantasy defends against the lack in the symbolic order, the "Other." For Lacan, the "Other" does not always refer to the symbolic order; importantly, it also refers to—as it does in many traditions of thought, from Hegelian phenomenology to feminist existentialism and postcolonial, ethnic, and queer studies—the subject apart from the self and over against which the self is established.

15. Evans, *An Introductory Dictionary to Lacanian Psychoanalysis*, 133.

16. Slavoj Žižek, *Looking Awry: An Introduction to Jacques Lacan through Popular Culture* (Cambridge, MA: MIT Press, 1992), 6.

17. Althusser, "Ideology and Ideological State Apparatuses," 163.

18. Lauren Berlant, *The Female Complaint: The Unfinished Business of Sentimentality in American Culture* (Durham, NC: Duke University Press, 2008), 14.

19. In Lacanian terms, fantasy also occupies some place of the Real: Jacques Lacan, *The Four Fundamental Concepts of Psycho-analysis*, ed. Jacques-Alain Miller, trans. Alan Sheridan (New York: W. W. Norton, 1981), 60.

20. Jacques Lacan, *The Seminar of Jacques Lacan. Book 7: The Ethics of Psychoanalysis, 1959–1960*, trans. Dennis Porter (New York: Norton, 1992), 99. As Lacan puts it, sublimation, a mode of fantasy, seeks to "colonize the field of *das Ding* with imaginary schemes." He then clarifies that this is exactly "how collective, socially accepted" fantasies work.

21. Gilles Deleuze and Félix Guattari, *Anti-Oedipus: Capitalism and Schizophrenia*, trans. Robert Hurley, Mark Seem, and Helen Lane (Minneapolis: University of Minnesota Press, 1983), 30.

22. Tim Dean, *Beyond Sexuality* (Chicago: University of Chicago Press, 2000), 260.

23. Fredric Jameson, *The Political Unconscious: Narrative as Socially Symbolic Act* (Ithaca, NY: Cornell University Press, 1982). Jameson, incidentally, understands the "political unconscious" specifically as a mediation of the Lacanian Real: Jameson, *The Political Unconscious*, 35.

24. Jacqueline Rose, *States of Fantasy* (Oxford: Oxford University Press, 1996), 4.

25. Rey Chow, *The Protestant Ethnic and the Spirit of Capitalism* (New York: Columbia University Press, 2002), 110. What Chow posits, to play out the metaphor I offer earlier, is the terrifying scenario that there is no police officer at all.

26. Chandan Reddy, *Freedom with Violence: Race, Sexuality and the U.S. State* (Durham, NC: Duke University Press, 2011), 240.

27. See the influential critique of national form as "imagined" in Benedict Anderson, *Imagined Communities: On the Origin and Spread of Nationalism* (London: Verso, 1983).

28. "Overseas expansion . . . relied on the creation of ambiguous spaces that were not quite foreign nor domestic, and it also created vast de-territorialized arenas in which to exercise military, economic and cultural power divorced from political annexation": Amy Kaplan, *The Anarchy of Empire in the Making of U.S. Culture* (Durham, NC: Duke University Press, 2002), 15.

29. Here I borrow from Julian Go's definitions of these terms, specifically within the context of the U.S. colonial state the Philippines: Julian Go, "Introduction," in *The American Colonial State in the Philippines*, ed. Julian Go and Anne Foster (Durham, NC: Duke University Press, 2003), 4–5.

30. Reddy, *Freedom with Violence*, 100.

31. Rose, *States of Fantasy*, 14.

32. Michel Foucault writes similarly, "I don't try to write an archaeology of sexual fantasies. I try to make an archaeology of discourse about sexuality, which is really the relationship between what we do, what we are forbidden to do in the field of sexuality, and what we are allowed, forbidden, or obliged to say about our sexual behavior. That's the point. It's not a problem of fantasy; it's a problem

of verbalization": Michel Foucault, "An Interview with Stephen Riggs," in *Ethics: Subjectivity and Truth*, ed. Paul Rabinow, trans. Robert Hurley et al. (New York: New Press, 1997), 125–26.

33. Michel Foucault, *The History of Sexuality, Volume 1: An Introduction*, trans. Robert Hurley (New York: Vintage, 1980), 18.

34. For an exposition of colonial discourse in Foucault's thinking, see Ann Stoler's classic *Race and the Education of Desire: Foucault's History of Sexuality and the Colonial Order of Things* (Durham, NC: Duke University Press, 1995).

35. Roderick Ferguson, *Aberrations in Black: Toward a Queer of Color Critique* (Minneapolis: University of Minnesota Press, 2003). I borrow the term "intracolonialism," which refers to the U.S. state's colonial practices in the management of ethnic peoples within the metropole, from Nicole Waligora-Davis, *Sanctuary: African Americans and Empire* (New York: Oxford University Press, 2011).

36. The works most influential to my understanding of intimacy here include the essays in Berlant, ed. *Intimacy*, ed. Lauren Berlant (Chicago: University of Chicago Press, 2000); Lisa Lowe, "The Intimacies of Four Continents," in *Haunted by Empire: Geographies of Intimacy in North American History*, ed. Ann Stoler (Durham, NC: Duke University Press, 2006), 191–212; Elizabeth Povinelli, *The Empire of Love: Toward a Theory, Genealogy, and Carnality* (Durham, NC: Duke University Press, 2006); Nayan Shah, *Stranger Intimacy: Contesting Race, Sexuality, and the Law in the North American West* (Berkeley: University of California Press, 2011); Ann Stoler, *Carnal Knowledge and Imperial Power: Race and the Intimate in Colonial Rule* (Berkeley: University of California Press, 2002); Ann Stoler, ed. *Haunted by Empire: Geographies of Intimacy in North American History* (Durham, NC: Duke University Press, 2006).

37. See Stoler, *Carnal Knowledge*, 9; Lowe, "The Intimacies of Four Continents," 193, 195, 202–3.

38. Jasbir K. Puar, *Terrorist Assemblages: Homonationalism in Queer Times* (Durham, NC: Duke University Press, 2007), 121.

39. Dylan Rodriguez, *Suspended Apocalypse: White Supremacy, Genocide, and the Filipino Condition* (Minneapolis: University of Minnesota Press, 2009), 3.

40. Hartman writes, "What concerns me here is the diffusion of terror and the violence perpetrated under the rubric of pleasure, paternalism, and property": Saidiya Hartman, *Scenes of Subjection: Terror, Slavery, and Self-Making in Nineteenth-Century America* (New York: Oxford University Press, 1997), 4.

41. Stoler, "Intimidations of Empire," in *Haunted by Empire: Geographies of Intimacy in North American History*, ed. Ann Stoler (Durham, NC: Duke University Press, 2006), 13.

42. Max Weber, *From Max Weber: Essays in Sociology*, ed. and trans. H. H. Gerth and C. Wright Mills (New York: Academic Press, 1974), 77–83.

43. Wendy Brown, *States of Injury: Power and Freedom in Late Modernity* (Princeton, NJ: Princeton University Press, 1995), 174–75. For a thorough discussion of the Spanish colonial state in the Philippines, see John Blanco, *Frontier Constitutions:*

Christianity and Colonial Empire in the Nineteenth Century Philippines (Berkeley: University of California Press, 2009).

44. Go, "Introduction," 5.
45. Blanco also finds more cogent the Foucauldian (rather than Weberian) understanding of the state when it comes to the colonial Philippines: Blanco, *Frontier Constitutions*, 47–51.
46. Go, "Introduction," 5, 7.
47. In saying that the economic boom exceeded the liberal developmentalist ethos, I refer to the numerous arguments made in popular pro-expansionist discourse that overproduction in the United States necessitated new consuming markets overseas. The U.S. occupation of the Philippines famously promised to lead to the Open Door Policy with China.
48. See esp. Michel Foucault, "Governmentality," in *The Foucault Effect: Studies in Governmentality with Two Lectures by and an Interview with Michel Foucault*, ed. Graham Burchell, Colin Gordon, and Peter Miller (Chicago: University of Chicago Press, 1991), 87–104.
49. Nancy Cott, *Public Vows: A History of Marriage and the Nation* (Cambridge, MA: Harvard University Press, 2000), 81.
50. Claudia Tate, *Domestic Allegories of Political Desire: The Black Heroine's Text at the Turn of the Century* (New York: Oxford University Press, 1992), 91.
51. Roderick Ferguson, "Of Our Normative Strivings: African American Studies and the Histories of Sexuality," *Social Text* 23, nos. 3–4 (Fall–Winter 2005): 85–100.
52. Somerville, *Queering the Color Line*, 9.
53. See Somerville, *Queering the Color Line*, 35.
54. Somerville, *Queering the Color Line*, 3.
55. The Page Law of 1875 legislated the exclusion of Chinese women (as well as other "degenerates"). The Tydings-McDuffie Act of 1934 granted the independence of the Philippines under federal law. On the canonical and brilliant discussion of these immigration acts as standing in for the contradiction between the U.S. state and capitalist production, see Lisa Lowe, *Immigrants Acts: On Asian American Cultural Politics* (Durham, NC: Duke University Press, 1996). For now classic monographs on early twentieth-century racial formation of what we now know as Asian Americans or Asian Pacific Islander Americans, see Sucheng Chan, *Asian Americans: An Interpretive History* (Boston, MA: Twayne, 1991); David Eng, *Racial Castration: Managing Masculinity in Asian America* (Durham, NC: Duke University Press, 2001); Robert G. Lee, *Orientals: Asian Americans in Popular Culture* (Philadelphia, PA: Temple University Press, 1999); Colleen Lye, *America's Asia: Racial Form and American Literature, 1893–1945* (Princeton, NJ: Princeton University Press, 2005); Gary Okihiro, *Cane Fires: The Anti-Japanese Movement in Hawaii, 1865–1945* (Philadelphia, PA: Temple University Press, 1995); Gary Okihiro, *Margins and Mainstreams: Asians in American history and Culture* (Seattle: University of Washington Press, 1994); David Palumbo-Liu, *Asian/American: Historical Crossings of a Racial Frontier* (Stanford, CA: Stanford University Press, 1995);

Alexander Sexton, *The Indispensable Enemy: Labor and the Anti-Chinese Movement* (Berkeley: University of California Press, 1971); Nayan Shah, *Contagious Divides: Epidemics and Race in San Francisco's Chinatown* (Berkeley: University of California Press, 2001); Ronald Takaki, *Strangers from a Different Shore* (Boston, MA: Little, Brown, 1989).

56. Cott, *Public Vows*, 136.

57. I borrow the term "strangers" from Nayan Shah, who has argued that scholars might move away from focusing on the state's restriction of immigration and instead look at the state's production of foreign "strangers": Shah, *Stranger Intimacy*.

58. See George Peffer, "Forbidden Families: Emigration Experiences of Chinese Women under the Page Law, 1875–1882," *Journal of American Ethnic History* 6, no. 1 (Fall 1986): 28–46; Shah, *Contagious Divides*; Jennifer Ting, "Bachelor Society: Deviant Heterosexuality and Asian American Historiography," in *Privileging Positions: The Sites of Asian American Studies*, ed. Gary Y. Okihiro, Marilyn Alquizola, Dorothy Fujita Rony, Wong K. Scott (Pullman: Washington State University Press, 1995), 271–80.

59. See Shah, *Stranger Intimacy*.

60. Drawing from Rubin's famous "charmed circle" of the sex value system, Luibhéid points out, "Spouses have been exempted from many exclusion and deportation laws, granted preference when numerical quota limits were imposed, and even exempted altogether from quota limitations. Such spousal privilege is consonant with the fact that dominant cultural standards suggest that 'sexuality that is "good," "normal," and "natural" should ideally be heterosexual, marital, monogamous, reproductive, and non-commercial'": Eithne Luibhéid, *Entry Denied: Controlling Sexuality at the Border* (Minneapolis: University of Minnesota Press, 2002), 55–56.

61. Peggy Pascoe, *What Comes Naturally: Miscegenation Law and the Making of Race in America* (New York: Oxford University Press, 2009).

62. Foucault, *The History of Sexuality, Volume 1*, 43.

63. The now classic monographs on the historical study of lesbian and gay identity in the U.S. metropole include George Chauncey, *Gay New York: Gender, Urban Culture, and the Making of the Gay Male World, 1890–1940* (New York: Basic Books, 1994); John D'Emilio, *Sexual Politics, Sexual Communities: The Making of a Homosexual Minority in the United States, 1940–1970* (Chicago: University of Chicago Press, 1983); Lillian Faderman, *Odd Girls and Twilight Lovers: A History of Lesbian Life in Twentieth Century-America* (New York: Penguin, 1992); Elizabeth Lapovsky Kennedy and Madeline D. Davis, *Boots of Leather, Slippers of Gold: The History of a Lesbian Community* (New York: Routledge, 1993); Esther Newton, *Cherry Grove, Fire Island: Sixty Years in America's First Gay and Lesbian Town* (Boston, MA: Beacon, 1993); Somerville, *Queering the Color Line*; Jennifer Terry, *An American Obsession: Science, Medicine, and Homosexuality in Modern Society* (Chicago: University of Chicago Press, 1999).

64. Margot Canaday, *The Straight State: Sexuality and Citizenship in Twentieth-Century America* (Princeton, NJ: Princeton University Press, 2009), 23.

65. Edward Munson, *The Theory and Practice of Military Hygiene* (New York: William Wood, 1901), 21.

66. For the demographic of the subjects of sexological discourse (in which these subjects are characterized as "elite"), see George Chauncey, "From Sexual Inversion to Homosexuality: Medicine and the Changing Conceptualization of Female Deviance," *Salmagundi* 58, no. 9 (Fall-Winter 1982): 114–46. See also the brilliant work on sexology's reliance on contemporary racial discourse in "Scientific Racism and the Invention of the Homosexual Body," in Somerville, *Queering the Color Line*, 15–38.

67. Canaday, *The Straight State*, 19–54.

68. Canaday, *The Straight State*, 21.

69. It is important to note, though, that even as state policing and suppression of the plurality of bodies proliferated at this time, subjects were not entirely powerless before the law. Indeed, as Shah traces, some groups managed to imagine social relations that exceeded state-enforced norms: see Shah, *Stranger Intimacy*.

70. Canaday, *The Straight State*, 29.

71. I paraphrase here the famous description of biopower, in Foucault, *The History of Sexuality*, 1:143.

72. The question as to why the United States went into the business of imperialist expansion in the Philippines has been long debated. For a historiographic review of this debate, see Ephraim K. Smith, "William McKinley's Enduring Legacy: The Historiographical Debate on the Taking of the Philippine Islands," in *Crucible of Empire: The Spanish American War and Its Aftermath*, ed. James Bradford (Annapolis, MD: Naval Institute Press, 1993), 205–49. Hoganson, moreover, shifts the debate from liberal economic and global positioning reasons to turn-of-the-century cultural politics around gender. For her redaction of historical reasoning, see Kristin Hoganson, *Fighting for American Manhood: How Gender Politics Provoked the Spanish-American and Philippine-American Wars* (New Haven, CT: Yale University Press, 1998), 7–8.

73. Alfred W. McCoy, *Policing America's Empire: The United States, the Philippines, and the Rise of the Surveillance State* (Madison: University of Wisconsin Press, 2009), 27.

74. For more on U.S. imperialism in Cuba, see Louis Perez, *The War of 1898: The United States and Cuba in History and Historiography* (Chapel Hill: University of North Carolina Press, 1998).

75. See Kaplan, *The Anarchy of Empire in the Making of U.S. Culture*, 146–70. See also José Capino, *Dream Factories of a Former Colony: American Fantasies, Colonial Cinema* (Minneapolis: University of Minnesota Press, 2010).

76. "Jingoism," remarked J. A. Hobson in 1902, "is merely the lust of the spectator": quoted in Kaplan, *The Anarchy of Empire in the Making of U.S. Culture*, 131.

77. Richard Drinnon, *Facing West: The Metaphysics of Indian-Hating and Empire Building* (Minneapolis: University of Minnesota Press, 1980).

78. William McKinley, "Message from the President of the United States, 56th Congress," December 21, 1898, U.S. Congress, 1st sess., 1899–1900, S. Doc. 208, 82–83.

79. For an elaboration of this claim, see Reddy, *Freedom with Violence*; Mimi Nguyen, *The Gift of Freedom: War, Debt, and Other Refugee Passages* (Durham, NC: Duke University Press, 2012).

80. Quoted in Paul A. Kramer, *The Blood of Government: Race, Empire, the United States, and the Philippines* (Chapel Hill: University of North Carolina Press, 2006), 88.

81. Reynaldo Ileto, "Outlines of Nonlinear Emplotment of Philippine History," in *The Politics of Culture in the Shadow of Capital*, ed. Lisa Lowe and David Lloyd (Durham, NC: Duke University Press, 1997), 100. I use the masculine "ilustrado" here because nearly all of the elite who held positions in the local government were men.

82. Ileto points out that not all anticolonial Philippine fighters were nationalist, which had progressivist connotations. Indeed, the first Philippine republic had to set itself against ambiguous "illicit associations" because they were seen as backward, superstitious, and thus contradictory to nationalist appeals to modernity and self-governance: Ileto, "Outlines of Nonlinear Emplotment of Philippine History."

83. The fantasy here, of course, was that such brutal measures presumed an a priori state merely acting out of emergency. On the U.S. state's deployment of "emergency" as a legitimation of violence, see Jesse Carr's excellent dissertation, "States of Exceptionalism: Race, Violence, and Governance," Ph.D. diss., University of Michigan, Ann Arbor, 2014.

84. Kramer, *The Blood of Government*, 152–53.

85. Quoted in Kramer, *The Blood of Government*, 153.

86. Quoted in Kramer, *The Blood of Government*, 154.

87. It's impossible to get an accurate count of Philippine fatalities as colonial records were varied and inaccurate. On the numbers of war, see Judith Butler, *Frames of War: When Is Life Grievable?* London: Verso, 2010, xx.

88. Oscar Campomanes, "The Politics of Imperial Amnesia," Invited lecture given at Illini Union, University of Illinois, Urbana-Champaign, April 19, 2005.

89. On the U.S. colonial military's management of cholera epidemic and the racialized bodies that perpetuated it, see Warwick Anderson, *Colonial Pathologies: American Tropical Medicine, Race, and Hygiene in the Philippines* (Durham, NC: Duke University Press, 2006); Reynaldo Ileto, "Cholera and the Origins of the American Sanitary Order in the Philippines," in *Imperial Medicine and Indigenous Societies*, ed. David Arnold (Manchester: Manchester University Press, 1988), 125–47; Ileto, "Outlines of Nonlinear Emplotment of Philippine History."

90. Hence the title of Samuel K. Tan's *The Filipino-American War: 1899–1913* (Quezon City: University of the Philippines Press, 2002).

91. Rick Baldoz, *The Third Asiatic Invasion: Empire and Migration in Filipino America, 1898–1946* (New York: New York University Press, 2011), 47.

92. See Go, "Introduction," 12.

93. The Tydings-McDuffie Act declared that "the Philippines shall be considered a foreign country" and at the same time, following legislation established against Asian migrants, set an annual quota on migration to fifty persons. This quota was

the lowest among possible immigrants: Mae M. Ngai, *Impossible Subjects: Illegal Aliens and the Making of Modern America* (Princeton, NJ: Princeton University Press, 2004), 97.

94. For an excellent social history of this later period, see Linda España-Maram, *Creating Masculinity in Los Angeles's Little Manila: Working-Class Filipinos and Popular Culture, 1920s–1950s* (New York: Columbia University Press, 2006).

95. Vicente Rafael, *White Love and Other Essays in Filipino History* (Durham, NC: Duke University Press, 2000), 21.

96. I thank Leela Fernandes for pointing out how this trope of marriage was not typically used in other colonial contexts.

97. Hoganson, *Fighting for American Manhood*, 137.

98. Quoted in Hoganson, *Fighting for American Manhood*, 138.

99. "Encourages Matrimony in the Philippines," *St. Louis Republic* (St. Louis, MO), May 5, 1904, 1.

100. *Oxford English Dictionary*, 3rd online ed., s.v. "Benevolence."

101. Benito M. Vergara Jr., *Displaying Filipinos: Photography and Colonialism in Early 20th Century Philippines* (Quezon City: University of the Philippines Press, 1995); Slavoj Žižek, *Tarrying with the Negative: Kant, Hegel, and the Critique of Ideology* (Durham, NC: Duke University Press, 1993), 90.

102. Baldoz, *The Third Asiatic Invasion*, 14. Hawaiian sugar planters began recruiting Philippine laborers to that state in 1906.

103. Isaac, *American Tropics*, 6.

104. "Filipino Can't Vote," *New York Times*, October 29, 1904, 3.

105. "Filipinos Not Citizens," *The Globe* (Boston, MA), November 3, 1904, 6.

106. See Baldoz, *The Third Asiatic Invasion*.

107. "Letter from Manila," *Kansas City Journal* (Kansas City, MO), February 12, 1899, 13.

108. "Filipino Refugees Tell Queer Yarns," *San Francisco Call*, January 13, 1899, 4.

109. "Admiral Dewey Again in His Native Land," *Salt Lake Herald*, September 27, 1899, 1.

110. "Features of Manila," *Omaha Illustrated Bee*, March 4, 1900, 8.

111. Frank G. Carpenter, "Queer Human and Animal Sprigs in Our Philippine Territory," *Atlanta Constitution*, May 3, 1902, 9.

112. Kramer, *The Blood of Government*, 67.

113. "Uncle Sam's Pygmies are the Slaves of the Philippines," *St. Louis Republic*, St. Louis, MO, April 20, 1902, 53.

114. Frank G. Carpenter, "Among the Bagobas: A Queer Tribe of the Southern Philippines, Who Sacrifice Human Beings to Their Gods," *Atlanta Constitution*, July 8, 1900, A7.

115. G. W. Drake, "He Believes in Expansion," *New York Times*, February 12, 1899, 4.

116. See Chauncey, *Gay New York*. For a useful discussion of "queer" during the same period, see also Scott Herring, *Queering the Underworld: Slumming, Literature, and the Undoing of Lesbian and Gay History* (Chicago: University of Chicago Press), 2007, 21–22.

117. "Are a Queer Lot," *Des Moines Daily News*, October 10, 1899, 7.

118. "The Native Filipino a Queer Character: Women More than Men Manage General Affairs," *Los Angeles Times*, February 6, 1902, 4.

119. See Somerville, *Queering the Color Line*, 15–38; Chauncey, *Gay New York*, 13.

120. Richard Johnson, "My Life in the U.S. Army, 1899 to 1922" (1969), quoted in Cynthia Marasigan, " 'Between the Devil and the Deep Sea': Ambivalence, Violence and African American Soldiers in the Philippine American War and Its Aftermath," Ph.D. diss., University of Michigan, Ann Arbor, 2010, 142–43.

121. See Siobhan Somerville, "Queer," in *Keywords for American Cultural Studies*, ed. Bruce Burgett and Glenn Hendler (New York: New York University Press, 2007), 188.

122. See Cathy Cohen's brilliant "Punks, Bulldaggers, and Welfare Queens: The Radical Potential of Queer Politics?" GLQ 3, no. 4 (May 1997): 437–65; Ferguson, *Aberrations in Black*; Gayatri Gopinath, *Impossible Desires: Queer Diasporas and South Asian Public Cultures* (Durham, NC: Duke University Press, 2005); David Eng, Judith/Jack Halberstam, José Esteban Muñoz, eds. *What's Queer about Queer Studies Now?* Special issue of *Social Text* 84–5/23, nos. 3–4 (2005); Reddy, *Freedom with Violence*; Manalansan, *Global Divas*; Ponce, *Beyond the Nation*; Somerville, *Queering the Color Line*.

123. Butler, *Frames of War*, xiii. Butler's understanding of framing here accords with the arguments around U.S. imperial war and presentation by a range of postcolonial and ethnic studies scholars. See, e.g., Sylvia Chong, *The Oriental Obscene: Violence and Racial Fantasy* (Durham, NC: Duke University Press, 2011); Trinh T. Minh-ha, *When the Moon Waxes Red: Representation, Gender, and Cultural Politics* (New York: Routledge, 1991).

124. Walter Benjamin, "Theses on the Philosophy of History," in *Illuminations: Essays and Reflections*, ed. Hannah Arendt (New York: Schocken Books, 1986), 254.

125. I thank Maria Cotera, Rod Ferguson, Joe Ponce, Siobhan Somerville, and Ruby Tapia for helping me work through these points.

126. Anjali Arondekar, *For the Record: On Sexuality and the Colonial Archive in India* (Durham, NC: Duke University Press, 2009), 15.

127. Stuart Hall, "Signification, Representation, Ideology: Althusser and the Post-Structuralist Debates," *Critical Studies in Mass Communication* 2, no. 2 (June 1985): 91–114.

128. Lowe, *Immigrant Acts*, x.

CHAPTER 1. RACIAL-SEXUAL GOVERNANCE

1. J. Neil Garcia, *Philippine Gay Culture: Binibae to Bakla, Sihalis to MSM* (1996), repr. ed. (Quezon City: University of the Philippines Press, 2009), 184.

2. William Eskridge, *Dishonorable Passions: Sodomy Laws in America 1861–2003* (New York: Penguin, 2008), 50.

3. My discussion about the colonial state in the Philippines draws variously from the recent research in Julian Go and Anne Foster, *The American Colonial State in the Philippines: Global Perspectives* (Durham, NC: Duke University Press, 2003); Julian Go, *American Empire and the Politics of Meaning: Elite Political Cultures in*

the Philippines and Puerto Rico during U.S. Colonialism (Durham, NC: Duke University Press, 2008), John Blanco, *Frontier Constitutions: Christianity and Colonial Empire in the Nineteenth Century Philippines* (Berkeley: University of California Press, 2009), Alfred W. McCoy, *Policing America's Empire: The United States, the Philippines, and the Rise of the Surveillance State* (Madison: University of Wisconsin Press, 2009), and Alfred W. McCoy and Francisco A. Sarano, eds., *The Colonial Crucible and the Making of the Modern American State* (Madison: University of Wisconsin Press, 2009).

4. See McCoy, *Policing America's Empire.*

5. Foucault, *The History of Sexuality,* 1:101.

6. Nayan Shah, *Stranger Intimacy: Contesting Race, Sexuality, and the Law in the North American West* (Berkeley: University of California Press, 2011); George Chauncey, *Gay New York: Gender, Urban Culture, and the Making of the Gay Male World, 1890–1940* (New York: Basic Books, 1994); Eskridge, *Dishonorable Passions.*

7. Slavoj Žižek, "Philosophy, the 'Unknown Knowns,' and the Public Use of Reason," *Topoi* 25, nos. 1–2 (2006): 136. Žižek here discusses the Abu Ghraib prison photograph scandal.

8. "Acquisition of the Philippines demanded the new category of 'unincorporation,' which demanded a novel set of economic, administrative and juridical boundaries between the U.S. home government and the colonial apparatus overseas": Go, "Introduction," 9.

9. This is not at all to say that the United States did not have many precedents of colonial expansion: westward, settler territorialization throughout the nineteenth century, the settler colonial conquest of the northern half of Mexico in 1848, the purchase of Alaska in 1867, and the annexation of Hawai'i in 1898 all attest to the might of the Anglo-Saxon doctrine of manifest destiny. Still while these territorial sites always had a prospect of becoming incorporated into the U.S. as states, the status of the newly acquired colonial properties was yet to be determined by the imperial-colonial state.

10. William Willoughby, *Territories and Dependencies of the United States* (New York: Century, 1905), 172. Even today, many scholars regard U.S. presence in the Philippines as a colonial experiment, repeating the language used at the turn of the last century.

11. See Go and Foster, *The American Colonial State in the Philippines*; McCoy, *Policing America's Empire*; Patricio Abinales and Donna Amoroso, *State and Society in the Philippines* (Lanham, MD: Rowman and Littlefield, 2005); Go, *American Empire and the Politics of Meaning.* For the production of the state in the Philippines under Spanish colonial rule, see Blanco, *Frontier Constitutions.*

12. McCoy, *Policing America's Empire,* 28–29, 34.

13. McCoy, *Policing America's Empire,* 28.

14. For an examination of these cases, see Efrén Rivera Ramos, "The Legal Construction of American Colonialism: The Insular Cases (1901–1922)," *Revista Jurídica Universidad de Puerto Rico* 65 (1996): 225–328; Owen Lynch, "The U.S. Constitution

and Philippine Colonialism: An Enduring and Unfortunate Legacy," in *Colonial Crucible and the Making of the Modern American State*, ed. Alfred McCoy and Francisco Scarano (Madison: University of Wisconsin Press, 2009), 353–64.

15. Such ambiguity and arbitrariness around the legal status of the colonial territories was compounded by an ambiguity in national status within the context of the U.S. imperialism's ascendancy onto the world stage. In an oft-quoted statement, Justice Edward Douglass White, writing of the Insular Case of *Downes v. Bidwell* (1901), articulated this ambiguity even as he sought to resolve it: "Whilst in an international sense Porto Rico was not a foreign country, since it was subject to sovereignty of and owned by the United States, it was foreign to the United States in a domestic sense, because the island had not been incorporated into the United States, but was merely appurtenant thereto as a possession": quoted in Christina Duffy Burnett and Burke Marshall, "Between the Foreign and the Domestic: The Doctrine of Territorial Incorporation, Invented and Reinvented," in *Foreign in a Domestic Sense: Puerto Rico, American Expansion, and the Constitution* (Durham, NC: Duke University Press, 2001), 1.

16. Go, "Introduction," 10.

17. Though appearing in an article on the second page of the *New York Times*, this phrase popped up on the front page of several local newspaper stories at the same time. See "Respite in Hostilities," *New York Times*, April 7, 1899; "Rebellion in Negros," *Daily Northwestern* (Oshkosh, WI), April 7, 1899; "Filipinos Have a Chance to Digest the Proclamation," *Austin Daily Herald* (Austin, MN), April 7, 1899; "Given Krag-Jorenson Rifles," *Dubuque Daily Herald* (Dubuque, IA), April 7, 1899.

18. There are many instances from the popular press recounting how colonial administrators punished sexual misconduct or immorality, especially regarding what we now call heterosexual behavior. A blurb in the *Washington Times*, for example, mentions that President Roosevelt had approved the dismissal by court-martial of Second Lieutenant Lawrence E. Grennan, another officer in charge of the Philippine Scouts, for "immoral conduct": "Sentence Approved," *Washington Times*, May 2, 1904. A story appearing in *The Des Moines Daily Capital* two weeks later, though underscoring Grennan's "conduct unbecoming an officer and a gentleman," clarifies that the U.S. officer had proposed marriage to "the wife of a Filipino," threatening to have the woman's husband jailed for her refusal: "Wanted the Wife of a Filipino," *Des Moines Daily Capital*, May 16, 1904.

19. Paul A. Kramer, "The Military-Sexual Complex: Prostitution, Disease, and the Boundaries of Empire during the Philippine-American War," *Asia-Pacific Journal: Japan Focus*, July 6, 2012, http://japanfocus.org/-Paul_A_-Kramer/3574.

20. See Ken De Bevoise, *Agents of Apocalypse: Epidemic Disease in the Colonial Philippines* (Princeton, NJ: Princeton University Press, 1995), 69–93.

21. As Kramer describes the scandal, "Activists made venereal inspection into a problem in diverse ways, each attempting to employ it to advance its agenda. For 'social purity' reformers, regulation 'licensed' vice in several senses, threatening soldiers' moral and physical health and that of the society to which they would return.

Suffragists cast the policy as the natural by-product of a state without women's moralizing influence. Anti-colonialists connected it to broader fears of bodily and political 'corruption.' For all of them, adoption of regulation signaled a tragic collapse of national exceptionalism": Kramer, "The Military-Sexual Complex."

22. H. M. J. (*Howard Malcolm Jenkins*), "Purifying Great Cities," *Friends Intelligencer*, vol. 57, no. 49, December 8, 1900, 882.

23. No evidence has emerged, furthermore, suggesting that any of the Philippine sex workers were men, as in the major cities in the U.S. metropole.

24. Warwick Anderson, *Colonial Pathologies: American Tropical Medicine, Race, and Hygiene in the Philippines* (Durham, NC: Duke University Press, 2006), 2; Paul A. Kramer, "Jim Crow Science and the 'Negro Problem' in the Occupied Philippines, 1898–1914," in *Race Consciousness*, ed. Judith Jackson Fossett and Jeffrey A. Tucker (New York: New York University Press, 1997), 227–46; Cynthia Marasigan, "'Between the Devil and the Deep Sea': Ambivalence, Violence and African American Soldiers in the Philippine American War and Its Aftermath," Ph.D. diss., University of Michigan, Ann Arbor, 2010.

There are several possible reasons that colonial administrators never attempted to legislate against miscegenation. First, legislating against cross-racial marriage would have involved administrators' acknowledging publicly that such marriages were occurring. Such an acknowledgment would have added fuel to many U.S. nativist, white-supremacist anti-expansionists' claims that colonial contact would pollute the "race." Second, it would have meant trying to define "whiteness" explicitly in the Philippine context; such a project would have proved a logical and social-political nightmare (i.e., did "whiteness" mean American? European? What about all those European commercial agents married to Filipinas?). Third, the relative smallness of the "white" American colonial civilian population with respect to the Philippine population made interracial marriage insignificant to colonial administrators. Finally, and this possibility seems to be the most important factor, Americans there sensed that Philippine elites were aware of Jim Crow and did not want to be treated like black people. Informal moral policing (such as the kind I trace here) could accomplish the desired goals of racial-sexual governance without alienating Filipino elites. I thank Paul Kramer for outlining this historical point: Paul A. Kramer, e-mail to the author, August 26, 2010.

25. One U.S. official in Hong Kong, for example, claimed, "There is not an industry in the [Philippine] islands that will not be ruined if Chinese labor is not permitted": Consul-General Wildman, report to the Secretary of State, November 22, 1898, quoted in "Exclusion Laws—Representations against Reenactment as Affecting the United States and Territories, and Extension to the Philippine Islands," in *Foreign Relations of the United States with the Annual Message of the President Transmitted to Congress* (Washington, DC: U.S. Government Printing Office, 1902), 94. That administrators in the United States and the Philippines would claim that the Chinese population posed a threat to labor is a curious projection of hysterical nativist claims onto the native labor force. See also Richard Chu, *Chinese and Chinese*

Mestizos of Manila: Family, Identity, and Culture, 1860s–1930s (Boston, MA: Brill, 2010).

26. This language comes from Emma Blair and James Robertson's massive translation and collection of early Spanish colonial documents, *The Philippine Islands, 1493–1803* (Cleveland, OH: A. H. Clark, 1903), 107. As Alfred McCoy argues, it is unlikely that U.S. officials used this work in state policy: McCoy, *Policing America's Empire*, 43.

The late nineteenth-century Philippine nationalist hero José Rizal, who famously railed against Spanish abuses, also attributed sodomy to the Chinese but claimed that Filipino men resisted such practices: see Racquel A. G. Reyes, *Love, Passion and Patriotism: Sexuality and the Philippine Propaganda Movement, 1882–1892* (Seattle: University of Washington Press, 2008), 212–15.

27. See Nayan Shah, *Contagious Divides: Epidemics and Race in San Francisco's China-town* (Berkeley: University of California Press, 2001), esp. 77–104.

28. Michael Meyers Shoemaker, *Quaint Corners of Ancient Empires: South India, Burma, and Manila* (New York: G. P. Putnam's Sons, 1899), 178.

29. I borrow this phrase from Joseph Boone, "Vacation Cruises; or, The Homoerotics of Orientalism," PMLA 110 (January 1995): 89–100.

30. Between 1848 and 1900, municipalities in twenty-one U.S. states passed laws against cross-dressing. In 1863, San Francisco passed its anti–cross-dressing law. Since California vagrancy laws seem to have been adapted by colonial state administrators in the Philippines, as I suggest later in the chapter, it is significant that this law was not transmitted to the archipelago: see Clare Sears, *Arresting Dress: Cross-Dressing, Law, and Fascination in Nineteenth-Century San Francisco* (Durham, NC: Duke University Press, 2014).

The scarcity of records of policing cross-dressing is all the more surprising given the fact that Emilio Aguinaldo, the general of Philippine anticolonial forces and thus the most famous *insurrecto* in the metroimperial imagination, was widely reputed to have instructed his guerrilla army to dress as women at U.S. check-points. I discuss this point further in chapter 3.

31. As Chauncey points out, although sodomy laws had been on the books since the beginning of the U.S. republic as vestiges of English statutes, only twenty-two sod-omy prosecutions occurred in New York City from 1796 to 1873. The number of prosecutions had increased markedly by the 1880s, so that by the 1890s "between fourteen [and] thirty-eight men were arrested *every year* for sodomy or the 'crime against nature'": Chauncey, *Gay New York*, 140.

32. Eskridge's *Dishonorable Passions* offers a clear and impressive account of these transformations.

33. *U.S. v. Cuna*, 12 Phil. 241, G.R. No. L-4504, December 15, 1908.

34. U.S. War Department, Division of Customs and Insular Affairs, *The Translation of the Penal Code in Force in the Philippines* (Washington, DC: U.S. Government Printing Office, 1900).

35. The enforcement of the Spanish Penal Code persisted well into the decade after the war, according to the *Manual for the Philippine Constabulary* (Manila: Bureau

of Printing, 1911), 71. On the mixed Spanish and U.S. legal traditions of the Philippine colonial state, see Soliman Santos, "Common Elements in the Philippine Mixed Legal System," *Australian Journal of Asian Law* 2, no. 1 (2000): 34–52.

36. U.S. War Department, Division of Customs and Insular Affairs, *The Translation of the Penal Code in Force in the Philippines*, 89–92.

37. See Paul Boyer, *Urban Masses and Moral Order, 1820–1920* (Cambridge, MA: Harvard University Press, 1978); John D'Emilio and Estelle B. Freedman, *Intimate Matters: A History of Sexuality in America* (Chicago: University of Chicago Press, 1997); Chauncey, *Gay New York*; Shah, *Stranger Intimacy*.

38. "Ordinance No. 27," in U.S. War Department, Bureau of Insular Affairs, *Third Annual Report of the Philippine Commission to the Secretary of War* (Washington, DC: U.S. Government Printing Office, 1903), 1213.

39. "Ordinance No. 28," in U.S. War Department, Bureau of Insular Affairs, *Third Annual Report of the Philippine Commission to the Secretary of War* (Washington, DC: U.S. Government Printing Office, 1903), 1213.

40. U.S. Secretary of War, *Annual Reports of the War Department for the Fiscal Year Ended June 30, 1903*, vol. 8 (Washington, DC: U.S. Government Printing Office, 1903), 215–216.

41. Philippine Vagrancy Act 519 shares the language of the vagrancy legislation enacted in the California Penal Code of 1872: see *Penal Code of the State of California Adopted February 14, 1872, with Amendments up to and Including those of the Forty-First Session of the Legislature, 1915* (San Francisco: Bancroft Whitney, 1915), 380–81. Significantly, by 1855 California statutes had already included language around the "infamous crime against nature" and "assault to commit sodomy": Eskridge, *Dishonorable Passions*, 388.

42. Shah, *Stranger Intimacy*, 132.

43. José Dávila-Caballero, "Discrimen por orientación sexual: El denominado estatuto de sodomía de Puerto Rico," *Revista Jurídica Universidad de Puerto Rico* 69 (2000): 1193–94. Significantly, Dávila-Caballero points out that Article 278 of Puerto Rico's Penal Code was modeled after California's. On contemporary implications of this legislation, see Juana Maria Rodriguez's excellent *Sexual Futures, Queer Gestures, and Other Latina Longings* (New York: New York University Press, 2014), 69–98.

44. *The Municipal Code and the Provincial Government Act, Being Act No. 82, Entitled "A General Act for the Organization of Municipal Governments in the Philippine Islands" and Act No. 83, Entitled "A General Act for the Organization of Provincial Governments in the Philippine Islands* (Manila: Bureau of Public Printing, 1905), 27.

45. U.S. War Department, Bureau of Insular Affairs, *Report of the Commissioner of Public Health for the Philippine Islands for the Year Ended September 1, 1903* (Manila: Bureau of Public Printing, 1904), 164.

46. Lee Edelman, "Tearooms and Sympathy; or, The Epistemology of the Water Closet," in *The Lesbian and Gay Studies Reader*, ed. Henry Abelove, Michèle Aina Barale, and David Halperin (New York: Routledge, 1993), 562.

47. Alec R. Webb, "Philippine Islands. Report by Consul Webb, of Manila," in *Special Consular Reports. Volume X* (Washington, DC: Government Printing Office, 1893), 547.
48. Shah, *Stranger Intimacy*, 88.
49. U.S. v. Pablo Trinidad, record no. 3023, January 16, 1907, in *Official Gazette*, vol. 5, no. 35, 480.
50. U.S. v. Pablo Trinidad.
51. This understanding of vagrancy law accords with the famous Marxian critique in William Chambliss, "A Sociological Analysis of the Law of Vagrancy," *Social Problems* 12 (Summer 1964): 67–77.
52. *Report of the Philippine Commission, 1903*, quoted in Frank Hindman Golay, *Face of Empire: United States-Philippine Relations, 1898–1946* (Madison: University of Wisconsin Press, 1998), 95–96. See also McCoy, *Policing America's Empire*, 103.
53. McCoy, *Policing America's Empire*, 103.
54. My "sideways" reading of these two events follows the genealogical practice in Siobhan Somerville, "Queer Loving," GLQ 11, no. 3 (2005): 335–70.
55. Foucault, *History of Sexuality*, 1:143.
56. McCoy, *Policing America's Empire*, 103.
57. U.S. War Department, Bureau of Insular Affairs, *Fourth Annual Report of the Philippine Commission 1903* (Washington: Government Printing Office, 1904), 141.
58. Ignacio Villamor, *Criminality in the Philippine Islands, 1903–1908* (Manila: Bureau of Printing, 1909), 54.
59. Villamor, *Criminality in the Philippine Islands*, 73. Between 1903 and 1907, reports Villamor, crimes against decency and public morals had been steadily decreasing, but in 1908 they "made a sudden leap." Incidences of "rape and adultery," Villamor reported, "increased about 20 per cent over the previous year, while seduction, corruption of minors, abduction, bigamy, and public scandal increased about 5 per cent." The attorney-general's explanation for the escalation of these crimes reflects Foucault's critique of the repressive hypothesis. "It must be remembered," Villamor advised, "that in October 1907, Act No. 1773 was enacted by the Philippine Commission, wherein it is provided that the crimes of adultery, rape, and abduction shall be prosecuted as public crimes. This Act, to a certain extent, increased the number of cases filed by provincial fiscals for such crimes." In other words, since laws produced the crimes against public morals as such, charges proliferated because there was now a specific target for the constabulary.
60. Villamor, *Criminality in the Philippines*, 73.
61. Villamor, *Criminality in the Philippines*, 75; emphasis added.
62. Note, moreover, that it seems unthinkable to this fiscal that women in this bedroom scenario might sleep too "closely" or "promiscuously." As in much of my archive, the possibility of women's same-sex relations is rendered "impossible," as Gayatri Gopinath has used this term. See *Impossible Desires: Queer Diasporas and South Asian Public Cultures* (Durham, NC: Duke University Press, 2005).

63. I thank Paul Kramer and Alfred McCoy for advising me on the hypotheses I offer here. Any misguided speculation is mine.

64. See Vicente Rafael, *White Love and Other Events in Filipino History* (Durham, NC: Duke University Press, 2000); Paul A. Kramer, *The Blood of Government: Race, Empire, the United States, and the Philippines* (Chapel Hill: University of North Carolina Press, 2006); Go and Foster, *The American Colonial State in the Philippines*.

65. Kramer, "The Military-Sexual Complex."

66. De Bevoise, *Agents of Apocalypse*, 84.

67. De Bevoise, *Agents of Apocalypse*, 84–95.

68. Quoted in De Bevoise, *Agents of Apocalypse*, 85.

69. Aaron Belkin, *Bring Me Men: Military Masculinity and the Benign Façade of American Empire, 1898–2001* (New York: Columbia University Press, 2012); Anderson, *Colonial Pathologies*.

70. Edward L. Munson, *The Theory and Practice of Military Hygiene* (New York: William Wood, 1901), 27 (hereafter, *Military Hygiene*).

71. Munson, *Military Hygiene*, 413.

72. Munson, *Military Hygiene*, 21.

73. Munson, *Military Hygiene*, 910.

74. The phrase "gratification of passion" is Munson's. The phrase "*nisus generativus*" appears in such disparate scientific discourses as Havelock Ellis's *Studies in the Psychology of Sex*, vol. 2 (Philadelphia, PA: F. A. David, 1900), 77, and the Research Laboratory of the Royal College of Physicians of Edinburgh's *Report of Investigations on the Life History of Salmon*, ed. Noël Paton (Glasgow: James Hedderwick and Sons, 1898), 169.

75. Percy M. Ashburn, *The Elements of Military Hygiene: Especially Arranged for Officers and Men of the Line* (Boston, MA: Houghton Mifflin, 1909), 27 (hereafter, *Elements*). Ashburn oddly sanctions "'wet dreams' and involuntary seminal emissions" as healthy, morally acceptable, and manhood-preserving ways to relieve soldiers' acute urges to perpetuate the race.

76. Ashburn, *Elements*, 129. For more on neurasthenia and masculinity in the colonial context, see Gail Bederman, *Manliness and Civilization: A Cultural History of Gender and Race in the United States, 1880–1917* (Chicago: University of Chicago Press, 1996); Anderson, *Colonial Pathologies*.

77. Ashburn, *Elements*, 338. The psychiatric categorization of those soldiers practicing sodomy had shifted from depression to psychopathy by 1917: see Margot Canaday, *The Straight State: Sexuality and Citizenship in Twentieth-Century America* (Princeton, NJ: Princeton University Press, 2009), 55–90.

78. Ashburn, *Elements*, 282.

79. Ashburn, *Elements*, 294.

80. Assistant Adjutant General John J. Pershing, August 31, 1900, in *General Orders and Circulars Issued from Headquarters Department of Mindanao and Jolo*, Special Orders, no. 73, August 31, 1900, n.p. Widick was charged under Article 62 of the

Articles of War; the article, although concerned with general criminality in the military, made no reference to sodomy until 1907, as I point out.

81. U.S. War Department, Office of the Judge Advocate General, "Articles of War," in *A Digest of Opinions of the Judge Advocates General of the Army* (Washington, DC: U.S. Government Printing Office, 1912), 147. This regulation is contested by the *Officers' Manual*, which states, "When the evidence is conclusive that an enlisted man is guilty of sodomy or any other crime against nature, it is generally better, for the good of the service, to apply for his discharge without honor, than to expose the service to the scandal of public trial. . . . But when the evidence is not absolutely conclusive . . . in order that no injustice may be done to him, he should be brought to trial, and given his day in court": James A. Moss, *Officers' Manual* (Fort Leavenworth, KS: U.S. Cavalry Association, 1909), 205.

82. U.S. War Department, *A Manual for Courts-Martial, Courts of Inquiry, and of Other Procedure under Military Law* (Washington, DC: U.S. Government Printing Office, 1910), 6.

83. See Canaday, *The Straight State*; Belkin, *Bring Me Men*; William Eskridge, *Gaylaw: Challenging the Apartheid of the Closet* (Cambridge, MA: Harvard University Press, 2002).

84. Edward M. Coffman, *The Regulars: The American Army, 1898–1941* (Cambridge, MA: Harvard University Press, 2007), 81, 448, n. 57.

85. Chauncey, *Gay New York*, 140.

86. Canaday, *The Straight State*, 55.

87. Eskridge, *Gaylaw*, 392, n. 103.

88. See, e.g., Randy Shilts, *Conduct Unbecoming: Gays and Lesbians in the U.S. Military* (New York: St. Martin's Press, 1993), 15; Craig A. Rimmerman, ed., *Gay Rights, Military Wrongs: Political Perspectives on Lesbians and Gays in the Military* (New York: Routledge, 1996), 5; Janice H. Laurence and Michael D. Matthews, eds., *The Oxford Handbook of Military Psychology* (New York: Oxford University Press, 2012), 345. Many gay and lesbian activists who fought for the repeal of "Don't Ask, Don't Tell" have cited this regulation as the origin.

CHAPTER 2. UNMENTIONABLE LIBERTIES

1. "Army and Navy Gossip," *Washington Post*, June 5, 1910, 2.

2. "May Be Sensational Developments in the Philippines," *New York Daily Tribune*, June 4, 1910, 13.

3. "Army and Navy Gossip" (1910), 2.

4. "Captain Reese's Sentence Commuted," *Evening Post* (New York), April 8, 1911, 34.

5. "Dropped from Army Pay Rolls," *Galveston Daily News*, September 7, 1912, n.p.

6. Harry Hill Bandholtz to Major-General Leonard Wood, memorandum, May 12, 1910, Harry Hill Bandholtz Papers, Bentley Historical Library, University of Michigan, Ann Arbor (hereafter, Bandholtz Papers), reel 3, 3.

7. I draw here from Halperin's definition of "active sodomy": David Halperin, "How to Do the History of Male Homosexuality" *GLQ* 6, no. 1 (2000): 92.

8. Alfred McCoy seems to take the charges of "rough" and "brutal treatment" to heart in his recent description of Reese's sexual crime. "A scouts commander in Palawan, Capt. Boss Reese, raped a dozen of his Filipino soldiers in a series of drunken rages": Alfred W. McCoy, *Policing America's Empire: The United States, the Philippines, and the Rise of the Surveillance State* (Madison: University of Wisconsin Press, 2009, 103). I do not necessarily contest McCoy's retroactive description of Reese's actions as "rape," although the hierarchical structures that rape connotes should be attended to. The fact that Reese was the ranked superior of the men with whom he had sex with might lead one to regard the sex act as inherently nonmutual and perhaps coercive, and the "active," penetrating role might thus be regarded as inherently "brutal."

9. "May Be Sensational Developments in the Philippines," 13. See Gayle Rubin, "Thinking Sex: Notes for a Radical Theory of the Politics of Sexuality," in *The Lesbian and Gay Studies Reader*, ed. Henry Abelove, Michèle Aina Barale, and David Halperin (New York: Routledge, 1993), 11.

10. On the recruitment of Filipinos for the imperial Philippine Scouts, see Paul A. Kramer, *The Blood of Government: Race, Empire, the United States, and the Philippines* (Chapel Hill: University of North Carolina Press, 2006), 113–14.

11. Ann Stoler, *Along the Archival Grain: Epistemic Anxieties and Colonial Common Sense* (Princeton, NJ: Princeton University Press, 2009), 1. Stoler here discusses colonial Indonesia.

12. "Scouts Rout Filipinos," *New York Times*, March 28, 1903, 5; "Rewards for Brave Scouts," *New York Times*, April 5, 1903, 13.

13. "San Miguel Died Game," *Daily Star* (Fredericksburg, VA), May 5, 1903, 1. The phrase "near-suicidal assault" comes from the patriotic description of the battle in Matthew Westfall, *The Devil's Causeway: The True Story of America's First Prisoners of War in the Philippines, and the Heroic Expedition Sent to their Rescue* (Guilford, CT: Lyons Press, 2012), 391.

14. Captain E. M. Joss to General H. H. Bandholtz, letter, May 27, 1910, Bandholtz Papers.

15. Slavoj Žižek, "Philosophy, the 'Unknown Knowns,' and the Public Use of Reason," *Topoi* 25, nos. 1–2 (2006): 136. Žižek here discusses the Abu Ghraib prison photograph scandal.

16. Jean-François Lyotard, *The Differend: Phrases in Dispute*, trans. Georges Van Den Abbeele (Minneapolis: University of Minnesota Press, 1988), 10. Other scholars working in critical race studies, postcolonial studies, gender studies, and sexuality studies—or their intersections—have also found Lyotard's concept powerful: see, e.g., Gayatri Spivak's "History," a revision of her canonical essay "Can the Subaltern Speak?" in *A Critique of Postcolonial Reason: Toward a History of a Vanishing Present* (Cambridge, MA: Harvard University Press, 1999), 198–311; Richard Delgado and Jean Stefancic, *Critical Race Theory: An Introduction* (New York: New York University Press, 2001), 44; Joseph Valente, *James Joyce and the Problem of Justice: Negotiating Sexual and Colonial Difference* (Cambridge: Cambridge University Press, 1995); Lynne Huffer, "Queer Victory, Feminist Defeat? Sodomy and Rape

in *Lawrence v. Texas*," in *Feminist and Queer Legal Theory: Intimate Encounters, Uncomfortable Conversations*, ed. Martha Albertson Fineman, Jack E. Jackson, Adam P. Romero (Burlington, VT: Ashgate, 2009), 411–32.

17. Lyotard, *The Differend*, 9.

18. Lyotard, *The Differend*, 13.

19. "Army and Navy Gossip," *Washington Post*, June 9, 1912, 2.

20. Michel Foucault, *The History of Sexuality, Volume 1: An Introduction*, trans. Robert Hurley (New York: Vintage, 1980).

21. Harry Hill Bandholtz to Major-General W. H. Carter, letter, May 16, 1910, Bandholtz Papers, n.p.

22. Bandholtz to Wood (May 12, 1910); emphasis added.

23. For other examples of the houseboy trope in the colonial imaginary, see Eng-Beng Lim's *Brown Boys and Rice Queens: Spellbinding Performance in the Asias* (New York: New York University, 2013).

24. I draw here from the discussion of the act of penetration as signifying one man's superordinate status over another in Halperin, "How to Do the History of Male Homosexuality," 94.

25. George Chauncey, arguing that the homosexual–heterosexual binary that now hegemonically structures our contemporary understanding of sexual identities only began to hold sway during the middle of the twentieth century, has suggested that during the late nineteenth century and early twentieth century, deviance from or inversion of one's ascribed gender status was more indicative of perversion or abnormality than was the participation in same-sex acts. As Chauncey puts it, "The abnormality (or 'queerness') of the 'fairy' [i.e., the 'effeminate' man] was defined as much by his 'womanlike' character or 'effeminacy' as his solicitation of male sexual partners; the 'man' who responded to his solicitations—no matter how often—was not considered abnormal, a 'homosexual,' so long as he abided by masculine gender conventions. Indeed the centrality of effeminacy to the representation of the 'fairy' allowed many conventionally masculine men, especially unmarried men living in sex-segregated immigrant communities, to engage in sexual activity with other men without risking stigmatization and the loss of their status as 'normal men'": George Chauncey, *Gay New York: Gender, Urban Culture, and the Making of the Gay Male World, 1890–1940* (New York: Basic Books, 1994), 13.

26. Halperin, "How to Do the History of Male Homosexuality," 95–96.

27. Not only were Filipinos barred from officer ranks, but only three African American men were promoted to officer status within the Philippine Scouts: see Cynthia Marasigan, "'Between the Devil and the Deep Sea': Ambivalence, Violence and African American Soldiers in the Philippine American War and Its Aftermath," Ph.D. diss., University of Michigan, Ann Arbor, 2010, 427.

28. Here I mean to expand on the famous account of gender performativity in Judith Butler, *Gender Trouble: Feminism and the Subversion of Identity* (New York: Routledge, 1990).

29. Office of the Judge Advocate General to the Adjutant General of the Army, letter, March 2, 1911, in Court-martial of Capt. Boss Reese, Case Files 71051 and 75876; Court-Martial Case Files, 1809–1938; Records of the Office of the Judge Advocate General (Army), Record Group 153; National Archives Building, Washington, DC (hereafter, Reese Papers), n.p.

30. Major J. T. Dickman, quoted in Judge Advocate General (Enoch Crowder) to the Adjutant General, letter, July 8, 1912, 3, in Reese Papers.

31. On the widespread perception among colonial administrators that all Philippine natives could become *insurrectos*, see Vicente Rafael, *White Love and Other Events in Filipino History* (Durham, NC: Duke University Press, 2000); Warwick Anderson, *Colonial Pathologies: American Tropical Medicine, Race, and Hygiene in the Philippines* (Durham, NC: Duke University Press, 2006); Kramer, *The Blood of Government*.

32. Bandholtz to Wood (May 12, 1910), 3.

33. Joss to Bandholtz (May 27, 1910).

34. *United States v. Captain Boss Reese, P.S.*, General Court-Martial, P.I., 1911, Record of Trial (hereafter, *Reese*), 703, in Reese Papers.

35. Bandholtz to Wood (May 12, 1910), 3; Judge Advocate General's Office to Adjutant General of the Army, letter, December 30, 1910, 12, in Reese Papers.

36. *Record of Investigation of Charges against Captain Boss Reese, Philippine Scouts*, Manila, P.I., Major-General W. P. Duvall and Captain S. D. Rockenbach presiding, January 17, 1910, 211, in Reese Papers.

37. Judge Advocate General's Office to Adjutant General of the Army (December 30, 1910), 18, in Reese Papers.

38. Deposition of Joseph Theodore Dickman, Inspector General, n.p., in Reese Papers; Judge Advocate General to Adjutant General (July 8, 1912), 2, in Reese Papers.

39. First Lieutenant James I. Thorne, physician in Medical Reserve Corps, to George B. Davis, Judge Advocate General, letter, November 7, 1909, cited in Judge Advocate General's Office to Adjutant General of the Army (December 30, 1910), 1–3, in Reese Papers. According to one witness who lived in the barracks with Reese and Thorne (one First Lieutenant Charles Long, a dental surgeon), the barracks were called "the bachelor quarters": *Reese*, 456.

40. Thorne to Davis, cited in Judge Advocate General's Office to Adjutant General of the Army (December 30, 1910), 1, in Reese Papers.

41. Thorne to Davis, cited in Judge Advocate General's Office to Adjutant General of the Army (December 30, 1910), 2, in Reese Papers; the bizarre emphases are Thorne's.

42. *Reese*, 1006.

43. Deposition of Luis Malonso, Fifth Company, Philippine Scouts, n.p., Reese Papers.

44. *Reese*, 812.

45. Deposition of Sergeant Apolonio Ducut, Fourth Company, Philippine Scouts, in Reese Papers, n.p.; deposition of Sergeant Rafael Reyes, Fourth Company, Philippine Scouts, in Reese Papers, n.p.

46. *Reese*, 1012.

47. *Reese*, 1012.

48. *Reese*, 1012–13.

49. *Reese*, 974, 980.

50. *Reese*, 980.

51. *Reese*, 980.

52. *Reese*, 47.

53. Judge Advocate General to Adjutant General (July 8, 1912), 16, in Reese Papers. "Pederasty" here would have been used interchangeably with "sodomy."

54. *Reese*, 992–93.

55. *Reese*, 862.

56. James Thorne, Medical Reserve Corps, Affidavit collected by J. T. Dickman, Inspector General, Zamboanga, P.I., December 14, 1909, 6, in Reese Papers.

57. *Reese*, 1013.

58. *Reese*, 1013.

59. Judge Advocate General to Adjutant General (July 8, 1912), 16–17, in Reese Papers.

60. Judge Advocate General to Adjutant General (July 8, 1912), 16, in Reese Papers.

61. *Reese*, 852.

62. See Jonathan Ned Katz, *The Invention of Heterosexuality* (1995), repr. ed. (Chicago: University of Chicago Press, 2007), 95.

63. *Reese*, 1007. This narrative, based on witness statements, comes from the prosecution's closing statements.

64. Foucault, *The History of Sexuality*, 1:45.

65. Memo by President William H. Taft, September 5, 1912, in Reese Papers, n.p.

66. See Sandra Gunning, *Race, Rape, and Lynching: The Red Record of American Literature, 1890–1912* (New York: Oxford University Press, 1996); Saidiya Hartman, *Scenes of Subjection: Terror, Slavery, and Self-Making in Nineteenth-Century America* (New York: Oxford University Press, 1997); Hannah Rosen, *Terror in the Heart of Freedom: Citizenship, Sexual Violence, and the Meaning of Race in the Post-Emancipation South* (Chapel Hill: University of North Carolina Press, 2009). This phrase is from Rosen, *Terror in the Heart of Freedom*, 8. One might also think here of the dismissal in the metropole of Chinese testimonies against white men, established by *People of California v. George W. Hall*, 62 Cal. 2d 104 (1855).

67. Report by Major T. R. Rivers, Inspector-General, Philippines Division, cited in Judge Advocate General's Office to Adjutant General of the Army (December 30, 1910), 13, in Reese Papers.

68. Major S. D. Rockenbach to Adjutant General, Philippines Division, letter, December 31, 1909, quoted in Judge Advocate General's Office to Adjutant General of the Army (December 30, 1910), 10, in Reese Papers.

69. Deposition of Major General William P. Duvall, U.S. Army, cited in *Record of Court of Inquiry, Boss Reese, Philippine Scouts*, January 12, 1910, 6, in Reese Papers.

70. Judge Advocate General's Office to Adjutant General of the Army (December 30, 1910), 20, in Reese Papers.

71. *Reese*, 979–80.

72. Judge Advocate General's Office to Adjutant General of the Army (December 30, 1910), 25, in Reese Papers.

73. Lyotard, *The Differend*, 9.

74. Judge Advocate General's Office to Adjutant General of the Army (December 30, 1910), 20–22, in Reese Papers.

75. Judge Advocate General to Adjutant General (July 8, 1912), 2, in Reese Papers; U.S. War Department, Office of the Judge Advocate General, "Articles of War," in *A Digest of Opinions of the Judge Advocates General of the Army* (Washington, DC: U.S. Government Printing Office, 1912), 140; emphasis in original removed.

76. *Reese*, 1018.

77. Judge Advocate General to Adjutant General (July 8, 1912), 17.

78. Judge Advocate General to Adjutant General (July 8, 1912), 20–21.

79. Cited in copy of the data made by Lt. Thorne M.R.C., 1909, 5, in Reese Papers.

80. Statement of Private Tomas Magat, Fourth Company, Philippine Scouts, n.p., in Reese Papers.

81. Affidavit of Private Tomas Magat, Fourth Company, Philippine Scouts, in *Record of Investigation of Charges against Captain Boss Reese*, 7, in Reese Papers.

82. Lyotard, *The Differend*, 13.

83. Quoted in David Halperin, *Saint Foucault: Towards a Gay Hagiography* (New York: Oxford University Press, 1995), 94.

84. Statement of Corporal Roman Cortez, Fourth Company, Philippine Scouts, n.p., in Reese Papers.

85. In his affidavit, Malonso states: "On the night of October 31, 1909, Captain Reese unbuttoned my breeches. His trousers were already unbuttoned and he took hold of my hand to put it on his privates. I pulled my hand away and said 'It is not the custom of the Filipinos to do this.' Afterward he tried to get next to me, and I rolled over on the ground to that he could not do it. I was not too drunk but what I could remember [was] that he did not accomplish the act" ("Statement of Musician Luis Malonso, Fifth Company, Philippine Scouts," collected by Inspector-General Major J. T. Dickman for investigation of Captain Boss Reese, Philippine Scouts, December 8–9, 1909, in Reese Papers).

86. Luis Malonso, Fifth Company, Philippine Scouts, in *Record of Investigation of Charges against Captain Boss Reese*, 2–3, in Reese Papers. The captain whose name Malonso cannot remember is, as we know, Menz.

87. U.S. Philippine Commission, "Act 190," in *Annual Reports of the War Department: Public Laws and Resolutions Passed by the Philippine Commission* (Washington, DC: U.S. Government Printing Office, 1901), 427.

88. Lyotard, *The Differend*, 10.

89. *Reese*, 1017.

90. *Reese*, 843.

91. *Reese*, 843, 855, 863. The terms "hot stuff" and "cocksucker" are both attributed in the court-martial transcript to Reese.

92. *Reese*, 983.

93. See Anne Fausto-Sterling's brilliant *Sexing the Body: Gender Politics and the Construction of Sexuality* (New York: Basic Books, 2000), esp. 31–36. See also Laurence Senelick, "Enlightened by Morphodites: Narratives of the Fairground Half-and-Half," *Amerikastudien/American Studies* 44, no. 3 (Winter 1999): 357–78.

94. On the rarity of "true" hermaphrodites and their increased disappearance in late nineteenth-century biomedical discourse, see Fausto-Sterling, *Sexing the Body*, esp. 37–39.

95. On the bakla, see Martin Manalansan, *Global Divas: Filipino Gay Men in the Diaspora* (Durham, NC: Duke University Press, 2003); Bobby Benedicto, "The Haunting of Gay Manila: Global Space-Time and the Specter of Kabaklaan," GLQ 14, nos. 2–3 (2008): 317–38; J. Neil Garcia, *Philippine Gay Culture: Binibae to Bakla, Sihalis to MSM* (1996), repr. ed. (Quezon City: University of the Philippines Press, 2009). Although I describe the bakla's sexual attraction here, I do not fold the "bakla" into a sexual category as it is first and foremost a gender category.

96. "Perverse presentism" refers to a model of historical analysis "that avoids the trap of simply projecting contemporary understandings back in time, but one that can apply insights from the present to the conundrums of the past": Judith/Jack Halberstam, *Female Masculinity* (Durham, NC: Duke University Press, 1998), 53.

97. The court's assumption is not surprising. The word "bakla," as several queer Philippine scholars have demonstrated, has been historically untranslatable within both Spanish and U.S. colonial regimes; indeed, "bakla" continued to be mistranslated as "hermaphrodite" in a Tagalog-English dictionary as late as 1972.

98. Foucault, *The History of Sexuality*, 1:101.

99. Garcia's influential and important work *Philippine Gay Culture*, which traces the genealogy and cultural specificity of the bakla from pre-Spanish colonial periods to the 1990s, does not discuss the U.S. colonial period. Garcia does, however, briefly cite an ethnography from 1922 that identifies "effeminate cross-dressing" in the U.S. colonial Philippines: see Fay-Cooper Cole, *The Tinguian: Social, Religious and Economic Life of a Philippine Tribe* (Chicago: Field Museum of Natural History, 1922). 480, n. 4. As far as I know, Cole's anthropological study is, until now, the earliest citation of such an identification.

Morphodite's appearance in the archive will, one hopes, serve as a source of interest for further historical studies of the baklas in the early U.S. colonial Philippines. At the very least, that the figure went by the name "Morphodite" suggests a self-styling reminiscent of the more contemporary bakla figures that Manalansan beautifully tracks in *Global Divas*.

100. I draw here from Dipesh Chakrabarty's conceit in *Provincializing Europe: Postcolonial Thought and Historical Difference* (Princeton: Princeton University Press, 2000).

101. Michel Foucault, "Questions of Method," in *The Foucault Effect: Studies in Governmentality: With Two Lectures by and an Interview with Michel Foucault*, ed. Graham Burchell, Colin Gordon, and Peter Miller (Chicago: University of Chicago Press, 1991), 76.

102. Foucault, "Questions of Method," 76.

103. Reese died on October 6, 1912, coded in the files as a "civilian" and "ex-captain" and was buried at Clark Cemetery in Luzon: report submitted to the Quartermaster General, "Report of Internment of REESE, Boss"; Miranda Gerholt, e-mail message to author, August 15, 2013.

104. My use of the term "reservation" is drawn from the report by exposition administrators: Major William. H. Johnston, "The Battalion of Philippine Scouts," in *Report of the Philippine Exposition Board to the Louisiana Purchase Exposition and Official List of Awards Granted by the Philippine International Jury at the Philippine Government Exposition* (St. Louis: Greeley Printery of St. Louis, 1904), 26.

105. *Report of the Philippine Exposition Board,* 7. On the Philippine Constabulary Band's demonstration of civilization through their virtuoso performances with the African American band leader Walter Loving, see the chapter "Walter Loving and the Philippine Constabulary Band Play the 1904 St. Louis World's Fair," in Marasigan, "Between the Devil and the Deep Sea," 429–87.

106. Richard von Krafft-Ebing, *Psychopathia Sexualis, with Special Reference to Contrary Sexual Instinct,* trans. Charles Gilbert Chaddock (Philadelphia, PA: F. A. Davis, 1894), 2. For a discussion tracing Krafft-Ebing's possible sources about the "Malays of the Philippines," see Racquel A. G. Reyes, *Love, Passion and Patriotism: Sexuality and the Philippine Propaganda Movement, 1882–1892* (Seattle: University of Washington Press, 2008), 198–200.

107. Indeed, newspaper coverage of Reese's charge in St. Louis recounted his heroics in the Philippines, in which even a thigh wound incurred in battle did not prevent him from staving off attacks from the six Philippine insurgents who rushed him: "Lieutenant Reese at Home," *Atlanta Constitution,* May 17, 1904, 1; "Lieut. Reese Soon to Leave," *Atlanta Constitution,* March 12, 1905, 28.

CHAPTER 3. MENACING RECEPTIVITY

1. Michel Foucault, *The History of Sexuality, Volume 1: An Introduction,* trans. Robert Hurley (New York: Vintage, 1980), 36.

2. Sumathi Ramaswamy, "Introduction," in *Empires of Vision: A Reader,* ed. Sumathi Ramaswamy and Martin Jay (Durham, NC: Duke University Press, 2014), 5.

3. The cartoons assembled in *The Forbidden Book* were first shown in "Colored: Black' n White Filipinos in American Popular Media, 1896–1907," an exhibition at PUSOD in Berkeley, California, and later toured throughout the state. It was also featured at Sangandan 2003, an international conference in the Philippines: Abe Ignacio, Enrique de le Cruz, Jorge Emmanuel, and Helen Toribio, eds., *The Forbidden Book: The Philippine-American War in Political Cartoons* (San Francisco, CA: T'Boli, 2004).

4. See Roland Barthes, "The Death of the Author" (1967), in *Image-Music-Text,* trans. Stephen Heath (New York: Hill and Wang, 1977), 142–48, and the description of the "author-function" in Michel Foucault, "What Is an Author?" (1969), in *Language, Counter-Memory, Practice: Selected Essays and Interviews,* ed. Donald F. Bouchard (Ithaca, NY: Cornell University Press, 1980), 113–48.

5. W. J. T. Mitchell, quoted in Nerissa Balce, "The Filipina's Breast: Savagery, Docility, and the Erotics of American Empire," *Social Text* 24, no. 2 (Summer 2006): 103.

6. Roger Fischer, *Them Damned Pictures: Explorations in American Political Cartoon Art* (New Haven, CT: Archon, 1996), 71.

7. Fischer, *Them Damned Pictures*, 71.

8. Donald Dewey, *The Art of Ill Will: The Story of American Political Cartoons* (New York: New York University Press, 2007), 32.

9. Fischer, *Them Damned Pictures*, 72.

10. Kerry Soper, "From Swarthy Ape to Sympathetic Everyman and Subversive Trickster: The Development of Irish Caricature in American Comic Strips between 1890 and 1920," *Journal of American Studies* 39, no. 2 (August 2005): 260.

11. Michael Hunt, *Ideology and Foreign Policy* (New Haven, CT: Yale University Press, 1987).

12. Margo Machida, *Unsettled Visions: Contemporary Asian American Artists and the Social Imaginary* (Durham, NC: Duke University Press, 2008), 63.

13. Stephen Hess and Milton Kaplan, *The Ungentlemanly Art: A History of Political Cartoons*, 2d ed. (New York: Macmillan, 1975), 122; Dewey, *The Art of Ill Will*, 39–45.

14. Fischer, *Them Damned Pictures*, 72.

15. Soper, "From Swarthy Ape to Sympathetic Everyman and Subversive Trickster," 268.

16. Fischer, *Them Damned Pictures*, 122. As Rebecca Edwards argues, cartoons indexed a periodical's financial success, and thus, the size and socioeconomic class of its audience: Rebecca Edwards, "Politics as Social History: Political Cartoons in the Gilded Age," *OAH Magazine of History* 13, no. 4 (Summer 1999): 15.

The liberal, pro-Republican *Judge*, which printed several of the cartoons I examine here, had reached a circulation of fifty thousand by the early 1890s. In 1898, a single issue cost ten cents. The anti-imperialist *Life* had a circulation of fifty thousand by 1890; by 1902, circulation exceeded sixty-five thousand. Although *Life* also cost ten cents per issue, its audience, judging from the advertisements for cameras, automobiles, and top-shelf liquor, was upper middle class: Martha Patterson, *The American New Woman Revisited: A Reader, 1894–1930* (New Brunswick, NJ: Rutgers University Press, 2008), 52, 81, 287.

17. Ubiquitous images of the naked, primitive Filipina and Filipino body played an unstable but critical role in U.S. popular consciousness, affecting even those figures that would seek later to separate themselves from the masses, the "high modernists": see Ronald Bush, "The Presence of the Past: Ethnographic Thinking/Literary Politics," in *Prehistories of the Future: The Primitivist Project and the Culture of Modernism*, ed. Elazar Barkan and Bush (Stanford, CA: Stanford University Press, 1995), 23–41.

18. For an example of the proliferation of photographs, see Jonathan Best, *A Philippine Album: American Era Photographs, 1900–1930* (Makati, Philippines: Bookmark, 1998). See also Mark Rice, *Dean Worcester's Fantasy Islands: Photography, Film, and the Colonial Philippines* (Ann Arbor, MI: University of Michigan Press, 2014); Nerissa Balce, *Body Parts of Empire: Abjection, Filipino Images, and the American Public* (Ann Arbor, MI: University of Michigan Press, forthcoming).

19. Kristin Hoganson, *Consumers' Imperium: The Global Production of American Domesticity, 1865–1920* (Chapel Hill: University of North Carolina Press, 2007), 85.

20. Asterio Favis, "Hunt-Igorot Incident," *The Filipino* 1, no. 6 (November 1906): 27. Wild East shows also traveled in the Philippines.

21. "Editorial Section," *Wichita Daily Eagle* (Wichita, Kansas), February 14, 1904, 13.

22. Du Bois describes double-consciousness as the "sense of always of looking at one's self through the eyes of others, of measuring one's soul by the tape of a world that looks on in amused contempt and pity": W. E. B. Du Bois, *The Souls of Black Folk*, (1903), repr. ed. (New York: Vintage, 1990), 8.

23. Philippine Government Students (PGS), "United States Queries," *Filipino Students' Magazine* 1, no. 2 (June 1905): 34.

24. I borrow this phrase from Mimi Thi Nguyen, "The Biopower of Beauty: Humanitarian Imperialisms and Global Feminisms in an Age of Terror," *Signs* 36, no. 2 (Winter 2011): 359–83, and Minh-ha Pham, "The Right to Fashion in the Age of Terror," *Signs* 36, no. 2 (Winter 2011): 359–83.

25. As Kristin Hoganson has argued, U.S. imperial war in fact resulted from anxieties around white masculinity in the metropole: Kristin Hoganson, *Fighting for American Manhood: How Gender Politics Provoked the Spanish-American and Philippine-American Wars* (New Haven, CT: Yale University Press, 1998).

26. Ignacio et al., *The Forbidden Book*, 73.

27. Ignacio et al., *The Forbidden Book*, 80. In January 1900, the *Sunday Globe* (Boston, MA) had a circulation of 255,705: see *Printers' Ink*, vol. 30, no. 9 (February 28, 1900), 39.

28. See Cynthia Marasigan, " 'Between the Devil and the Deep Sea': Ambivalence, Violence and African American Soldiers in the Philippine American War and Its Aftermath," Ph.D. diss., University of Michigan, Ann Arbor, 2010.

29. Monica Miller, *Slaves to Fashion: Black Dandyism and the Styling of Black Diasporic Identity* (Durham, NC: Duke University Press, 2010), 16.

30. Miller, *Slaves to Fashion*, 158.

31. I borrow this term from Barbara Webb, "The Black Dandyism of George Walker: A Case Study in Genealogical Method," *Drama Review* 45, no. 4 (2001): 7.

32. On the cultural resistance of the black dandy, see Miller, *Slaves to Fashion*; Elisa Glick, "Harlem's Queer Dandy: African-American Modernism and the Artifice of Blackness," *MFS Modern Fiction Studies* 49, no. 3 (2003): 414–42; Camille Forbes, "Dancing with 'Racial Feet': Bert Williams and the Performance of Blackness," *Theatre Journal* 56, no. 4 (2004): 603–25; David Krasner, *Resistance, Parody, and Double Consciousness in African American Theatre, 1895–1910* (New York: St. Martin's Press, 1997); Eric Lott, *Love and Theft: Blackface Minstrelsy and the American Working Class* (New York: Oxford University Press, 1995).

33. Lott, *Love and Theft*, 57.

34. As Alan Sinfield has argued, "The [Oscar Wilde] trials helped to produce a major shift in the perceptions of the scope of same-sex passion. At that point, the entire, vaguely disconcerting nexus of effeminacy, leisure, idleness, immorality, luxury,

insouciance, decadence and aestheticism, with which Wilde was perceived, variously, as instantiating, was transformed into a brilliantly precise image": Alan Sinfield, *The Wilde Century: Effeminacy, Oscar Wilde, and the Queer Moment* (New York: Columbia University Press, 1994), 3. The supposed degeneracy of white American masculinity in the last decade of the nineteenth century was symptomatized in part, as Mary Blanchard argues, by the Gilded Age's popular turn to Wildean aestheticism. Wilde's flamboyant style inspired many men's disturbing (because effeminate) interests in Oriental robes, decorative embroidery, and interior design: see Mary Warner Blanchard, *Oscar Wilde's America: Counterculture in the Gilded Age* (New Haven, CT: Yale University Press, 1998).

35. Jennifer Terry, *An American Obsession: Science, Medicine, and Homosexuality in Modern Society* (Chicago: University of Chicago Press, 1999), 37.

36. Margot Canaday, *The Straight State: Sexuality and Citizenship in Twentieth-Century America* (Princeton, NJ: Princeton University Press, 2009), 22.

37. See Gail Bederman, *Manliness and Civilization: A Cultural History of Gender and Race in the United States, 1880–1917* (Chicago: University of Chicago Press, 1996); Hoganson, *Fighting for American Manhood*; Amy Kaplan, *The Anarchy of Empire in the Making of U.S. Culture* (Durham, NC: Duke University Press, 2002).

38. Neville Hoad captures elegantly the odd temporality of the dandy, showing how evolutionary discourse located the figure both in the past and the future: Neville Hoad, "Arrested Development or the Queerness of Savages: Resisting Evolutionary Narratives of Difference," *Postcolonial Studies* 3, no. 2 (2000): 137.

39. Hoad, "Arrested Development or the Queerness of Savages," 137.

40. Ignacio et al., *The Forbidden Book*, 134–35. Still other cartoons depict anti-Senator George Frisbee Hoar as a "woman" or in blackface and the famous anti-imperialist Mark Twain in "brownface," dressed in "Filipino" native garb: Ignacio et al., *The Forbidden Book*, 137, 144–45, 149.

41. See Hoganson, *Fighting for American Manhood*, esp. 156–80.

42. "Aguinaldo's Wife," *Intermountain and Colorado Catholic Reader* (Salt Lake City), February 17, 1900, 7; emphasis added.

43. Aguinaldo's alleged instructions are reprinted in U.S. Senate, "Proclamation of Aguinaldo" in *Affairs in the Philippine Islands: Hearings before the Committee of the Philippines of the United States Senate* (Washington, DC: U.S. Government Printing Office, 1902), 522–24. The same instructions were previously printed in full in the U.S. press: see, e.g., "Aguinaldo's Orders to Kill Americans," *New York Times*, October 5, 1900.

44. In the late nineteenth century, a man's wearing red socks, something of a flamboyant wardrobe choice, often "spelled effeminacy and decadence, and hinted strongly of increasingly popularized notions of degeneracy": George Haggerty, ed., *Gay Histories and Cultures: An Encyclopedia*. New York: Garland, 2000, 94. George Chauncey cites white gloves as part of the self-styling of some 1890s fairies: George Chauncey, *Gay New York: Gender, Urban Culture, and the Making of the Gay Male World, 1890–1940* (New York: Basic Books, 1994, 52).

45. The speaker of a short poem, "A Hint to a Musician" (1898), directly addresses Aguinaldo, using the musical instruments as a source for innuendo to address the "public" concern of Philippine assimilation: "The public waits to know/What will be your repertory/When you play your piccolo." The speaker also cites Aguinaldo's attempts at fashionability: "You have a golden whistle/and a chance to put on style." The poem was reprinted from the *Washington Star* in the *Corning Journal* (Corning, NY), September 21, 1898, 2.

46. Editorial, *Lawrence World Journal* (Lawrence, KS), February 10, 1899, 2.

47. On the bodily comportment of fairies, see Chauncey, *Gay New York*, 55. Chauncey notes that even as these signals used to identify "homosexuality" were stereotypical, many men wanting to participate in same-sex behavior relied on such signals among themselves.

48. Apart from Aguinaldo, the cartoon figures, from left to right, William Jennings Bryan (Democratic Party presidential candidate from Nebraska), Richard Croker (Democratic Tammany Hall boss and betrayer of Bryan's ticket, after uneasily supporting the candidate), Carl Shurz (former Republican Party senator and secretary of the interior and critic of Croker), and John Altgeld (a Progressivist leader in the Democratic Party and former governor of Illinois).

49. See Chauncey, *Gay New York*, esp. 48–51.

50. Chauncey, *Gay New York*, 33–34.

51. Michael Meyers Shoemaker, *Quaint Corners of Ancient Empires: South India, Burma, and Manila* (New York: G. P. Putnam's Sons, 1899), 178; emphasis in original removed.

52. "The Mazet Board Begins to Probe," *New York Times*, April 9, 1899, 2.

53. See Danielle Robinson, "The Ugly Duckling: The Refinement of Ragtime Dancing and the Mass Production of Marketing of Modern Social Dance," *Dance Research* 28, no. 2 (Winter 2010): 189. It is not clear whether "kiky" actually signifies what Audre Lorde's variantly spelled "Ky-Ky" does, but the similarity convinces me. In any event, there is clearly an "immorality" or "perversion," based on gender-sexual deviance, attributed to this term: see Audre Lorde, *Zami: A New Spelling of My Name—A Biomythography* (Berkeley, CA: Crossing Press, 1982), 178, 208, 225.

54. Nguyen, "The Biopower of Beauty," 375.

55. The project of masculinist U.S. imperialism not only allowed for the possible entry of colonized others into the nation. It also, as Amy Kaplan argues, threatened to disrupt abroad the racial segregation recently legalized in the metropole: Kaplan, *The Anarchy of Empire*, 124–25.

56. Hunt offers a slightly different, though not incompatible, genealogy of cartoons' figuring former Spanish colonies as children: Hunt, *Ideology and U.S. Foreign Policy*, 61.

57. Ignacio et al., *The Forbidden Book*, 60, 72.

58. Ignacio et al., *The Forbidden Book*, 22, 28.

59. The phrase "white love" comes from Vicente Rafael, *White Love and other Events in Filipino History* (Durham, NC: Duke University Press, 2000).

60. See Ivan Crozier, "Philosophy in the English Boudoir: Havelock Ellis, *Love and Pain*, and the Sexological Discourses on Algophilia," *Journal of the History of Sexuality* 13, no. 3 (2004): 275–305.

61. Crozier, "Philosophy in the English Boudoir," 283.

62. Quoted in Crozier, "Philosophy in the English Boudoir," 276

63. Jean Laplanche and J. B. Pontalis note Krafft-Ebing's naming of sadism in *The Language of Psycho-Analysis*, trans. Donald Nicholson-Smith (New York: W. W. Norton, 1973), 401.

64. "American Woman Visits Queer Corners of World," *Tensas Gazette*, September 11, 1914, 8.

65. "Ponder This Child Problem," *Tensas Gazette*, September 11, 1914, 8.

66. Ignacio et al., *The Forbidden Book*, 85.

67. Ignacio et al., *The Forbidden Book*, 40.

68. Theodore Roosevelt, "At the Founders' Day Banquet of the Union League, Philadelphia, PA, November 22, 1902," in *A Compilation of the Messages and Speeches of Theodore Roosevelt: 1901–1905*, ed. Alfred Henry Louis (New York: Bureau of National Literature and Art, 1906), 189.

69. Ignacio et al., *The Forbidden Book*, 109.

70. Ignacio et al., *The Forbidden Book* 104.

71. Jasbir K. Puar and Amit S. Rai, "Monster, Terrorist, Fag: The War on Terrorism and the Production of Docile Bodies," *Social Text* 20, no. 3 (2002): 117–48.

72. Such allegedly infinite reproductive capabilities historically have informed the abstraction of the Filipina and Filipino laborer, not to mention the "Oriental" laborer writ large. As Colleen Lye has argued, "As the phantasmatically cheapening body capitalism strives to universalize, the coolie represents a biological impossibility and a numerical abstraction, whose social domination means that the robust American body will have disappeared": Colleen Lye, *America's Asia: Racial Form and American Literature, 1893–1945* (Princeton, NJ: Princeton University Press, 2005), 57.

73. *Collier's Weekly* at the time boasted a circulation of 197,000 copies per week. See *American Newspaper Dictionary* (New York: Geo. P. Rowell, 1900), 780.

74. Ignacio et al., *The Forbidden Book*, 104. This cartoon seems to allude to the infamous shooting of a Filipino soldier by Private William Grayson on February 4, 1899, which is conventionally held as the provocation of the Philippine-American War.

75. This cartoon represents something of an innovation in the representation of the Philippine insurrecto body, as it is one among a series of caricatures that drew on the romanticization of death in the U.S. colonial arena in Frederick Remington's painting *The Charge of the Rough Riders at San Juan Hill* (1898). Remington's patriotic painting would so please Theodore Roosevelt's imperialist aesthetic that Roosevelt included it in the book-length account of his exploits during the Cuban American War: see Theodore Roosevelt, *The Rough Riders* (New York:

Charles Scribner's Sons, 1899), 132. That same year, several cartoons would riff off this memento mori, though moving the setting from a battlefield in Cuba to one in the Philippines and replacing the dying white soldier with a "Filipino": see "United States Soldier—If I Can Catch This Fellow I'll Deliver the Goods," *Chicago Record*, February 18, 1899, and "Aguinaldo Illustrates the Latest Popular Song," *Chicago Record*, November 24, 1899. I thank Amanda Healy for identifying these predecessors.

76. Slavoj Žižek, *The Sublime Object of Ideology* (London: Verso, 1989), 134.

77. Žižek, *The Sublime Object of Ideology*, 134–35.

78. Saidiya Hartman, *Scenes of Subjection: Terror, Slavery, and Self-Making in Nineteenth-Century America* (New York: Oxford University Press, 1997), 25. I write this at a time when this same fantasmatic, genocidal logic motivates white supremacist violence against countless black bodies in the U.S. metropole. Remember the murder of black eighteen-year-old Michael Brown in Ferguson, Missouri, by a police officer that imagined that Brown grew *stronger* and *bigger* with each bullet boring into his body. Remember the murder of Aiyana Jones, the seven-year-old girl from Detroit, Michigan, who was shot in her bed during a police raid. Remember the murder of fifty-year-old Walter Scott, in North Charleston, South Carolina, by an officer who shot him eight times in the back and would plant (not a sword) but a taser on Scott's lifeless body. Remember the murder of ninety-two-year-old Kathryn Johnson of Atlanta, Georgia, who was shot at thirty-nine times by police officers. It's not coincidence that the cartoon examined here is called "The First *Black* Bored in the Philippines." This is blackness in the metroimperial fantasy. We are compelled to see over and over again the transhistorical production—the *conservation*—of what Ruth Wilson Gilmore has called black vulnerability to premature death, the unmitigated and unashamed brutality of white supremacist terrorism, the banality of U.S. imperial subjection.

79. Lauren Berlant has recently used the phrase "sensed but always missed" to describe the Lacanian Real: Lauren Berlant, *Desire/Love* (Brooklyn, NY: Punctum Books, 2012), 54.

80. Žižek, *The Sublime Object of Ideology*, 132.

81. Žižek, *The Sublime Object of Ideology*, 134.

82. Ignacio et al., *The Forbidden Book*, 125.

83. Ignacio et al., *The Forbidden Book*, 103.

84. This image in particular explicitly evokes Hans Holbein's drawing *The Tyranny of Schoolmasters* (circa 1515), which depicts the eponymous figure birching a disobedient student.

85. Ignacio et al., *The Forbidden Book*, 110.

86. Ignacio et al., *The Forbidden Book*, 103. Contemporaneous political cartoons' depictions of nativist violence against Chinese characters—most notably, for example, those used by the Workingmen's Party of California—share in this tropology of white violence penetrating the racial bottom. I thank Jesse Carr for bringing these tropes to my attention.

87. René Girard understands sadism's slippage into masochistic identification: see René Girard, *Violence and the Sacred*, trans. Patrick Gregory (Baltimore, MD: Johns Hopkins University Press), 1977.

88. Ignacio et al., *The Forbidden Book*, 103.

89. Gilles Deleuze, *Masochism: Coldness and Cruelty* (1967), trans. Jean McNeil, repr. ed. (New York: Zone Books, 1991), 18–20.

90. Sara Ahmed, *Willful Subjects* (Durham, NC: Duke University Press, 2014), 2.

91. Deleuze, *Masochism*, 19.

92. Meg Wesling, *Empire's Proxy: American Literature and U.S. Imperialism in the Philippines* (New York: New York University Press, 2011), 2.

93. Quoted in Paul A. Kramer, *The Blood of Government: Race, Empire, the United States, and the Philippines* (Chapel Hill: University of North Carolina Press, 2006), 2.

94. Quoted in Deleuze, "Coldness and Cruelty," 20.

95. We might see this scene as an instance of U.S. empire's "pedophiliac Western modernity": Eng-Beng Lim, *Brown Boys and Rice Queens: Spellbinding Performance in the Asias* (New York: New York University, 2013), 4.

96. Chauncey, *Gay New York*, 52.

97. Ignacio et al., *The Forbidden Book*, 87.

98. One might recall Leo Bersani's famous rendering of heteronomative culture's fantasy of gay male sex, the "seductive and intolerable image of a grown man, legs high in the air, unable to refuse the suicidal ecstasy of being a woman": Leo Bersani, "Is the Rectum a Grave?" *October* 43 (1987): 212.

99. Warwick Anderson, *Colonial Pathologies: American Tropical Medicine, Race, and Hygiene in the Philippines* (Durham, NC: Duke University Press, 2006), 106.

100. Anderson, *Colonial Pathologies*, 106, 117.

101. Anderson, *Colonial Pathologies*, 106.

102. Anderson, *Colonial Pathologies*, 60.

103. Anderson, *Colonial Pathologies*, 107.

104. Anderson, *Colonial Pathologies*, 110.

105. D. A. Miller, "Anal Rope," in *Inside/Out: Lesbian Theories, Gay Theories*, ed. Diana Fuss (New York: Routledge, 1991), 134.

106. Dean, *Beyond Sexuality*, 267.

107. Anderson, *Colonial Pathologies*, 111.

108. To put this differently: if, as Žižek has argued, "excrement is *objet a* [i.e., the paradoxical object/cause of desire] in the precise sense of the non-symbolizable surplus that remains after the body is symbolized," then in the Filipino bottom we find U.S. imperial colonialism's *objet a*, the impossible object-cause of imperial fantasy and desire: *The Metastases of Enjoyment* (London: Verso, 1994), 179. Such a psychoanalytic reading of imperial desire draws from Anderson's borrowing of the Freudian term in characterizing American colonial physicians as "retentive," even as Anderson himself does not read psychoanalytically: see Anderson, *Colonial Pathologies*, 71, 106, 111.

109. Hartman, *Scenes of Subjection*, 7.

110. Ignacio et al., *The Forbidden Book*, 126.

111. See Rick Baldoz, *The Third Asiatic Invasion: Empire and Migration in Filipino America, 1898–1946* (New York: New York University Press, 2011).

112. Here I draw from Ann Cvetkovich's discussion of femme discourses around sex, in which "receptivity," which involves the bottom's power and work, "replaces 'passivity' so as to make the role of the 'bottom' less stigmatized. . . . So impoverished is the language of sexual power, especially the loss of sexual power, that it can only be translated into an active/passive dichotomy, where passivity is always stigmatized": Ann Cvetkovich, *An Archive of Feelings: Trauma, Sexuality, and Lesbian Public Archives* (Durham, NC: Duke University Press, 2003), 58–59.

113. To be clear, I am not suggesting that these cartoons somehow recuperate the subjecthood, power, or pleasure out of abject racialized bottomhood, as one sees in the recent work by brilliant scholars working at the convergence of race and sexuality: see, e.g., Nguyen Tan Hoang, *A View from the Bottom: Asian American Masculinity and Sexual Representation* (Durham, NC: Duke University Press, 2014); Joon Oluchi Lee, "Joy of the Castrated Boy," *Social Text* 23, nos. 3–4 (Fall-Winter 2005): 35–56; Amber Musser, *Sensational Flesh: Race, Power, and Masochism* (New York: New York University Press, 2014); Jennifer Nash, *The Black Body in Ecstasy: Reading Race Reading Pornography* (Durham, NC: Duke University Press, 2014); Darieck Scott, *Extravagant Abjection: Blackness, Power, and Sexuality in the African American Literary Imagination* (New York: New York University Press, 2010); Kathryn Bond Stockton, *Beautiful Bottom, Beautiful Shame: Where "Black" Meets "Queer"* (Durham, NC: Duke University Press, 2006).

CHAPTER 4. EPIDEMIC OF INTIMACIES

1. Roosevelt significantly qualifies this declaration, however, saying that it "did not apply" "in the country inhabited by Moro tribes": Theodore Roosevelt, "A Proclamation," July 4, 1902, in *A Compilation of the Messages and Papers of the Presidents: 1789–1902*, ed. James D. Richardson (New York: Bureau of National Literature and Art, 1903), 393.

2. Quoted in Michael Salman, *The Embarrassment of Slavery: Controversies over Bondage and Nationalism in the American Colonial Philippines* (Berkeley: University of California Press, 2001), 36–37.

3. Salman, *The Embarrassment of Slavery*, 44

4. George Ade, *The Sultan of Sulu: An Original Satire in Two Acts* (New York: R. H. Russell, 1903), unpaginated note. Further citations to this work are in parentheses in the text.

5. The handsome Colonel Budd also evokes, as Joe Ponce reminded me, the eponymous and often queered protagonist of *Billy Budd, Sailor*, even as Melville's posthumously published novela appeared in print decades later.

6. Henry Wonham, "'I Want a Real Coon': Mark Twain and Late-Nineteenth-Century Ethnic Caricature," *American Literature* 72, no. 1 (March 2000): 121.

7. Michael Warner, "Irving's Posterity," ELH 67, no. 3 (Fall 2000): 773.

8. Eve Sedgwick, *Epistemology of the Closet* (Berkeley: University of California Press, 1991), esp. 182–212; Nayan Shah, *Contagious Divides: Epidemics and Race in San Francisco's Chinatown* (Berkeley: University of California Press, 2001).

9. Fred Kelly, *George Ade, Warmhearted Satirist* (New York: Bobbs-Merrill, 1947), 217.

10. Albert Agsforth, "Hoosier Humorist, Three Letters," *American Scholar* 56, no. 4 (Autumn 1987): 570.

11. See, e.g., George Ade, *The America of George Ade (1866–1944)*, ed. Jean Shepherd (New York: Putnam, 1960); George Ade, *The Best of George Ade*, ed. A. L. Lazarus (Bloomington: Indiana University Press, 1985); George Ade, *Letters of George Ade*, ed. Terrence Tobin (West Lafayette, IN: Purdue University Press, 1973); George Ade, *Stories of Chicago* (1941), ed. Franklin Meine, repr. ed. (Urbana: University of Illinois Press, 2003); Lee Coyle, *George Ade* (New York: Twayne, 1964); James Demuth, *Small Town Chicago: The Comic Perspective of Finley Peter Dunne, George Ade, Ring Lardner* (Port Washington, NY: Kennikat Press, 1980); Kelly, *George Ade, Warmhearted Satirist*; Fred Kelly, *The Permanent Ade: The Living Writings of George Ade* (Indianapolis: Bobbs-Merrill, 1947). One exception is Timothy Spears, *Chicago Dreaming: Midwesterners and the City, 1871–1919* (Chicago: University of Chicago Press, 2005).

12. U.S. Senate, *Treaty with the Sultan of Sulu*, 56th Cong., 1st sess., S. Doc. 136, 1900, 16.

13. Article 3 reads, "The rights and dignities of His Highness the Sultan and his datos [Moro for "chiefs"] shall be fully respected; the Moros shall not be interfered with on account of their religion; all their religious customs shall be respected, and no one shall be persecuted on account of his religion": U.S. Senate, *Treaty with the Sultan of Sulu*, 4. Critics of the treaty at the time often cited this article as evidence of U.S. administrators' hands-off policy concerning polygamy.

14. U.S. Senate, *Treaty with the Sultan of Sulu*, 109.

15. Paul A. Kramer, *The Blood of Government: Race, Empire, the United States, and the Philippines* (Chapel Hill: University of North Carolina Press, 2006), 208–14.

16. Theodore William Noyes, *Oriental America and Its Problems* (Washington, DC: Judd and Detweiler, 1903), 40.

17. Irving Reems, "From the Far East," *Princeton Union* (Princeton, MN), January 4, 1900, 1.

18. Kristin Hoganson, *Consumers' Imperium: The Global Production of American Domesticity, 1865–1920* (Chapel Hill: University of North Carolina Press, 2007).

19. Marilla Weaver, "The Women of Sulu: The Oppressed Sex in the South Philippines," *Wichita Eagle*, July 7, 1901, 16.

20. Clare Sears, "Electric Brilliancy: Cross-Dressing Law and Freak Show Displays in Nineteenth-Century San Francisco," *Women's Studies Quarterly* 36, nos. 3–4 (Fall-Winter 2008): 172.

21. "Sherman on Sulus: America Has about the Same Protectorate as Spain," *Los Angeles Times*, November 1, 1899, 2. The classical historical accounts of Muslim populations in the southern Philippines include, for example, Cesar Majul, *Muslims in the Philippines* (Quezon City: University of the Philippines Press, 1973); Salman,

The Embarrassment of Slavery; Samuel K. Tan, *Sulu under American Military Rule, 1899–1913* (Manila: University of the Philippines, 1967).

22. Margherita Arlina Hamm, "Philippine Customs and Oddities," *The Independent* (New York), April 6, 1899, 51. On Hamm's prominence among female journalists in the fin-de-siècle United States, see Alice Fahs, *Out on Assignment: Newspaper Women and the Making of Modern Public Space* (Chapel Hill: University of North Carolina Press, 2011).

23. Hamm, "Philippine Customs and Oddities." I hope to demonstrate how U.S. Islamophobia around the "Terrifying Muslim," to borrow Junaid Rana's phrase, remains largely unchanged in metropolitan imaginary. Hamm's descriptions of the *juramentado* training recall the popular press's grainy footage of "terrorists" training for "jihad" on various obstacle courses following the September 11 attacks. For the roots and routes of this terror, see Junaid Rana, *Terrifying Muslims: Race, and Labor in the South Asian Diaspora* (Durham, NC: Duke University Press, 2011).

24. "Running Amuck in the Philippines: A Queer Form of Insanity to Which the Natives are Sometimes Subject," *Red Cloud Chief* (Red Cloud, NE), April 6, 1900, 2. This image clearly borrows from the famous cover of *Judge* (July 9, 1898) depicting the "Spanish Brute."

25. Frank G. Carpenter, "Uncle Sam's Slaves," *Evening Star* (Washington, DC), June 23, 1900, 21.

26. Cited in "The Twin Evils," *Newark Daily Advocate* (Newark, OH), November 20, 1899, 2.

27. Bruce Burgett, "On the Mormon Question: Race, Sex, and Polygamy in the 1850s and 1990s," *American Quarterly* 57, no. 1 (March 2005): 75–102; Nancy Bentley, "Marriage as Treason: Polygamy, Nation, and the Novel," in *The Futures of American Studies*, ed. Donald Pease and Robyn Wiegman (Durham, NC: Duke University Press, 2002).

28. Burgett, "On the Mormon Question," 76.

29. Burgett, "On the Mormon Question," 84–85.

30. Lieber, quoted in Burgett, "On the Mormon Question," 86. Lieber's fear of "Africanization" might come from the fact that informal polygamy was not uncommon among early nineteenth-century slave communities: see Edward Curtis, *Muslims in America: A Short History* (New York: Oxford University Press, 2009), 15.

31. Bentley, "Marriage as Treason," 345.

32. Nancy Cott, *Public Vows: A History of Marriage and the Nation* (Cambridge, MA: Harvard University Press, 2000), 137.

33. Bentley, "Marriage as Treason," 345.

34. "Polygamy," *Washington Post*, December 27, 1898, 4.

35. Cott, *Public Vows*, 139.

36. "It Is a Very Queer Thing," *Dubuque Daily Herald* (Dubuque, IA), October 6, 1900, 4.

37. D. A. Recrem, "Polygamy in History," *Washington Post*, December 24, 1899, 13.

38. Editorial, *Hornellsville Weekly Tribune* (Hornellsville, NY), October 27, 1899, 4.

39. "Rank Discrimination," *Virginian Pilot* (Norfolk, VA), August 22, 1900, 4.

40. Mark Rifkin, *When Did Indians Become Straight? Kinship, the History of Sexuality and Native Sovereignty* (New York: Oxford University Press, 2011), 173.

41. See Jack Brenner, "Howells and Ade," *American Literature* 38, no. 2 (May 1966): 199.

42. George Ade, *George Ade's "Stories of Benevolent Assimilation,"* ed. Perry Gianakos (Quezon City, Philippines: New Day, 1985), 13.

43. Ade, *George Ade's "Stories of Benevolent Assimilation,"* 15.

44. Much of the biography in this section is extracted from Kelly, *George Ade, Warmhearted Satirist.*

45. Kelly, *George Ade, Warmhearted Satirist,* 164.

46. Brenner, "Howells and Ade," 198.

47. "Many Places of Amusement Changed Bills Last Night," *St. Louis Republic,* September 8, 1902, 6.

48. For a history of Savage's production history, see Jim McPherson, "The Savage Innocents. Part 1, King of the Castle: Henry W. Savage and the Castle Square Opera Company," *Opera Quarterly* 18, no. 4 (Autumn 2002): 503–33; Jim McPherson, "The Savage Innocents. Part 2: On the Road with Parsifal, Butterfly, the Widow, and the Girl," *Opera Quarterly* 19, no. 1 (Winter 2003): 28–63.

49. "George Ade's Operetta," *The Sun* (New York), December 30, 1902, 7. A reviewer from the *New York Tribune* also reported that the play "was listened to with considerable relish" but disparaged Wathall's music, saying that "at least [it] drove nobody away": "The Sultan of Sulu," *New York Tribune,* December 30, 1902, 7. The music, while pleasant enough, is indeed unremarkable, so I do not analyze it here. One can find a recent interpretation of the *Sultan,* performed by the Canton Comic Opera Company (Canton, OH) in 2009, on Youtube.

50. Ade's original stage directions are marked by brackets; for the sake of clarity, here and throughout the chapter, I cite Ade's stage directions in parentheses.

51. Kelly, *George Ade, Warmhearted Satirist,* 59.

52. One might think of the "most ingenious paradox" that the protagonist of Gilbert and Sullivan's *The Pirates of Penzance* (1880), Frederick, must grapple with: set to be released on his twenty-first birthday from the contracted custody of the pirates who raised him, Frederick is shocked by the fact that, because he was born on February 29, during a leap year, he is, at twenty-one, but "a little boy of five!"

53. See Kristyn Moon, *Yellowface: Creating the Chinese in American and Popular Music and Performance, 1850s–1920s* (New Brunswick, NJ: Rutgers University Press, 2005).

54. Gerald Bordman, *American Musical Theatre* (New York: Oxford University Press, 1978), 188.

55. Bordman, *American Musical Theatre,* 220.

56. Helen Heran Jun, *Race for Citizenship: Black Orientalism and Asian Uplift from Pre-Emancipation to Neoliberal America* (New York: New York University Press, 2011), 17–18.

57. Titles include *The Runaways* (1903), *The Isle of Spice* (1904), *Fantana* (1905), and Ade's own *The Shogun* (1904): see Bordman, *American Musical Theatre,* 188.

58. Christina Klein, *Cold War Orientalism: Asia in the Middlebrow Imagination, 1945–1961* (Berkeley: University of California Press, 2003), 9.

59. On Moulan's blackface stardom, see Bordman, *American Musical Theatre*, 206. As Moon documents, the efforts to pass as "authentically" Chinese were keenly developed: Moon, *Yellowface*, 117. Still, that Moulan did not play the role in yellow face or brown face does not attest to a lack of Orientalist performance. As documented in Noyes, *Oriental America and Its Problems*, 43, the Sultan met with the American colonial administrators wearing a "European suit of light gray, with white shirt and collar"—hardly "Oriental."

60. "F. Moulan and G. L. Fox: Striking Resemblance between the Two Comedians," *New York Tribune*, April 26, 1903, 5. More to my point regarding not practicing brown face, the reporter notes that Moulan "applied the usual coloring [presumably 'white'] to his face."

61. To be sure, the original production of *The Sultan of Sulu* did not avoid blackface. Ki-Ram's "slaves," as production photos attest, were clearly, and clearly problematically, white actors in minstrel makeup. On the cultural "authenticity" that objects furnished oriental productions, see Josephine Lee, *The Japan of Pure of Invention: Gilbert and Sullivan's The Mikado* (Minneapolis: University of Minnesota Press, 2010), esp. 3–38.

62. "The Theatre," *Evening Star* (Washington, DC), September 29, 1903, 16.

63. Salman, *The Embarrassment of Slavery*, 45.

64. U.S. Senate, *Treaty with the Sultan of Sulu*, 32–33.

65. Andrew Ross, "Uses of Camp," in *Camp: Queer Aesthetics and the Performing Subject, a Reader*, ed. Fabio Cleto (Ann Arbor: University of Michigan Press, 1999), 320.

66. Such language resembles that used by Noyes when he deems the historical figure of Datto Mandi, the Sultan's neighbor and rival, "the most attractive and apparently the most forceful of the dattos whom [he] met": Noyes, *Oriental America and Its Problems*, 51.

67. Michel Foucault, *The History of Sexuality, Volume 1: An Introduction*, trans. Robert Hurley (New York: Vintage, 1980), 23.

68. Ade constantly tinkered with and had multiple drafts of the libretto. The phrase "full of the oil of joy" comes from the version he had most control over—and, indeed, the one he considered part of his "private archives": see George Ade, *Verses and Jingles* (Indianapolis: Bobbs-Merrill, 1911), 2. Ade's discussion of Savage's editorial is documented in the preface to *Verses and Jingles* (emphasis added).

69. The third stanza in the good-bye poem "Au Revoir" includes the lines, "Never those happy strolls/In the evening's purple bliss, /When two immortal souls/Blended—to part like this!": *The Lover's Poetic Companion and Valentine Writer* (London: Ward, Lock, and Tyler, 1875, 91. A front-page story in the *San Antonio Light*, meanwhile, recounts the "romance" between one Miss Della Paris and Mr. C. A. Lewis by stating, "Friendship ripened into love rapidly and *the world was one kaledoscope [sic] of purple bliss*": "Kansas Romance Has Climax in San Antonio," *San Antonio Light*,

May 5, 1911, 1. Curiously, the reporter, clearly borrowing quite liberally from Ade's libretto, likens "purple bliss" of romance to "climax."

70. Carlos Bulosan, *America Is in the Heart* (1943) (Seattle: University of Washington Press, 1973), 159. For a "queer" reading of this passage, see Melinda L. de Jesus, "Rewriting History, Rewriting Desire: Reclaiming Queerness in Carlos Bulosan's *American Is in the Heart* and Bienvenido Santos' *The Scent of Apples*," *Journal of Asian American Studies* 5, no. 2 (June 2002): 91–111.

71. George Chauncey, *Gay New York: Gender, Urban Culture, and the Making of the Gay Male World, 1890–1940* (New York: Basic Books, 1994), 49.

72. Howard Chudacoff, *The Age of the Bachelor: Creating an American Subculture* (Princeton, NJ: Princeton University Press, 2000), 97.

73. Chudacoff, *The Age of the Bachelor.*

74. Chudacoff, *The Age of the Bachelor,* 75.

75. Scott Herring, *Queering the Underworld: Slumming, Literature, and the Undoing of Lesbian and Gay History* (Chicago: University of Chicago Press, 2007), 25–66.

76. Quoted in Chudacoff, *The Age of the Bachelor,* 75.

77. José Esteban Muñoz, *Disidentifications: Queers of Color and the Politics of Performance* (Minneapolis: University of Minnesota Press, 1999), 31.

78. Kelly, *George Ade, Warmhearted Satirist,* 151. The largely oral history of the Chicago Athletic Club has only recently been recounted in print: see Jill Austin, Jennifer Brier, Jessica Herczeg-Konecny, and Anne Parsons, "When the Erotic Becomes Illicit: Struggles over Displaying Queer History at a Mainstream Museum: Struggles over Displaying Queer History at a Mainstream Museum," *Radical History Review* 113 (Spring 2012): 192.

79. Kelly, *George Ade, Warmhearted Satirist,* 164.

80. Quoted in Kelly, *George Ade, Warmhearted Satirist,* 164.

81. See Chauncey, *Gay New York,* 25.

82. "Just George Ade's Way," *Goodwin's Weekly* (Salt Lake City, UT), April 4, 1903, 4.

83. Kelly, *George Ade, Warmhearted Satirist,* 217–18.

84. Kelly, *George Ade, Warmhearted Satirist,* 218.

85. Othello famously describes himself as "one that loved not wisely but too well": *Othello* 5.2.344. I thank Valerie Traub for pointing out Ade's allusion.

86. George Ade, "The Joys of Single Blessedness," in *Single Blessedness and Other Observations* (Garden City, NY: Doubleday Page, 1922), 1–2. Further citations to this work are in parentheses in the text.

87. Gayle Rubin, "Thinking Sex: Notes for a Radical Theory of the Politics of Sexuality," in *The Lesbian and Gay Studies Reader,* ed. Henry Abelove, Michèle Aina Barale, and David Halperin (New York: Routledge, 1993), 3–44; Christopher Nealon, *Foundlings: Lesbian and Gay Historical Emotion before Stonewall* (Durham, NC: Duke University Press, 2001).

88. McCutcheon, who won a Pulitzer Prize in 1932, often drew (non-pornographic) cartoons featuring Chicago figures engaged in same-sex intimacy: Jill Austin and

Jennifer Brier, eds., *Out in Chicago: LGBT History at the Crossroads* (Chicago, IL: Chicago History Museum, 2012).

89. See Kelly, *George Ade, Warmhearted Satirist*, 205–9; Ade, *Letters of George Ade*, 160.

90. See Austin, et al., "When the Erotic Becomes Illicit," 192–93. Ade has recalled fondly his first meeting with "Mr. Wells" in Chicago, saying, "I met you one fine, cool, bracing date last autumn on the West Side. . . . I believe you were wearing a light overcoat. . . . We went back to the Athletic Club in a taxi, and after a pleasant steaming, we took the shower and jumped into the pool": quoted in Kelly, *George Ade, Warmhearted Satirist*, 208.

91. See Austin and Brier, *Out in Chicago*, n.p.

92. Kelly, *George Ade, Warmhearted Satirist*, 185.

93. Cheng, *The Melancholy of Race*, 42, 71.

94. Such recognition affirms Jack/Judith Halberstam's hypothesis about "the strangely similar constructions of non-metropolitan queer sexualities in the United States and nonmetropolitan sexualities in other parts of the world": Jack/Judith Halberstam, *In a Queer Time and Place: Transgender Bodies, Subcultural Lives* (New York: New York University Press, 2005), 37.

95. "The Sultan of Sulu and His Comic Opera Court," *Omaha Illustrated Bee*, November 26, 1900, 12.

CHAPTER 5. CERTAIN PECULIAR TEMPTATIONS

1. Pacifico Laygo, "On the Battlefield," *Filipino Students' Magazine* 1, no. 3 (September 1905): 14–16.

2. Laygo, "On the Battlefield," 16.

3. As there were both female and male Philippine students, I refer to the collective Philippine students as pensionadas/os, even if they were known only by the masculine "pensionados."

4. The *Filipino Students' Magazine* was renamed *Philippine Review* in July 1907.

5. Notable exceptions are Kimberly Alidio, "Student Migrations: Racialized Bodies, Cosmopolitan Nationalism and the 'New Filipino,'" in "Between Civilizing Mission and Ethnic Assimilation: Racial Discourse, U.S. Colonial Education and Filipino Ethnicity, 1901–1946," Ph.D. diss., University of Michigan, Ann Arbor, 2001, 91–129; Alexander A. Calata, "The Role of Education in Americanizing Filipinos," in *Mixed Blessings: The Impact of the American Colonial Experience on Politics and Society in the Philippines*, ed. Hazel M. McFerson (Westport, CT: Greenwood Press, 2002), 89–98. Susan Harris has recently examined how some of the more prominent Philippine political actors—namely, Emilio Aguinaldo and Apolinario Mabini— responded to U.S. imperial conquest: see Susan Harris, *God's Arbiters: Americans and the Philippines*. New York: Oxford University Press, 2011, 178–96.

6. David Barrows was the general superintendent of education in the Philippines and, later, professor, dean, and president of the University of California, Berkeley. Erving Winslow was the secretary of the Anti-Imperialist League; Benjamin Ide

Wheeler was the president of the University of California, Berkeley; Moorfield Storey was the author of a book on U.S. colonial war crimes during the Philippine-American War and the president of the national Anti-Imperialist League; and William Lloyd Garrison II was the secretary of the American Free Trade League.

7. On the pensionados/os more generally, see Calata, "The Role of Education in Americanizing Filipinos"; Barbara Posadas, "Transnational and Higher Education: Four Filipino Chicago Case Studies," *Journal of American Ethnic History* 32, no. 2 (Winter 2013): 7–37; Barbara Posadas and Roland Guyotte, "Unintentional Immigrants: Chicago's Filipino Foreign Students Become Settlers, 1900–1941," *Journal of American Ethnic History* 9, no. 2 (Spring 1990): 26–48; Noel Teodoro, "*Pensionados* and Workers: The Filipinos in the United States, 1903–1956," *Asian and Pacific Migration Journal* 8, nos. 1–2 (1999): 157–78.

On scholarship concerned with immigrating Filipino laborers from the early to the middle of the twentieth century, see, e.g., Catherine Ceniza Choy, *Empire of Care: Nursing and Migration in Filipino American History* (Durham, NC: Duke University Press, 2002); Denise Cruz, *Transpacific Femininities: The Making of the Modern Filipina* (Durham, NC: Duke University Press, 2012); Linda España-Maram, *Creating Masculinity in Los Angeles's Little Manila: Working-Class Filipinos and Popular Culture, 1920s–1950s* (New York: Columbia University Press, 2006); Dorothy Fujita-Rony, *American Workers, Colonial Power: Philippine Seattle and the Transpacific West, 1919–1941* (Berkeley: University of California Press, 2002); Susan Koshy, *Sexual Naturalization: Asian Americans and Miscegenation* (Stanford, CA: Stanford University Press, 2005); Dawn Bohulano Mabalon, *Little Manila Is in the Heart: The Making of the Filipina/o American Community in Stockton, California* (Durham, NC: Duke University Press, 2013); Leti Volpp, "American Mestizo: Filipinos and Antimiscegenation Laws in California," *University of California, Davis, Law Review* 33 (2000): 795–835. For an excellent study of the careers of later generations of *pensionados*, see Augusto Fauni Espiritu, *The Five Faces of Exile: The Nation and Filipino Americans*. Stanford, CA: Stanford University Press, 2005.

8. Benjamin Ide Wheeler to Ponciano Reyes, letter, in "Suggests Politics Should Be Relegated," *San Francisco Call*, May 25, 1906, 40.

9. "Filipino Students Want Freedom," *San Francisco Call*, October 25, 1906, 4.

10. Koshy, *Sexual Naturalization*, 95.

11. This phrase is from Michel Foucault, *The History of Sexuality, Volume 1: An Introduction*, trans. Robert Hurley (New York: Vintage, 1980), 140. Of biopower, Foucault writes: "Such a power has to qualify, measure, appraise, and hierarchize, rather than display itself in its murderous splendor," 144.

12. Rick Baldoz, *Third Asiatic Invasion: Empire and Migration in Filipino America, 1898–1946* (New York: New York University Press, 2011), 9.

13. Foucault, *The History of Sexuality*, 1:119.

14. Anjali Arondekar's questions, "How is the history of sexuality recorded in the colonial moment, and how are we returning to that moment to produce a counter-record of that history? . . . How does one think through the current privileged

lexicon of erasure, silence, and recovery within a colonial context . . . whose archival instantiations emphasize the centrality rather than liminality of the race/sex nexus?" inform my confessed expectation: see Anjali Arondekar, *For the Record: On Sexuality and the Colonial Archive in India* (Durham, NC: Duke University Press, 2009), 14.

15. Ann Stoler, *Race and the Education of Desire: Foucault's History of Sexuality and the Colonial Order of Things* (Durham, NC: Duke University Press, 2005), 39.

16. Calata, "The Role of Education in Americanizing Filipinos," 92.

17. U.S. Philippine Commission, "Act 854," In *Acts of the Philippine Commission [Acts 425–949, Inclusive]* (Washington, DC: U.S. Government Printing Office, 1904), 668–70.

18. William Alexander Sutherland, *Not By Might: The Epic of the Philippines* (Las Cruces, NM: Southwest, 1953), 28.

19. Here I follow Pierre Bourdieu's understanding of both social and cultural capital: see Pierre Bourdieu, *Distinction: A Social Critique of the Judgment of Taste*, trans. Richard Nice (Cambridge, MA: Harvard University Press, 1984).

20. "Father's Write-Up Pleases," *Berkeley Daily Gazette*, January 6, 1905, 2.

21. "Buencamino Proposes a Plan," *Omaha Daily Bee*, June 7, 1902, 3.

22. "Will Edit Filipino Magazine," *Berkeley Daily Gazette*, January 9, 1905, 2.

23. On the establishment of social and cultural capital in Philippine colonial education, see James Gonzales, "Colonial Education and Filipino Student Immigration in the Early Twentieth Century: 1900 to 1934," Master's thesis, University of San Diego, 1999; John Schumacher, *The Propaganda Movement, 1880–1895: The Creation of a Filipino Consciousness, the Making of the Revolution* (Manila: Ateneo de Manila University Press, 1997).

24. Alidio, "Student Migrations," 92.

25. Benedict Anderson, "Cacique Democracy in the Philippines," *New Left Review* 169 (May 1998): 3–33.

26. "Captured by Filipinos," *Arizona Republican* (Phoenix), August 2, 1904, 4.

27. "Interesting Students," *Aberdeen Herald* (Aberdeen, WA), December 12, 1904, 3.

28. Editorial, *Deseret Evening News* (Salt Lake City, UT), June 26, 1907, 4.

29. Editorial, *Omaha Daily Bee*, April 4, 1906, 4.

30. Associated Press, "Don't Like Filipinos," *Daily Press* (Newport News, VA), February 24, 1905, 2.

31. "Four Filipino Students Shut Out from Dupont Manual Training High School, Louisville," *Salt Lake Tribune*, July 7, 1904, 8.

32. Editorial, *San Francisco Call*, October 14, 1903, 6.

33. "Social and Personal," *Washington Post*, July 6, 1905, 7.

34. "Berkeley Girl Won by Young Filipino: Becomes Islander's Bride," *San Francisco Call*, February 20, 1906," 1. The pensionado editors esteem the wedding "the happiest of all events connected with the Filipino colony in California": "Our Congratulations," *Filipino Students' Magazine* 2, no. 3 (March 1906): 33.

35. "Tribute of Respect," *Evening Star* (Washington, DC), April 13, 1907, 12.

36. "Taft Party in the Philippines," *Salt Lake Tribune*, September 24, 1905, 16.
37. "Aimed at Filipino Students," *Bemidji Daily Pioneer* (Bemidji, MN), February 24, 1905, 1; "Hits Filipino Lovers," *Valentine Democrat* (Valentine, NE), March 2, 1905, 2; "Indiana Parents Want No Dusky Sons-in-Law," *San Francisco Call*, February 24, 1905, 5.
38. Sutherland, *Not by Might*, 129. A similar story emerged in St. Louis in March 1905, when a local coffee merchant filed for divorce, claiming "alienation of his wife's affections by a Filipino": "Said on the Side," *Evening World* (New York), March 3, 1905, 14.
39. Volpp, "American Mestizo"; España-Maram, *Creating Masculinity in Los Angeles's Little Manila*; Ruby Tapia, " 'Just Ten Years Removed from a Bolo and a Breech-cloth': The Sexualization of the Filipino 'Menace,' " in *Positively No Filipinos Allowed: Building Communities and Discourse*, ed. Antonio Tiongson, Edgardo Gutierrez, and Ricardo Gutierrez (Philadelphia, PA: Temple University Press, 2006), 61–71.
40. Tapia, "Just Ten Years Removed from a Bolo and a Breech-cloth," 69.
41. "Filipino Suitors Ask Fair Deal: Little Brown Brother Wants to Be Little Brown Brother-in-Law," *Evening Statesman* (Walla Walla, WA), March 9, 1905, 2.
42. For an excellent study of Filipino men's marriages within the metropole to both white and nonwhite women, see Maria Paz Gutierra Esguerra, "Interracial Romances of American Empire: Migration, Marriage, and Law in Twentieth Century California," Ph.D. diss., University of Michigan, Ann Arbor, 2013.
43. "Our Purpose," *Filipino Students' Magazine* 1, no. 1 (1905): 1.
44. Editorial, *Filipino Students' Magazine* 1, no. 2 (1905): 5.
45. Warwick Anderson, *Colonial Pathologies: American Tropical Medicine, Race, and Hygiene in the Philippines* (Durham, NC: Duke University Press, 2006), 181.
46. J. P. Katigbak, "Filipino Youth and the Engineering Profession," *Filipino Students' Magazine* 1, no. 1 (April 1905): 10.
47. Pacifico Laygo, "Municipal Sanitation in the Philippines," *Filipino Students' Magazine* 1, no. 4 (December 1905): 21–22.
48. Untitled poem, *Filipino Students' Magazine* 1, no. 1 (April 1905): 25.
49. The poem was later reproduced, again anonymously, in Phineas Garrett, ed., *The Speaker's Garland, Comprising 100 Choice Elections*, vol. 8 (Philadelphia, PA: Penn Publishing, 1892), 235.
50. Lorenzo Onrubia, "Education in the Philippine Islands," *Filipinos Students' Magazine* 1, no. 1 (April 1905): 24–5.
51. Onrubia, "Education in the Philippine Islands," 25.
52. José Esteban Muñoz, *Disidentifications: Queers of Color and the Politics of Performance* (Minneapolis: University of Minnesota Press, 1999), 31. "A disidentification," Muñoz explains elsewhere, "is neither an identification nor a counter-identification—it is a working on, with, and against a form at a simultaneous moment": José Esteban Muñoz, " 'Feeling Brown': Ethnicity and Affect in Ricardo Bracho's *The Sweetest Hangover (and Other STDs)*," *Theatre*

Journal 52, no. 1 (March 2000): 70. We have seen this disidentificatory process before: whereas George Ade the bachelor disidentified with the Sultan of Sulu the polygamist (chapter 4), here the pensionadas/os disidentify with African Americans.

53. As William Gatewood's collection of letters from African American soldiers fighting in the Philippine-American War attests, Filipinos themselves were often called "niggers" by the white troops: William B. Gatewood, *"Smoked Yankees" and the Struggle for Empire: Letters from Negro Soldiers, 1898–1902* (Urbana: University of Illinois Press, 1971).

54. Lisa Lowe, *Immigrant Acts: On Asian American Cultural Politics* (Durham, NC: Duke University Press, 1996), 72–73; Lisa Lowe, "Literary Nomadics in Francophone Allegories of Postcolonialism: Pham Van Ky and Tahar Ben Jelloun," *Yale French Studies* 82 (1993): 43–61.

55. "No More of Negro Troops," *Philippine Review* 3, no. 3 (1907): 134.

56. On African Americans' sympathies with colonial Filipinos, see William B. Gatewood, *Black Americans and the White Man's Burden* (Urbana: University of Illinois Press, 1975); Gatewood, *"Smoked Yankees" and the Struggle for Empire*; Cynthia Marasigan, "'Between the Devil and the Deep Sea': Ambivalence, Violence and African American Soldiers in the Philippine American War and Its Aftermath," Ph.D. diss., University of Michigan, Ann Arbor, 2010; George Marks, ed., *Black Press Views American Imperialism, 1898–1900*. New York: Arno, 1971.

57. On the newspaper reports of black soldiers' raping of Filipinas, see Marasigan, "Between the Devil and the Deep Sea," 58–59.

58. Marasigan, "Between the Devil and the Deep Sea," 59.

59. "Seeks an Exhibit," *Filipino Students' Magazine* 2, no. 4 (December 1906): 10.

60. "Wrong Ideas about Filipinos," *Filipino Students' Magazine* 1, no. 2 (June 1905): 6.

61. Favis became chief editor of *The Filipino* in this issue, replacing William Sutherland, who announced that he would take "some time" off from both his position of superintendent over the pensionados and editor of the journal "to collect exhibits for the Philippine Exhibit at the Jamestown Exposition (1907)": "Our Superintendent," *The Filipino* 1, no. 6 (December 1906): 6.

62. Asterio Favis, "Hunt-Igorot Incident," *The Filipino* 1, no. 6 (November 1906): 27–28.

63. Vicente Rafael, *White Love and Other Events in Filipino History* (Durham, NC: Duke University Press, 2000), 26.

64. "Igorrotes in the Shows," *Filipino Students' Magazine* 2, no. 2 (July 1906): 2–3.

65. "Truth versus Falsehood," *Philippine Review* 3, no. 1 (March 1907): 2. Here the editors replace "Wild" with "Uncivilized."

66. Lowe, "Literary Nomadics in Francophone Allegories of Postcolonialism," 44.

67. Sutherland, *Not by Might*, 8.

68. "Feminism in the Philippines," *Philippine Students' Magazine* 2, no. 3 (October 1906): 1–2.

69. Rafael, *White Love and Other Events in Filipino History*, 48.

70. Nellie L. Pritchard, "The American Girl," *Philippine Review* 3, no. 5 (December 1907): 177–78.

71. Pritchard, "The American Girl," 177.

72. Pritchard, "The American Girl." 177.

73. Pritchard, "The American Girl." 177.

74. Quoted in M. P. de Veyra, "The Filipino Woman," *Filipino Students' Magazine* 2, no. 3 (October 1906): 14.

75. de Veyra, "The Filipino Woman," 15.

76. William Ju Sabro Iwami, "Criticism on 'A Defence of the Filipino' by an American Lady, and a Defence of Japanese Women," *Filipino Students' Magazine* 2, no. 2 (July 1906): 29–31.

77. See, e.g., the editorial "Wrong Ideas," *Filipino Students' Magazine* 2, no. 4 (November 1906); P. Taga Sulong, "The Truth about the Filipinos," *Filipino Students' Magazine* 1, no. 4 (December 1906): 17–18.

78. "Filipino Japanese Relations," *Philippine Review* 3, no. 3 (July 1907): 116. See also "Fear the Japanese: Filipinos See Ulterior Purpose in Forming New Society," *San Francisco Call*, July 10, 1907, 6.

79. Genoveva Llamas, "Domestic Science," *Philippine Review* 3, no. 5 (December 1907): 179.

80. Llamas, "Domestic Science," 179.

81. N. M. Lisos, "From Our Girls," *The Filipino* 1, no. 6 (December 1906): 30–32.

82. Amy Kaplan, "Manifest Domesticity," *American Literature* 70, no. 3 (September 1998): 581–606.

83. Lisos, "From Our Girls," 31. On the performative nature of gender and sexual identification, I draw from Judith Butler, *Gender Trouble: Feminism and the Subversion of Identity* (New York: Routledge, 1990).

84. Siobhan Somerville, "Notes toward a Queer History of Naturalization," *American Quarterly* 57, no. 3 (2005): 668.

85. Glenn May, *Social Engineering in the Philippines: The Aims, Execution, and Impact of American Colonial Policy, 1900–1913* (Westport, CT: Greenwood Press, 1980).

86. Foucault, *The History of Sexuality*, 1:118.

87. Hubert Dreyfus and Paul Rabinow. *Michel Foucault: Beyond Structuralism and Hermeneutics*, 2d ed. (Chicago: University of Chicago Press, 1983), 141.

88. Philippine Government Students, "United States Queries," *Filipino Students' Magazine* 1, no. 2 (June 1905): 34; 2, no. 2 (July 1906): 22; 2, no. 3 (October 1906): 26.

89. Foucault, *The History of Sexuality*, 1:46.

90. U.S. Public Health Service, *Manual for the Mental Examination of Aliens* (1918), quoted in Margot Canaday, *The Straight State: Sexuality and Citizenship in Twentieth-Century America* (Princeton, NJ: Princeton University Press, 2009), 33.

91. Gervasio Santos, "The Dangers of College Life," *The Filipino* 1, no. 6 (December 1906): 28–29; emphasis added.

92. "Wolves" were normatively gendered (masculine) men who preferred sex with male sexual partners; "punks" were physically slighter youths who let himself be

used sexually by older, more powerful men, the wolves, in exchange for money, protection, or other forms of support: George Chauncey, *Gay New York: Gender, Urban Culture, and the Making of the Gay Male World, 1890–1940*. New York: Basic Books, 1994, 87–88.

93. Ann Stoler, *Carnal Knowledge and Imperial Power: Race and the Intimate in Colonial Rule* (Berkeley: University of California Press, 2002), 2.

94. Nayan Shah, "Policing Privacy, Migrants, and the Limits of Freedom," *Social Text* 23, nos. 3–4 (Fall-Winter 2005): 277.

95. Michael Warner, quoted in Shah, "Policing Privacy, Migrants, and the Limits of Freedom," 280.

96. Andres Aguilar, "A Vision That Was Not Altogether a Vision," *The Filipino* 1, no. 1 (January 1906): 25–27.

97. I say "popular" because the nighttime attack scene by insurrectos on a U.S. military camp was frequently staged as a mock battle at the St. Louis World's Fair in 1904. This mock battle was in turn anticipated by the *Globe-Democrat*, which said, "The insurrectos will make a night attack on the American camp. Intrenchments [sic] are being thrown up, artillery will be brought into action and many features of actual war was carried out in realistic style. . . . The engagement will end in the repulse of the insurrectos": quoted in Marasigan, "Between the Devil and the Deep Sea," 407.

98. Slavoj Žižek, *The Sublime Object of Ideology* (London: Verso, 1989), 45.

99. Žižek, *The Sublime Object of Ideology*.

100. Aguilar, "A Vision That Was Not Altogether a Vision," 25.

101. It's hard, here, not to note a similarity and incongruity between Aguilar's narration and Luis Malonso's heartbreaking testimony in chapter 2.

102. Abstracts of Spanish-American War, Philippine-American War, and China Relief Expedition, Military and Naval Service Records, 1898–1902, New York State Adjutant General's Office, Albany, NY, n.p.

103. I borrow this phrase from José Esteban Muñoz, *Cruising Utopia: The Then and There of Queer Futurity* (New York: New York University Press, 2009).

104. Laygo, "On the Battlefield," 16.

105. Rafael, *White Love and Other Events in Filipino History*, 19.

106. James Henry Kyner, ed., *Odes, Hymns and Songs of the G.A.R.* (Omaha: Herald Printing, 1880), 90–91; John Davis Billings, *Hardtack and Coffee; or, The Unwritten Story of Army Life* (Boston, MA: George M. Smith, 1888), 223–24; *Military History and Reminiscenes of the Thirteenth Regiment of Illinois Volunteer Infantry in the Civil War in the United States, 1861–1865* (Chicago: Women's Temperance Publishing Association, 1892), 671–72.

On the nineteenth-century genre of male-male "romantic friendships," see Axel Nissen, *Manly Love: Romantic Friendship in American Fiction* (Chicago: University of Chicago Press, 2009). Laygo's story is all the more exceptional in the face of the literature Nissen traces because much of almost all of it was written by and featured middle- and upper-class white men: Nissen, *Manly Love*, 23.

107. Michel Foucault, *"Society Must Be Defended": Lectures at the Collège de France, 1975–1976*, ed. Maura Bertani and Alessando Fontana, trans. David Macey (New York: Picador, 2003), 8.

108. Koshy, *Sexual Naturalization*, 96.

109. Rey Chow, and Jasbir Puar after her, theorize the "ascendancy of whiteness" in U.S. imperial culture: Rey Chow, *The Protestant Ethnic and the Spirit of Capitalism* (New York: Columbia University Press, 2002), 3; Jasbir K. Puar, *Terrorist Assemblages: Homonationalism in Queer Times* (Durham, NC: Duke University Press, 2007).

110. Quoted in Sutherland, *Not by Might*, 37.

CONCLUSION

1. Michel Foucault, *"Society Must Be Defended": Lectures at the Collège de France, 1975–1976*, ed. Maura Bertani and Alessandro Fontana, trans. David Macey (New York: Picador, 2003), 7–8; emphasis added.

2. Foucault, *"Society Must Be Defended,"* 8.

3. Martin Joseph Ponce, *Beyond the Nation: Diasporic Filipino Literature and Queer Reading* (New York: New York University Press, 2012), 18.

4. I borrow this phrase from Elizabeth Povinelli, who uses it to describe Foucault's genealogy: Elizabeth Povinelli, "The Will to Be Otherwise/The Effort of Endurance," *South Atlantic Quarterly* 113, no. 3 (Summer 2012): 455.

5. George Chauncey, *Gay New York: Gender, Urban Culture, and the Making of the Gay Male World, 1890–1940* (New York: Basic Books, 1994), 23, 48.

6. Louis Sullivan, *From Female to Male: The Life of Jack Bee Garland* (Boston, MA: Alyson Press, 1990), 13, 154–55, 158, 164.

7. Quoted in Sullivan, *From Female to Male*, 19.

8. Sullivan, *From Female to Male*, 37.

9. Sullivan, *From Female to Male*, 42.

10. Quoted in Sullivan, *From Female to Male*, 40.

11. Sullivan, *From Female to Male*, 86–89; Chauncey, *Gay New York*, 88; *Cassell's Dictionary of Slang*, 2d ed. (London: Cassell, 2005), s.v., "Gaycat," 571.

12. See, e.g., Liz Stevens and Estelle Freedman, dirs., *She Even Chewed Tobacco*, documentary slideshow, 1983; Gayle Rubin, "Of Catamites and Kings: Reflections on Butch, Gender, and Boundaries," in *The Transgender Studies Reader*, ed. Susan Stryker and Stephen White (New York: Routledge, 2006), 476.

13. Quoted in Sullivan, *From Female to Male*, 76.

14. Sullivan, *From Female to Male*, 85.

15. Quoted in Sullivan, *From Female to Male*, 120.

16. "Americanizing Manila," *Indianapolis Journal*, June 20, 1900, 11.

17. Sullivan, *From Female to Male*, 131. My fact checking here is drawn from chapter 1.

18. Sullivan, *From Female to Male*, 134.

19. Sullivan, *From Female to Male*, 135.

20. Sullivan, *From Female to Male*, 135.

21. Sullivan, *From Female to Male*, 138.

22. Sullivan, *From Female to Male*, 3.

23. Brice Smith, "'Yours in Liberation': Lou Sullivan and the Construction of FTM Identity," Ph.D. diss., University of Wisconsin, Milwaukee, 2010, 292. Bérubé's comment is from a blurb on the back cover of Sullivan, *From Female to Male*.

24. Nan Alamilla Boyd, "Bodies in Motion: Lesbian and Transsexual Histories," in *A Queer World: The Center for Lesbian and Gay Studies Reader*, ed. Martin Duberman (New York: New York University Press, 1997), 139.

25. Boyd, "Bodies in Motion," 139.

26. Boyd, "Bodies in Motion," 139.

27. Sullivan, *From Female to Male*, 118.

28. Emily Skidmore points out this disavowal by Garland: Emily Skidmore, "Exceptional Queerness: Defining the Boundaries of Normative U.S. Citizenship, 1876–1936," Ph.D. diss., University of Illinois, Urbana-Champaign, 2011, 222–23.

29. Foucault, *"Society Must Be Defended,"* 268.

30. Foucault, *"Society Must Be Defended,"* 8.

31. Foucault, *"Society Must Be Defended,"* 8.

32. Chandan Reddy, for example, has quite provokingly examined the U.S. nation-state's historical enactment of freedom *with* violence. This book has begun to trace, in turn, U.S. imperialism's historical conduct of violence with intimacy.

Abinales, Patricio, and Donna Amoroso. *State and Society in the Philippines*. Lanham, MD: Rowman and Littlefield, 2005.

Ade, George. *The America of George Ade (1866–1944)*, ed. Jean Shepherd. New York: Putnam, 1960.

———. *The Best of George Ade*, ed. A. L. Lazarus. Bloomington: Indiana University Press, 1985.

———. *George Ade's "Stories of Benevolent Assimilation,"* ed. Perry Gianakos. Quezon City, Philippines: New Day, 1985.

———. "The Joys of Single Blessedness." In *Single Blessedness and Other Observations*, 1–22. Garden City, NY: Doubleday Page, 1922.

———. *Letters of George Ade*, ed. Terrence Tobin. West Lafayette, IN: Purdue University Press, 1973.

———. *Stories of Chicago* (1941), ed. Franklin Meine, repr. ed. Urbana: University of Illinois Press, 2003.

———. *The Sultan of Sulu: An Original Satire in Two Acts*. New York: R. H. Russell, 1903.

———. *Verses and Jingles*. Indianapolis, IN: Bobbs-Merrill, 1911.

Agsforth, Albert. "Hoosier Humorist, Three Letters." *American Scholar* 56, no. 4 (Autumn 1987): 565–73.

Aguilar, Andres. "A Vision That Was Not Altogether a Vision." *The Filipino* 1, no. 1 (January 1906): 25–27.

Alexander, M. Jacqui. *Pedagogies of Crossing: Meditations on Feminism, Sexual Politics, Memory, and the Sacred*. Durham, NC: Duke University Press, 2005.

Alidio, Kimberly. "Between Civilizing Mission and Ethnic Assimilation: Racial Discourse, U.S. Colonial Education, and Filipino Ethnicity." Ph.D. diss., University of Michigan, Ann Arbor, 2001.

———. "Student Migrations: Racialized Bodies, Cosmopolitan Nationalism and the 'New Filipino,'" in "Between Civilizing Mission and Ethnic Assimilation: Racial

Discourse, U.S. Colonial Education and Filipino Ethnicity, 1901–1946," 91–129. Ph.D. diss., University of Michigan, Ann Arbor, 2001.

Althusser, Louis. "Ideology and Ideological State Apparatuses." In *Lenin and Philosophy and Other Essays*, trans. Ben Brewster, 127–86. London: New Left Books, 1969.

American Newspaper Dictionary. New York: Geo. P. Rowell, 1900.

Anderson, Benedict. "Cacique Democracy in the Philippines." *New Left Review* 169 (May 1998): 3–33.

———. *Imagined Communities: On the Origin and Spread of Nationalism*. London: Verso, 1983.

Anderson, Warwick. *Colonial Pathologies: American Tropical Medicine, Race, and Hygiene in the Philippines*. Durham, NC: Duke University Press, 2006.

Arondekar, Anjali. *For the Record: On Sexuality and the Colonial Archive in India*. Durham, NC: Duke University Press, 2009.

Ashburn, Percy M., *The Elements of Military Hygiene: Especially Arranged for Officers and Men of the Line*. Boston, MA: Houghton Mifflin, 1909.

Austin, Jill, and Jennifer Brier, eds. *Out in Chicago: LGBT History at the Crossroads*. Chicago, IL: Chicago History Museum, 2012.

Austin, Jill, Jennifer Brier, Jessica Herczeg-Konecny, and Anne Parsons. "When the Erotic Becomes Illicit: Struggles over Displaying Queer History at a Mainstream Museum." *Radical History Review* 113 (Spring 2012): 187–97.

Balce, Nerissa. *Body Parts of Empire: Abjection, Filipino Images, and the American Public*. Ann Arbor, MI: University of Michigan Press, forthcoming.

———. "The Filipina's Breast: Savagery, Docility, and the Erotics of American Empire." *Social Text* 24, no. 2 (Summer 2006): 89–110.

Baldoz, Rick. *The Third Asiatic Invasion: Empire and Migration in Filipino America, 1898–1946*. New York: New York University Press, 2011.

Barthes, Roland. "The Death of the Author" (1967). In *Image-Music-Text*, trans. Stephen Heath, 142–48. New York: Hill and Wang, 1977.

Bederman, Gail. *Manliness and Civilization: A Cultural History of Gender and Race in the United States, 1880–1917*. Chicago: University of Chicago Press, 1996.

Belkin, Aaron. *Bring Me Men: Military Masculinity and the Benign Façade of American Empire, 1898–2001*. New York: Columbia University Press, 2012.

Benedicto, Bobby. "The Haunting of Gay Manila: Global Space-Time and the Specter of Kabaklaan." *GLQ* 14, nos. 2–3 (2008): 317–38.

Benjamin, Walter. "Theses on the Philosophy of History." In *Illuminations: Essays and Reflections*, ed. Hannah Arendt, 253–64. New York: Schocken Books, 1986.

Bentley, Nancy. "Marriage as Treason: Polygamy, Nation, and the Novel." In *The Futures of American Studies*, ed. Donald Pease and Robyn Wiegman, 341–70. Durham, NC: Duke University Press, 2002.

Berlant, Lauren. *Desire/Love*. Brooklyn, NY: Punctum Books, 2012.

———. *The Female Complaint: The Unfinished Business of Sentimentality in American Culture*. Durham, NC: Duke University Press, 2008.

———. ed. *Intimacy*. Chicago: University of Chicago Press, 2000.

Bersani, Leo. "Is the Rectum a Grave?" *October* 43 (1987): 197–222.

Best, Jonathan. *A Philippine Album: American Era Photographs, 1900–1930*. Makati, Philippines: Bookmark, 1998.

Billings, John Davis. *Hardtack and Coffee; or, The Unwritten Story of Army Life*. Boston, MA: George M. Smith, 1888.

Blair, Emma Helen, and James Alexander Robertson. *The Philippine Islands, 1493–1803*, 52 vols. Cleveland, OH: A. H. Clark, 1903.

Blanchard, Mary Warner. *Oscar Wilde's America: Counterculture in the Gilded Age*. New Haven, CT: Yale University Press, 1998.

Blanco, John. *Frontier Constitutions: Christianity and Colonial Empire in the Nineteenth Century Philippines*. Berkeley: University of California Press, 2009.

Boone, Joseph. "Vacation Cruises; or, the Homoerotics of Orientalism." *PMLA* 110 (January 1995): 89–100.

Bordman, Gerald. *American Musical Theatre*. New York: Oxford University Press, 1978.

Bourdieu, Pierre. *Distinction: A Social Critique of the Judgment of Taste*, trans. Richard Nice. Cambridge, MA: Harvard University Press, 1984.

Boyd, Nan Alamilla. "Bodies in Motion: Lesbian and Transsexual Histories." In *A Queer World: The Center for Lesbian and Gay Studies Reader*, ed. Martin Duberman, 134–52. New York: New York University Press, 1997.

Boyer, Paul. *Urban Masses and Moral Order, 1820–1920*. Cambridge, MA: Harvard University Press, 1978.

Brenner, Jack. "Howells and Ade." *American Literature* 38, no. 2 (May 1966): 198–207.

Brown, Wendy. *States of Injury: Power and Freedom in Late Modernity*. Princeton, NJ: Princeton University Press, 1995.

Bulosan, Carlos. *America Is in the Heart* (1943). Seattle: University of Washington Press, 1973.

Burgett, Bruce. "On the Mormon Question: Race, Sex, and Polygamy in the 1850s and 1990s." *American Quarterly* 57, no. 1 (March 2005): 75–102.

Burnett, Christina Duffy, and Burke Marshall. "Between the Foreign and the Domestic: The Doctrine of Territorial Incorporation, Invented and Reinvented." In *Foreign in a Domestic Sense: Puerto Rico, American Expansion, and the Constitution*, 1–38. Durham, NC: Duke University Press, 2001.

Bush, Ronald. "The Presence of the Past: Ethnographic Thinking/Literary Politics." In *Prehistories of the Future: The Primitivist Project and the Culture of Modernism*, ed. Elazar Barkan and Bush, 23–41. Stanford, CA: Stanford University Press, 1995.

Butler, Judith. *Frames of War: When Is Life Grievable?* London: Verso, 2010.

———. *Gender Trouble: Feminism and the Subversion of Identity*. New York: Routledge, 1990.

Calata, Alexander A. "The Role of Education in Americanizing Filipinos." In *Mixed Blessings: The Impact of the American Colonial Experience on Politics and Society in the Philippines*, ed. Hazel M. McFerson, 89–98. Westport, CT: Greenwood Press, 2002.

Campomanes, Oscar. "Filipinos in the United States and Their Literature of Exile." In *Reading the Literatures of Asian America*, ed. Shirley Geok-lin Lim and Amy Ling, 49–78. Philadelphia, PA: Temple University Press, 1992.

———. "The Politics of Imperial Amnesia and the Making of U.S. Modernity." Invited lecture given at Illini Union, University of Illinois, Urbana-Champaign, April 19, 2005.

Canaday, Margot. *The Straight State: Sexuality and Citizenship in Twentieth-Century America*. Princeton, NJ: Princeton University Press, 2009.

Capino, José. *Dream Factories of a Former Colony: American Fantasies, Colonial Cinema*. Minneapolis: University of Minnesota Press, 2010.

Carr, Jesse. "States of Exceptionalism: Race, Violence, and Governance." Ph.D. diss., University of Michigan, Ann Arbor, 2014.

Chakrabarty, Dipesh. *Provincializing Europe: Postcolonial Thought and Historical Difference*. Princeton, NJ: Princeton University Press, 2000.

Chambliss, William. "A Sociological Analysis of the Law of Vagrancy." *Social Problems* 12 (Summer 1964): 67–77.

Chan, Sucheng. *Asian Americans: An Interpretive History*. Boston, MA: Twayne, 1991.

Chauncey, George. "From Sexual Inversion to Homosexuality: Medicine and the Changing Conceptualization of Female Deviance." *Salmagundi* 58, no. 9 (Fall-Winter 1982): 114–46.

———. *Gay New York: Gender, Urban Culture, and the Making of the Gay Male World, 1890–1940*. New York: Basic Books, 1994.

Cheng, Anne Anlin. *The Melancholy of Race: Psychoanalysis, Assimilation, and Hidden Grief*. New York: Oxford University Press, 2000.

Chong, Sylvia. *The Oriental Obscene: Violence and Racial Fantasy*. Durham, NC: Duke University Press, 2011.

Chow, Rey. *The Protestant Ethnic and the Spirit of Capitalism*. New York: Columbia University Press, 2002.

Choy, Catherine Ceniza. *Empire of Care: Nursing and Migration in Filipino American History*. Durham, NC: Duke University Press, 2002.

Chu, Richard. *Chinese and Chinese Mestizos of Manila: Family, Identity, and Culture, 1860s–1930s*. Boston, MA: Brill, 2010.

Chudacoff, Howard. *The Age of the Bachelor: Creating an American Subculture*. Princeton, NJ: Princeton University Press, 2000.

Chuh, Kandice. *Imagine Otherwise: On Asian Americanist Critique*. Durham, NC: Duke University Press, 2003.

Coffman, Edward M. *The Regulars: The American Army, 1898–1941*. Cambridge, MA: Harvard University Press, 2007.

Cohen, Cathy. "Punks, Bulldaggers, and Welfare Queens: The Radical Potential of Queer Politics?" *GLQ* 3, no. 4 (May 1997): 437–65.

Cole, Fay-Cooper. *The Tinguian: Social, Religious and Economic Life of a Philippine Tribe*. Chicago: Field Museum of Natural History, 1922.

Cott, Nancy. *Public Vows: A History of Marriage and the Nation.* Cambridge, MA: Harvard University Press, 2000.

Court-martial of Capt. Boss Reese, Case Files 71051 and 75876; Court-Martial Case Files, 1809–1938; Records of the Office of the Judge Advocate General (Army), Record Group 153; National Archives Building, Washington, DC.

Coyle, Lee. *George Ade.* New York: Twayne, 1964.

Crozier, Ivan. "Philosophy in the English Boudoir: Havelock Ellis, *Love and Pain*, and the Sexological Discourses on Anglophilia." *Journal of the History of Sexuality* 13, no. 3 (2004): 275–305.

Cruz, Denise. *Transpacific Femininities: The Making of the Modern Filipina.* Durham, NC: Duke University Press, 2012.

Curtis, Edward. *Muslims in America: A Short History.* New York: Oxford University Press, 2009.

Cvetkovich, Ann. *An Archive of Feelings: Trauma, Sexuality, and Lesbian Public Archives.* Durham, NC: Duke University Press, 2003.

Dávila-Caballero, José. "Discrimen por orientación sexual: El denominado estatuto de sodomía de Puerto Rico." *Revista Jurídica Universidad de Puerto Rico* 69 (2000): 1185–266.

Dean, Tim. *Beyond Sexuality.* Chicago: University of Chicago Press, 2000.

De Bevoise, Ken. *Agents of Apocalypse: Epidemic Disease in the Colonial Philippines.* Princeton, NJ: Princeton University Press, 1995.

de Jesus, Melinda L. "Rewriting History, Rewriting Desire: Reclaiming Queerness in Carlos Bulosan's *American Is in the Heart* and Bienvenido Santos' *The Scent of Apples.*" *Journal of Asian American Studies* 5, no. 2 (June 2002): 91–111.

Deleuze, Gilles. *Masochism: Coldness and Cruelty* (1967), trans. Jean McNeil, repr. ed. New York: Zone Books, 1991.

Deleuze, Gilles, and Félix Guattari. *Anti-Oedipus: Capitalism and Schizophrenia,* trans. Robert Hurley, Mark Seem, and Helen Lane. Minneapolis: University of Minnesota Press, 1983.

Delgado, Richard, and Jean Stefancic. *Critical Race Theory: An Introduction.* New York: New York University Press, 2001.

Demuth, James. *Small Town Chicago: The Comic Perspective of Finley Peter Dunne, George Ade, Ring Lardner.* Port Washington, NY: Kennikat Press, 1980.

D'Emilio, John. "Capitalism and Gay Identity." In *The Lesbian and Gay Studies Reader,* ed. Henry Abelove, Michèle Aina Barale, and David Halperin, 467–76. New York: Routledge, 1993.

———. *Sexual Politics, Sexual Communities: The Making of a Homosexual Minority in the United States, 1940–1970.* Chicago: University of Chicago Press, 1983.

D'Emilio, John, and Estelle B. Freedman. *Intimate Matters: A History of Sexuality in America.* Chicago: University of Chicago Press, 1997.

Dewey, Donald. *The Art of Ill Will: The Story of American Political Cartoons.* New York: New York University Press, 2007.

Dreyfus, Hubert, and Paul Rabinow. *Michel Foucault: Beyond Structuralism and Hermeneutics*, 2d ed. Chicago: University of Chicago Press, 1983.

Drinnon, Richard. *Facing West: The Metaphysics of Indian-Hating and Empire Building.* Minneapolis: University of Minnesota Press, 1980.

Du Bois, W. E. B. "Present Outlook for the Darker Races of Mankind" (1900). In *The Oxford W. E. B. Du Bois Reader*, ed. Eric J. Sundquist, 47–54. New York: Oxford University Press, 1996.

———. *The Souls of Black Folk* (1903), repr. ed. New York: Vintage, 1990.

Edelman, Lee. "Tearooms and Sympathy; or, The Epistemology of the Water Closet." In *The Lesbian and Gay Studies Reader*, ed. Henry Abelove, Michèle Aina Barale, and David Halperin, 553–576. New York: Routledge, 1993.

Editorial. *Filipino Students' Magazine* 1, no. 2 (1905): 5–7.

Edwards, Rebecca. "Politics as Social History: Political Cartoons in the Gilded Age." *OAH Magazine of History* 13, no. 4 (Summer 1999): 11–15.

Ellis, Havelock. *Studies in the Psychology of Sex*, vol. 2. Philadelphia, PA: F. A. David, 1900.

Eng, David. *Racial Castration: Managing Masculinity in Asian America.* Durham, NC: Duke University Press, 2001.

Esguerra, Maria-Paz Gutierra. "Interracial Romances of American Empire: Migration, Marriage, and Law in Twentieth Century California." Ph.D. diss., University of Michigan, Ann Arbor, 2013.

Eskridge, William. *Dishonorable Passions: Sodomy Laws in America 1861–2003.* New York: Penguin, 2008.

———. *Gaylaw: Challenging the Apartheid of the Closet.* Cambridge, MA: Harvard University Press, 2002.

España-Maram, Linda. *Creating Masculinity in Los Angeles's Little Manila: Working-Class Filipinos and Popular Culture, 1920s–1950s.* New York: Columbia University Press, 2006.

Espiritu, Augusto Fauni. *The Five Faces of Exile: The Nation and Filipino Americans.* Stanford, CA: Stanford University Press, 2005.

Evans, Dylan. *An Introductory Dictionary to Lacanian Psychoanalysis.* London: Routledge, 1996.

Faderman, Lillian. *Odd Girls and Twilight Lovers: A History of Lesbian Life in Twentieth Century-America.* New York: Penguin, 1992.

Fahs, Alice. *Out on Assignment: Newspaper Women and the Making of Modern Public Space.* Chapel Hill: University of North Carolina Press, 2011.

Fajardo, Kale. *Filipino Crosscurrents: Oceanographies of Seafaring, Masculinities, and Globalization.* Minneapolis: University of Minnesota Press, 2011.

Fausto-Sterling, Anne. *Sexing the Body: Gender Politics and the Construction of Sexuality.* New York: Basic Books, 2000.

Favis, Asterio. "Hunt-Igorot Incident." *The Filipino* 1, no. 6 (November 1906): 26–28.

"Feminism in the Philippines." *Filipino Students' Magazine* 2, no. 3 (October 1906): 1–2.

Ferguson, Roderick. *Aberrations in Black: Toward a Queer of Color Critique*. Minneapolis: University of Minnesota Press, 2003.

———. "Of Our Normative Strivings: African American Studies and the Histories of Sexuality." *Social Text* 23, nos. 3–4 (Fall–Winter 2005): 85–100.

"Filipino Japanese Relations." *Philippine Review* 3, no. 3 (July 1907): 116.

Fischer, Roger. *Them Damned Pictures: Explorations in American Political Cartoon Art*. North Haven, CT: Archon, 1996.

Forbes, Camille. "Dancing with 'Racial Feet': Bert Williams and the Performance of Blackness." *Theatre Journal* 56, no. 4 (2004): 603–25.

Foucault, Michel. "An Interview with Stephen Riggs." In *Ethics: Subjectivity and Truth*, ed. Paul Rabinow, trans. Robert Hurley et al., 121–34. New York: New Press, 1997.

———. "Governmentality." In *The Foucault Effect: Studies in Governmentality with Two Lectures by and an Interview with Michel Foucault*, ed. Graham Burchell, Colin Gordon, and Peter Miller, 87–104. Chicago: University of Chicago Press, 1991.

———. *The History of Sexuality, Volume 2: The Uses of Pleasure*, trans. Robert Hurley. New York: Vintage, 1990.

———. "Questions of Method." In *The Foucault Effect: Studies in Governmentality: With Two Lectures by and an Interview with Michel Foucault*, ed. Graham Burchell, Colin Gordon, and Peter Miller, 73–86. Chicago: University of Chicago Press, 1991.

———. *"Society Must Be Defended": Lectures at the Collège de France, 1975–1976*, ed. Maura Bertani and Alessandro Fontana, trans. David Macey. New York: Picador, 2003.

———. "What Is an Author?" (1969). In *Language, Counter-Memory, Practice: Selected Essays and Interviews*, ed. Donald F. Bouchard, 113–48. Ithaca, NY: Cornell University Press, 1980.

Freud, Sigmund. *The Origins of Psychoanalysis: Letters to Wilhelm Fleiss, Drafts and Notes, 1887–1902*, ed. Marie Bonaparte, Anna Freud, Ernst Kris. New York: Basic Books, 1954.

Fujita-Rony, Dorothy. *American Workers, Colonial Power: Philippine Seattle and the Transpacific West, 1919–1941*. Berkeley: University of California Press, 2002.

Garcia, J. Neil. *Philippine Gay Culture: Binibae to Bakla, Sihalis to MSM* (1996), repr. ed. Quezon City: University of the Philippines Press, 2009.

Gatewood, William B. *Black Americans and the White Man's Burden*. Urbana: University of Illinois Press, 1975.

———. *"Smoked Yankees" and the Struggle for Empire: Letters from Negro Soldiers, 1898–1902*. Urbana: University of Illinois Press, 1971.

Gilbert, William, and Arthur Sullivan. *The Pirates of Penzance; or, The Slave of Duty: An Entirely Original Comic Opera in Two Acts*. London, 1911.

Girard, René. *Violence and the Sacred*, trans. Patrick Gregory. Baltimore, MD: Johns Hopkins University Press, 1977.

Glick, Elisa. "Harlem's Queer Dandy: African-American Modernism and the Artifice of Blackness." *MFS Modern Fiction Studies* 49, no. 3 (2003): 414–42.

Go, Julian. *American Empire and the Politics of Meaning: Elite Political Cultures in the Philippines and Puerto Rico during U.S. Colonialism.* Durham, NC: Duke University Press, 2008.

———. "Introduction." In *The American Colonial State in the Philippines,* ed. Julian Go and Anne Foster, 1–42. Durham, NC: Duke University Press, 2003.

Go, Julian, and Anne L. Foster, eds. *The American Colonial State in the Philippines: Global Perspectives.* Durham, NC: Duke University Press, 2003.

Gonzales, James. "Colonial Education and Filipino Student Immigration in the Early Twentieth Century: 1900 to 1934." Master's thesis, University of San Diego, 1999.

Gopinath, Gayatri. *Impossible Desires: Queer Diasporas and South Asian Public Cultures.* Durham, NC: Duke University Press, 2005.

Gunning, Sandra. *Race, Rape, and Lynching: The Red Record of American Literature, 1890–1912.* New York: Oxford University Press, 1996.

Haggerty, George, ed. *Gay Histories and Cultures: An Encyclopedia.* New York: Garland, 2000.

Halberstam, Judith/Jack. *Female Masculinity.* Durham, NC: Duke University Press, 1998.

———. *In a Queer Time and Place: Transgender Bodies, Subcultural Lives.* New York: New York University Press, 2005.

Hall, Stuart. "Signification, Representation, Ideology: Althusser and the Post-Structuralist Debates." *Critical Studies in Mass Communication* 2, no. 2 (June 1985): 91–114.

Halperin, David. "How to Do the History of Male Homosexuality." *GLQ* 6, no. 1 (2000): 87–123.

———. *Saint Foucault: Towards a Gay Hagiography.* New York: Oxford University Press, 1995.

Harris, Susan. *God's Arbiters: Americans and the Philippines.* New York: Oxford University Press, 2011.

Hartman, Saidiya. *Scenes of Subjection: Terror, Slavery, and Self-Making in Nineteenth-Century America.* New York: Oxford University Press, 1997.

Herring, Scott. *Queering the Underworld: Slumming, Literature, and the Undoing of Lesbian and Gay History.* Chicago: University of Chicago Press, 2007.

Hess, Stephen, and Milton Kaplan. *The Ungentlemanly Art: A History of Political Cartoons,* 2d ed. New York: Macmillan, 1975.

Hindman Golay, Frank. *Face of Empire: United States-Philippine Relations, 1898–1946.* Madison: Center for Southeast Asian Studies, University of Wisconsin Press, 1998.

Hoad, Neville. "Arrested Development or the Queerness of Savages: Resisting Evolutionary Narratives of Difference." *Postcolonial Studies* 3, no. 2 (2000): 133–58.

Hoang, Nguyen Tan. *A View from the Bottom: Asian American Masculinity and Sexual Representation.* Durham, NC: Duke University Press, 2014.

Hoganson, Kristin. *Consumers' Imperium: The Global Production of American Domesticity, 1865–1920.* Chapel Hill: University of North Carolina Press, 2007.

———. *Fighting for American Manhood: How Gender Politics Provoked the Spanish-American and Philippine-American Wars.* New Haven, CT: Yale University Press, 1998.

Huffer, Lynne. "Queer Victory, Feminist Defeat? Sodomy and Rape in *Lawrence v. Texas.*" In *Feminist and Queer Legal Theory: Intimate Encounters, Uncomfortable Conversations*, ed. Martha Albertson Fineman, Jack E. Jackson, Adam P. Romero, 411–32. Burlington, VT: Ashgate, 2009.

Hunt, Michael. *Ideology and U.S. Foreign Policy*. New Haven, CT: Yale University Press, 1987.

Ignacio, Abe, Enrique de le Cruz, Jorge Emmanuel, and Helen Toribio, eds. *The Forbidden Book: The Philippine-American War in Political Cartoons*. San Francisco, CA: T'Boli, 2004.

"Igorrotes in the Shows." *Filipino Students' Magazine* 2, no. 2 (July 1906): 2–3.

Ileto, Reynaldo. "Cholera and the Origins of the American Sanitary Order in the Philippines." In *Imperial Medicine and Indigenous Societies*, ed. David Arnold, 125–48. Manchester: Manchester University Press, 1988.

———. "Outlines of Nonlinear Emplotment of Philippine History." In *The Politics of Culture in the Shadow of Capital*, ed. Lisa Lowe and David Lloyd, 98–131. Durham, NC: Duke University Press, 1997.

Isaac, Allan Punzalan. *American Tropics: Articulating Filipino America*. University of Minnesota Press, 2006.

Iwami, William Ju Sabro. "Criticism on 'A Defence of the Filipino' by an American Lady, and a Defence of Japanese Women." *Filipino Students' Magazine* 2, no. 2 (July 1906): 29–31.

Jameson, Fredric. *The Political Unconscious: Narrative as Socially Symbolic Act*. Ithaca, NY: Cornell University Press, 1982.

Jenkins, Howard Malcolm (H. M. J.). "Purifying Great Cities." *Friends Intelligencer* 57, no. 49 (December 8, 1900): 882.

Johnston, Major William H. "The Battalion of Philippine Scouts." In *Report of the Philippine Exposition Board to the Louisiana Purchase Exposition and Official List of Awards Granted by the Philippine International Jury at the Philippine Government Exposition*. St. Louis: Greeley Printery of St. Louis, 1904.

Jun, Helen Heran. *Race for Citizenship: Black Orientalism and Asian Uplift from Pre-Emancipation to Neoliberal America*. New York: New York University Press, 2011.

The Anarchy of Empire in the Making of U.S. Culture. Durham, NC: Duke University Press, 2002.

Kaplan, Amy. "Manifest Domesticity." *American Literature* 70, no. 3 (September 1998): 581–606.

Katigbak, J. P. "Filipino Youth and the Engineering Profession." *Filipino Students' Magazine* 1, no. 1 (April 1905): 10.

Katz, Jonathan Ned. *The Invention of Heterosexuality* (1995), repr. ed. Chicago: University of Chicago Press, 2007.

Kelly, Fred. *George Ade, Warmhearted Satirist*. New York: Bobbs-Merrill, 1947.

———. *The Permanent Ade: The Living Writings of George Ade*. Indianapolis, IN: Bobbs-Merrill, 1947.

Klein, Christina. *Cold War Orientalism: Asia in the Middlebrow Imagination, 1945–1961.* Berkeley: University of California Press, 2003.

Koshy, Susan. *Sexual Naturalization: Asian Americans and Miscegenation.* Stanford, CA: Stanford University Press, 2005.

Krafft-Ebing, Richard von. *Psychopathia Sexualis, with Special Reference to Contrary Sexual Instinct,* trans. Charles Gilbert Chaddock. Philadelphia, PA: F. A. Davis, 1894.

Kramer, Paul A. *The Blood of Government: Race, Empire, the United States, and the Philippines.* Chapel Hill: University of North Carolina Press, 2006.

———. "Jim Crow Science and the 'Negro Problem' in the Occupied Philippines, 1898–1914." In *Race Consciousness,* ed. Judith Jackson Fossett and Jeffrey A. Tucker, 227–46. New York: New York University Press, 1997.

———. "The Military-Sexual Complex: Prostitution, Disease, and the Boundaries of Empire during the Philippine-American War." *Asia-Pacific Journal: Japan Focus,* July 6, 2012. http://japanfocus.org/-Paul_A_-Kramer/3574.

Krasner, David. *Resistance, Parody, and Double Consciousness in African American Theatre, 1895–1910.* New York: St. Martin's Press, 1997.

Kyner, James Henry, ed. *Odes, Hymns and Songs of the G.A.R.* Omaha, NE: Herald Printing, 1880.

Lacan, Jacques. *The Four Fundamental Concepts of Psycho-analysis,* ed. Jacques-Alain Miller, trans. Alan Sheridan. New York: W. W. Norton, 1981.

———. *The Seminar of Jacques Lacan.* Book 7: *The Ethics of Psychoanalysis, 1959–1960,* trans. Dennis Porter. New York: Norton, 1992.

Laplanche, Jean, and J. B. Pontalis. *The Language of Psycho-Analysis,* trans. Donald Nicholson-Smith. New York: W. W. Norton, 1973.

Lapovsky Kennedy, Elizabeth, and Madeline D. Davis. *Boots of Leather, Slippers of Gold: The History of a Lesbian Community.* New York: Routledge, 1993.

Laurence, Janice H., and Michael D. Matthews, eds. *The Oxford Handbook of Military Psychology.* New York: Oxford University Press, 2012.

Laygo, Pacifico. "Municipal Sanitation in the Philippines." *Filipino Students' Magazine* 1, no. 4 (December 1905): 21–22.

———. "On the Battlefield." *Filipino Students' Magazine* 1, no. 3 (September 1905): 14–16.

Lee, Robert G. *Orientals: Asian Americans in Popular Culture.* Philadelphia, PA: Temple University Press, 1999.

Lee, Joon Oluchi. "Joy of the Castrated Boy." *Social Text* 23, nos. 3–4 (Fall-Winter 2005): 35–56.

Lee, Josephine. *The Japan of Pure of Invention: Gilbert and Sullivan's The Mikado.* Minneapolis: University of Minnesota Press, 2010.

Lenin, Vladimir. *Imperialism, the Highest Stage of Capitalism: A Popular Outline* (1916), repr. ed. New York: International Publishers, 1969.

Lim, Eng-Beng. *Brown Boys and Rice Queens: Spellbinding Performance in the Asias.* New York: New York University, 2013.

Lisos, N. M. "From Our Girls." *The Filipino* 1, no. 6 (December 1906): 30–32.

Llamas, Genoveva. "Domestic Science." *Philippine Review* 3, no. 5 (December 1907): 9.

Lorde, Audre. *Zami: A New Spelling of My Name—A Biomythography*. Berkeley, CA: Crossing Press, 1982.

Lott, Eric. *Love and Theft: Blackface Minstrelsy and the American Working Class*. New York: Oxford University Press, 1995.

The Lover's Poetic Companion and Valentine Writer. London: Ward, Lock, and Tyler, 1875.

Lowe, Lisa. *Immigrant Acts: On Asian American Cultural Politics*. Durham, NC: Duke University Press, 1996.

———. "The Intimacies of Four Continents." In *Haunted by Empire: Geographies of Intimacy in North American History*, ed. Ann Stoler, 191–212. Durham, NC: Duke University Press.

———. "Literary Nomadics in Francophone Allegories of Postcolonialism: Pham Van Ky and Tahar Ben Jelloun." *Yale French Studies* 82 (1993): 43–61.

Luibhéid, Eithne. *Entry Denied: Controlling Sexuality at the Border*. Minneapolis: University of Minnesota Press, 2002.

Lye, Colleen. *America's Asia: Racial Form and American Literature, 1893–1945*. Princeton, NJ: Princeton University Press, 2005.

Lynch, Owen. "The U.S. Constitution and Philippine Colonialism: An Enduring and Unfortunate Legacy." In *Colonial Crucible and the Making of the Modern American State*, ed. Alfred McCoy and Francisco Scarano, 353–64. Madison: University of Wisconsin Press, 2009.

Lyotard, Jean-François. *The Differend: Phrases in Dispute*, trans. Georges Van Den Abbeele. Minneapolis: University of Minnesota Press, 1988.

Mabalon, Dawn Bohulano. *Little Manila Is in the Heart: The Making of the Filipina/o American Community in Stockton, California*. Durham, NC: Duke University Press, 2013.

Machida, Margo. *Unsettled Visions: Contemporary Asian American Artists and the Social Imaginary*. Durham, NC: Duke University Press, 2008.

Majul, Cesar. *Muslims in the Philippines*. Quezon City: University of the Philippines Press, 1973.

Manalansan, Martin. *Global Divas: Filipino Gay Men in the Diaspora*. Durham, NC: Duke University Press, 2003.

Manual for the Philippine Constabulary. Manila: Bureau of Printing, 1911.

Marasigan, Cynthia. "'Between the Devil and the Deep Sea': Ambivalence, Violence and African American Soldiers in the Philippine American War and Its Aftermath." Ph.D. diss., University of Michigan, Ann Arbor, 2010.

Marks, George, ed. *Black Press Views American Imperialism, 1898–1900*. New York: Arno, 1971.

May, Glenn. *Social Engineering in the Philippines: The Aims, Execution, and Impact of American Colonial Policy, 1900–1913*. Westport, CT: Greenwood Press, 1980.

McCoy, Alfred W. *Policing America's Empire: The United States, the Philippines, and the Rise of the Surveillance State*. Madison: University of Wisconsin Press, 2009.

McCoy, Alfred W., and Francisco A. Scarano, eds. *The Colonial Crucible and the Making of the Modern American State*. Madison: University of Wisconsin Press, 2009.

McKinley, William. "Message from the President of the United States, 56th Congress," December 21, 1898. U.S. Congress, 1st sess., 1899–1900, S. Doc. 208, 82–83.

McPherson, Jim. "The Savage Innocents. Part 1, King of the Castle: Henry W. Savage and the Castle Square Opera Company." *Opera Quarterly* 18, no. 4 (Autumn 2002): 503–33.

———. "The Savage Innocents. Part 2: On the Road with Parsifal, Butterfly, the Widow, and the Girl." *Opera Quarterly* 19, no. 1 (Winter 2003): 28–63.

Military History and Reminiscences of the Thirteenth Regiment of Illinois Volunteer Infantry in the Civil War in the United States, 1861–1865. Chicago: Women's Temperance Publishing Association, 1892.

Miller, D. A. "Anal Rope." In *Inside/Out: Lesbian Theories, Gay Theories*, ed. Diana Fuss, 119–41. New York: Routledge, 1991.

Miller, Monica. *Slaves to Fashion: Black Dandyism and the Styling of Black Diasporic Identity*. Durham, NC: Duke University Press, 2010.

Moon, Kristyn. *Yellowface: Creating the Chinese in American and Popular Music and Performance, 1850s–1920s*. New Brunswick, NJ: Rutgers University Press, 2005.

Moss, James A. *Officers' Manual*. Fort Leavenworth, KS: U.S. Cavalry Association, 1909.

The Municipal Code and the Provincial Government Act, Being Act No. 82, Entitled "A General Act for the Organization of Municipal Governments in the Philippine Islands" and Act No. 83, Entitled "A General Act for the Organization of Provincial Governments in the Philippine Islands." Manila: Bureau of Public Printing, 1905.

Muñoz, José Esteban. *Cruising Utopia: The Then and There of Queer Futurity*. New York: New York University Press, 2009.

———. *Disidentifications: Queers of Color and the Politics of Performance*. Minneapolis: University of Minnesota Press, 1999.

———. "'Feeling Brown': Ethnicity and Affect in Ricardo Bracho's *The Sweetest Hangover (and Other STDs)*." *Theatre Journal* 52, no. 1 (March 2000): 67–79.

Munson, Edward. *The Theory and Practice of Military Hygiene*. New York: William Wood, 1901.

Nash, Jennifer. *The Black Body in Ecstasy: Reading Race Reading Pornography*. Durham, NC: Duke University Press, 2014.

Nealon, Christopher. *Foundlings: Lesbian and Gay Historical Emotion before Stonewall*. Durham, NC: Duke University Press, 2001.

Newton, Esther. *Cherry Grove, Fire Island: Sixty Years in America's First Gay and Lesbian Town*. Boston, MA: Beacon, 1993.

Ngai, Mae M. *Impossible Subjects: Illegal Aliens and the Making of Modern America*. Princeton, NJ: Princeton University Press, 2004.

Nguyen, Mimi Thi. "The Biopower of Beauty: Humanitarian Imperialisms and Global Feminisms in an Age of Terror." *Signs* 36, no. 2 (Winter 2011): 359–83.

———. *The Gift of Freedom: War, Debt, and Other Refugee Passages*. Durham, NC: Duke University Press, 2012.

Nissen, Axel. *Manly Love: Romantic Friendship in American Fiction*. Chicago: University of Chicago Press, 2009.

"No More of Negro Troops." *Philippine Review* 3, no. 3 (1907): 134.

Noyes, Theodore William. *Oriental America and Its Problems*. Washington, DC: Judd and Detweiler, 1903.

Okihiro, Gary. *Cane Fires: The Anti-Japanese Movement in Hawaii, 1865–1945*. Philadelphia, PA: Temple University Press, 1995.

———. *Margins and Mainstreams: Asians in American History and Culture*. Seattle: University of Washington Press, 1994.

Omi, Michael, and Howard Winant. *Racial Formation in the United States: From the 1960s to the 1990s*, 2d ed. New York: Routledge, 1994.

Onrubia, Lorenzo. "Education in the Philippine Islands." *Filipino Students' Magazine* 1, no. 1 (April 1905): 24–25.

"Ordinance No. 27." In U.S. War Department, Bureau of Insular Affairs, *Third Annual Report of the Philippine Commission to the Secretary of War*. Washington, DC: U.S. Government Printing Office, 1903.

"Ordinance No. 28." In U.S. War Department, Bureau of Insular Affairs, *Third Annual Report of the Philippine Commission to the Secretary of War*. Washington, DC: U.S. Government Printing Office, 1903.

"Our Congratulations." *Filipino Students' Magazine* 2, no. 3 (March 1906): 33.

"Our Purpose." *Filipino Students' Magazine* 1, no. 1 (1905): 1.

"Our Superintendent." *The Filipino* 1, no. 6 (December 1906): 6.

Palumbo-Liu, David. *Asian/American: Historical Crossings of a Racial Frontier*. Stanford, CA: Stanford University Press, 1995.

Pascoe, Peggy. *What Comes Naturally: Miscegenation Law and the Making of Race in America*. New York: Oxford University Press, 2009.

Patterson, Martha. *The American New Woman Revisited: A Reader, 1894–1930*. New Brunswick, NJ: Rutgers University Press, 2008.

Peffer, George. "Forbidden Families: Emigration Experiences of Chinese Women under the Page Law, 1875–1882." *Journal of American Ethnic History* 6, no. 1 (Fall 1986): 28–46.

Penal Code of the State of California Adopted February 14, 1872, with Amendments up to and Including those of the Forty-First Session of the Legislature, 1915. San Francisco: Bancroft Whitney, 1915.

Perez, Louis. *The War of 1898: The United States and Cuba in History and Historiography*. Chapel Hill: University of North Carolina Press, 1998.

Pham, Minh-ha. "The Right to Fashion in the Age of Terror." *Signs* 36, no. 2 (Winter 2011): 359–83.

Philippine Government Students. "United States Queries." *Filipino Students' Magazine* 1, no. 2 (June 1905): 34.

———. "United States Queries." *Filipino Students' Magazine* 2, no. 2 (July 1906): 22.

——. "United States Queries." *Filipino Students' Magazine* 2, no. 3 (October 1906): 26.

Ponce, Martin Joseph. *Beyond the Nation: Diasporic Filipino Literature and Queer Reading.* New York: New York University Press, 2012.

Posadas, Barbara. "Transnational and Higher Education: Four Filipino Chicago Case Studies." *Journal of American Ethnic History* 32, no. 2 (Winter 2013): 7–37.

Posadas, Barbara, and Roland Guyotte. "Unintentional Immigrants: Chicago's Filipino Foreign Students Become Settlers, 1900–1941." *Journal of American Ethnic History* 9, no. 2 (Spring 1990): 26–48.

Povinelli, Elizabeth. *The Empire of Love: Toward a Theory, Genealogy, and Carnality.* Durham, NC: Duke University Press, 2006.

——. "The Will to Be Otherwise/The Effort of Endurance." *South Atlantic Quarterly* 113, no. 3 (Summer 2012): 453–75.

Pritchard, Nellie L. "The American Girl." *Philippine Review* 3, no. 5 (December 1907): 177–78.

Puar, Jasbir K. *Terrorist Assemblages: Homonationalism in Queer Times.* Durham, NC: Duke University Press, 2007.

Puar, Jasbir K., and Amit S. Rai. "Monster, Terrorist, Fag: The War on Terrorism and the Production of Docile Bodies." *Social Text* 20, no. 3 (2002): 117–48.

Rafael, Vicente. *White Love and Other Events in Filipino History.* Durham, NC: Duke University Press, 2000.

Ramaswamy, Sumathi. "Introduction." In *Empires of Vision: A Reader,* ed. Sumathi Ramaswamy and Martin Jay, 1–22. Durham, NC: Duke University Press, 2014.

Rana, Junaid. *Terrifying Muslims: Race, and Labor in the South Asian Diaspora.* Durham, NC: Duke University Press, 2011.

Reddy, Chandan. *Freedom with Violence: Race, Sexuality and the U.S. State.* Durham, NC: Duke University Press, 2011.

Research Laboratory of the Royal College of Physicians of Edinburgh. *Report of Investigations on the Life History of Salmon,* ed. Paton, Noël. Glasgow: James Hedderwick and Sons, 1898.

Reyes, Racquel A. G. *Love, Passion and Patriotism: Sexuality and the Philippine Propaganda Movement, 1882–1892.* Seattle: University of Washington Press, 2008.

Rice, Mark. *Dean Worcester's Fantasy Islands: Photography, Film, and the Colonial Philippines.* Ann Arbor, MI: University of Michigan Press, 2014.

Rifkin, Mark. *When Did Indians Become Straight? Kinship, the History of Sexuality and Native Sovereignty.* New York: Oxford University Press, 2011.

Rimmerman, Craig A., ed. *Gay Rights, Military Wrongs: Political Perspectives on Lesbians and Gays in the Military.* New York: Routledge, 1996.

Rivera Ramos, Efrén. "The Legal Construction of American Colonialism: The Insular Cases (1901–1922)." *Revista Juridica Universidad de Puerto Rico* 65 (1996): 225–328.

Robinson, Danielle. "The Ugly Duckling: The Refinement of Ragtime Dancing and the Mass Production of Marketing of Modern Social Dance." *Dance Research* 28, no. 2 (Winter 2010): 179–99.

Rodriguez, Dylan. *Suspended Apocalypse: White Supremacy, Genocide, and the Filipino Condition*. Minneapolis: University of Minnesota Press, 2009.

Rodriguez, Juana Maria. *Sexual Futures, Queer Gestures, and Other Latina Longings*. New York: New York University Press, 2014.

Roosevelt, Theodore. "A Proclamation," July 4, 1902. In *A Compilation of the Messages and Papers of the Presidents: 1789–1902*, ed. James D. Richardson, 392–94. New York: Bureau of National Literature and Art, 1903.

———. "At the Founders' Day Banquet of the Union League, Philadelphia, PA, November 22, 1902." In *A Compilation of the Messages and Speeches of Theodore Roosevelt: 1901–1905*, ed. Alfred Henry Louis, 184–89. New York: Bureau of National Literature and Art, 1906.

———. *The Rough Riders*. New York: Charles Scribner's Sons, 1899.

Rose, Jacqueline. *States of Fantasy*. Oxford: Oxford University Press, 1996.

Rosen, Hannah. *Terror in the Heart of Freedom: Citizenship, Sexual Violence, and the Meaning of Race in the Post-Emancipation South*. Chapel Hill: University of North Carolina Press, 2009.

Ross, Andrew. "Uses of Camp." In *Camp: Queer Aesthetics and the Performing Subject, a Reader*, ed. Fabio Cleto, 308–399. Ann Arbor: University of Michigan Press, 1999.

Rubin, Gayle. "Of Catamites and Kings: Reflections on Butch, Gender, and Boundaries." In *The Transgender Studies Reader*, ed. Susan Stryker and Stephen White, 471–81. New York: Routledge, 2006.

———. "Thinking Sex: Notes for a Radical Theory of the Politics of Sexuality." In *The Lesbian and Gay Studies Reader*, ed. Henry Abelove, Michèle Aina Barale, and David Halperin, 3–44. New York: Routledge, 1993.

———. "The Traffic in Women: Notes on the 'Political Economy' of Sex" (1975). In *The Second Wave: A Reader in Feminist Theory*, ed. Linda Nicholson, 27–62. New York: Routledge, 1997.

Salman, Michael. *The Embarrassment of Slavery: Controversies over Bondage and Nationalism in the American Colonial Philippines*. Berkeley: University of California Press, 2001.

Santos, Gervasio. "The Dangers of College Life." *The Filipino* 1, no. 6 (December 1906): 28–29.

Santos, Soliman. "Common Elements in the Philippine Mixed Legal System." *Australian Journal of Asian Law* 2, no. 1 (2000): 34–52.

Schumacher, John. *The Propaganda Movement, 1880–1895: The Creation of a Filipino Consciousness, the Making of the Revolution*. Manila: Ateneo de Manila University Press, 1997.

Scott, Darieck. *Extravagant Abjection: Blackness, Power, and Sexuality in the African American Literary Imagination*. New York: New York University Press, 2010.

Sears, Clare. *Arresting Dress: Cross-Dressing, Law, and Fascination in Nineteenth-Century San Francisco*. Durham, NC: Duke University Press, 2014.

———. "Electric Brilliancy: Cross-Dressing Law and Freak Show Displays in Nineteenth-Century San Francisco." *Women's Studies Quarterly* 36, nos. 3–4 (Fall-Winter 2008): 170–87.

Sedgwick, Eve. *The Epistemology of the Closet*. Berkeley: University of California Press, 1991.

"Seeks an Exhibit." *Filipino Students' Magazine* 2, no. 4 (December 1906): 10.

Senelick, Laurence. "Enlightened by Morphodites: Narratives of the Fairground Half-and-Half." *Amerikastudien/American Studies* 44, no. 3 (Winter 1999): 357–78.

Sexton, Alexander. *The Indispensable Enemy: Labor and the Anti-Chinese Movement*. Berkeley: University of California Press, 1971.

Shah, Nayan. *Contagious Divides: Epidemics and Race in San Francisco's Chinatown*. Berkeley: University of California Press, 2001.

———. "Policing Privacy, Migrants, and the Limits of Freedom." *Social Text* 23, nos. 3–4 (Fall-Winter 2005): 275–384.

———. *Stranger Intimacy: Contesting Race, Sexuality, and the Law in the North American West*. Berkeley: University of California Press, 2011.

Shilts, Randy. *Conduct Unbecoming: Gays and Lesbians in the U.S. Military*. New York: St. Martin's Press, 1993.

Shoemaker, Michael Meyers. *Quaint Corners of Ancient Empires: South India, Burma, and Manila*. New York: G. P. Putnam's Sons, 1899.

Sinfield, Alan. *The Wilde Century: Effeminacy, Oscar Wilde, and the Queer Moment*. New York: Columbia University Press, 1994.

Skidmore, Emily. "Exceptional Queerness: Defining the Boundaries of Normative U.S. Citizenship, 1876–1936." Ph.D. diss., University of Illinois, Urbana-Champaign, 2011.

Smith, Brice. "'Yours in Liberation': Lou Sullivan and the Construction of FTM Identity." Ph.D. diss., University of Wisconsin, Milwaukee, 2010.

Smith, Ephraim K. "William McKinley's Enduring Legacy: The Historiographical Debate on the Taking of the Philippine Islands." In *Crucible of Empire: The Spanish American War and Its Aftermath*, ed. James Bradford, 205–49. Annapolis: Naval Institute Press, 1993.

Somerville, Siobhan. "Notes toward a Queer History of Naturalization." *American Quarterly* 57, no. 3 (2005): 659–75.

———. "Queer." In *Keywords for American Cultural Studies*, ed. Bruce Burgett and Glenn Hendler, 187–90. New York: New York University Press, 2007.

———. *Queering the Color Line: Race and the Invention of Homosexuality in American Culture*. Durham, NC: Duke University Press, 2000.

———. "Queer Loving." *GLQ* 11, no. 3 (2005): 335–70.

Soper, Kerry. "From Swarthy Ape to Sympathetic Everyman and Subversive Trickster: The Development of Irish Caricature in American Comic Strips between 1890 and 1920." *Journal of American Studies* 39, no. 2 (August 2005): 257–96.

Spears, Timothy. *Chicago Dreaming: Midwesterners and the City, 1871–1919*. Chicago: University of Chicago Press, 2005.

Spivak, Gayatri Chakravorty. "History." In *A Critique of Postcolonial Reason: Toward a History of a Vanishing Present*, 198–311. Cambridge, MA: Harvard University Press, 1999.

Stockton, Kathryn Bond. *Beautiful Bottom, Beautiful Shame: Where "Black" Meets "Queer."* Durham, NC: Duke University Press, 2006.

Stoler, Ann. *Along the Archival Grain: Epistemic Anxieties and Colonial Common Sense.* Princeton, NJ: Princeton University Press, 2009.

—. *Carnal Knowledge and Imperial Power: Race and the Intimate in Colonial Rule.* Berkeley: University of California Press, 2002.

—, ed. *Haunted by Empire: Geographies of Intimacy in North American History.* Durham, NC: Duke University Press, 2006.

—. "Intimidations of Empire," in *Haunted by Empire: Geographies of Intimacy in North American History,* ed. Ann Stoler, 1–22. Durham, NC: Duke University Press, 2006.

—. *Race and the Education of Desire: Foucault's History of Sexuality and the Colonial Order of Things.* Durham, NC: Duke University Press, 1995.

Sullivan, Louis. *From Female to Male: The Life of Jack Bee Garland.* Boston, MA: Alyson Press, 1990.

Sulong, P. Taga. "The Truth about the Filipinos." *Filipino Students' Magazine* 1, no. 4 (December 1906): 17–18.

Sutherland, William Alexander. *Not by Might: The Epic of the Philippines.* Las Cruces, NM: Southwest, 1953.

Tadiar, Neferti. *Fantasy Production: Sexual Economies and Other Philippine Consequences for the New World Order.* Hong Kong: Hong Kong University Press, 2006.

Takaki, Ronald. *Strangers from a Different Shore.* Boston, MA: Little, Brown, 1989.

Tan, Samuel K. *The Filipino-American War: 1899–1913.* Quezon City: University of the Philippines Press, 2002.

—. *Sulu under American Military Rule, 1899–1913.* Manila: University of the Philippines, 1967.

Tapia, Ruby. "'Just Ten Years Removed from a Bolo and a Breech-cloth': The Sexualization of the Filipino 'Menace.'" In *Positively No Filipinos Allowed: Building Communities and Discourse,* ed. Antonio Tiongson, Edgardo Gutierrez, and Ricardo Gutierrez, 61–71. Philadelphia, PA: Temple University Press, 2006.

Tate, Claudia. *Domestic Allegories of Political Desire: The Black Heroine's Text at the Turn of the Century.* New York: Oxford University Press, 1992.

Teodoro, Noel. "*Pensionados* and Workers: The Filipinos in the United States, 1903–1956." *Asian and Pacific Migration Journal* 8, nos. 1–2 (1999): 157–78.

Terry, Jennifer. *An American Obsession: Science, Medicine, and Homosexuality in Modern Society.* Chicago: University of Chicago Press, 1999.

Ting, Jennifer. "Bachelor Society: Deviant Heterosexuality and Asian American Historiography." In *Privileging Positions: The Sites of Asian American Studies,* ed. Gary Y. Okihiro, Marilyn Alquizola, Dorothy Fujita Rony, and K. Scott Wong, 271–80. Pullman: Washington State University Press, 1995.

Trinh T. Minh-ha. *When the Moon Waxes Red: Representation, Gender, and Cultural Politics.* New York: Routledge, 1991.

"Truth versus Falsehood." *Philippine Review* 3, no. 1 (March 1907): 2.

U.S. Philippine Commission. "Act 190." In *Annual Reports of the War Department: Public Laws and Resolutions Passed by the Philippine Commission.* Washington, DC: U.S. Government Printing Office, 1901.

————. "Act 854." In *Acts of the Philippine Commission [Acts 425–949, Inclusive]*, 668–70. Washington, DC: U.S. Government Printing Office, 1904.

U.S. Secretary of War. *Annual Reports of the War Department for the Fiscal Year Ended June 30, 1903*, vol. 3. Washington, DC: U.S. Government Printing Office, 1903.

U.S. Senate. "Proclamation of Aguinaldo." In *Affairs in the Philippine Islands: Hearings before the Committee of the Philippines of the United States Senate*, 522–24. Washington, DC: U.S. Government Printing Office, 1902.

————. *Treaty with the Sultan of Sulu*. 56th Cong., 1st sess., S. Doc. 136, 1900.

U.S. War Department. *A Manual for Courts-Martial, Courts of Inquiry, and of Other Procedure under Military Law*. Washington, DC: U.S. Government Printing Office, 1910.

U.S. War Department, Bureau of Insular Affairs. *Fourth Annual Report of the Philippine Commission 1903*. Washington, DC: U.S. Government Printing Office, 1904.

————. *Report of the Commissioner of Public Health for the Philippine Islands for the Year Ended September 1, 1903*. Manila: Bureau of Public Printing, 1904.

U.S. War Department, Division of Customs and Insular Affairs. *The Translation of the Penal Code in Force in the Philippines*. Washington, DC: U.S. Government Printing Office, 1900.

U.S. War Department, Office of the Judge-Advocate General. "Articles of War." In *A Digest of Opinions of the Judge Advocates General of the Army*. Washington, DC: U.S. Government Printing Office, 1912.

Untitled poem. *Filipino Students' Magazine* 1, no. 1 (April 1905): 25.

Valente, Joseph. *James Joyce and the Problem of Justice: Negotiating Sexual and Colonial Difference*. Cambridge: Cambridge University Press, 1995.

Vergara Jr., Benito M. *Displaying Filipinos: Photography and Colonialism in Early 20th Century Philippines*. Quezon City: University of the Philippines Press, 1995.

Veyra, M.P. de. "The Filipino Woman." *Filipino Students' Magazine* 2, no. 3 (October 1906): 14.

Villamor, Ignacio. *Criminality in the Philippine Islands, 1903–1908*. Manila: Bureau of Printing, 1909.

Volpp, Leti. "American Mestizo: Filipinos and Antimiscegenation Laws in California." *University of California, Davis, Law Review* 33 (2000): 795–835.

Waligora-Davis, Nicole. *Sanctuary: African Americans an Empire*. New York: Oxford University Press, 2011.

Warner, Michael. "Irving's Posterity." ELH 67, no. 3 (Fall 2000): 773–99.

Webb, Alec. "Philippine Islands. Report by Consul Webb, of Manila," in *Special Consular Reports. Volume X*, 547–49. Washington, DC: Government Printing Office, 1893.

Webb, Barbara. "The Black Dandyism of George Walker: A Case Study in Genealogical Method." *Drama Review* 45, no. 4 (2001): 7–24.

Weber, Max. *From Max Weber: Essays in Sociology*, ed. and trans. H. H. Gerth and C. Wright Mills. New York: Academic Press, 1974.

Wesling, Meg. *Empire's Proxy: American Literature and U.S. Imperialism in the Philippines*. New York: New York University Press, 2011.

Westfall, Matthew. *The Devil's Causeway: The True Story of America's First Prisoners of War in the Philippines, and the Heroic Expedition Sent to their Rescue*. Guilford, CT: Lyons Press, 2012.

Willoughby, William. *Territories and Dependencies of the United States*. New York: Century, 1905.

Wonham, Henry. "'I Want a Real Coon': Mark Twain and Late-Nineteenth-Century Ethnic Caricature." *American Literature* 72, no. 1 (March 2000): 117–52.

"Wrong Ideas." *Filipino Students' Magazine* 2, no. 4 (November 1906): 3.

"Wrong Ideas about Filipinos." *Filipino Students' Magazine* 1, no. 2 (June 1905): 6.

Young, Elliot. "Red Men, Princess Pocahontas, and George Washington: Harmonizing Race Relations in Laredo at the Turn of the Century." *Western Historical Quarterly* 29, no. 1 (Spring 1998): 48–85.

Žižek, Slavoj. "Introduction: The Spectre of Ideology." In *Mapping Ideology*, ed. Slavoj Žižek, 1–32. London: Verso, 1994.

———. *Looking Awry: An Introduction to Jacques Lacan through Popular Culture*. Cambridge, MA: MIT Press, 1992.

———. *The Metastases of Enjoyment*. London: Verso, 1994.

———. "Philosophy, the 'Unknown Knowns,' and the Public Use of Reason." *Topoi* 25, nos. 1–2 (2006): 137–42.

———. *The Sublime Object of Ideology*. London: Verso, 1989.

———. *Tarrying with the Negative: Kant, Hegel, and the Critique of Ideology*. Durham, NC: Duke University Press, 1993.

Benjamin, Walter, 31
Bentley, Nancy, 142
Berlant, Lauren, 6–7
Bérubé, Allan, 208
Beveridge, Albert, 122–24
biopolitics, 102, 171
biopower, 48–49
black dandy (Filipino figure), 101, 102–7, 129
Bocobo, Jorge, 202
Boston Globe (newspaper), 26
Boston Sunday Globe (newspaper), 103–4, 104
bottom, Filipino men's: excrement and, 126–27, 242n108; fixation on, 100, 105–6; punishing, in cartoons, 120–27; as sublime object, 127–28, 130
Bowery Neighborhood (NYC), 111
Boyd, Nan, 208
Brown, Wendy, 12
Bryan, William Jennings, 110–11
Buencamino, Felipe, 173
Buencamino, Felipe, Jr., 173–74, 177
Bulosan, Carlos, 157, 170–71
Bureau of Insular Affairs (U.S. War Department), 39
Burgett, Bruce, 141
Butler, Judith, 30, 33

Calandria, Andres, 75, 84
Canaday, Margot, 13, 17–18, 38, 106
Carson, Adam, 44
Chauncey, George, 157, 230n25
Cheng, Anne, 163
Chicago Evening Post (newspaper), 182
Chicago Record (newspaper), *120*, 120–22, 144, 145
Chinese Exclusion Act (1882), 41
Chinese immigrants, 15–16, 41
Chow, Rey, 8
Chudacoff, Howard, 136, 159
Chuh, Kandice, 4
citizenship, 14, 15, 24, 26, 126, 188
Clevenger, Shobal Vail, 113
Cohen, Cathy, 29

Collier's Weekly (magazine), 116–18, *117*
colonialism, use of term, 9
Colonial Pathologies (Anderson), 126
colonianormativity, 92–93, 95, 209
Cortez, Roman, 75, 84, 85
Cott, Nancy, 142
Criminality in the Philippine Islands, 1903–1908 (Villamor), 49–50
cross-dressing. *See* anti-cross-dressing laws
Crowder, Enoch, 82–83
cruising. *See* gay cruising
Cruthers, Margaret Alberta, 175
Cuba, 4, 19, 20, 39, 98
Cuban-American War (1898), 18, 97
Cvetkovich, Ann, 243n112

"Dangers of College Life, The" (Santos), 191–92, 201
Davis (senator), 176
Davis, George, 74
Dean, Tim, 7–8, 127
De Bevoise, Ken, 53
de Court, Julian, 73
degenerate, use of term, 36, 106
degenerescence theory, 188–89
Deleuze, Gilles, 7, 123
D'Emilio, John, 2
Des Moines Daily News (newspaper), 28
Dewey, George, 27
Dickman, J. T., 74, 75
differend, use of term, 68–69, 81–82, 84–85
Dreyfus, Hubert, 189
Drinnon, Richard, 180
Du Bois, W. E. B., 4, 9
Dubuque Daily Herald (newspaper), 143
Ducut, Apolonio, 75–76, 77, 84

"Education in the Philippine Islands" (Onrubia), 178
Edwards, Rebecca, 236n16
effeminacy, 67, 90, 105–6, 109, 129, 157, 174, 230n25
Elements of Military Hygiene, The (Ashburn), 56–57, 76

Eng, David, 29
England, 153
España-Maram, Linda, 176
Evening Gazette (newspaper), 206
Evening Mail (newspaper), 205–6
Evening Star (newspaper), 141
eventalization, 92
exceptionalism. *See* U.S. exceptionalism
excrement, native, 126–27, 242n108
ex propio vigore doctrine, 39

"Fables in Slang" (Ade), 144
fairy, use of term, 90, 106, 230n25
Fanon, Franz, 178–79, 183
fantasy: cultural, 4–6, 102, 187; functions of, 5–7, 9–10; imperial, 9social; imperial, 7–8
Favis, Asterio, 101, 181
female domesticity ethos, 183–89
femininity, 108–9, 184
feminism, resistance to, 185–86
Ferguson, Roderick, 10, 13, 29
Filipino, The (magazine), 169, 170, 181, 198, 201
Filipino Students' Magazine, 101, 169, 170, 173, 177–78, 180, 182, 184, 186, 189
"First Pensionados, The" (Olivar), 201–2
Fischer, Roger, 97–98
Flower Drum Song (musical), 163
Foster, Anne, 39
Foucault, Michel, 65, 69; on biopower, 49, 209, 250n11; on degenerescence theory, 188–89; on eventalization, 92; on homosexuality, 16–17; on knowledge production, 203–4, 209; on pleasure, 85; on power, 12, 96; on sexuality, 10, 16–17, 27, 155, 171, 213–14n32; on sodomy, 37; on state racism, 171; on surveillance, 190
Freedman's Bureau, 14
Freud, Sigmund, 113, 195, 212n10

Galveston News (newspaper), 64
Garland, Jack Bee "Bean," 205–9
Garrison, William Lloyd, 169
gay cruising, 193, 198

gender: Filipino conventions, 28–29, 185; nonnormative, 29, 106, 138; normative, 13, 71–72, 139, 187–88, 189; transman example, 205–9
Germany, 153
Go, Julian, 12, 25, 39
Gopinath, Gayatri, 29, 226n62
Guam, 4, 20, 39, 98, 103
Guattari, Félix, 7
guerrilla warfare. *See under insurrectos,* Philippine
Guevara, Rafael, 75

Hadji Mohmammad Jamalul Kiram (sultan), 131–32, 141, 154
Halberstam, Jack/Judith, 29, 90, 249n94
Hall, Stuart, 96
Halperin, David, 71
Hamm, Margherita, 139
Harper's Weekly (magazine), 98, 141
Hartman, Saidiya, 11, 128
Havana, Cuba, 19–20
Hawai'i, 4, 25–26, 39, 103, 221n9
Hearst, William Randolph, 19, 98
heterosexuality, use of term, 16–17, 205
History of Sexuality, The (Foucault), 10, 16, 209
Hoar, George Frisbie, 122, 124
Hoganson, Kristin, 3, 217n72
homosexuality: bachelorhood and, 136; as degenerate, 106; exclusion in military, 60; gay cruising, 193, 198; use of term, 16–17, 58–59, 65, 205
Hornellsville Weekly Tribune (newspaper), 143
Howells, William Dean, 144
Hunt, William, 181

Igorots people, 101, 180–82
Ileto, Reynaldo, 25, 218n82
immigrant exclusion, 15–16, 142
imperialism. *See* U.S. imperialism
incorporation, doctrine of, 39
Insular Cases, 39

U.S. exceptionalism, 19, 21, 24, 52, 208, 222–23n21

U. S. imperialism: anti-imperialists, 22, 26, 28, 107–10, 112, 132, 135–36, 144–45, 169, 177–79; benevolent assimilation and, 9, 18–19, 21, 41, 115, 121–22; as capitalism, 2; cultural fantasies, 4–6, 60–61, 102, 187; defense of, 83; desire to be ruled, 39–40; Du Bois on, 4; global dominance and, 210; intimacies and, 1–2, 204; on model minorities, 177–83; national disavowal of, 60; as paternalistic, 24; in political cartoons, 96–100, 124–26, 204; on polygamy, 132, 135; public image of, 70; St. Louis World's Fair as, 93–94; sublime object of, 112–19, 130; surveillance and, 25; tentative character of, 38–43; unknown knowns of, 37, 67; use of term, 6, 9; violence with intimacy in, 257n32. *See also* metroimperial culture; U.S. colonial state

U.S. Medical Commission, 40

U.S. metropole: Filipinos in, 26, 104, 171, 177–83, 189; masculinity in, 19, 100, 106–7, 111–12, 202; on polygamy, 142; queer in, 29; racial-sexual governance in, 3, 10, 12–18, 40, 43; racial-sexual transgression in, 138; slavery in, 80; sodomy laws, 35–37, 44–45; use of term, 9; violence toward blacks in, 241n78. *See also* metroimperial culture

U.S. military: vs. *insurrectos*, 18–24, 53, 65, 131, 167, 194, 201, 255n97; racial-sexual governance in, 22; sodomy within, 53–61

U.S. Public Health Service, 190

U.S. Supreme Court, 26, 39

U.S. War Department, 39, 44, 58, 64

Utah, 141–42, 143

Vagrancy Act 519 (Philippine Commission), 225n41

vagrancy laws, 36–37, 45–49, 51

venereal disease. *See* sexually transmitted disease

Vergara, Benito, 25

Villamor, Ignacio, 49–50

Virginia Pilot (newspaper), 143

"Vision That Was Not Altogether a Vision, A" (Aguilar), 194–99, 201

Volpp, Leti, 176

Washington, D.C., 63

Washington Post (newspaper), 64, 69, *120*, 120–21, 142, 143

Wathall, Alfred, 145, 160

Weaver, Marilla, 138–39

Weber, Max, 12

Wells, Orson Collins, *164*

Wesling, Meg, 124

Weyler, Valeriano, 19

Wheeler, Benjamin Ide, 169, 170

White, Edward Douglass, 222n15

whiteness, 15, 68, 72, 97–98, 107, 142, 223n24, 256n109

white supremacy, 4, 13, 16, 84, 92, 208

Wichita Daily Eagle (newspaper), 101, 138

Widick, Albert A., 58

Wilde trials, 237–38n34

Winslow, Erving, 169

Wood, Leonard, 70

Wretched of the Earth, The (Fanon), 183

yellow journalism, 19, 98

Žižek, Slavoj, 6, 25, 37, 67, 117–18, 195, 197, 242n108